HOW THINGS WORK

By Steve Parker
Illustrated by Alex Pang

Miles Kelly

First published in 2010 by Miles Kelly Publishing Ltd
Harding's Barn, Bardfield End Green, Thaxted, Essex, CM6 3PX, UK

This edition printed 2014

4 6 8 10 9 7 5

Publishing Director: *Belinda Gallagher*
Creative Director: *Jo Cowan*
Design Concept: *Simon Lee*
Design: *Rocket Design*
Cover Designer: *Rob Hale*
Junior Designer: *Kayleigh Allen*
Assistant Editor: *Claire Philip*
Indexer: *Gill Lee*
Production Manager: *Elizabeth Collins*
Reprographics: *Stephan Davis, Anthony Cambray*
Assets: *Lorraine King*
Consultants: *John and Sue Becklake*

ISBN 978-1-78209-710-5

Printed in China

British Library Cataloguing-in-Publication Data
A catalogue record for this book is available from the British Library

MADE WITH PAPER FROM
A SUSTAINABLE FOREST

www.mileskelly.net
info@mileskelly.net

HOW THINGS WORK

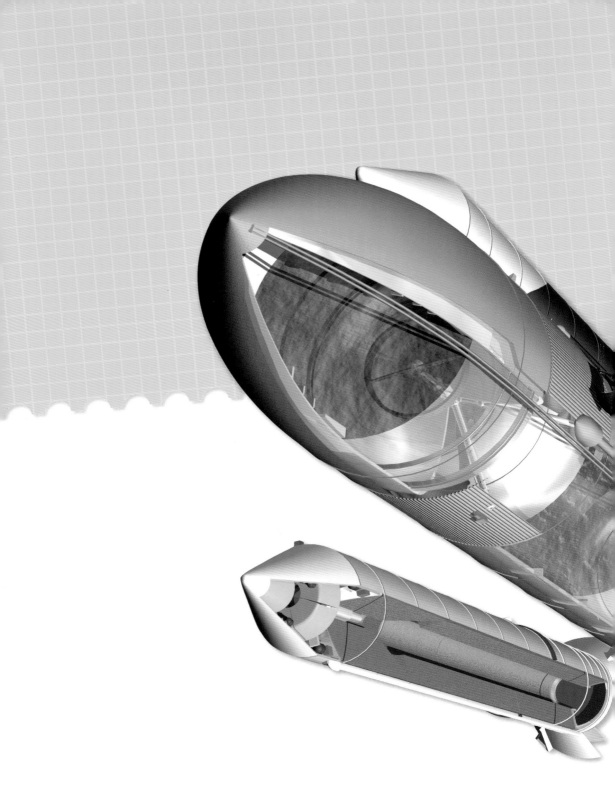

CONTENTS

GADGETS

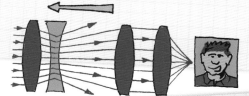

CARS, TRUCKS AND BIKES

EMERGENCY VEHICLES

SPEED MACHINES

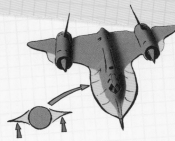

MILITARY MACHINES

GIANT MACHINES

ENERGY AND POWER

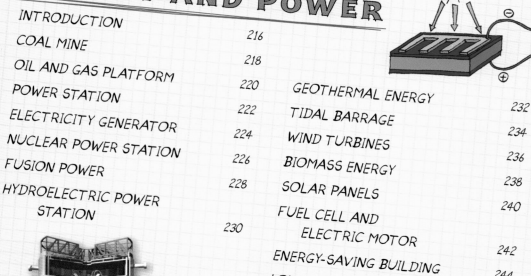

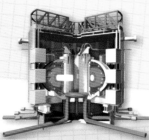

SHIPS AND SUBMARINES

AIRCRAFT

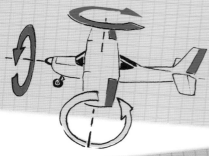

SPACE EXPLORATION

GADGETS

INTRODUCTION

People have always loved gadgets. In ancient times, alongside important tools and machines such as levers and wheels, people also invented gadgets, gizmos, widgets and devices to make life easier and more fun. Many gadgets were novelties that came and went, used just for entertainment. But others took on more serious uses and became part of everyday life, such as the abacus, alarm clock and microwave oven.

A skilled abacus user can work out sums almost as fast as a skilled electronic calculator user.

HIGHER TECH

The story of gadgets follows the march of technology. The calculator began thousands of years ago as rows of pebbles, then wooden beads on wires, followed by hand-cranked mechanical versions, and then an electric motor design. From the 1940s, electronics and microchips not only shrank the calculator to pocket size but also started a whole new area for gizmology. It has led to the ultimate gadget of our times – the computer.

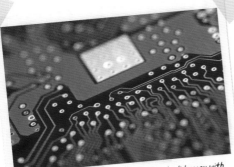

Mass-produced printed circuit boards did away with the labour-intensive task of installing wires by hand.

Personal music players are small enough to be carried wherever we go.

SMALL IS BIG

Drive motor

Platter

Actuator arm

Read/write head

Power supply socket

A computer hard drive can be as small as a postage stamp.

The market for new gadgets seems endless. Adverts continually announce smaller size, less weight, better batteries, easier controls and more add-ons and features. Sometimes existing parts are miniaturized for a new use, like the micro versions of computer hard drives developed for personal music players. In other cases a different area of technology is devised, such as 'flash' digital memory sticks or pens for music players.

Wide open spaces are recorded by a camcorder microchip smaller than your fingernail.

SIZE MATTERS

Some technologies resist the shrinking trend. Optical or light-based gadgets such as cameras and camcorders have to be a certain size, otherwise they could not handle enough light rays from the real world to record and show us the scene.

Manipulating light rays makes things look nearer or farther.

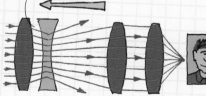

Concave lens to front

Camera zoom lens at telephoto setting

Concave lens to rear

Camera zoom lens at wide-angle setting

NO LIMITS?

Will there come a time when all possible gadgets have been invented? That's very doubtful. Few people 25 years ago predicted the success of sports-playing computers that keep you active, brain-training video consoles, car satnavs and internet-enabled, do-everything mobile phones. What will the next 25 years bring? Perhaps a new generation of plug-in brain chips, a TV screen fitted inside the eyeball and thought-wave communicators.

We can be sure of one thing — people will always want the most cutting-edge gadgets, so the well-worn phrase "I want one of those" will always survive!

There are even gadgets to cause you brain strain, such as this Nintendo DS gaming device.

CALCULATOR

Long ago, people did sums and calculations with pencil and paper, or used a machine as big as a table with lots of gears – or in their heads. In the 1960s came hand-held calculators, which were among the first small electronic gadgets. Today they are found in almost every room in offices, schools, factories and homes.

Eureka!

A calculating machine called the abacus was used in ancient Greece and Rome over 2000 years ago. It had rows of pebbles or beads in grooves on a table or in sand.

Whatever next?

Scientists are testing foldable calculators, with the keys and display built into thin, flexible cloth like a small handkerchief.

Cover The outer cover is usually made of hard plastic, able to resist scratches and knocks.

Microchips are also called ICs, integrated circuits, because they contain microscopic components, such as transistors and resistors, already 'integrated' on one wafer-like chip of silicon.

✳ PORTABLE POWER

Early calculators had LED (light-emitting diode) displays that needed plenty of battery power. With the introduction of LCD screens, which use much less electricity, enough power for a small calculator could be provided by a photovoltaic cell, or solar cell, which turns light energy into electricity. Most modern gadgets have built-in secondary electrical cells – rechargeable batteries that can be plugged into the mains.

PCB (Printed Circuit Board) Electronic components are linked by metal strips 'printed' onto a board made of a green plastic-like substance that is an electrical insulator (does not carry electricity).

Microprocessor The 'brain' of any electronic device is a chip called the microprocessor, or CPU, central processing unit. It carries out calculations from instructions fed into it via the keys.

Batteries range in size from smaller than a button to bigger than a suitcase

The most complex microprocessors or CPUs have more than ten million components on a chip as small as this 'o'.

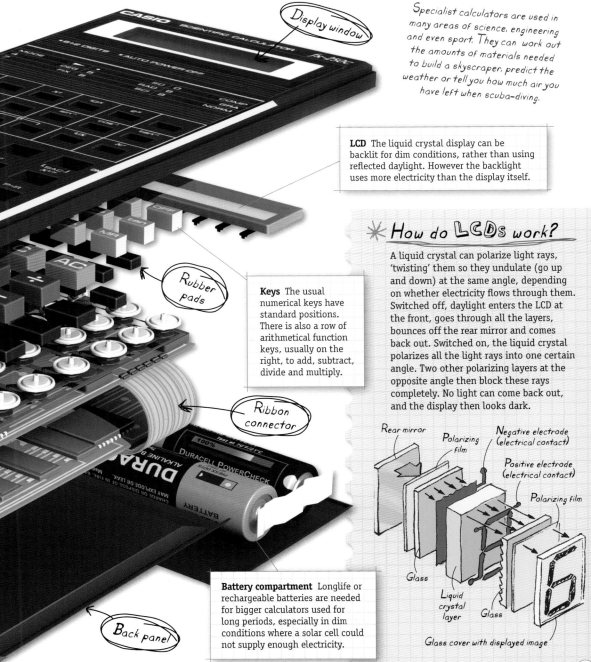

Display window

Specialist calculators are used in many areas of science, engineering and even sport. They can work out the amounts of materials needed to build a skyscraper, predict the weather or tell you how much air you have left when scuba-diving.

LCD The liquid crystal display can be backlit for dim conditions, rather than using reflected daylight. However the backlight uses more electricity than the display itself.

Rubber pads

Keys The usual numerical keys have standard positions. There is also a row of arithmetical function keys, usually on the right, to add, subtract, divide and multiply.

Ribbon connector

Back panel

Battery compartment Longlife or rechargeable batteries are needed for bigger calculators used for long periods, especially in dim conditions where a solar cell could not supply enough electricity.

✳ How do LCDs work?

A liquid crystal can polarize light rays, 'twisting' them so they undulate (go up and down) at the same angle, depending on whether electricity flows through them. Switched off, daylight enters the LCD at the front, goes through all the layers, bounces off the rear mirror and comes back out. Switched on, the liquid crystal polarizes all the light rays into one certain angle. Two other polarizing layers at the opposite angle then block these rays completely. No light can come back out, and the display then looks dark.

Rear mirror

Polarizing Film

Negative electrode (electrical contact)

Positive electrode (electrical contact)

Polarizing film

Glass

Liquid crystal layer

Glass

Glass cover with displayed image

FLAT SCREEN

Flat screens are in computer monitors, TVs and closed-circuit TV, displays on digital cameras, camcorders, satnav units and phones, and many other devices. There are two main kinds of flat screen technology – LCD (see page 15) and plasma (see below). Flat screens took over in the 1990s from older, heavier, box-like, glass-screen displays known as CRTs, cathode ray tubes. A CRT uses far more electricity than a flat screen.

Eureka!

The first purely electronic television systems, with no moving parts, were developed in the 1920s–30s by Hungarian engineer Kalman Tihanyi and Russian-American inventor Vladimir Zworykin.

Clear cover

Screen format Most flat screens have a 16:9 aspect ratio for widescreen viewing, where the screen height is 9/16ths of its width.

✳ How do PLASMA SCREENS work?

A plasma screen has millions of tiny compartments or cells, and two sets or grids of wire-like electrodes at right angles to each other. Each cell can be 'addressed' by sending electric pulses along two particular electrodes that cross at the cell. The electric pulse heats the cell's gas into a form called plasma, and this makes an area of coloured substance, the phosphor, glow for a split second. Millions of pulses every second at different 'addresses' all over the screen build up the overall picture.

Remote sensor A small infrared sensor detects the invisible IR (heat) beam from the remote-control handset.

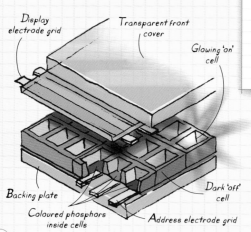

Display electrode grid
Transparent front cover
Glowing 'on' cell
Backing plate
Dark 'off' cell
Coloured phosphors inside cells
Address electrode grid

Stand

The biggest LCD flat screens measure 108 in or 274 cms. That's the distance from corner to corner diagonally across the screen, which is the traditional way of sizing screens.

In 1925, Scottish inventor John Logie Baird built a part-mechanical TV system, used by the BBC from 1924-1937.

Whatever next?

HD or High Definition screens have five to six times more tiny coloured dots (pixels) than a standard flat screen. This gives a sharper, clearer, more colourful image and smoother, less jerky movements.

The QuadHD flat screen has four to five times as many tiny coloured dots (pixels) than an HD flat screen – but whether most people have good enough eyesight to tell the difference is unlikely.

Receiver A TV's receiver unit is part of the electronic circuit board. It tunes into different channels and filters and strengthens the signals received by the aerial, ready for electronic processing. Computer monitors receive their signals already processed and so lack a receiver.

Ventilation slots The outer casing needs slots at the rear to allow heat to escape, otherwise the thermal cutout makes the screen go blank to prevent components overheating.

Electronics A typical HD flat screen TV has more than 1000 microchips and other components.

Most LCD flat screens use TFTs, thin-film transistors. The transistor components for producing coloured dots in the pixels are made within the thickness of the transparent screen.

✳ DIGITAL BROADCASTING

Older television broadcasting was called analogue, where the information for the pictures and sounds was carried by the varying strength of the radio wave signals. In digital broadcasting the information is coded in the form of on-off signals, millions every second. Radio waves used for one analogue channel can carry up to ten digital channels.

Dishes receive digital signals direct from satellites in space

Frame and backing The outer frame keeps the screen rigid and secure and wraps around the electronics at the rear. Some flat screens are less than 2.5 cm deep.

PERSONAL COMPUTER

Since the 1970s, personal computers have progressed from machines as big as a fridge that only the wealthy could afford, to small, neat packages found on and under desks in almost every home. A 'personal' computer, or PC, is usually stand-alone, which means it works by itself without being connected into a network with shared devices such as servers and other computers.

Eureka!

The first successful personal computer was the Commodore PET (Personal Electronic Transactor) in 1972. IBM's home computer, the IBM PC, was introduced in 1981 and set the standard for the computing industry.

Whatever next?

Moore's Law says that computer power – the number of components on a microchip and how fast they work – doubles about every two years. Devised by Gordon Moore in 1965, it is still holding true today.

Cooling fan

RAM (Random Access Memory) chips

Many modern computers have wireless peripherals (connected devices) that use short-range radio waves, such as the Bluetooth system, to carry information. This gets rid of trailing wires and allows them to be moved easily.

CPU The Central Processing Unit, or computer's 'brain', is connected to several other microchips. It carries out the main processing – altering data (information) according to the instructions from the application (program).

Card Smaller PCBs known as 'cards' deal with signals going in and out, for example, to the display screen from the graphics card, and to the loudspeakers from the sound card.

Hard drive The main memory disc that stores information permanently as micro-spots of magnetism is known as the hard disc or hard drive (see page 32).

✳ How do KEYBOARDS work?

All kinds of press-button or key-activated gadgets, from mobile phones to super computers, rely on a simple piece of technology similar to a light switch. Under each key are two pieces of metal conductor separated by a small gap. Pressing the key pushes them together so electricity flows. Each key has its own code of electrical pulses. A flexible membrane cover keeps out dust and sometimes even spilt drinks.

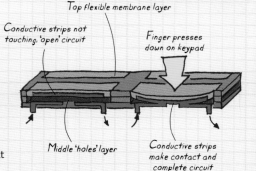

Top flexible membrane layer

Conductive strips not touching, 'open' circuit

Finger presses down on keypad

Middle 'holes' layer

Conductive strips make contact and complete circuit

Motherboard The main PCB (printed circuit board), which carries most of the major microchips, and the connectors for other, smaller PCBs, is often called the motherboard.

Optical drive trays CDs (compact discs) and DVDs (digital versatile discs) are inserted here where they work using light. A laser beam 'reads' tiny pits in their shiny surfaces (see page 37).

A typical home computer costs one-quarter of its price 20 years ago – and it is ten times more powerful.

Flat screen monitor

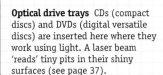

The INTERNET

The global system of computers linked into an international network is known as the Internet. It began as a limited network for the US military in 1969, was widened to research centres and universities in the 1970s, taken up by businesses in the 1980s, and opened for public access in the 1990s.

Pages and documents viewed on the Internet form the World Wide Web.

IBM's 'Roadrunner', located at Los Alamos National Laboratory in New Mexico, USA, is currently the world's fastest super computer.

Keyboard This is the main input device, allowing information to enter the computer as codes for alphanumerics – letters, numbers and symbols such as + and &.

Mouse A laser beam or a rolling ball on the underside track the movements of the mouse. This makes the cursor or insertion point on the screen move in a similar way. The wireless mouse works by a Bluetooth short-wave radio link and so has no wire 'tail'.

Home computing did not really catch on until early games machines appeared such as the Atari 2600 (1977) and Sinclair ZX Spectrum (1982). They could play games in full colour and with sound – amazing for the time!

DIGITAL CAMERA

A camera makes a permanent visual record of a scene, person or object. Most cameras have a lens to focus the light rays for a clear image. A digital stills camera (recording a 'still' split-second moment in time) turns the pattern of light rays into on-off electronic signals stored in a microchip.

Eureka!

Early digital cameras included the Fuji DS-1P of 1988 and the Dycam M1 of 1990. Kodak introduced its first digi-cam in 1991 with the DCS-100.

Whatever next?

Early digital cameras recorded images of about one megapixel. For a typical camera in the 2000s this rose to six megapixels, then eight. It will continue to rise as CCD chips improve.

Digital cameras may not capture such detail or colour variation as photographic film cameras. However they can show you the image being stored, delete it if need be and hold many more images than a roll of film.

Autofocus An invisible infrared beam bounces off the object in front of the camera, which detects the time taken for it to return. This shows the object's distance for lens focusing.

Aperture This hole is made larger or smaller to let in more or less light, depending on brightness conditions.

'Take' button

✳ MEGAPIXELS and RESOLUTION

A megapixel is one million pixels, and pixels, or 'picture elements', are tiny areas or spots in the whole picture. Each pixel is made up of red, green and blue light. In various combinations these produce all other colours, and all together they make white. Packing more pixels into a given area makes the image clearer and more detailed, which is known as going from low resolution to high resolution.

Lens The lens system has several curved pieces of glass or plastic that move forwards or backwards to focus the image, depending on the object's distance.

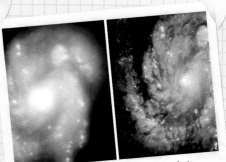

A space galaxy at low resolution (left) and higher resolution (right)

Shutter Pressing the 'take' button opens a door-like flap for a split second to allow light through to the CCD (see page 24).

Battery

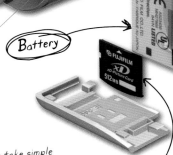

Memory card

Many digital cameras can take simple sequences of moving images or videos, and record sound too.

A traditional camera stores images as patterns of silver-containing chemical changes on a flexible cellulose-based roll of photographic film.

Viewfinder A small LCD display shows the view that the lens sees, which is the image that will be stored.

Screen

Image processor

FUJIFILM

F700 DIGITAL CAMERA

Flash

CCD chip

The smallest digital cameras are the size of shirt buttons – and that includes a transmitter to send pictures by radio waves to a receiver up to one km away.

✳ How do LENSES work?

As light rays pass from air to glass, they bend or refract. A concave lens (thinner in the middle) makes them refract outwards, or diverge. A convex lens (bulging in the middle) makes them refract inwards, or converge, to a focal point where they form a clear image, as in a camera.

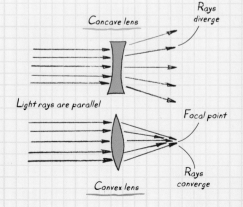

Concave lens
Rays diverge
Light rays are parallel
Focal point
Rays converge
Convex lens

CAMCORDER

The camcorder is a camera-recorder specialized to take video – very fast split-second sequences of still images that look like moving pictures – and record them for later playback. It also records sounds at the time, which are linked in time, or synched (synchronized), to the images. Some camcorders record on magnetic tape, either analogue or digitally. Others are digital, using very small hard drives or electronic microchips in memory cards.

Eureka!

The first video cameras were cinema cameras using photographic film. Made in the 1880s, they recorded early movies or cinema 'motion pictures'. Small hand-held versions became popular from the 1950s.

Whatever next?

A light-detecting electronic chip that works as a simple video camera could one day be put into the eye, so you can make a permanent record of everything you see.

Zoom gears A small electric motor and gearing system move the lenses so that the camera can focus and zoom in to show a small area larger (see right).

Lens cover

✳ SATELLITE VIDEOPHONE

Satvidphones have a radio link, not into the local telecom or cellphone network as used by mobile phones, but direct to a satellite orbiting in space. The transmitter-receiver is housed in a laptop-sized case. A headset carries the camera to record the view, the microphone for sound and a display screen and headphones, either for what is being recorded, or to relay video and sound sent through the satellite link to the wearer.

Casing The scratchproof outer casing gives some protection against knocks.

Main processors The main microchips process the digital signals from the CCD into a form that is easily stored in the memory device.

The headset camera (left) records what is in front of the person's face

The highest-quality digital formats include MiniDV and Digital Betacam. They lose much less quality when the video recording is later copied and edited, compared to an analogue recording.

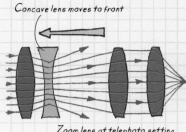

Concave lens moves to front

Zoom lens at telephoto setting

Concave lens moves to rear

Zoom lens at wide-angle setting

Microphone A small microphone (see page 28) picks up sounds during image recording. On some cameras it can be detached for accurate aiming, linked to the camcorder by a wire or radio waves.

Early camcorders were developed for television, being small and lightweight for 'on-the-spot' reporting and recording.

Viewfinder The LCD screen allows you to see what has been recorded and delete it, or 'edit' it by picking out only the parts you want to save.

✳ How does ZOOM work?

Zooming in, or telephoto, enlarges a portion of the scene, at the same time showing a relatively smaller area of the whole scene. Zooming out to wide-angle takes in more of the scene but reduces its magnification so things look smaller. The zoom system uses a moveable concave lens (one that is thinner in the centre than around the edges) to spread out or diverge the light rays (see page 21). Some zooms are worked by an electric motor, others are twisted or pulled by hand.

Battery

LCD display

USB memory stick

Screen controls The screen has brightness, contrast, colour balance and other controls. You can adjust these to view it comfortably out in the glaring sunshine or indoors in a darkened room.

Most photographic film video cameras take 24 separate still pictures or frames every second. Camcorders usually take 30 frames per second. When the recording is played back, your eyes cannot see the individual frames separately. Your brain blurs them together to give the impression of smooth movement.

Webcams (World Wide Web cameras) are small, simple video cameras that do not record their images but feed them straight into a computer or digital network.

SCANNER

The key to digital technology is to turn anything – pictures, videos, sounds, speech, written words and numbers – into coded sequences of on-off electrical pulses. We write these as the digits (numbers) 1 and 0, and they are the 'language' of computers. An image scanner 'digitizes' a picture by detecting the colour and brightness of every tiny spot, one spot after another, and converting this information to digital code.

Eureka!

The first image scanners appeared in the 1960s, as part of the work to develop body scanners for medical use. They were taken up by businesses in the 1980s and became available for home use in the early 1990s.

Whatever next?

Three-dimensional (3D) scanners consist of two digital cameras mounted on a frame. They are moved over and around an object, to make a 3D view in the computer memory.

Scan technology involves looking at and detecting a row of tiny areas in a straight line, then moving along slightly and doing the same for the next line, and so on – usually thousands of times.

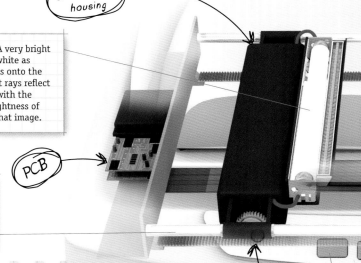

Drive motor housing

Light source A very bright light, as pure white as possible, shines onto the image. Its light rays reflect off the image with the colour and brightness of every part of that image.

PCB

Rail The scan head slides to and fro along a metal guide rail. It is driven by a toothed belt that meshes to a sprocket (gear wheel) for very accurate movement.

Drive gear

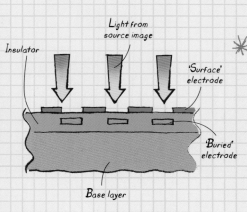

Insulator

Light from source image

'Surface' electrode

'Buried' electrode

Base layer

✳ How does a CCD CHIP work?

A CCD (charge-coupled device) is a microchip with millions of tiny wire-like electrodes forming a criss-cross grid. When a ray of light hits the area or boundary between two neighbouring electrodes, it causes a particle called an electron (an outer part of an atom) to jump between them. This causes a tiny pulse of electric current at that point on the chip – light has been converted into electricity.

Control buttons The scanner has some manual controls, such as to 'home' the scan head, to scan only a small area or to make a direct copy. Most of the controls are in the computer application to which it is linked.

The detail that a scanner picks up is measured as dpi, dots per inch. This shows how many dots of colour are detected in a line one inch (2.54 cm) long.

Tray

Direct output (copy)

If large areas of an image are the same colour, the computer can save memory by giving them all a shortened version of the code for that colour, rather than the full code for every tiny spot of the area. This is one way of compressing a computer file to make it smaller.

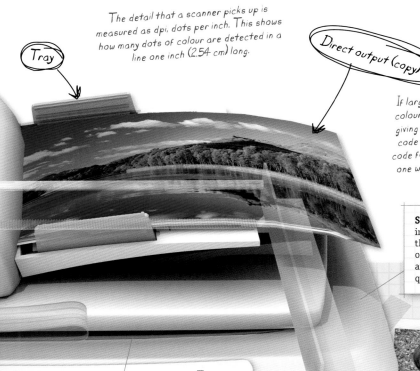

Sealed case The scanner's internal parts are sealed to keep them dust-proof, since build-up of dust on the mirrors, lenses and CCD would greatly affect the quality of the scan.

A red shirt is changed to blue – or the other way around?

Power button

Flatbed The image is laid flat on a glass sheet for flatbed scanning. Some scanners have a different design where the image is wrapped around a drum that revolves past the scan head. Drum scanners can produce a far more detailed scan.

Main housing Inside the scanner's main case is a mirror that reflects light that has already been reflected from the image. The mirror reflects the light towards the CCD, which turns the patterns of colour and brightness in the light rays into a corresponding pattern of electronic digital signals.

✳ VSFX

Using keyboard instructions, computers can change or process words. The same can be done with pictures, known as image processing or visual special effects (VSFX). For example, the computer can be instructed to change all areas of a certain shade of red in an image to a blue colour.

PRINTER

A typical home printer makes 'hard copy' – a version or copy of what is on the computer screen, on a sheet of paper or card where it is permanent or 'hard'. Printer technology is in some ways the opposite of the image scanner (see page 24). The printer builds up the image as many tiny dots of ink forming a long row or line, and then another line next to it, and so on.

Eureka!

Computer printers for home use were developed in the 1960s. The print head had a grid-like set or matrix of tiny pins that pressed an inked ribbon onto paper, similar to old typewriter technology. This was called the dot-matrix printer. It could only produce marks the colour of the ribbon.

Whatever next?

Skin printers are small rollers that squirt out ink as they pass over the skin. They make images of any kind, usually from washable inks – like having an almost instant temporary tattoo.

Cover

Rollers Driven by an electric motor, the roller system moves the paper past the print head a strip at a time and the print head produced each strip of the image.

There are two main types of design for inkjet print heads. In the fixed-head version the nozzles are permanent and need cleaning occasionally. In the disposable head type a new set of nozzles comes with each cartridge of ink or toner.

Output

A laser beam heats the powder in a 3D printer chamber

*3D magic

Instead of the usual two-dimensional or 2D printing on a flat surface, 3D printing builds up solid objects layer by layer, with depth or height as the third dimension. A powder spreads out in the printer chamber, then a laser warms it only in the area of the print, so its particles stick together. The next layer is added on top, and as the same happens, this layer also fuses to the one below. When the layering is complete, the loose powder is removed. This method is used for 'fabbing' or prefabricating – making models and prototypes of complex shapes.

Output tray Printed sheets pile up here. It is wise to let them dry separately, uncovered, where air can get to the ink. Otherwise they may smudge as they slide and press together.

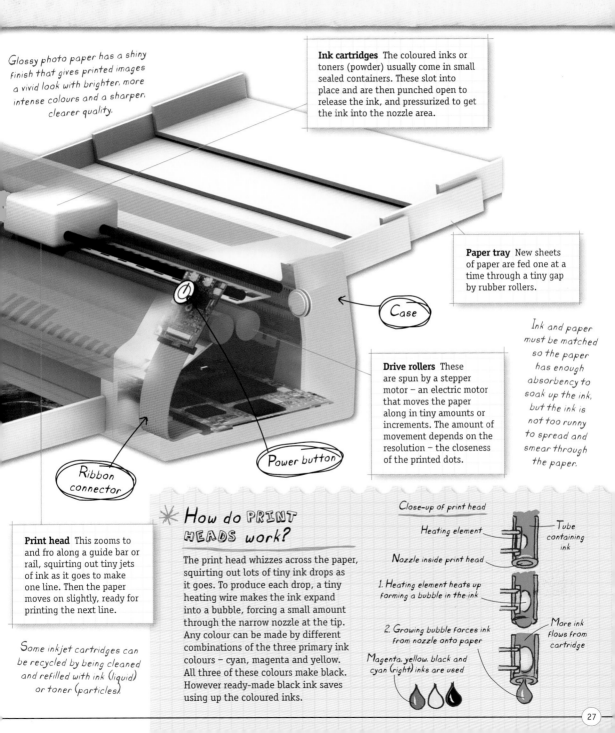

Glossy photo paper has a shiny finish that gives printed images a vivid look with brighter, more intense colours and a sharper, clearer quality.

Ink cartridges The coloured inks or toners (powder) usually come in small sealed containers. These slot into place and are then punched open to release the ink, and pressurized to get the ink into the nozzle area.

Paper tray New sheets of paper are fed one at a time through a tiny gap by rubber rollers.

Case

Ink and paper must be matched so the paper has enough absorbency to soak up the ink, but the ink is not too runny to spread and smear through the paper.

Drive rollers These are spun by a stepper motor – an electric motor that moves the paper along in tiny amounts or increments. The amount of movement depends on the resolution – the closeness of the printed dots.

Power button

Ribbon connector

Print head This zooms to and fro along a guide bar or rail, squirting out tiny jets of ink as it goes to make one line. Then the paper moves on slightly, ready for printing the next line.

Some inkjet cartridges can be recycled by being cleaned and refilled with ink (liquid) or toner (particles).

✳ How do PRINT HEADS work?

The print head whizzes across the paper, squirting out lots of tiny ink drops as it goes. To produce each drop, a tiny heating wire makes the ink expand into a bubble, forcing a small amount through the narrow nozzle at the tip. Any colour can be made by different combinations of the three primary ink colours – cyan, magenta and yellow. All three of these colours make black. However ready-made black ink saves using up the coloured inks.

Close-up of print head

Heating element

Nozzle inside print head

Tube containing ink

1. Heating element heats up forming a bubble in the ink

2. Growing bubble forces ink from nozzle onto paper

More ink flows from cartridge

Magenta, yellow, black and cyan (right) inks are used

RADIO MICROPHONE

A microphone changes patterns of sound waves into similar patterns of tiny electrical signals, which are fed into an amplifier to make them stronger. The long wire trailing from an ordinary microphone to the amplifier means that performers cannot move about with freedom – and they might even trip over it. The radio microphone sends its signals to the amplifier by radio waves.

Eureka!

The first microphones were in the first telephones, made by Alexander Graham Bell and his co-workers in the 1870s. By the 1920s bigger, better microphones were in regular use for radio broadcasts.

Whatever next?

A small pellet-like microphone can be placed in a false tooth to transmit what you say by radio – but you have to turn it down when you eat!

Performers often check a microphone by saying 'testing, one, two'. These words contain common voice sounds, such as 'sss' and a hard 't'.

Body or barrel

Batteries The barrel or main body of the microphone is shaped for grip in the hand and so is ideal for housing the batteries. A warning light shines when battery power begins to fade. To save the batteries the mike can be switched to 'mute', which means it goes silent but is ready for use again in an instant.

Transmitter and antenna The radio transmitter sends out coded radio waves from its antenna (aerial), carrying the sound information to a receiver that is usually less than 100 metres away.

Hand grip

In a hospital, a Bluetooth microphone links by radio to its base next door

✳ What is BLUETOOTH?

To avoid too many tangled and trailing wires, electrical devices can send information between themselves using radio waves, known as 'wireless'. Bluetooth is not the name of a particular make or type of device. It is the 'label' for the way the information is coded into radio signals, and a standard for the speed, quality, strength and reliability of the short-range wireless system. All Bluetooth devices can communicate or 'talk' to each other in the standard way, rather than different manufacturers using their own systems that did not communicate.

'Bugs' are small listening devices made up of a tiny microphone and radio transmitter. They are often used for spying and secret investigations.

As well as moving-coil microphones there are many other kinds including condenser, laser, electrostatic, carbon-granule and piezoelectric mikes. Each has its own benefits, such as light weight, durability or high quality sound reproduction.

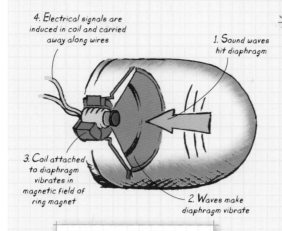

4. Electrical signals are induced in coil and carried away along wires

1. Sound waves hit diaphragm

3. Coil attached to diaphragm vibrates in magnetic field of ring magnet

2. Waves make diaphragm vibrate

✳ How do MICROPHONES work?

There are many kinds of microphones. Many in regular stage use are called dynamic or moving-coil mikes and work by the process of electromagnetic induction. Sound waves make a wire coil vibrate within a magnetic field. This movement of a wire near a magnet causes, or induces, electrical currents to flow in the wire. The pattern of the current is the same as the pattern of sound waves. The opposite process, known as the electromagnetic effect, is used in a loudspeaker (see page 30).

Magnetic coil The coil attached to the diaphragm is wound from many turns of ultra-thin wire. The more turns it has, the stronger the electrical signals it generates, and so the clearer the sounds are.

A unidirectional microphone picks up sounds from only one direction.

Muffler or guard A foam cover over the diaphragm prevents the wind and air currents from rattling the diaphragm. But at the same it is acoustically transparent, allowing through sound waves from the air around.

Permanent magnet

Head

PCBs Printed circuit boards filter, convert and clean up the electrical signals from the wire coil, ready to feed to the transmitter.

Diaphragm The thin, flexible diaphragm shakes very fast, or vibrates, when sound waves bounce off it. This makes the wire coil attached to it vibrate with a similar pattern of movements.

An omnidirectional mike detects sounds from all directions.

LOUDSPEAKERS

A loudspeaker or 'speaker' turns electrical signals into corresponding patterns of sound waves – the opposite of a microphone (see page 28). To make the electrical signals strong enough to power a loudspeaker, they usually have to be boosted or increased by an amplifier or 'amp'.

Eureka!

Like early microphones, the first loudspeakers were developed by Alexander Graham Bell and his colleagues for the first telephones, during the 1870s.

Whatever next?

Tiny Bluetooth-type radio earphones could be implanted into the human ear and activated by brainwaves. It may then be possible to switch on a radio link and listen just by thinking.

Unlike many modern electronic devices, loudspeakers are analogue. They use electrical signals of varying strength rather than on-off digital signals.

The massive speakers at big events need thousands of watts of power, while the tiny ones in earphones need just a few thousandths of a watt.

Coil The wire coil inside the magnet, also known as the voice coil, has many turns of very thin wire. This makes it move as much as possible even with very weak electrical signals

Ring magnet

1. Electrical signals are sent to the speaker

3. Diaphragm connected to coil enlarges the vibrations, causing sound

2. Magnet and coil attached to diaphragm convert electrical signals into vibrations

4. Sound travels from speaker out into air

Stand

Diaphragm Also called the cone, this is usually made of stiff plastic or specially treated card. It has a flexible outer rim so it can vibrate freely within its frame.

✳ How do MOVING-COIL LOUDSPEAKERS work?

A loudspeaker uses the opposite principle to electromagnetic induction, which is known as the electromagnetic effect. When an electric current passes through a wire coil, this becomes an electromagnet with its own magnetic field. In a speaker the field interacts with the constant field of a ring-shaped permanent magnet around it, alternately pulling (attraction) and pushing (repulsion). This makes the coil vibrate, which it passes its vibrations to the diaphragm, which then produces the sound waves.

The name 'loudspeaker' can be used for the box, cabinet or container housing one or more actual speaker units, which are then known as 'drivers'.

✳ Tiny SPEAKERS

Earphones are tiny loudspeakers, small enough to fit in the ear. The magnets in earphones are made of special alloys, or combinations of metals that have a very strong magnetic field but are also light and not damaged by knocks and vibrations. These alloys include the rare metals samarium and cobalt, which make earphones with powerful low frequencies for a deep bass sound. Headphones have slightly larger speakers and padded cups that fit over the ears to keep out unwanted sounds.

Earphones let us listen without disturbing others too much

Tweeter This smaller loudspeaker produces shrill notes or high frequencies such as cymbals and the 'sss' sounds of the voice.

Subwoofer loudspeakers or subs produce some sound waves that are too deep or low for the human ear to detect. However we can 'feel' them in our bodies as a deep thud or thump.

Grill A protective covering stops damage to the loudspeaker or driver unit but lets sound waves pass through unaffected.

Now Playing
1 of 14
Dani California
Red Hot Chili Peppers
Stadium Arcadium
3:27   1:15
MENU
iPod
Dock

Woofer The larger loudspeaker produces deep notes or low frequencies such as drums and bass guitars.

Apart from moving-coil or dynamic loudspeakers there are also electrostatic, ribbon and piezoelectric (crystal-based) types for special applications.

Some very high-quality loudspeaker systems have five driver units for different frequencies or pitches of sound: subwoofer, woofer, midrange, tweeter and ultratweeter.

PERSONAL MUSIC PLAYER

Various manufacturers make portable personal music players, also called digital audio players. Those produced by Apple are called iPods, while many others are known by the general name of MP3 players. The term 'MP3' refers to the way the sounds are changed into digital code and 'compressed' to take up less memory space without loss of quality.

Eureka!

The iPod took little more than one year to develop, under the close eye of Apple chief Steve Jobs. It was launched in 2001 with the catchphrase '1000 songs in your pocket' and has been a best seller ever since.

Whatever next?

MP4 is faster to transfer than MP3, works with audio and video, takes up even less memory and is more suitable for streaming (transferring 'live' in real time) over the Internet.

MP3 stands for mpeg audio layer 3. The 'mpeg' part is Moving Pictures Expert Group. It refers to a team of electronics experts who worked out how images and sounds could be changed into digital electronic form using a series of mathematical sums and formulas known as algorithms.

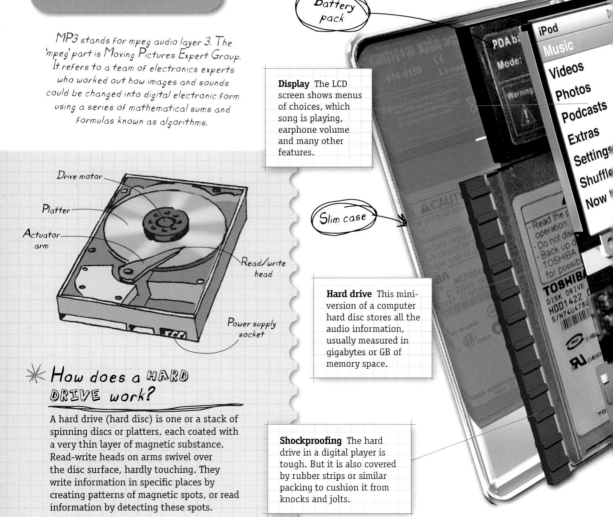

Battery pack

Display The LCD screen shows menus of choices, which song is playing, earphone volume and many other features.

Slim case

Drive motor

Platter

Actuator arm

Read/write head

Power supply socket

Hard drive This mini-version of a computer hard disc stores all the audio information, usually measured in gigabytes or GB of memory space.

iPod
Music
Videos
Photos
Podcasts
Extras
Settings
Shuffle
Now

✳ How does a HARD DRIVE work?

A hard drive (hard disc) is one or a stack of spinning discs or platters, each coated with a very thin layer of magnetic substance. Read-write heads on arms swivel over the disc surface, hardly touching. They write information in specific places by creating patterns of magnetic spots, or read information by detecting these spots.

Shockproofing The hard drive in a digital player is tough. But it is also covered by rubber strips or similar packing to cushion it from knocks and jolts.

Some digital music players with display screens have video games such as Brick, Solitaire and Music Quiz.

Flash memory is non-volatile, which means it doesn't need an electricity supply to 'refresh' or maintain it. It should stay in a microchip for years with no electrical power.

Album artwork

Motherboard

✳ FLASHY MEMORY

Some MP3 players use flash memory, which is a microchip that holds information that can be deleted and reprogrammed. Flash memory chips or 'sticks' are smaller and cheaper than a tiny hard drive or microdrive, but hold less information. However they also use less electricity and so allow batteries to last longer than with a microdrive. Most flash chips are protected in plastic cases and plug into the USB (universal serial bus) socket of a player, computer or network.

The USB memory stick plugs into many electronic devices

Click wheel Play and pause, skip forwards or back, volume, choose a menu item, and return to the previous menu are carried out by pressing or stroking parts of this wheel, rather than by pressing a row of buttons.

Touch-sensors A series of flat components called capacitors detects when an object, such as a finger, is near and which way it moves. The presence of the object alters the amount of electricity that the capacitor can hold.

The forerunner of the iPod/MP3 player was the portable laser-based CD player. It was more than ten times bigger and heavier than an MP3 player. Moving it often made the compact disc skip.

33

VIDEO GAMES CONSOLE

Computer games consoles and video games machines have been around since the 1960s. Early versions had just a few games, like 'tennis' with two bats and a ball – in black and white! The latest consoles have hundreds of games in stunning fast-action 3D colour. You can play yourself, or against friends, or online with someone on the other side of the world.

Eureka!

The first computer game using graphics – pictures and symbols rather than words – was noughts-and-crosses in 1952. 'Tennis' followed in 1958, and the first true computer game SpaceWar! arrived in 1962.

Whatever next?

Some people say video games should have built-in 'rest periods' where the game stops for ten minutes every hour, for health reasons and to prevent people getting obsessed.

SONY PLAYSTATION

One of the most popular games ever was Space Invaders. It was launched in 1978 in video gaming arcades and then for home machines. No other arcade game has been played so much.

Main board

✳ Virtual WORLDS

Video 'games' on the Internet have become so detailed and complex that they are almost like leading an alternative existence in the virtual world of computing. Avatars (a name derived from the Hindu religion) are characters or representations that gamers use for themselves, varying from human-like forms to animals, monsters, robots, machines or simple symbols or icons.

Chips The many microchips include a clock chip that ensures all the circuits work together properly and signals are sent between them on time.

Video games consoles are now in the seventh generation with models such as the Sony PlayStation 3, Microsoft Xbox 360 and Nintendo Wii.

Gamers gather at big meetings to play the latest releases

Optical disc drive Advanced games machines can play DVDs and Blu-ray discs, and so be used as a disc player to watch movies on a high-definition (HD) television or computer display.

PLAYSTATION

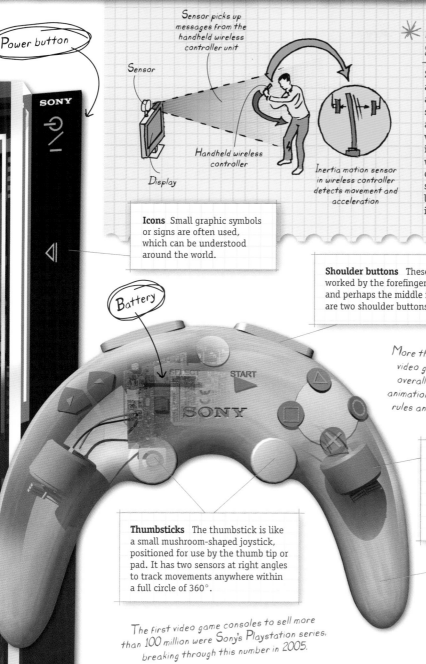

Power button

Sensor picks up messages from the handheld wireless controller unit

Sensor

Handheld wireless controller

Display

Inertia motion sensor in wireless controller detects movement and acceleration

SONY

✳ How do MOTION SENSORS work?

Some handheld controllers, such as Nintendo's 'Wii-mote', are able to sense movements and send information to the console about the player's actions. One version has a tiny gyroscope inside, which is a spinning weight that resists being tilted or moved. Others have flexible strips or weights on springs that lag behind when the controller is moved about.

Icons Small graphic symbols or signs are often used, which can be understood around the world.

Battery

Shoulder buttons These buttons are worked by the forefinger (first finger) and perhaps the middle finger if there are two shoulder buttons.

SELECT   START

SONY

More than 100 people work on a typical video game, with teams developing the overall appearance, the graphics and animations, the music and sounds and the rules and strategies of the game itself.

Force feedback A small electric motor with an offset weight spins to shake or vibrate the handset, for example, if you drive your racing car off the track onto rough ground.

Thumbsticks The thumbstick is like a small mushroom-shaped joystick, positioned for use by the thumb tip or pad. It has two sensors at right angles to track movements anywhere within a full circle of 360°.

Controller Buttons on the wireless controller make choices from menus, move items around the screen, open and close doors and boxes, fire guns and other actions, depending on the game.

The first video game consoles to sell more than 100 million were Sony's Playstation series, breaking through this number in 2005.

HOME CINEMA

A trip to the real cinema is an exciting event, to watch the new blockbuster movie on the big screen with loud sound all around. But in the past 20 years home cinemas have become bigger and better. The key parts are a widescreen display or television, a sound system with several loudspeakers, and the movie itself, usually on a DVD player.

Eureka!

The first CDs were sold in the early 1980s. They were used for audio (sound), usually recorded music. Computer engineers then used them to store words, pictures and software, applications or programs, and data files. In recent years they have been partly replaced for data storage by devices such as mini hard drives, microdrives and memory cards, chips or sticks.

Whatever next?

Scientists are in the process of developing holographic displays where the scenes and objects are projected as coloured lights in three dimensions, including true depth rather than the illusion of depth on a flat screen.

Blu-ray discs look like bluish versions of a CD or DVD. They use blue laser light, which can read tinier spots than the usual red DVD laser. This enables the Blu-ray disc to hold more information – 25 or even 50 GB, for movies in HD (high-definition).

Speakers In a standard 5:1 loudspeaker set-up there is one subwoofer for very deep sounds that can be positioned almost anywhere, left and right front speakers for stereo effect, a central front speaker to 'fill the gap' for sounds coming from the middle, and left and right rear speakers for 'surround sound'.

Many modern smash-hit movies such as WALL-E use CGI

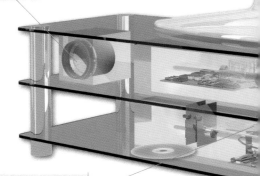

✳ SUPER-REAL

Many spectacular films use CGI, computer generated images, either for special effects amid real-life action or for an entire animated movie. Characters and scenes are built up as three-dimensional net-like 'meshes' in computer memory, showing their basic shapes. The meshes can be manipulated and changed according to mathematical rules, such as when a character walks along.

DVD player A standard DVD holds about 4.7 GB (gigabytes), which is up to six times more information than a CD. That's enough for colour pictures and sound for more than two hours of movie.

The first cinema screening was in Paris, France, in 1895. Brothers August and Louis Lumière showed ten 50-second films they had made, including one of workers leaving their factory.

Plasma flat screen

Wide screen The wide screen format of 16:9 (see page 16) has the correct proportions of width to height to fit neatly in our field of vision – the complete area we can see with both eyes.

✳ How do CDs and DVDs work?

Compact discs and digital versatile (or video) discs are optical – they use light. Each disc has a spiral track of tiny hollows or pits with flat areas, called lands, between. The sequence of pits and lands contains the digitally coded information. As the disc spins, a laser beam reflects off the pits but not the lands. The flashes of reflection are picked up by a detector.

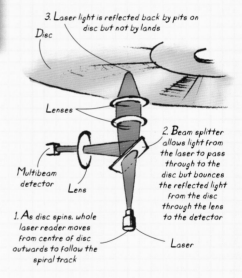

3. Laser light is reflected back by pits on disc but not by lands

Disc

Lenses

2. Beam splitter allows light from the laser to pass through to the disc but bounces the reflected light from the disc through the lens to the detector

Multibeam detector

Lens

1. As disc spins, whole laser reader moves from centre of disc outwards to follow the spiral track

Laser

Component shelving

Connecting cables There are several types of connecting cables including elongated 21-pin SCART plugs, component video leads with red, green and blue plugs, small round S-video plugs, DVI (Digital Visual Interface) plugs as used for computer monitors, and the latest 19-pin HDMI (High-Definition Multimedia Interface) design.

Sound system Audio information from the DVD is fed into the sound system, which has controls such as volume (loudness), bass (deep notes), treble (high notes), balance (left or right speakers) and fade (front to rear speakers).

VIRTUAL REALITY

Reality is real. Virtuality is not – but it seems real to our senses such as vision, hearing and touch. The best virtual reality or VR systems feed information such as sights, sounds and movements to the human brain and trick it into believing that things are real and actually exist, rather than being artificial or 'pretend'. VR can be used for fun and entertainment, and for serious purposes such as training pilots to fly and surgeons to carry out medical operations.

Eureka!

Some of the first VR machines were flight simulators for pilots and air crew. In World War II (1939–1945) the Celestial Navigation Trainer, a massive machine at 13.7 metres high, could hold an entire bomber aircraft crew training for night-time missions.

Whatever next?

As VR equipment becomes faster and more complicated, more body senses can be stimulated. Tiny pellets of different odours can be released from the headset, for example, the smell of smoke when training firefighters to tackle a virtual inferno.

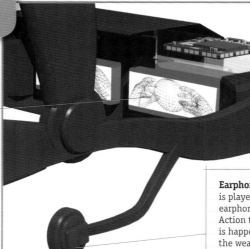

Screens Two screens give slightly different views of the scene, just like human eyes. The brain merges these into one three-dimensional view.

The Virtual Cocoon Room stimulates all the senses to take the person on a tour of anywhere in the world, from the African grasslands to a deep cave.

Earphones Stereo sound is played through the earphones or headphones. Action that looks as if it is happening to the left of the wearer is accompanied by sounds that are louder in the left earpiece.

✳ VIRTUALLY FLYING

Full motion flight simulators not only show a widescreen view of what is outside, which changes according to which way the pilot guides the 'aircraft'. The simulator or 'sim' also leans, tilts and shakes using powerful, fast-acting hydraulic pistons underneath, to recreate the movements of the aircraft. It can make a beginner feel very airsick!

Pilots train in a Boeing 727 'sim'

Virtual surgery can be extended into tele-surgery or remote surgery, where a surgeon in one place works a console that controls robot equipment operating on the patient in another place.

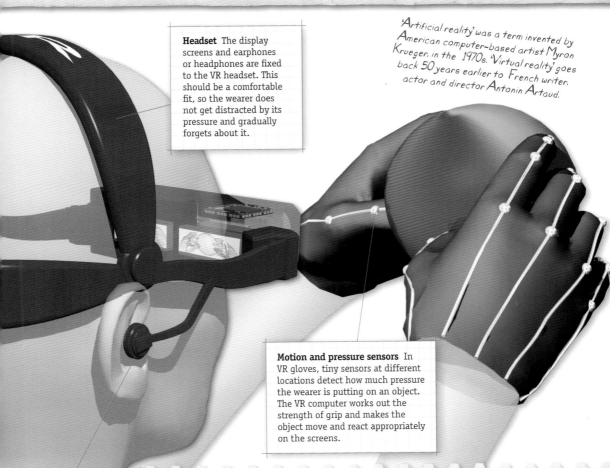

Headset The display screens and earphones or headphones are fixed to the VR headset. This should be a comfortable fit, so the wearer does not get distracted by its pressure and gradually forgets about it.

'Artificial reality' was a term invented by American computer-based artist Myron Krueger, in the 1970s. 'Virtual reality' goes back 50 years earlier to French writer, actor and director Antonin Artaud.

Motion and pressure sensors In VR gloves, tiny sensors at different locations detect how much pressure the wearer is putting on an object. The VR computer works out the strength of grip and makes the object move and react appropriately on the screens.

Wireless link The VR headset, gloves and perhaps even a whole body suit are linked by radio to the main console, so that the wearer can move and react freely.

The first VR headsets were built in the late 1960s. They were so heavy that they had to be hung from a frame above to avoid crushing the wearer!

✳ How does STEREO VISION work?

Human eyes each see a slightly different view of the world, known as stereoscopic vision. The closer an object, the more different these views. By comparing them, the brain works out the distance of the object. A VR headset's screens show two different views, one for each eye, with no area of overlap as when looking at a normal TV screen. The brain combines the separate views so that objects look and 'feel' as if they are near or far.

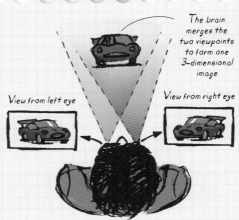

The brain merges the two viewpoints to form one 3-dimensional image

View from left eye

View from right eye

MOBILE PHONE

It's hard to imagine life without the 'mobile' or cellphone. Yet just 20 years ago these handy gadgets were three times bigger and cost five times more – and text messaging was almost unknown. Today's models do not so much shrink in size, as they did in the past. Rather they pack in more and more functions, such as games, camera, video and sound recording, satnav, Bluetooth short-range wireless link, Internet access, music player, radio and television.

Eureka!

In the 1980s, early 'mobile' phones were the size of house bricks and just as heavy. Apart from progress in microchips and radio circuits, one of the main advances has been batteries that are smaller and lighter but last many times longer.

Whatever next?

Technically it is possible to make a mobile phone smaller than your little finger. However the screen, icons and buttons would be too small to see or manipulate. Advances in voice control may overcome this problem.

In 2008 about two mobile phones in every five sold were made by Nokia.

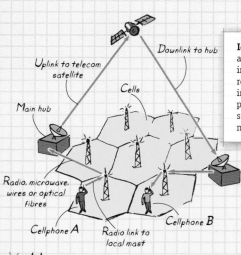

Uplink to telecom satellite

Downlink to hub

Cells

Main hub

Radio, microwave, wires or optical fibres

Cellphone A

Radio link to local mast

Cellphone B

Icons An icon is a small picture, image or symbol representing information or a particular function such as 'Send text message'.

✳ How do CELLPHONES work?

Each area or cell has a radio transmitter-receiver mast that regularly sends out its identification code. A cellphone detects the strongest code and sends outgoing talk or text messages to it. The mast links by radio, microwaves or wires to a main hub, which communicates with the whole telecom network including satellites. The network finds the receiver cellphone and sends the message to the nearest mast – which could be in the next cell!

In clean, flat, open areas, a typical mobile phone has a range of about 40 km to the nearest transmitter-receiver mast.

NiMH cell The nickel-metal hydride cell is a small but powerful and long-lasting rechargeable battery. Larger versions power electric cars and trucks.

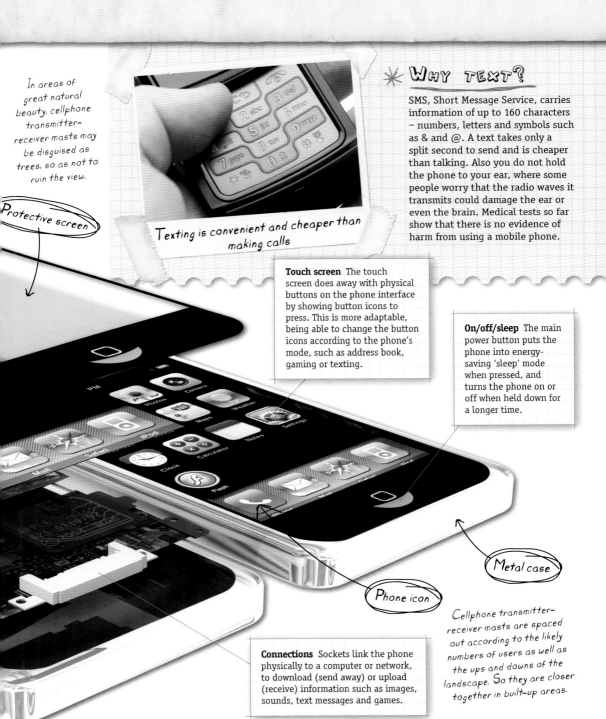

In areas of great natural beauty, cellphone transmitter-receiver masts may be disguised as trees, so as not to ruin the view.

Protective screen

Texting is convenient and cheaper than making calls

WHY TEXT?

SMS, Short Message Service, carries information of up to 160 characters – numbers, letters and symbols such as & and @. A text takes only a split second to send and is cheaper than talking. Also you do not hold the phone to your ear, where some people worry that the radio waves it transmits could damage the ear or even the brain. Medical tests so far show that there is no evidence of harm from using a mobile phone.

Touch screen The touch screen does away with physical buttons on the phone interface by showing button icons to press. This is more adaptable, being able to change the button icons according to the phone's mode, such as address book, gaming or texting.

On/off/sleep The main power button puts the phone into energy-saving 'sleep' mode when pressed, and turns the phone on or off when held down for a longer time.

Metal case

Phone icon

Cellphone transmitter-receiver masts are spaced out according to the likely numbers of users as well as the ups and downs of the landscape. So they are closer together in built-up areas.

Connections Sockets link the phone physically to a computer or network, to download (send away) or upload (receive) information such as images, sounds, text messages and games.

SATELLITE NAVIGATION SYSTEM

Satellite navigation describes the use of a GPS receiver to pinpoint or 'fix' your location, and navigate your way from place to place. GPS is the Global Positioning System – a network of about 30 satellites 22,200 kilometres high in space, orbiting the Earth twice daily – plus the radio links, computers and other equipment that control and co-ordinate them. A GPS receiver detects signals from the satellites and displays its own position or location on a screen.

Eureka!

The first global navigation system was Transit in the 1960s. It had five satellites, took two minutes to make a 'fix' and had a best accuracy of about 100 metres.

In some cars with tinted windows and heated windscreens, the metal in the tints and heating elements can prevent satellite radio signals from reaching the GPS unit inside.

Whatever next?

The USA developed the main GPS we use today, but other nations and groups are building their own systems. These include China's Compass, Russia's Glosnass and India's IRNSS. The European Union, in partnership with several other countries, is developing the Galileo GPS.

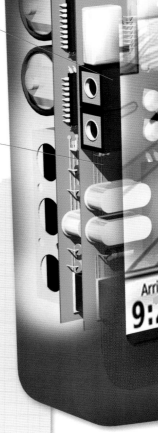

Batteries

Changes high in the Earth's atmosphere, especially in the layer called the ionosphere (from 50 to 1000 km) can bend or weaken GPS satellite signals. Making corrections for this problem is a big challenge for GPS designers.

Receiver The receiver unit compares the available satellite signals and 'locks on' to the three strongest or most suitable ones.

Components Among the many chips inside, SIDRAM (synchronous dynamic random access memory) holds temporary information that can be changed fast. It is linked or 'synched' to the other components so that it supplies its information almost instantly on demand. In a GPS receiver, fractions of thousandths of a second are very important.

Arri
9:

✳ How does GPS work?

At any place on Earth's surface, a GPS receiver can 'see' in a clear line three or more of the system's satellites, high above in space, and so receive signals from them. Each satellite continuously transmits its own identity and also the exact time. Radio waves go fast, but there is a slight time difference between them reaching the receiver, because they are different distances from it. The receiver works out the delay in time from each satellite and compares them, to know its distance from them and so work out its own position on Earth's surface.

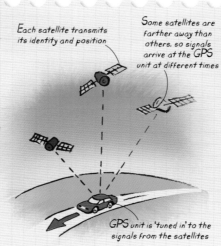

Each satellite transmits its identity and position

Some satellites are farther away than others, so signals arrive at the GPS unit at different times

GPS unit is 'tuned in' to the signals from the satellites

Antenna (aerial) As well as an in-built antenna, the wires that connect the unit to an electricity supply may also be used to receive radio signals. The circuits are designed to detect radio signals from all available GPS satellites, and to minimize the signals from other sources such as television, radio and mobile phone networks.

DGPS is used to map a glacier and follow global warming

✳ NEVER LOST AGAIN

As the name 'global' suggests, GPS works anywhere in the world – even in frozen polar wastes or on remote mountaintops, where there is no mobile phone network. Its accuracy depends partly on the cost of the receiver, with its complex circuits to compare satellite signals, but is usually to within a few metres. Even better accuracy is obtained from a receiver that can also detect radio signals from one or more transmitters on land, known as DGPS, differential GPS.

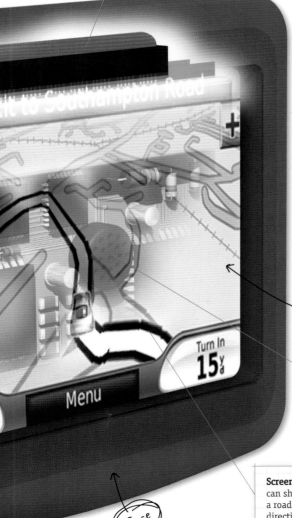

Anti-glare touch screen

Speaker Most GPS units can 'talk' using pre-recorded words to give instructions such as 'At the next road junction, turn left'. On many receivers there is a choice of voices and accents.

The main GPS was developed by the USA for military use, with secretly coded satellite signals. It was made available to anyone by altering the codes following a terrible aircraft disaster in 1983 when 269 people died.

Screen The LCD colour display can show various images, often a road map of the area showing direction of travel with the receiver at the lower centre.

Case

CARS, TRUCKS AND BIKES

INTRODUCTION

The wheel was invented about 6000 years ago in western Asia. Initially it was a potter's wheel, used for shaping clay bowls and vases. By 3500 years ago, wheels were in use on wagons and chariots pulled by horses, oxen or slaves. It took another 3300 years to invent wheeled vehicles with engines. Just before them, the first bicycles appeared. They had no pedals – you pushed your feet against the ground. Then came personal engine-driven transport, and we have never looked back – except to see who is behind.

The penny-farthing bicycle of the 1870s had direct drive, with pedals attached to the wheel.

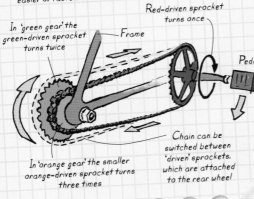
Bicycle gears make pedalling easier or faster, but not both.

In 'green gear' the green-driven sprocket turns twice

Red-driven sprocket turns once

Frame

Pedal

In 'orange gear' the smaller orange-driven sprocket turns three times

Chain can be switched between 'driven' sprockets, which are attached to the rear wheel

ON THE ROAD

The first pedal-powered bicycles and engine-driven cars and motorcycles appeared towards the end of the 1800s. Most transport was still animal-drawn and roads were little more than dirt tracks with sharp stones and deep holes. Many early cars were steam- or electric-powered, and most were hand-built in the tradition of horse-drawn carriages.

MOTORING FOR ALL

In 1908 the American Ford Motor Company introduced an assembly line where lots of identical cars could be put together from already-made parts. Suddenly, vehicles were cheaper and demand grew. By the 1950s some cars were huge, covered with shiny chrome and lined with leather. Real mass motoring took hold in the 1960s with smaller 'budget' cars such as the VW Beetle and the Mini.

The British Mini was not only a very small car but also a fashion item and symbol of the 1960s.

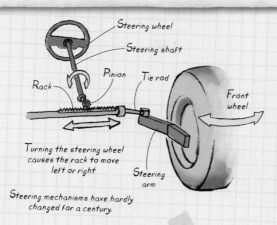

Steering wheel
Steering shaft
Rack
Pinion
Tie rod
Front wheel
Steering arm

Turning the steering wheel causes the rack to move left or right

Steering mechanisms have hardly changed for a century.

BRANCHING OUT

As road vehicles became more powerful and more reliable, they evolved into new kinds. Today there are huge lorries to transport loads, emergency vehicles such as fire appliances and breakdown services, all-wheel-drive off-roaders and pick-ups to carry almost anything. More gears, better brakes, stronger engines and smoother suspension help to make these vehicles more efficient and the ride more comfortable. Whether dashing to the shops in the family car, messing about on bicycles, boarding the school bus or cruising the empty freeway, road vehicles are vital in our daily lives.

THE RACE IS ON!

Any new way of going places meant that people wanted to be there first. Cycling races and motor sports blossomed, from rallying to track events to dragster duels. In today's Formula One, super-fast cars that cost tens of millions race in front of the biggest audiences on the planet.

Massive road trains are used to transport goods across the vast open areas of Australia.

Motor vehicles have come a long way in a century, but with fossil fuels running out and global warming on the increase, could we live without them?

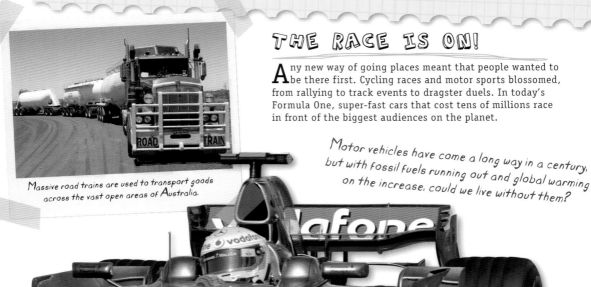

More than 600 million TV viewers watch each Formula One race.

MOUNTAIN BIKE

The overall design of the bicycle has hardly changed for more than 100 years. It is made up of many simple machines or basic mechanical devices such as levers, wheels and axles, pulleys, gears and springs. A bicycle also gives its rider exercise to stay healthy, and because it has no engine and polluting exhaust gases, it's excellent for the environment.

Mountain-biking became an official Olympic sport in 1996 – 100 years after ordinary cycle racing.

Eureka!

The first bicycles were developed in Germany and France during the 1810s. However they had no pedals. Riders had to push the ground with their feet to 'scoot' along.

Whatever next?

Electric bicycles are predicted to become much more popular, complete with a see-through, bubble-like cover to keep you dry.

Spring suspension When the rear wheel goes over a bump, its frame tilts up and squeezes a large spring to absorb the shock.

Gear changer A device called the derailleur moves the chain sideways from one sprocket to another, to change gear.

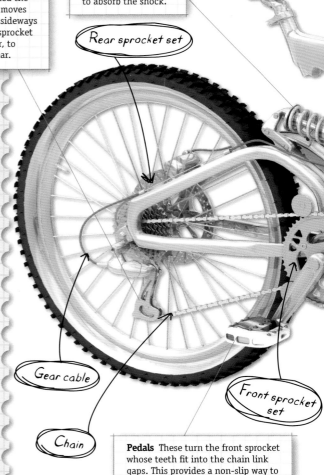

Rear sprocket set

Medium-sized green 'driven' sprocket turns two times (lower gear)

Large red 'driver' sprocket turns once

Frame

Pedal

Small orange 'driven' sprocket turns three times (higher gear)

Driven sprockets are attached to the rear wheel

Chain can be switched between 'driven' sprockets

Gear cable

Front sprocket set

Chain

Pedals These turn the front sprocket whose teeth fit into the chain link gaps. This provides a non-slip way to turn the rear sprocket.

✳ How do CHAIN AND SPROCKET GEARS work?

A bicycle's rear sprockets or cogs have different numbers of teeth. In a low gear, each turn of the front sprocket (attached to the pedals) means the rear sprocket (attached to the wheel) turns twice. You don't go very far for one turn of the front sprocket but pedalling is less effort. In a higher gear, the chain moves to a smaller sprocket. This turns three times for one turn of the front sprocket. So you go farther for each turn of the pedals but pedalling is more effort. The idea is to change gear to keep your pedalling speed and effort constant, at the best rate for you.

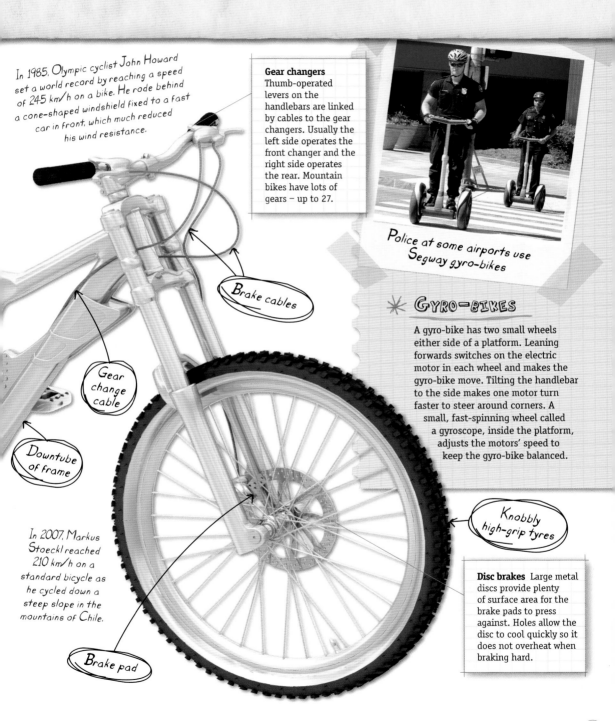

In 1985, Olympic cyclist John Howard set a world record by reaching a speed of 245 km/h on a bike. He rode behind a cone-shaped windshield fixed to a fast car in front, which much reduced his wind resistance.

Gear changers
Thumb-operated levers on the handlebars are linked by cables to the gear changers. Usually the left side operates the front changer and the right side operates the rear. Mountain bikes have lots of gears – up to 27.

Police at some airports use Segway gyro-bikes

✳ GYRO-BIKES

A gyro-bike has two small wheels either side of a platform. Leaning forwards switches on the electric motor in each wheel and makes the gyro-bike move. Tilting the handlebar to the side makes one motor turn faster to steer around corners. A small, fast-spinning wheel called a gyroscope, inside the platform, adjusts the motors' speed to keep the gyro-bike balanced.

Brake cables

Gear change cable

Downtube of frame

In 2007, Markus Stoeckl reached 210 km/h on a standard bicycle as he cycled down a steep slope in the mountains of Chile.

Brake pad

Knobbly high-grip tyres

Disc brakes Large metal discs provide plenty of surface area for the brake pads to press against. Holes allow the disc to cool quickly so it does not overheat when braking hard.

ROAD RACE BICYCLE

The road race bicycle is the specialist long-distance machine of the cycling world. It's much lighter than a commuter or mountain bike and is more stripped-down and simpler too, with fewer moving parts to go wrong. The best road-racers easily cover 200 kilometres in one day, even in bad weather.

Eureka!

The first bicycles had solid wood or metal wheel rims, then solid rubber tyres – not very comfortable. The pneumatic or air-filled tyre was invented in 1887 by John Boyd Dunlop for his son's bicycle.

Ball bearings A typical bicycle has up to ten sets of ball bearings. Two in the head tube support the handlebars and front forks.

Head tube

Front fork

Racing handlebars Curled-down racing, or dropped handlebars, mean the rider leans forwards, head down. This causes less air resistance than sitting upright and allows the legs to press harder on the pedals.

✳ How do BALL BEARINGS work?

A bearing reduces rubbing or friction where one part of a machine moves against another. It decreases wear and lessens the movement energy lost as heat. In a ball bearing design, hard metal balls fit snugly between outer and inner ring-shaped parts called races. The balls can rotate in all directions, which spreads out both the wear over their surfaces and any heat from friction to prevent overheating.

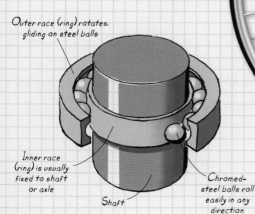

Outer race (ring) rotates, gliding on steel balls

Inner race (ring) is usually fixed to shaft or axle

Shaft

Chromed-steel balls roll easily in any direction

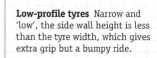

Low-profile tyres Narrow and 'low', the side wall height is less than the tyre width, which gives extra grip but a bumpy ride.

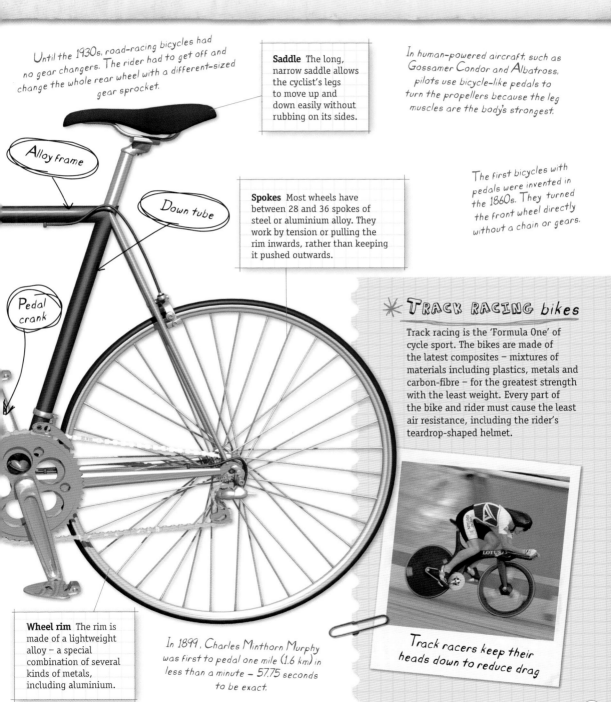

Until the 1930s, road-racing bicycles had no gear changers. The rider had to get off and change the whole rear wheel with a different-sized gear sprocket.

Saddle The long, narrow saddle allows the cyclist's legs to move up and down easily without rubbing on its sides.

In human-powered aircraft, such as Gossamer Condor and Albatross, pilots use bicycle-like pedals to turn the propellers because the leg muscles are the body's strongest.

Alloy frame

Down tube

Spokes Most wheels have between 28 and 36 spokes of steel or aluminium alloy. They work by tension or pulling the rim inwards, rather than keeping it pushed outwards.

The first bicycles with pedals were invented in the 1860s. They turned the front wheel directly without a chain or gears.

Pedal crank

✳ TRACK RACING bikes

Track racing is the 'Formula One' of cycle sport. The bikes are made of the latest composites – mixtures of materials including plastics, metals and carbon-fibre – for the greatest strength with the least weight. Every part of the bike and rider must cause the least air resistance, including the rider's teardrop-shaped helmet.

Wheel rim The rim is made of a lightweight alloy – a special combination of several kinds of metals, including aluminium.

In 1899, Charles Minthorn Murphy was first to pedal one mile (1.6 km) in less than a minute – 57.75 seconds to be exact.

Track racers keep their heads down to reduce drag

TOURING MOTORCYCLE

Long and low, the touring motorcycle is one of the coolest-looking machines on the road. It may not be the fastest on two wheels but it cruises the highways in great comfort. The bike has plenty of suspension to soak up the lumps and bumps and lots of power to overtake at speed and travel long distances.

Eureka!

In 1885 Gottlieb Daimler fitted his newly designed petrol engine into the frame of a wooden bicycle and invented the first motorcycle, the Reitwagen ('Riding Car'). Motorbikes went into mass production in 1894 with the 1500cc Hildebrand & Wolfmüller.

Whatever next?

Electric motorcycles and electric scooters become more popular and faster every year – the speed record is 270 kilometres per hour!

HARLEY DAVIDSON

'Bucket' seat

Cylinder cooling fins

Coil spring damper suspension

Exhaust pipes These long tubes mean exhaust gases are directed out of the engine so that it works more efficiently. They also reduce or muffle the engine's noise.

☀ How does COIL SPRING DAMPER suspension work?

Spring suspension absorbs holes, bumps and other rough parts of the road. However when a spring is squeezed and then allowed to push and lengthen again, it tends to 'bounce' back, shortening and lengthening several times. This is reduced by adding a hydraulic damper inside the spring. It's a tube filled with sealed-in oil, into which a smaller tube slides like a telescope. The thick oil slows down and smooths out any fast sliding movements to reduce or dampen the 'bounce' effect.

Upper mounting fixes to motorcycle frame

Oil-filled damper reduces the 'bounce' caused by the spring

Strong coil spring compresses as the vehicle goes over a bump

Lower mounting fixes to wheel's suspension arm

Transmission A series of gears transfers the engine's turning power to the drive belt and then on to the rear wheel.

Some motorcycles have a small sidecar for passengers, complete with its own wheel.

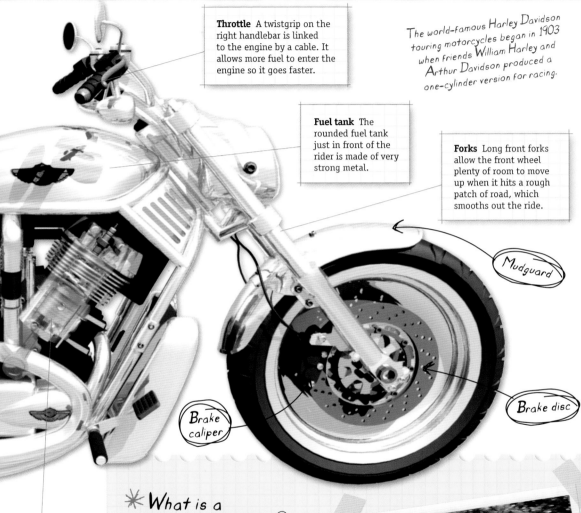

Throttle A twistgrip on the right handlebar is linked to the engine by a cable. It allows more fuel to enter the engine so it goes faster.

The world-famous Harley Davidson touring motorcycles began in 1903 when friends William Harley and Arthur Davidson produced a one-cylinder version for racing.

Fuel tank The rounded fuel tank just in front of the rider is made of very strong metal.

Forks Long front forks allow the front wheel plenty of room to move up when it hits a rough patch of road, which smooths out the ride.

Mudguard

Brake caliper

Brake disc

Engine The two-cylinder 1584cc engine is low down between the two wheels, which makes the motorcycle more stable and less likely to tip over sideways.

✳ What is a MAXI-SCOOTER?

Scooters usually have smaller wheels than motorcycles and streamlined coverings called fairings over most of the vehicle. Older scooters were not very fast or well-balanced. New maxi-scooters are faster, more comfortable, safer, change gear automatically and can be fitted with a petrol engine or electric motor.

Maxi-scooters make ideal runabouts

SUPERBIKE

Few road machines can accelerate (pick up speed) or travel as fast as the superbike – a high-powered, souped-up motorcycle. These fierce-looking machines are road versions of even faster track-racing motorcycles. Because of their great power, light weight and sensitive steering, they are tricky to ride and definitely not for the beginner.

Eureka!

Before the 1950s, riders had to kick-start their motorcycles by pushing down a pedal to turn over the engine. On most modern bikes this is done by an electric motor, as in a car.

Whatever next?

Motorcycle stunt riders are always inventing new tricks – such as speeding off a jump ramp and somersaulting two or three times.

A typical racing superbike can reach an amazing 300 km/h – but on the track, not on ordinary roads!

Windscreen The clear toughened plastic screen makes air flow up and over the rider at high speed.

Clutch lever The clutch disconnects the engine from the gearbox so the rider can change gear without damaging the spinning cogs inside (see page 58).

Brake pad presses on disc

Steel brake disc

Hydraulic fluid pushes a piston that presses the brake pad against the disc

Brake pipe

Disc rotates with wheel

✳ How do BRAKES work?

A disc brake has a large metal disc attached to the wheel. Brake pads made of very hard material, such as composite ceramic, press on this to cause friction and slow down the disc's rotation. The force to push the pads onto the disc may come from a cable attached to the brake lever. Or it can be hydraulic, from oil that is forced at high pressure from the brake lever or brake pedal along the brake pipe.

Brake disc

Streamlined fairing

Radiator scoop This low opening collects air to flow over the radiator just behind it, which contains the water that keeps the engine cool.

Since the Superbike World Championships began in 1988, makers Honda and Ducati have won all but two of the yearly titles.

Apart from being a nickname for a fast bike, 'Superbike' is also an official category of motorcycle racing for engines up to 1200cc.

✳ QUAD BIKES

A mix of car and motorcycle, quad bikes have four wheels but no main body or covering for the rider. A quad bike is difficult to handle because it tends to tip over if the rider steers around a corner too fast. It's great fun for riding over muddy fields and rough tracks.

Quad bikes have plenty of suspension

Exhaust

Swingarm The U-shaped swingarm tilts up and down at its joint with the frame so the rear wheel can move up and down as part of the suspension.

Tyres Racing superbikes have smooth or 'slick' tyres with no pattern or tread for good grip at high speed.

Three-spoked wheel

Water-cooled engine

Gear pedal Depending on which gear the motorcycle is already in, flipping the foot pedal up or down changes to the next gear.

Lightweight alloy wheels

SALOON CAR

The typical saloon car has been around for about 100 years and its basic design has hardly changed. It has four wheels, an engine in a compartment at the front that drives the front or rear wheels, two front seats and two or three rear seats in the main body. It also has a separate luggage compartment, or boot, at the rear.

Eureka!

The first petrol-engined automobile or 'car' (motorized carriage) was built by Karl Benz in 1885. It only had three wheels, the front one being steered by a lever.

Whatever next?

Cars of the future may drive themselves using GPS (satellite navigation) and radio links to a massive central computer.

Engine Typical family cars have engines from 2000cc (two litres) upwards. Usually there are four or six cylinders, one behind the other. The V8 shown here has two rows of four cylinders at a 'V' angle (see page 61).

Front suspension Upper and lower suspension arms allow the front wheels to move up and down.

* How do PETROL ENGINES work?

A petrol engine has a piston that moves up and down inside a cylinder. It works in four stages, or strokes.

1. Inlet The piston moves down and sucks a mixture of fuel and air into the cylinder through an inlet valve.

2. Compression The piston moves up and squashes (compresses) the mixture.

3. Combustion An electric spark plug makes the mixture explode, forcing the piston down.

4. Exhaust The piston goes back up and pushes the burnt mixture out through an exhaust valve. The piston's movements turn the engine's crankshaft, by a con-rod.

Headlight

Radiator grill

In the early 20th century, the fastest cars were steam-powered or electric.

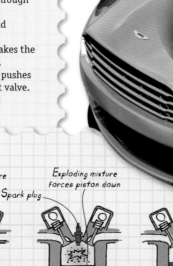

Fuel mixture enters engine through inlet valve

Inlet valve closes and piston moves up, compressing fuel mixture

Exploding mixture forces piston down

Spark plug

Exhaust valve opens, burnt mixture leaves as exhaust gases

Cylinder

Piston

Con-rod

Con-rod turns crankshaft

Crankcase

Stroke 1   Crankshaft   Stroke 2   Stroke 3   Stroke 4

ASTON MARTIN SALOON

In 1908 the mass-produced Ford Model T or 'Tin Lizzy' meant that ordinary people could afford a car.

Rear transmission The prop shaft is linked by the gears to the rear half-shaft axles on the wheels.

Propeller shaft Many saloon cars are front wheel drive. In the rear wheel drive design (shown here), the propeller shaft carries the turning power from the gearbox, along the underside of the car to the rear wheels.

Alloy wheels

The most successful car of all time is the Toyota Corolla, which began production in 1966. More than 35 million have been sold.

In the 1960s the tiny Austin Mini was a 'must-have' fashion car, with a transverse engine driving the front wheels to save space.

An all-electric car gets a kerbside charge

✳ GREEN CARS

'Hybrid' cars have a small petrol engine and an electric motor with batteries. The car can run on electricity very quietly with no polluting exhaust fumes. If the batteries run down, the petrol engine switches on to recharge them. The petrol engine can also add power to the electric motor for more speed.

SUPER SPORTS CAR

For people with plenty of money, sports cars with powerful engines are the top road machines. They have little room for the week's shopping and would scrape along bumpy tracks, but they are sleek, speedy and striking. The low design and smooth lines allow the car to slip along with the least air resistance, which becomes more important as you travel faster.

Eureka!

The first wings appeared on sports cars and racing cars in the 1960s. They work like an upside-down aircraft wing to press the car downwards for better tyre grip and improved steering.

Whatever next?

Bugatti, maker of the world's leading supercar, the Veyron, plan a new model within five years to hold onto the sports car top spot.

The Bugatti Veyron was introduced in 2005 as the fastest production car in the world. It's also one of the most expensive, costing more than one million euros.

The Veyron is named after Pierre Veyron, the racing driver who won the 1939 Le Mans 24 Hour race in a Bugatti.

Retractable wing The rear wing is known as a spoiler. If you want to travel at speeds of between 200 and 370 kilometres per hour in the Veyron, a switch lowers the car and wing, which then disturbs air flow that might suck the car upwards.

W16 engine The W16 engine is a double version of the V8 engine, with 16 cylinders in four rows of four at an angle, like two overlapping Vs.

✳ How does a GEARBOX work?

A car gearbox has several sets of spinning gear wheels, or cogs. Some are on the layshaft, an 'extra' shaft between the drive shaft from the engine and the shaft to the road wheels. The gear change mechanism works by sliding the gear collar along a shaft so that it rotates to make the cogs fit together in different combinations. This makes the road wheels turn faster or slower for the same engine speed.

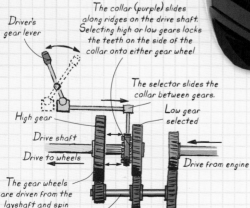

Driver's gear lever

The collar (purple) slides along ridges on the drive shaft. Selecting high or low gears locks the teeth on the side of the collar onto either gear wheel

The selector slides the collar between gears.

High gear

Low gear selected

Drive shaft

Drive to wheels

Drive from engine

The gear wheels are driven from the layshaft and spin free on the drive shaft until locked on by the collar

Layshaft

Exhaust pipe

Gearbox The seven-speed gearbox is computer controlled and can change gear in less than one-fifth of a second. The driver uses small gear-shift paddles next to the steering wheel.

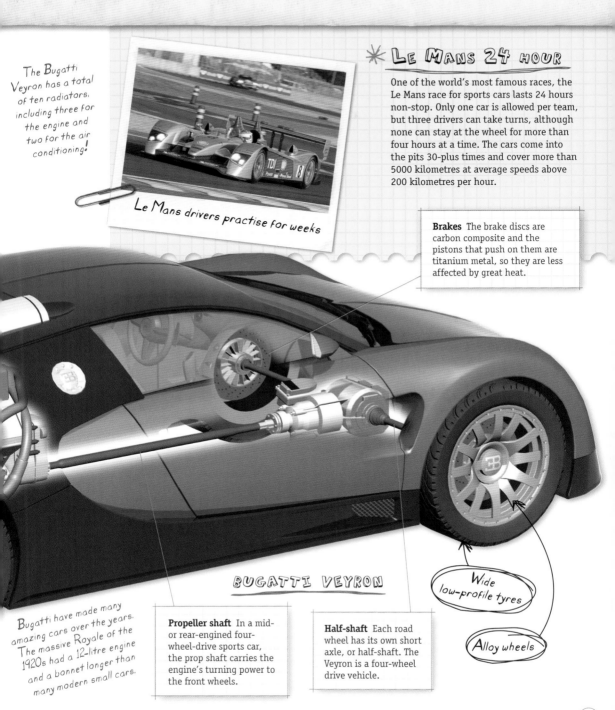

The Bugatti Veyron has a total of ten radiators, including three for the engine and two for the air conditioning!

Le Mans drivers practise for weeks

☀ LE MANS 24 HOUR

One of the world's most famous races, the Le Mans race for sports cars lasts 24 hours non-stop. Only one car is allowed per team, but three drivers can take turns, although none can stay at the wheel for more than four hours at a time. The cars come into the pits 30-plus times and cover more than 5000 kilometres at average speeds above 200 kilometres per hour.

Brakes The brake discs are carbon composite and the pistons that push on them are titanium metal, so they are less affected by great heat.

BUGATTI VEYRON

Bugatti have made many amazing cars over the years. The massive Royale of the 1920s had a 12-litre engine and a bonnet longer than many modern small cars.

Propeller shaft In a mid- or rear-engined four-wheel-drive sports car, the prop shaft carries the engine's turning power to the front wheels.

Half-shaft Each road wheel has its own short axle, or half-shaft. The Veyron is a four-wheel drive vehicle.

Wide low-profile tyres

Alloy wheels

F1 RACING CAR

Formula One cars are not the biggest racing machines, or the fastest, or the most powerful. But for all-round performance on a twisty track, speeding up and then braking hard to scream around corners, they cannot be beaten. An F1 car is built according to more than 1000 rules and regulations, from engine size to overall weight, the electronic sensors it must have, and using the same gearbox for four races in a row.

Eureka!

After many kinds of races with different cars and rules, the first F1 season was in 1950. There are about 18 races around the world in a year. Each race is more than 300 kilometres long but lasts less than two hours.

Whatever next?

The Rocket Racing League plans to hold races for rocket-powered cars and aircraft, each lasting between 60 and 90 minutes.

Telemetry Sensors for speed, brake temperature and many other features send information by radio signals to the team members in the pits.

Suspension arm The suspension arms swing to allow the wheel to move up and down.

Mirrors

Front wing The front wing produces about one-third of the down force of the rear wing. It keeps the front tyres pressed hard onto the track for accurate steering. The upright end plates direct air smoothly over the wheels.

An F1's engine is part of the car's structure, bolted to the driver's cockpit at the front, and the transmission and rear suspension at the back.

Nose cone

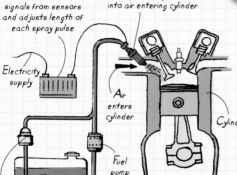

ECU (electronic control unit) receives signals from sensors and adjusts length of each spray pulse

Fuel injector squirts fuel into air entering cylinder

Electricity supply

Air enters cylinder

Cylinder

Fuel tank

Fuel pump

Fuel pressure regulator allows unused fuel back to the tank

✳ How does FUEL INJECTION work?

A fuel injector squirts fuel, under pressure from a fuel pump, into air being sucked into the cylinder. An electronic control unit calculates how much fuel per squirt, depending on sensor information such as air pressure, engine speed and how much oxygen is in the exhaust gases (which is linked to how much fuel is left unburnt).

Tyres There are tyres for dry conditions, wet conditions and intermediate (in between) are slicks with no tread pattern.

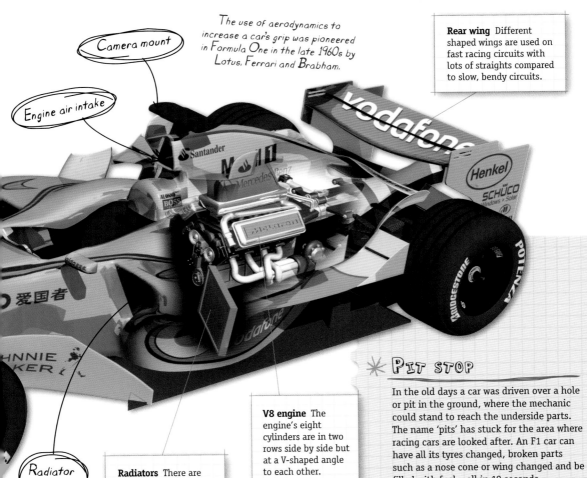

Camera mount

The use of aerodynamics to increase a car's grip was pioneered in Formula One in the late 1960s by Lotus, Ferrari and Brabham.

Engine air intake

Rear wing Different shaped wings are used on fast racing circuits with lots of straights compared to slow, bendy circuits.

Radiator air intake

Radiators There are two radiators, each in a pod on the side of the car next to the driver. They cool water that has circulated around the engine and picked up its heat.

V8 engine The engine's eight cylinders are in two rows side by side but at a V-shaped angle to each other.

The F1 engine can be up to 2.4 litres in size, has more than 5000 parts and produces over 900 horsepower – six times more than most family cars.

The F1 car's fuel tank is like a flexible bag made from the extremely strong material called Kevlar, as used in bullet-proof clothing.

✳ PIT STOP

In the old days a car was driven over a hole or pit in the ground, where the mechanic could stand to reach the underside parts. The name 'pits' has stuck for the area where racing cars are looked after. An F1 car can have all its tyres changed, broken parts such as a nose cone or wing changed and be filled with fuel – all in 10 seconds.

Pit crew refuel Lewis Hamilton's car

61

DRAGSTER

Dragster racing is the world's loudest, fastest form of motor racing – yet each race has only two competitors, no corners and lasts just a few seconds. The idea is to accelerate (pick up speed) as quickly as possible from a standing start, to be first across the finish line 402.3 metres (one-quarter of a mile) or 201 metres (one-eighth of a mile) away.

Eureka!

In 1951, Wally Parks had the idea of making unofficial and dangerous dragster-type street racing into an official sport. He founded the US National Hot Rod Association, which has run the sport since.

Whatever next?

Some drivers have experimented with jump ramps halfway along the drag strip (track) so that the race is half on the ground and half flying through the air!

Cockpit

Streamlined body The lightweight body is long, slim and tapering so that it slices through the air like an arrow.

Dragsters have just one gear – there's no time to change to a second one.

Twin 'meshing' impellers suck in and compress the air

Impellers spin around

Air blasted into carburettor

Roller bearing

Belt-driven pulley from engine drives first impeller

Gear on first impeller drives second impeller

Air sucked in   Casing

✳ How does a SUPERCHARGER work?

A supercharger forces air into the engine at high pressure so it carries extra fuel for greater speed and power. It consists of two screw-like devices called impellers that suck in air through an inlet and blast it from the outlet into the carburettor. The impellers are driven by a belt or chain from the engine. Turbochargers are similar but use a fan-like turbine rather than a direct mechanical drive (see page 68).

Front wheels The tiny front wheels mean less weight and air resistance. The front wing keeps them pushed onto the track.

Fuel tank

Front wing

The huge rear tyres on top-fuel dragsters wear out after about five races – less than 2 km. Ordinary car tyres usually last 30,000 km or more.

Smoke and flames at the 'burnout'

✳ WHACKY RACERS!

There are dozens of types or classes of dragster racing, depending on engine size and type of fuel. Before the start the enormous rear tyres are spun against the ground in a 'burnout' while the dragster stays still, to make them hot and sticky so they grip better.

Rear wing

Roll cage Drivers sit within a tubular metal frame or cage that gives protection if the dragster rolls over.

The fastest dragsters cross the finish line at more than 530 km/h – almost five times the British motorway speed limit.

Air intake manifold

Instrument panel

Supercharger

Short stub exhausts

Rear wheels The huge rear wheels have soft, slick (treadless) tyres. The driver and engine are both near the back so that their weight helps the tyres to press down and grip.

Top-fuel dragsters, the fastest type, use about 20 litres of fuel during the race, which is about 800 times more than a family car would use.

Supercharged V8 engine The largest engine in most races is 8.2 litres. Its supercharger means it can produce over 5000 horsepower.

Tubular alloy chassis The light but stiff chassis (the main framework) is made of various alloys or mixtures of metals.

4WD OFF-ROADER

A four-wheeled vehicle with four-wheel drive (4WD or 4x4) means that all four wheels are turned by engine power. A 4x2 vehicle has four wheels but only two are engine-powered, while 6x4 is a six-wheeled vehicle with engine power to four wheels. Four-wheel drive is best for ATVs – All-Terrain Vehicles that can go off-road and across almost any kind of terrain or ground, from soft sand to squashy mud to steep rocky slopes.

Eureka!

Car designers who built the first 4WD vehicles in the 1900s included Ferdinand Porsche, founder of the famous Porsche sports car and racing car organization. His first 4WD had an electric motor for each wheel. On some types of 4WDs all the four wheels steer, not just two.

Whatever next?

Military off-road vehicles have tested 4WDs with an extra two wheels that swing down to give added grip in the slippiest mud.

The Humvee's engine air intake, exhaust, electrical wires and similar parts are designed so that the vehicle can drive through water more than one metre deep.

Camouflage Military vehicles such as the Humvee are painted so they blend in with their surroundings. This is called camouflage.

Snorkel Air for the engine is sucked in through a tall pipe to avoid taking in water while crossing streams.

The military 4WD called the Humvee is used by US and other military forces around the world.

Lights

Radiator The radiator is well protected against damage from rocks by a strong metal plate underneath.

Tow points

☀ How does 4WD work?

In some cars a front engine drives the two rear wheels by a long propeller shaft. Most cars are front-wheel drive, with half-shafts at the front. The 4WD system combines the two so all four wheels turn under engine power. This gives much better grip on rough or slippery surfaces, especially when the tyres have a deep tread. The differential makes the two wheels it powers turn at different speeds, so when going around a corner, the outer one turns faster.

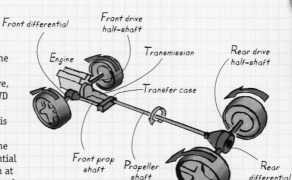

Front differential

Front drive half-shaft

Engine

Transmission

Rear drive half-shaft

Transfer case

Front prop shaft

Propeller shaft

Rear differential

Humvees are so tough they can be dropped by parachute from cargo planes.

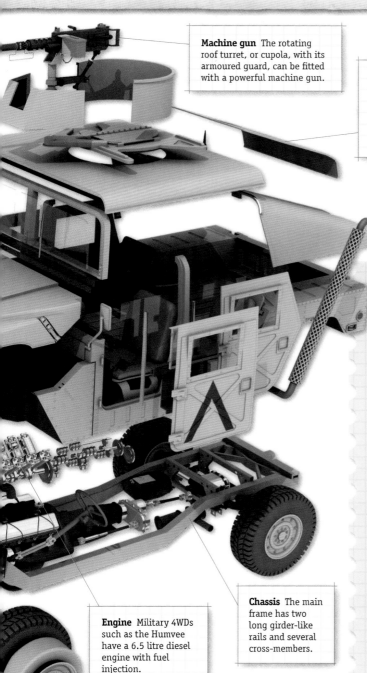

Machine gun The rotating roof turret, or cupola, with its armoured guard, can be fitted with a powerful machine gun.

Armour plating Thick, strong but light metal plates cover most of the bodywork to protect against bullets, land mines and other dangers.

The Humvee is named from its initials, HMMWV, meaning High Mobility Multi-purpose Wheeled Vehicle.

High exhaust

The Hummer can tackle any kind of difficult terrain

Engine Military 4WDs such as the Humvee have a 6.5 litre diesel engine with fuel injection.

Chassis The main frame has two long girder-like rails and several cross-members.

✳ MUSCLE-MACHINE!

The Humvee 4WD is available as a civilian (non-military) version – the Hummer 1. There are many other types of 4WDs used by farmers, foresters, ranchers, explorers, countryside workers and of course drivers keen on off-roading. Movie star and US politician Arnold Schwarzenegger has a 'green' Hummer that's been converted to run on non-polluting hydrogen fuel.

RALLY CAR

Rallies are tough races that can take place almost anywhere, from public roads (closed to everyday traffic for the event) to dirt tracks, forest trails, ice and snow, deserts and real racing circuits. A rally car is a special version of a normal production car that has a tuned-up engine and stronger mechanical parts.

Eureka!

Before satnav (satellite navigation), which uses GPS (the Global Positioning System of satellites), rally drivers sometimes got lost and ended up dozens of kilometres from the finish line.

Tough suspension The springs, shock absorber dampers and other suspension parts take a huge hammering on rallies.

The Dakar Rally is the longest, hardest race. It runs more than 10,000 km from European cities to Dakar, Senegal, in West Africa. Part of the race is across the Sahara Desert.

✳ ON THE SPEEDWAY

Stock cars are ordinary production cars with certain changes and modifications, as allowed by the rules, to compete on proper racing circuits. In the USA they roar around giant oval tracks called speedways as part of the NASCAR season – the National Association for Stock Car Auto Racing. NASCAR drivers can reach speeds of more than 300 kilometres per hour.

Stock cars on the NASCAR 'bowl'

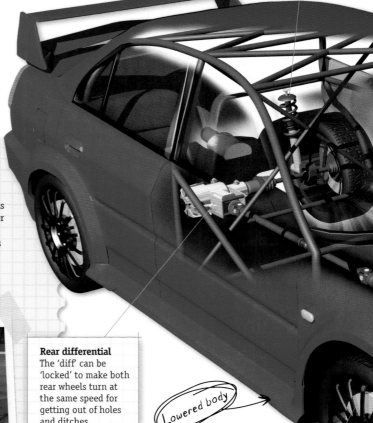

Rear differential The 'diff' can be 'locked' to make both rear wheels turn at the same speed for getting out of holes and ditches.

Lowered body

Rally cars are 4WD and based on 2-litre turbocharged engines.

Brakes Heavy duty brakes mean that rally drivers can brake at the last split second as they enter corners to clock up the fastest time.

Whatever next?

Inventors have built 'amphibious' cars that have wheels for normal road conditions, plus floats with propellers to travel through water like a boat.

Roll cage A framework of strong tubes inside the passenger compartment stops the sides or roof caving in if there's a crash.

The World Rally Championship consists of about 15 or 16 races all around the world.

Internal padding All hard objects near the driver and co-driver are padded to avoid injury when bouncing along rough roads.

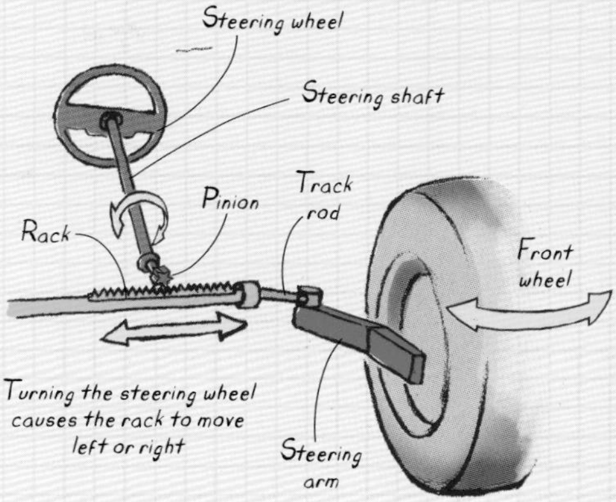

Steering wheel
Steering shaft
Pinion
Track rod
Rack
Front wheel
Turning the steering wheel causes the rack to move left or right
Steering arm

Steering rack and pinion

✳ How does STEERING work?

A car's steering wheel is fixed to a long shaft called a steering column, with a small gear called a pinion at its base. As the pinion turns it makes a rack – a long bar with teeth – slide left or right. Each end of the rack is linked to a smaller bar known as a track rod, which is attached by a ball joint to another bar, the steering arm, and this is attached to each front wheel hub. As the rack slides left or right, it moves the track rod and steering arm. The steering arm works as a lever to make the front wheels angle left or right.

Tuned transverse engine The engine is carefully adjusted, or tuned, so that it runs with the greatest power yet does not use too much fuel. This saves fuel weight and also reduces the number of refuelling stops.

Alternator (generator)

Spotlights

PICK-UP TRUCK

If you want to transport a heavy load, a pick-up truck is the ideal vehicle. These small but tough trucks have an open flat area called a load bed for their cargo. Some are two- or three-seaters with one row of seats, others have a second row behind the driver. The strengthened, stiffened rear suspension means the ride is not as comfortable as an ordinary car.

Eureka!

In the early years of motoring, people cut the rear body off a car and added a wooden platform to make a pick-up truck. The first mass-produced versions based on the Ford Model T were sold in 1925.

Whatever next?

Some pick-ups have a container that folds out and opens up to become a caravan-style living place or mobile home.

One travelling circus in the USA had an elephant specially trained to ride on the back of a pick-up truck.

Pick-up racing is a fast and furious motor sport where the modified trucks can speed along at more than 200 km/h.

Engine Most pick-ups have diesel engines. These are heavy and noisy but powerful and easy to adjust and maintain.

Tinted glass

✳ How does a TURBODIESEL work?

A diesel engine is similar to a petrol engine (see page 56) but it lacks spark plugs. The air-fuel mixture explodes in the cylinder because it gets hot from being squeezed so much. The turbocharger, or 'turbo', is similar to a supercharger (see page 62) but the impeller that forces extra air into the engine is worked by a fan-like turbine spun around by exhaust gases.

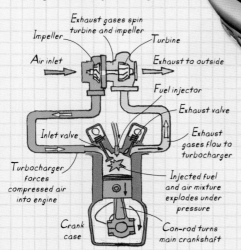

Exhaust gases spin turbine and impeller

Impeller — Turbine

Air inlet — Exhaust to outside

Fuel injector

Exhaust valve

Inlet valve

Exhaust gases flow to turbocharger

Turbocharger forces compressed air into engine

Injected fuel and air mixture explodes under pressure

Crank case

Con-rod turns main crankshaft

Foglights

Tyres Pick-ups have thick, wide, strong tyres to spread the weight, and knobbly tread to grip soft ground.

In Australia, pick-up trucks are often called 'utes' (utility vehicles).

Turbo

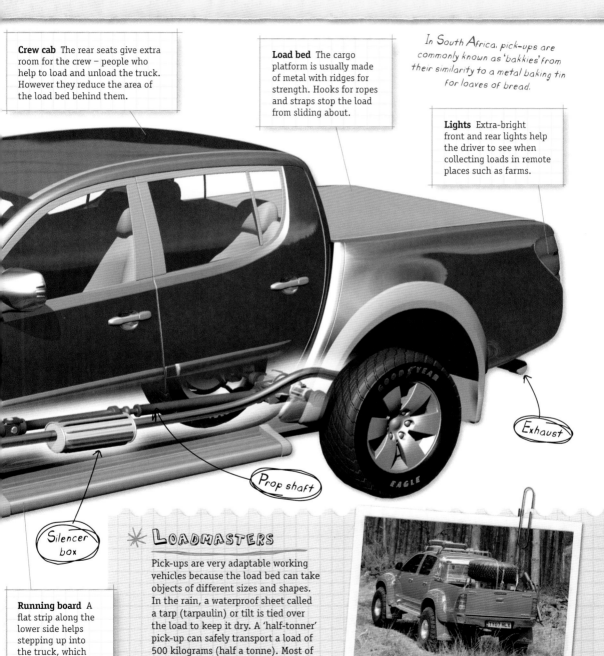

Crew cab The rear seats give extra room for the crew – people who help to load and unload the truck. However they reduce the area of the load bed behind them.

Load bed The cargo platform is usually made of metal with ridges for strength. Hooks for ropes and straps stop the load from sliding about.

In South Africa, pick-ups are commonly known as 'bakkies' from their similarity to a metal baking tin for loaves of bread.

Lights Extra-bright front and rear lights help the driver to see when collecting loads in remote places such as farms.

Exhaust

Prop shaft

Silencer box

Running board A flat strip along the lower side helps stepping up into the truck, which is higher than an ordinary car.

✳ LOADMASTERS

Pick-ups are very adaptable working vehicles because the load bed can take objects of different sizes and shapes. In the rain, a waterproof sheet called a tarp (tarpaulin) or tilt is tied over the load to keep it dry. A 'half-tonner' pick-up can safely transport a load of 500 kilograms (half a tonne). Most of the larger versions have a one tonne carrying capacity.

Pick-ups carry almost any cargo

CITY BUS

There are many kinds of passenger-carrying buses and coaches for different services. Some carry fewer people long distances in comfort, with soft seats and lots of legroom. Others pack in as many people as possible, often standing up, for short trips around towns and cities. In some places electric buses are replacing diesel-engined ones, to keep city streets quieter and the air cleaner.

Eureka!

The earliest 'buses' in the 1700s were horse-drawn wagons with two benches along the middle. The passengers sat back-to-back, facing sideways. There were no sides or roof to keep out the wind and rain.

Whatever next?

The latest long-distance buses have screens for computers or movies and earphones for music, like a long-haul passenger aircraft.

Automatic doors
The driver works buttons that make the passenger door swing open using an electric mechanism.

One of the world's biggest buses is the Superliner from Shanghai, China. At 25 m long it can carry up to 300 passengers and bend to go around corners.

Rack and pinion steering

An articulated bus in London

✳ BENDY BUSES

Many old cities have narrow streets and sharp corners unsuitable for long buses. The articulated (jointed) or 'bendy' bus, has a link in the middle so it can turn corners more tightly than a rigid one-piece vehicle. Some bendy buses have two links joining three sections. The driver keeps watch on the rear end using closed-circuit television cameras and a screen – CCTV.

Driver-only Most modern buses are driver-only. The driver collects the money and gives out tickets. Some buses have a driver and a conductor, who collects the fare.

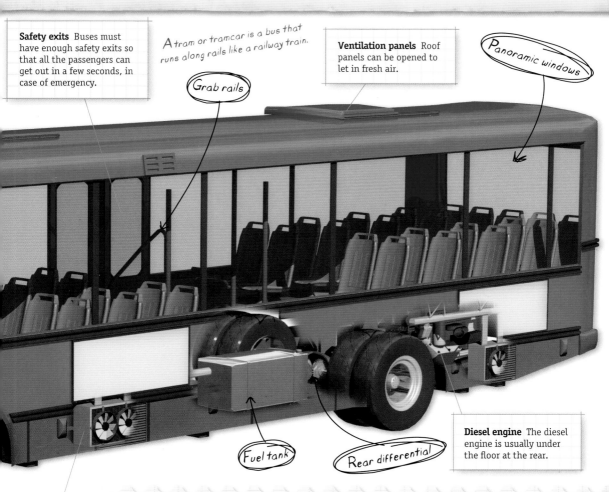

Safety exits Buses must have enough safety exits so that all the passengers can get out in a few seconds, in case of emergency.

A tram or tramcar is a bus that runs along rails like a railway train.

Grab rails

Ventilation panels Roof panels can be opened to let in fresh air.

Panoramic windows

Diesel engine The diesel engine is usually under the floor at the rear.

Fuel tank

Rear differential

Air conditioning The air inside the bus is heated or cooled depending on the outside temperature.

A trolley bus is an electric bus that gets its electricity from long 'arms' that touch overhead wires.

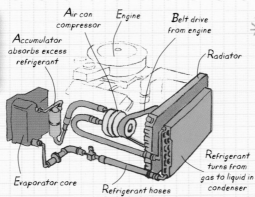

Air con compressor

Engine

Belt drive from engine

Accumulator absorbs excess refrigerant

Radiator

Evaporator core

Refrigerant hoses

Refrigerant turns from gas to liquid in condenser

✳ How does AIR CON work?

Air conditioning, or climate control, works in a similar way to a fridge. A compressor squeezes a gas, the refrigerant, flowing around a circuit of pipes. The compressed gas condenses and becomes a liquid and in the process gets hot. In the second part of the circuit the pressure is lower, so the liquid refrigerant expands and evaporates (turns back into a gas) and in the process becomes much colder.

ARTICULATED TRUCK

The 'artic' is a truck that is articulated, or jointed. The joint is between the front part – the tractor unit with the engine and driver's cab – and the rear part, or trailer, which carries the load. The joint allows the truck to go around tighter corners than a one-piece vehicle. It also means different kinds of trailers can be joined, or hitched, to the tractor unit.

Eureka!

The first artics were built in the 1910s by Charles Martin. He hitched a tractor-like truck to a wagon usually pulled by horses. Martin also invented the fifth wheel coupling between tractor unit and trailer (below).

Whatever next?

Most countries limit the size of trucks by their weight or length. However new super-highways could see trucks of 100 tonnes or more.

The ShockWave truck of Hawaii's Fire Department has two jet engines and can reach speeds of 600 km/h. It's only used for shows, not to race to real fires.

Trailer

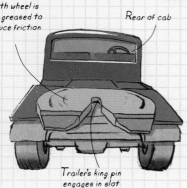

Fifth wheel is well greased to reduce friction

Rear of cab

Trailer's king pin engages in slot

✳ How does the FIFTH WHEEL work?

The 'fifth wheel coupling' is the joint or link between the tractor unit and trailer. It consists of a king pin or coupling pin on the lower front of the trailer that slides up on and then slots into the U-shaped fifth wheel on the rear of the tractor unit. The trailer can swing from side to side behind the tractor unit and also move by a small amount up or down to cope with bumpy roads.

Trailer stands
When the trailer is unhitched its front leans on these strong metal legs.

The Centipede truck is 55 m long and weighs 205 tonnes – the longest truck in regular work.

A road train is one tractor unit pulling several trailers, like a railway locomotive pulls several carriages. Some road trains are more than 1000 m long and weigh 1000-plus tonnes.

Roof fairing Even on a 40-tonne truck, smooth streamlining helps to lower air resistance. This increases speed and reduces fuel use.

In the USA, artics are called semi-trailer trucks, and the tractor unit is the towing engine.

Cab controls A big truck has ten gears for all conditions, from cruising the open road with no load to climbing a steep hill with 30-plus tonnes of cargo on the back.

Tractor unit

Sun visor

Fifth wheel

Engine Truck turbodiesel engines are 11, 13 or 16 litres, sometimes even more.

King pin

Fuel tank A family car's fuel tank holds around 70 litres. A big artic carries 500 litres, and sometimes over 2000 litres.

ICE ROAD TRUCKERS

Sometimes it's quicker for a car or truck to get to a remote place across a lake – provided it's frozen. Ice truckers specialize in carrying loads across the far north in winter, to faraway places such as mining centres and logging camps. The truckers keep in radio contact with each other about snowdrifts, cracks or melting ice.

An artic heads across a frozen lake

BREAKDOWN TRUCK

Everyone on the road fears a sudden breakdown. Soon after mass motoring began in the 1900s, specialized trucks were rescuing stranded drivers and recovering their broken vehicles. It's important to clear the road and get the vehicle out of danger, then take it to a suitable garage for repair. This may have to be done at night, in heavy rain or in thick fog or snow. Breakdown, recovery or tow trucks are strong, tough and able to cope with all conditions.

Eureka!

Mechanic Ernest Holmes built the first breakdown truck in 1915. He fixed three metal poles, a chain and a pulley to a 1913 Cadillac in Chattanooga, Tennessee, USA, and began the tow truck business.

Whatever next?

Motoring experts are working on 'intelligent' vehicle electronics to sense which part has broken and then radio the breakdown truck to bring it as soon as possible.

Powerful engine The turbodiesel engine must be powerful enough to move two vehicles, perhaps across soft ground if the broken-down one has veered off the road.

Visor

The world's biggest breakdown trucks are converted Caterpillar 793s, used in mines to recover giant haulage trucks weighing over 400 tonnes.

✳ How does a WINCH work?

A winch has a strong metal cable or wire that winds slowly onto a drum. Some breakdown truck winches are electric with a powerful motor worked by the truck's battery. Others are driven by the truck's engine. The turning speed is greatly reduced by gear cogs, so that as the turning speed goes down, the turning force or torque goes up. The cable winds very slowly but with huge force to drag or lift the broken-down vehicle.

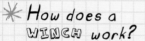

Large gear cog on drum shaft

Drum

Steel cable

Counterweight A very heavy vehicle at the truck's rear end might make the front end lift up, so the counterweight keeps the front end down.

Electric motor

Frame

Small gear cog on motor shaft

Air filter

The International Towing and Recovery Hall of Fame and Museum are in Chattanooga, USA, near where Ernest Holmes started the first breakdown truck business.

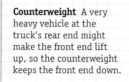

The AA, Automobile Association, started in 1905. Its patrol staff were equipped with two-way radios in the late 1940s. Before that, they phoned HQ regularly to find out if there were any breakdowns nearby.

Flashing lights

Winch The steel cable from the hoist hook winds slowly onto the winch drum.

Boom The boom (lift-arm or crane) is worked by two powerful hydraulic jacks. Its L-shaped end can be slotted underneath the front of a vehicle to raise it from beneath, instead of using the hook.

Britain's first motoring organization was the RAC (Royal Automobile Club), formed in 1897 for breakdown help. It introduced roadside emergency telephone boxes in 1912.

Hook

Ramps The rear ramps can be lowered to support the broken vehicle's front wheels.

Eight rear wheels spread load

Step

Tools A large tool compartment contains spanners, crowbars, screwdrivers, cutters and other essential equipment.

A flatbed (rollback or slide) truck recovers a broken-down car

✳ SLIDING UP AND ON

There are several kinds of breakdown or tow trucks. Some have crane-like booms to lift vehicles straight up out of ditches or rivers. Some have an arm and winch to drag the broken vehicle to safety. Others have a flat rear platform or flatbed that slides backwards and down onto the road, so the vehicle can be winched onto it. Then the platform slides back up.

FIRE ENGINE

Firefighting appliances, or trucks, (fire engines) may be first to arrive at big incidents – and not just fires, but floods, road accidents, people trapped down holes or in high places and even kittens in trees. The appliance sprays water or special types of chemical foam depending on the type of fire and what is burning, such as wood, plastic or fuels.

Eureka!

The first firefighting wagons were hauled by people, or horses, or both. Self-propelled appliances powered by steam engines were used in New York from 1841 and in London and other British cities from the 1850s.

Whatever next?

Fire crews carry out regular tests on new siren noises – although they warn people they are nearby – one sounds like a whining dog!

Flashing lights

Siren The siren is worked by an electric motor and fan that pumps air past a specially shaped hole into a tube, similar to blowing a trumpet.

✳ EXTENDING LADDERS

Multi-section ladders extend like a telescope mounted on a turntable on the fire vehicle. They can reach up to 30 metres – the 10th floor of a high-rise building. The crew member at the upper end of the ladder is in radio contact with the ladder operator below so that the ladder can be put into exactly the correct position. Spraying water or foam onto a fire from above is far more effective than from the side.

The extending ladder gets above the fire

Fire and ambulance crews refer to a call-out for an emergency as a 'shout'.

Engine The diesel engine is started regularly to make sure it works when needed.

Hoses One set of hoses connects to a nearby water supply to draw water in. Another set carries the water away to spray on the fire. The hoses wind onto reels turned by electric motors.

Mains supply pipes

Screw fittings link pipes

✳ How do HYDRAULICS work?

Hydraulic machinery, such as a fire appliance's cutters or extending ladder, works using high-pressure liquid (water or oil). Like a lever, the liquid changes a small force moving a long distance into a big force moving a short distance. The small force presses on a narrow piston to create pressure throughout the fluid. This pushes a wider piston with greater force because of its larger surface area.

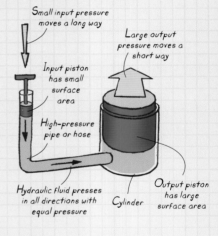

Small input pressure moves a long way

Large output pressure moves a short way

Input piston has small surface area

High-pressure pipe or hose

Hydraulic fluid presses in all directions with equal pressure

Cylinder

Output piston has large surface area

Wheel hub

London's Fire Brigade has more than 250 appliances including 30 aerial ladder platforms.

Control panel The switches and other controls are for the main pumps that force water or foam along the hose, showing its pressure and flow rate.

Some fire appliances have pumps so powerful they can spray a distance of more than 70 m.

Tools The standard appliance carries a host of useful tools including powerful hydraulic cutters and spreaders worked by high-pressure hoses from the diesel engine.

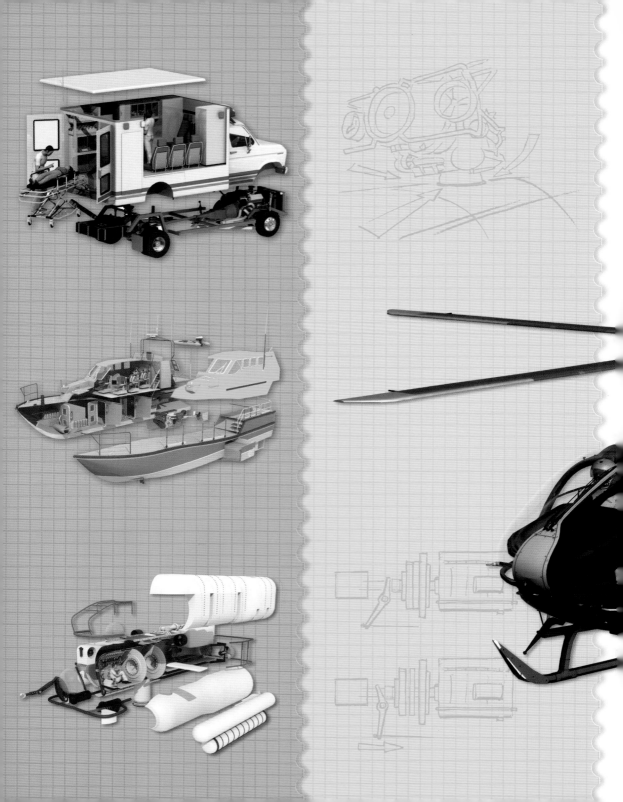

EMERGENCY VEHICLES

INTRODUCTION

Long ago, there were no emergency services – no paramedics, firefighters or lifeboat crews. People put out their own fires, and risked their lives in doing so. Crime was rife as there was no organized police force, and without ambulances people often died before reaching hospital. Even when emergency services were available, there was no quick way of summoning them. From the 1870s the telephone made getting help much quicker. So did people living in growing cities, as this brought them closer to emergency centres.

Police cars must be fast and reliable. Back in 1948 this German Volkswagen fitted the bill.

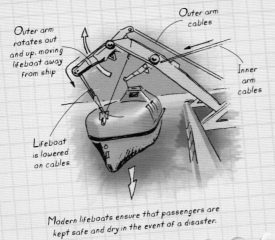

Outer arm cables

Outer arm rotates out and up, moving lifeboat away from ship

Inner arm cables

Lifeboat is lowered on cables

Modern lifeboats ensure that passengers are kept safe and dry in the event of a disaster.

DISASTER AT SEA

The tragic sinking of the huge liner *Titanic* in 1912, which caused the deaths of more than 1500 people, brought great changes to the way people responded to emergencies – especially at sea. From that time all ships had to carry enough lifeboats for everyone on board. They also had to keep their radio room open all day, every day, because the newly invented radio network was the fastest way to call for help if catastrophe struck, and it still is.

MERCY MISSION

Aircraft are much faster than cars or boats. Helicopters in particular need no roads or runways. They are often first to arrive at a disaster scene such as an earthquake zone or flood. Their relief effort brings urgent supplies such as medicines, food and water. The helicopters take away the most seriously injured people – and are soon back again. As road and rail links are repaired, trucks and trains can take over these tasks.

An aid helicopter delivers emergency supplies. Every minute counts, so the ground crew spring into action.

LAW AND ORDER

Burglary, car theft, noisy neighbours, broken-down trucks, angry fights, road accidents – police officers are called out to attend a range of very different situations. Fast vehicles, expert drivers, flashing lights and wailing sirens mean that their help has arrived. Police organize other emergency services so they all work together. They also tape off the scene, move along bystanders who stop to stare, and make sure that in the confusion, no one tries to commit a crime.

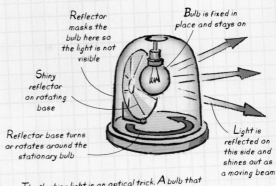

Reflector masks the bulb here so the light is not visible

Bulb is fixed in place and stays on

Shiny reflector on rotating base

Reflector base turns or rotates around the stationary bulb

Light is reflected on this side and shines out as a moving beam

The flashing light is an optical trick. A bulb that really flashed on-off would soon go 'pop'.

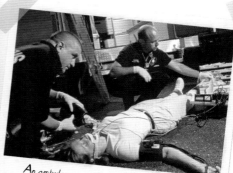

Firefighters get as close as possible to assess the blaze, put out the flames and save people and property.

SAVING LIVES

The biggest tragedy is losing a life. The first few seconds and minutes of a medical emergency are the most precious, so paramedics try to get there super-fast. Then the ambulance crews take over and rush the patient to the emergency staff back at the medical centre. All of these highly trained people are dedicated to saving lives, treating injuries and getting patients on the road to recovery.

An ambulance and its crew provide emergency treatment, helping to save a life in the balance.

Emergency services have to respond rapidly, so it's important that the vehicles and equipment they use continue to break the boundaries of technology.

POLICE MOTORCYCLE

Able to weave through traffic, squeeze along narrow paths and cross rough ground, its engine revving and siren screaming, the police motorcycle is often first to an emergency. Its rider is an expert at assessing the scene in seconds, and then sending radio messages back to base about the situation and which emergency services to summon. The bike is equipped and maintained to the highest standard – and environmentally clean too.

Eureka!

Practical motorcycles went on sale in Europe in 1894. About 14 years later they were in use by police in US cities such as Detroit, Michigan and Portland, Oregon. Their speed through crowded streets meant a boom in crime-solving.

Whatever next?

Jet-powered motorbikes are the fastest two-wheeled vehicles. However control at high speed on a rough surface is a problem.

One of the best-selling items in the famous Lego toy range is its model police motorcycle and rider.

Windshield

Mirror

Light

Fuel tank

Gearbox

An officer uses his motorcycle for cover during training

✳ In the SADDLE

Police motorcyclists undergo years of training in how to ride fast but safely, and how to get through hold-ups such as traffic jams. They become expert on their favourite machine, and can demonstrate amazing control. But the bike is more than just a way to travel. It is a mini-control centre for organizing help, a carrier of emergency equipment, and a barrier in case of danger such as thrown objects or gunfire.

V-twin Each of the two cylinders has cooling fins (ridges) on the outside and a sliding piston inside. The cylinders are set at an angle to each other in a design known as the V-twin.

The main makes of motorcycle used by police forces worldwide include Harley-Davidson of the USA, BMW of Germany (the chief make in Europe), and the Japanese manufacturers Yamaha, Kawasaki and Honda.

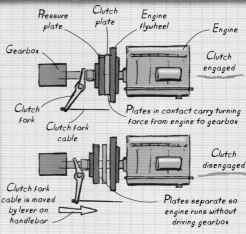

Pressure plate

Clutch plate

Engine flywheel

Engine

Gearbox

Clutch engaged

Clutch fork

Clutch fork cable

Plates in contact carry turning force from engine to gearbox

Clutch disengaged

Clutch fork cable is moved by lever on handlebar

Plates separate so engine runs without driving gearbox

Locker Important equipment such as maps, torches and tools are safe from rain and dirt inside the top locker.

Panniers Roomy side containers astride the rear wheel are known as panniers. Items inside must be fixed securely and the two panniers should be equal weight, otherwise they might unbalance the rider.

Speed camera

✳ How do CLUTCHES work?

A clutch allows the turning power of the engine to drive the gearbox – or not. A motorcycle's clutch lever on the left handlebar works a lever-like fork that slides a disc-shaped pressure plate to and fro. When the clutch lever is pulled the fork slides this plate, which is attached to the gearbox, away from the clutch plate, which is constantly turned by the engine. The gearbox is now disconnected, or disengaged, from the engine. The rider changes gears then releases the clutch lever so the plates come together and the engine drives the gearbox again.

Flares

Equipment Specialized police equipment includes rolls of plastic tape to mark off an accident scene and keep people away, and emergency flares to light the area and show its location to approaching rescue crews.

Transmission After the clutch and gearbox, turning power is taken to the rear wheel either by sprockets and a chain, as on a bicycle, or by a rod-like spinning drive shaft.

Suspension A combination of coil springs and hydraulic dampers let the rear wheel move up and down to absorb road bumps and holes.

One of the stars of the 1973 movie 'Electra Glide in Blue' was the Harley-Davidson motorcyle model named the Electra Glide.

BOMB DISPOSAL ROBOT

Bombs and explosive devices become terrifyingly real when you have to crouch next to one to defuse it. Robots do this without risk to human life. Some disarm the bomb while trying to preserve it, so that experts can learn if the bomb-makers have any new tricks. Others carry the bomb to a safe place where it can be exploded. Most robots are remote controlled by personnel using radio signals from a safe distance.

Eureka!

Bomb disposal began in World War I (1914–18), partly because hastily produced bombs resulted in a higher proportion of duds and unexploded bombs on the battlefield. The first robots arrived in the 1970s to counter the threat of car bombs during The Troubles in Ireland.

Whatever next?

Future robots may be programmed with all the latest tricks so they can predict which booby-traps the bomb-makers will invent next.

Sniffers Various specialized sensors detect tiny amounts of substances floating in the air, including explosive chemicals. Different sensors are fitted depending on the chemicals suspected.

Many military robots now search for IEDs (improvised explosive devices) – usually roadside bombs.

One of the top multi-role combat robots is PackBot, with more than 2500 in action worldwide. It has two sets of tracks. Each rear track rotates on flippers in order to climb boulders and stairs.

✳ How do TRACKS steer?

Caterpillar or crawler tracks are used in many vehicles, from bomb disposal robots to giant tanks, bulldozers, diggers and other construction machines. Their many shoes, or plates, grip well and also spread the weight so the vehicle does not sink into soft ground and get stuck. The speeds of the two tracks are controlled separately, often by two handles or levers worked by the driver. Making one track turn faster than the other causes the vehicle to steer to the opposite side.

Electric drive system Most robots have electric motors to work the tracks and also the on-board arms and levers. The track ones are known as traction or propulsion motors and are slow-spinning but with huge turning power.

Drive wheel Usually only one wheel on each side is turned by the motor to move the track. The track itself then spins the other wheels.

Return roller

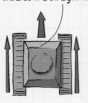
Both tracks running at the same speed move the vehicle forwards in a straight line

Speeding up the left track turns the vehicle to the right

If one track is driven forward, and the other drives in reverse, the vehicle spins around on the spot

Teeth

Road wheels The road wheels are allowed to turn at their own speed on their own axles, while distributing the robot's weight along the track.

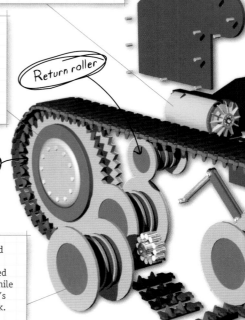

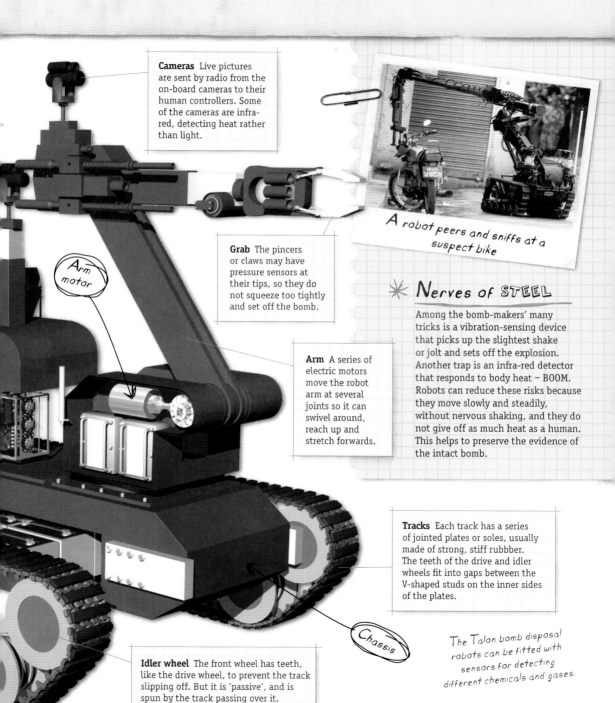

Cameras Live pictures are sent by radio from the on-board cameras to their human controllers. Some of the cameras are infra-red, detecting heat rather than light.

Arm motor

Grab The pincers or claws may have pressure sensors at their tips, so they do not squeeze too tightly and set off the bomb.

Arm A series of electric motors move the robot arm at several joints so it can swivel around, reach up and stretch forwards.

A robot peers and sniffs at a suspect bike

✳ Nerves of STEEL

Among the bomb-makers' many tricks is a vibration-sensing device that picks up the slightest shake or jolt and sets off the explosion. Another trap is an infra-red detector that responds to body heat – BOOM. Robots can reduce these risks because they move slowly and steadily, without nervous shaking, and they do not give off as much heat as a human. This helps to preserve the evidence of the intact bomb.

Tracks Each track has a series of jointed plates or soles, usually made of strong, stiff rubbber. The teeth of the drive and idler wheels fit into gaps between the V-shaped studs on the inner sides of the plates.

Chassis

The Talon bomb disposal robots can be fitted with sensors for detecting different chemicals and gases.

Idler wheel The front wheel has teeth, like the drive wheel, to prevent the track slipping off. But it is 'passive', and is spun by the track passing over it.

POLICE PATROL CAR

Apart from cruising highways to ensure that motorists drive more carefully, police vehicles also dash to road traffic accidents and other emergencies. The modern patrol car is packed with cameras, computers and other electronic gadgets. It has direct radio links to the regional control room and the computer databases for stolen or suspect vehicles and for people on the wanted list.

Eureka!

In 1899 the first police car went on patrol in Akron, Ohio, USA. It was powered by an electric motor and had a top speed of 26 kilometres per hour. Its first call was to pick up a drunken man on Main Street!

Whatever next?

The taser is a high-voltage dart on a long wire, fired at people to shock them out of troublesome behaviour. Versions are being tested that may be able to disable speeding or stolen cars.

The automatic number plate recognition identifies almost any car and its owner within a few seconds.

Bull bars The reinforced front guards or fenders are able to push other cars or knock down doors without damage to the car itself.

Dashboard computer The latest laptop links into the car's many computer systems for instant display of roads, suspects and other information.

Flashing lights

Camera

Wing mirrors

V8 engine

POLICE

✳ How do FLASHING LIGHTS work?

The 'flashing light' on many emergency vehicles works in various ways. In one design the light does not flash at all – it is a bulb that glows continuously. A shiny bowl-shaped reflector turns around it, making the bulb's beam whirl around. To an onlooker it appears to flash. This method overcomes the problem of burning out the bulb with continual flashes, and twisting its wires if the bulb itself spun around.

Reflector masks the bulb here so the light is not visible

Bulb is fixed in place and light stays on

Shiny reflector on rotating base

Light is reflected on this side and shines out as a moving beam

Reflector base turns or rotates around the stationary bulb

Disc drives On-board computer hard discs carry the latest information about stolen cars and wanted criminals, in case the patrol car's radio links are damaged or out of range.

Antenna (aerial) Much of the officers' work relies on them staying in contact with headquarters. So the car has several antennae to cope with different signal strengths and wavelengths according to radio conditions.

Italian motorway police have the world's fastest patrol cars – three ultra-speedy Lamborghini Gallardos. They can travel at over 300 km/h but rarely do. Their main duties are escorting medical emergencies and supplies, and raising awareness of motorway patrols. However one was 'totalled' (destroyed) in a crash in November 2009.

Stinger Stowed neatly in its box, the spiky stinger can be unloaded and unrolled in a few seconds (see below).

5 PCT 2582

COURTESY PROFESSIONALISM RESPECT

NYPD

✳ You've been STUNG!

The stinger or traffic spike strip is a row of sharp metal spikes unrolled across a roadway, sharp points upwards. Its aim is to puncture the tyres of a suspect vehicle passing over it. The spike design varies. Some shapes allow the tyres to go down gradually, so that the driver does not suffer four sudden 'blow-outs' and lose control. But this does not always work, giving the stinger the nickname of 'tyre-shredder'.

Disc brake

Chassis

Graphic markings Patrol cars must show their police force or department, unless the officers are working in secret or undercover, in which case they may be in an ordinary-looking 'unmarked car'.

A stinger is rolled up again after use

PARAMEDIC MOTORCYCLE

Like a micro ambulance on two wheels, the paramedic bike has emergency equipment and medication for the most life-threatening injuries and illnesses. The paramedic rider is trained not just in first aid but in many detailed procedures such as giving oxygen and and heart defibrillation (using a controlled electric shock to restore a normal heart rhythm).

Paramedic bikes may be used to rush human organs, such as hearts for transplant, to hospitals.

Eureka!

'Motorcycle ambulances' ridden by trained medics began saving lives during World War I (1914–18). But equipment such as defibrillators has only been portable and tough enough for on-site use since the 1980s.

Whatever next?

Heart monitors and similar gadgets send their readouts by radio to the nearest medical centre, where doctors advise the paramedic on urgent action.

Fairing

After a motorcyle accident, the paramedic arrives in less than three minutes

✳ FIRST on the SCENE

After a heart attack, stroke or similar event, the faster treatment comes, the greater the chances of saving life and a much improved outcome. The first 'platinum ten minutes' is when the paramedic and the kit carried on the bike can make so much difference, after speeding through traffic or along narrow lanes. The first hour is also known as the 'golden hour' – again, a vital time to identify the problem and give medication. When the ambulance arrives, it has more equipment and it can take the patient to hospital.

Front forks

Disc brake

Tyres The tubeless tyres are checked daily for the correct air pressure inside. Wrong pressure can make them wear too fast or unevenly and reduce their grip on the road surface.

Medication pack Various medicines and drugs are stowed in one pannier. They are always checked, replaced and updated as necessary after each trip.

Cardiac monitor The heart monitor shows a wavy line or trace, the ECG (electrocardiogram). This gives clues to the patient's health and whether a defibrillator is needed to 'shock' the heart back into a normal beating rhythm.

Oxygen Breathing difficulties are eased by oxygen from the cylinder delivered through a face mask. Pain-killing gases can also be given this way.

Fire extinguisher

Fluid packs Inside the containers are various types of blood replacement fluids, as well as medications already dissolved in liquid, perhaps to be administered through a 'drip' directly into a vein.

Some giant shopping malls and sports stadiums have indoor electric paramedic scooters. Noisy petrol engines would pollute the air with their dangerous exhaust fumes.

✳ How do TUBELESS TYRES work?

Inner tubes can cause problems if punctured – such as bursting like a balloon. A tubeless tyre, with no separate inner tube, is more likely to deflate gradually if punctured. The tubeless tyre's edges are two rounded rubber beads, each with a strong steel cable inside for strength. High pressure from the air in the tyre keeps each bead pressed against a recess in the wheel rim, for an airtight seal.

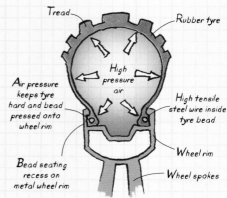

Tread

Rubber tyre

High pressure air

Air pressure keeps tyre hard and bead pressed onto wheel rim

High tensile steel wire inside tyre bead

Bead seating recess on metal wheel rim

Wheel rim

Wheel spokes

AMBULANCE

Ambulance drivers need a careful combination of speed and safety as they race to an emergency, sirens and lights warning other motorists to pull over. The vehicle contains the most important medical machines and drugs for critical cases. It also acts as a shelter where people who feel sick or faint can rest and be monitored, hopefully to recover.

Eureka!

Since the 14th century, horse-drawn wagons transported the injured and sick to the nearest physician – or mortuary. As these wagons evolved, they carried pills and potions to treat the casualties. The first motorized ambulance was used in 1899 in Chicago. From 1909 onwards they were mass produced.

Whatever next?

Advances in electronics mean that smarter heart and brain monitors analyze their own readings and help ambulance staff to identify illness.

Giant bus ambulances in Dubai can treat more than 50 patients.

Medical supplies The array of medications, usually kept in a locked cupboard, can treat most types of emergencies.

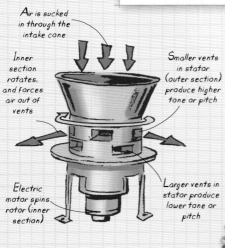

Air is sucked in through the intake cone

Inner section rotates, and forces air out of vents

Smaller vents in stator (outer section) produce higher tone or pitch

Electric motor spins rotor (inner section)

Larger vents in stator produce lower tone or pitch

✳ How do SIRENS work?

The pneumatic or air-based two-tone siren produces the familiar 'na-na-na-na' sound. An electric motor spins a collar-like inner section called the rotor within an outer stationary cylinder, the stator. The shape of the rotor sucks in air and blasts it out through vents in the stator. The spinning rotor alternately blocks then uncovers the vents in the stator, forcing out bursts of air, which are rapidly squeezed and stretched to make soundwaves. The rotor speed controls the overall pitch, high or low.

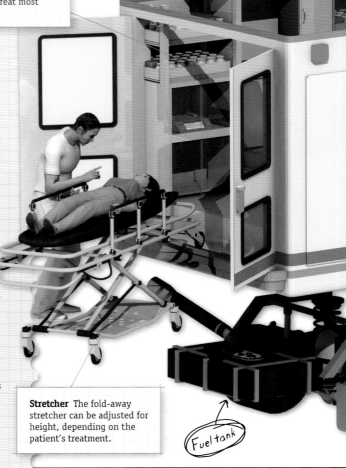

Stretcher The fold-away stretcher can be adjusted for height, depending on the patient's treatment.

Fuel tank

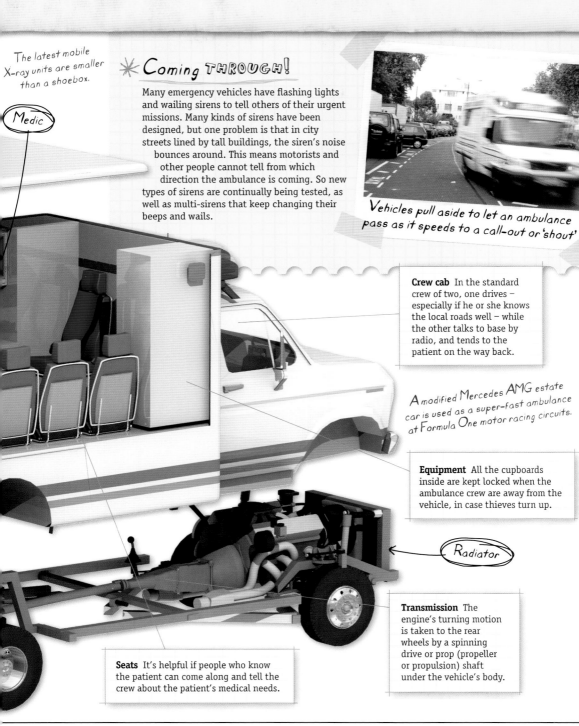

The latest mobile X-ray units are smaller than a shoebox.

✳ Coming THROUGH!

Many emergency vehicles have flashing lights and wailing sirens to tell others of their urgent missions. Many kinds of sirens have been designed, but one problem is that in city streets lined by tall buildings, the siren's noise bounces around. This means motorists and other people cannot tell from which direction the ambulance is coming. So new types of sirens are continually being tested, as well as multi-sirens that keep changing their beeps and wails.

Vehicles pull aside to let an ambulance pass as it speeds to a call-out or 'shout'

Medic

Crew cab In the standard crew of two, one drives – especially if he or she knows the local roads well – while the other talks to base by radio, and tends to the patient on the way back.

A modified Mercedes AMG estate car is used as a super-fast ambulance at Formula One motor racing circuits.

Equipment All the cupboards inside are kept locked when the ambulance crew are away from the vehicle, in case thieves turn up.

Radiator

Transmission The engine's turning motion is taken to the rear wheels by a spinning drive or prop (propeller or propulsion) shaft under the vehicle's body.

Seats It's helpful if people who know the patient can come along and tell the crew about the patient's medical needs.

OFFROAD RESCUE TRUCK

Emergencies do not always happen next to smooth roads. Out in the wild, climbers, trekkers and cavers run risks – and rely on off-roaders if there is an emergency. These vehicles have extra-strong suspension, extra-grip tyres, and extra-high ground clearance, which is the gap between the lowest part of the vehicle and the surface below.

Eureka!

Informal mountain rescue, by friends or local volunteers, has been around for centuries. Organized rescue teams began in the 1900s, with pack animals such as horses, mules or llamas. Motor vehicles became rugged enough to be used in the 1920s.

Whatever next?

Floating air-cushion vehicles – hovercraft – have been tested in remote rescue situations, but they are usually too difficult to control.

Fuel and water cans

The first Jeeps were built in 1940 for US military use.

The first Land Rovers were stars of the 1948 Amsterdam Motor Show in the Netherlands.

Roof rack Bulky but fairly lightweight items are carried here. Many mounting points (supports) spread the weight of the load around the whole roof area.

A Land Rover takes a steep, bumpy track in its stride

✳ OLD but RELIABLE

The Jeep and then the Land Rover vehicles date back to the 1940s. Inspired by the need to carry troops, supplies and casualties over rough ground in warfare, the Jeep quickly set the standard for toughness and ease of repair as a 4WD ATV (four-wheel-drive all-terrain vehicle). The Land Rover took the idea onto civilian roads with its simple design and fewer parts to go wrong. The steel-based chassis and the body parts made of aluminium-based alloys (combinations of metals) mean strength, lightness and no rusting.

Emergency equipment A first-aid paramedic pack of medicines, drugs and dressings, a lightweight carry-stretcher and other medical supplies are taken to most emergencies.

Flares

Mud flap

Steps

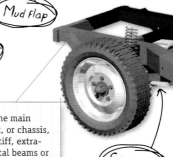

Chassis The main framework, or chassis, has very stiff, extra-strong metal beams or members compared to most road vehicles.

Stiffened suspension

The original Land Rovers are tough but not especially quiet or comfortable. So the company makes more luxurious 4WD models such as the Discovery and Freelander.

Bumps in the terrain force the wheel up and down

Damper attachment

Damper and spring smooth out the ride

Tyre

Spring

Steering arm

Damper

Drive from engine to wheel

Wheel

Lower wishbone

Wishbone pivots on bearings attached to chassis

Chassis

✳ How does SUSPENSION work?

As a wheel goes over a bump, it is forced upwards. To prevent it lifting the whole vehicle, it is mounted on V-shaped wishbones that are attached to the vehicle's chassis (main frame) by bearings. This allows the wishbone to swing or pivot up and down as the wheel rises and falls. However this system alone would make the chassis bounce up and down uncontrollably. A hydraulic damper or 'shock-absorber', consisting of a spring and a piston inside an oil-filled cylinder, resists the bounces and makes them smooth out very quickly.

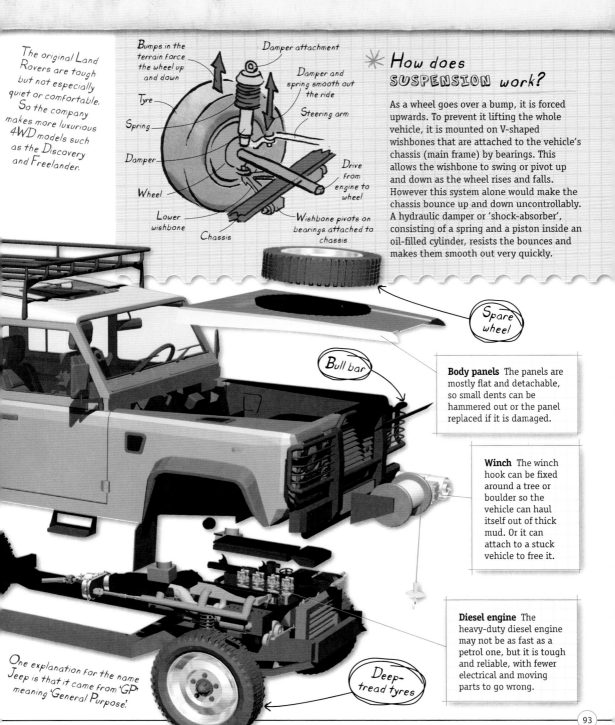

Spare wheel

Bull bar

Body panels The panels are mostly flat and detachable, so small dents can be hammered out or the panel replaced if it is damaged.

Winch The winch hook can be fixed around a tree or boulder so the vehicle can haul itself out of thick mud. Or it can attach to a stuck vehicle to free it.

Diesel engine The heavy-duty diesel engine may not be as fast as a petrol one, but it is tough and reliable, with fewer electrical and moving parts to go wrong.

One explanation for the name Jeep is that it came from 'GP' meaning 'General Purpose'.

Deep-tread tyres

FIRE TENDER

The fire tender doesn't just fight fires. It is an all-round emergency vehicle central to many kinds of incidents, from putting out unwanted campfires to assisting in major disasters such as earthquakes or explosions. Apart from the water pumps and hoses, its array of tools and equipment includes hammers, saws, chisels and cutters. It also has powerful lights for work at night or in dark places such as tunnels and underpasses.

Eureka!

Mechanical water pumps for fire tenders date back to the 18th century. The tender at that time was horsedrawn, the pump was human-powered. People pushed up and down on a large lever pivoted at its centre, like a see-saw.

Whatever next?

The flexible materials for hoses are continually being improved. A burst through a small crack could seriously injure someone nearby.

Emergency horns

Driver and co-driver cab
The driver uses all kinds of modern aids including satnav or GPS to find the best big-vehicle route to the emergency.

Radiator grille

✳ How does a RADIATOR work?

Petrol and diesel engines continually explode fuel inside, so they make huge amounts of heat. To prevent this causing damage, a coolant – mainly water plus anti-freeze chemicals – flows through a system of channels and spaces in the engine and takes in the heat. Its circuit continues into the metal radiator, which has hundreds of tiny flaps, or vanes, specialized to give off heat to the air around.

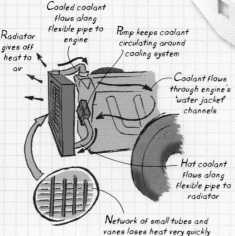

Cooled coolant flows along flexible pipe to engine

Pump keeps coolant circulating around cooling system

Radiator gives off heat to air

Coolant flows through engine's 'water jacket' channels

Hot coolant flows along flexible pipe to radiator

Network of small tubes and vanes loses heat very quickly

Road horns

The fastest working fire-fighting vehicle is a Nissan R35 Skyline car fitted with a large extinguisher tank in place of the rear seats. At the Nurburgring raceway near Cologne, Germany it puts out accidental fires and makes fuel spills safe.

Powerful engine Water and tools are very heavy, so a big fire tender ready to tackle a blaze may weigh more than 20 tonnes. This can limit its movements, for example, across small or weak bridges.

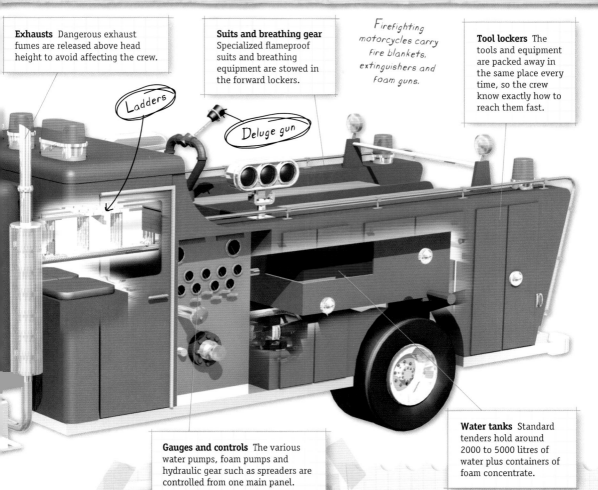

Exhausts Dangerous exhaust fumes are released above head height to avoid affecting the crew.

Suits and breathing gear Specialized flameproof suits and breathing equipment are stowed in the forward lockers.

Firefighting motorcycles carry fire blankets, extinguishers and foam guns.

Tool lockers The tools and equipment are packed away in the same place every time, so the crew know exactly how to reach them fast.

Ladders

Deluge gun

Gauges and controls The various water pumps, foam pumps and hydraulic gear such as spreaders are controlled from one main panel.

Water tanks Standard tenders hold around 2000 to 5000 litres of water plus containers of foam concentrate.

Specialized fire equipment includes turntable ladders, foam sprayers, water tanker trucks and 'cherry-picker' hydraulic platforms.

Holding the hose needs training for skill as well as strength

☀ Under PRESSURE

Enormous pressure is needed to make water shoot 50 metres or more onto the heart of a fire. As the water blasts forwards, it produces a reaction – an equal force in the opposite direction, causing the hose to jump backwards. Teams of firefighters brace themselves as the pressure is slowly turned up, to resist the reaction force and keep the hose steady. A dropped hose thrashes about on the ground, and the water pressure must be turned down before the team can get hold of it again.

AIRPORT FIRE-CRASH TENDER

One of the most intense emergencies is an aircraft fire. More than 500 people may be trapped inside the long metal tube of the fuselage, with hundreds of tonnes of highly flammable jet fuel all around. For major airports, regulations state that airport fire tenders – which can weigh more than 40 tonnes – must be at the scene, pumping foam, within two minutes. If the tenders are not available, for whatever reason, then no planes can take off or land.

Eureka!

Chemical fire-fighting foams were first developed in the late 19th century. They were mainly for fires at factories and depots handling petrol-type fuels for the rapidly growing car market.

Whatever next?

Putting out flames means starving them of oxygen in the air, which they need for burning. Very heavy inert gases can produce an invisible blanket to do this.

One of the main dry chemical fire-retarding powders is known as Purple K for its added violet dye colour.

Cannon The foam or water 'gun' is known as a cannon or monitor. It is aimed by the operator or co-driver inside the cab.

✳ How do PUNCTURE NOZZLES work?

If fuel leaks into an aircraft cabin, there is a massive risk that it may catch fire or even explode in a fireball. The puncture or piercing nozzle is a new system carried by some fire-crash tenders. A sharp nozzle on a telescopic arm can extend up to 20 metres from the tender and punch itself through the metal fuselage. A harmless chemical fire retardant is then pumped along the arm and through the nozzle into the inside of the fuselage.

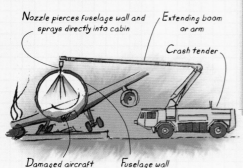

Nozzle pierces fuselage wall and sprays directly into cabin

Extending boom or arm

Crash tender

Damaged aircraft   Fuselage wall

Cab There may be room for five or more crew in the cab. Often there is an engineer who is an expert on the plane involved. He or she gives advice about danger points such as where the plane's fuel pipes run.

Heat-resistant bodywork

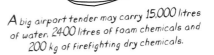

A big airport tender may carry 15,000 litres of water, 2400 litres of foam chemicals and 200 kg of firefighting dry chemicals.

Foam chemical tank The AFFF (aqueous fire-fighting foam) chemicals expand 100–200 times as they mix with water at the cannon to create the bubble barrier.

Exhaust

Tool racks Many of the tools are similar to those in a standard fire tender (see previous page), such as hydraulic cutters worked by high-pressure oil pumps driven by the vehicle's engine.

Airport tenders must have regular checks to see how long it takes them to race to the farthest corners of the airport.

Engine Such a massive vehicle, probably weighing more than 40 tonnes, needs a huge V8 turbodiesel engine to accelerate it to the crash site.

Tyres An aircraft emergency may happen anywhere at the airfield or airport. The tender must be able to cross grassy and rough areas with its low-pressure, high-grip tyres.

Multi-wheel drive

A layer of foam is sprayed over a fuel spill from a crashed plane

✳ Under the BLANKET

Water puts out many kinds of fires. But on flaming liquid fuels it mixes and flares up, creating yet more danger. Chemical foams called fire retardants are used instead. Two chemicals are mixed with water as they spray from the hose or cannon (monitor) to make a mass of bubbles that keep air away from the flammable liquid. Fuel tanks in the plane and fuel leaks or spills on the ground are all covered with a blanket of foam to prevent more flames.

FIREBOAT

Not just able to tackle fires and other emergencies on boats and ships, but also on oil rigs, dams, bridges, at waterfront warehouses, along harbours, ports and docks – the fireboat is an adaptable floating firefighter. This craft is often combined with a rescue vessel and first aid centre. Its massively powerful water/foam cannons, or monitors, can spray more than 100 metres.

Eureka!

In the 19th century steam-powered boats were adapted to spray water using steam-driven pumps. London's first self-propelled fireboat *Alpha II* went into service in 1900, and many other ports quickly followed.

Whatever next?

Taller booms are being developed that will allow water to be sprayed down into the centre or seat of the fire. This is much more effective at dousing flames.

The Warner L Lawrence fireboat in Los Angeles, USA, can spray water more than 120 m up into the air.

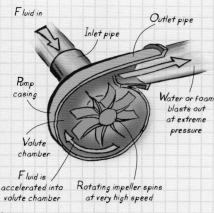

Fluid in

Inlet pipe

Outlet pipe

Pump casing

Water or foam blasts out at extreme pressure

Volute chamber

Fluid is accelerated into volute chamber

Rotating impeller spins at very high speed

✳ How do HIGH-PRESSURE PUMPS work?

One of the main high-pressure pumps for fluids – gases and liquids – is the centrifugal pump. Its rotating impeller is similar to an aircraft propeller but with blades that are slightly bent and not set at an angle. The impeller is spun at high speed by an electric motor, diesel or petrol engine, or steam turbine, and draws in fluid near its centre. The rotating blades fling the fluid outwards with so-called centrifugal force, into a doughnut-shaped space around – the volute chamber. Here, the peaks of pressure even out as the blades pass, and the fluid is forced away at steady pressure through the outlet.

Bridge The captain controls all aspects of the boat from this main control room. There are wrap-around windows for a wide view and radio communications with the boat's other rooms and crew members, including the firefighters.

Radar

Radio antennae

Deck water/foam cannon The forward deck-mounted cannon (monitor) is aimed at lower areas of a blaze.

Cannon deck

Lifebelts

Boom-mounted water/foam cannon A long two-part boom or articulated arm can lift this cannon many metres into the air, to attack a fire from a higher angle.

Bucket The boom cannon can be aimed by a person in the bucket (platform) or by remote control using the bucket-mounted camera.

Fireboats mark the arrival of Queen Mary 2 with coloured jet sprays

Big fireboats in large ports and harbours are manned and ready to go 24 hours each day. The crew live on board and have a rota or shift system called 'the watch' to make sure someone is always alert and ready to respond to an emergency.

Boom hydraulics Powerful hydraulic pistons raise and lower the boom at its 'elbow'.

✳ Wet WELCOME

Work on a fireboat is not all emergencies and disasters. When a special craft comes into harbour, such as a giant cruise liner on its first voyage, fireboats celebrate by lining the route and aiming welcome sprays high into the air. For really notable visits the water can be mixed with a dye (colouring substance) in the cannon, to make sprays in the colours of the ship's owners or its nationality.

Lifeboats

Bunks

Hatches Equipment and supplies are lowered through the trapdoor-like hatches in the main deck for storage on the lower decks.

Hull skins

Newer fireboats have a propulsion system called a cycloidal drive. A horizontal spinning wheel under the hull has paddle-like projections pointing downwards, like a waterwheel on its side. These paddles can twist to push the boat in any direction.

FIRE RESCU

Prop

Main engines Usually marine diesels, these spin the propeller. Separate engines power the cannons.

SHIP'S LIFEBOAT

For most people, lifeboats are never used, and stay as a comforting reminder that help is at hand should storms and rough seas strike. If the lifeboat is ever launched, it becomes a survival centre for all those on board. It must be strong and tough, with unsinkable construction, able to withstand high winds and ride out big waves, as well as provide shelter and supplies until rescue vessels reach the scene.

Eureka!

More than 3000 years ago, ancient Phoenician boats carried small wooden life rafts. International rules controlling lifeboats were strengthened following the tragic sinking of *RMS Titanic* in 1912. The giant liner carried more than 3000 people but had lifeboat spaces for only 1200.

Whatever next?

New lifeboats carry EPIRBs, or emergency position-indicating beacons – small devices that send out radio signals. Satellites detect these and inform the rescue services of the beacon's location.

Lifeboat drill (practice) is a familiar part of long-distance ship trips. Each person must go to a particular lifeboat position or station.

Raised bridge The person in charge of the lifeboat – usually a crew member – can see the surroundings and steer from here, as well as keep a check on the engine.

Radio equipment

Drinking water

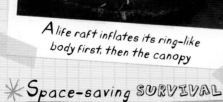

A life raft inflates its ring-like body first, then the canopy

Engine A small marine diesel engine provides power in some lifeboats. This allows the crew to steer away from dangers such as jagged rocks or sandbanks out at sea.

Rudder

✳ Space-saving SURVIVAL

Life rafts are blow-up or fold-out types of lifeboats. Their main advantage is that they save space on the ship, and they can also be stowed away in an aircraft in case it has to land or 'ditch' in water. Inflatable types blow up from compressed gas in a high-pressure canister or cylinder. As this happens the emergency radio beacon switches on to send out its locating signals. Life rafts do not have motors and propellers, but they often have oars or paddles. Modern lifeboats may well have a small engine.

Ballast tanks When the lifeboat is launched, these chambers in the bottom of the hull automatically fill with water. This provides weight or ballast low down, which makes the boat stable and stops it tipping over.

Flares and gun
The flare gun fires bright-burning emergency flares (similar to fireworks) high into the air. They float down on a small parachute.

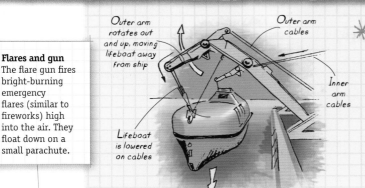

Outer arm rotates out and up, moving lifeboat away from ship

Outer arm cables

Inner arm cables

Lifeboat is lowered on cables

✳ How are LIFEBOATS launched?

A davit is a crane-like structure that lowers items over an edge to drop straight down. On ships the davits are usually folded along the sides to save deck space. In an emergency, they pivot on cables and lean outwards, either as one arm, or with inner and outer arms. These are let out by cables worked by electric winches. The lifeboat is then lowered carefully on another set of cables.

Cover This keeps out rain, spray, cold, winds and fierce sun. Some lifeboats have a foldaway canvas-type cover, others are equipped with a rigid plastic-type version.

Harnesses

The giant liner Queen Mary 2 has 37 lifeboats, each holding more than 100 people.

Diving gear Scuba equipment allows a diver to check the lifeboat hull or rescue someone from the water.

Grab handles

Hull The main hull is constructed from lightweight metal alloys or a composite material such as GRP, glass-reinforced plastic.

OFFSHORE LIFEBOAT

If a ship gets into trouble at sea, conditions are probably already difficult, with strong winds and crashing waves. Offshore lifeboats must withstand these problems, and more, to carry out their missions as the crew push their craft to its limits. One of the most important features is self-righting (see panel below), when a lifeboat that is tipped over by a giant wave turns to become upright again.

Eureka!

The world's oldest lifeboat organization is the UK's RNLI, Royal National Lifeboat Institution. It was founded in 1824 and on average carries out more than 20 rescues every day.

Whatever next?

Amphibious rescue craft are being tested along swampy areas of coastline where neither boats nor all-terrain vehicles can go.

The person in charge of the offshore lifeboat is called the coxwain. There is usually a second coxwain who can take over when needed.

Bridge and cabin The crew may have to strap themselves into their seats in very rough seas. They all wear lifejackets and survival-type suits in case they are swept overboard.

Wipers

Sprung seats

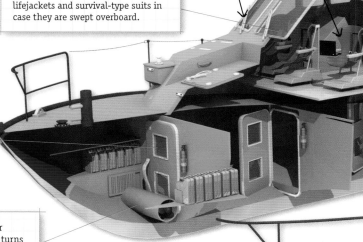

Bulkheads A series of cross-walls or bulkheads from the bow (front) to the stern (rear) divide the boat into a row of watertight compartments. Closing the door seals off each compartment. If one compartment leaks, the water cannot spread into the others.

Bow thrusters A small propellor or water-jet on each side at the front turns the bow left or right, for manoeuvring in tight corners or keeping the boat steady in strong currents and tides.

1. Full ballast tank keeps weight low and lifeboat stable

Righting tank   Ballast tank

2. A big wave knocks the boat over and water starts to flow into the righting tank

3. The weight of water in the righting tank keeps the boat turning

Ballast tank tips boat

4. After almost a full turn water in the righting tank flows into the ballast tank again

*How does SELF-RIGHTING work?

One method for self-righting involves a ballast tank and one or more off-centre righting tanks. Normally the weight of water in the very low ballast tank, in the bottom of the hull, keeps the lifeboat floating upright. If it tilts, this water flows into a righting tank, which puts the lifeboat off balance and makes it continue to spin around. The only stable position is when all the water flows once again into the ballast tank.

The RNLI's Severn Class lifeboats are 17 m long and weigh around 40 tonnes.

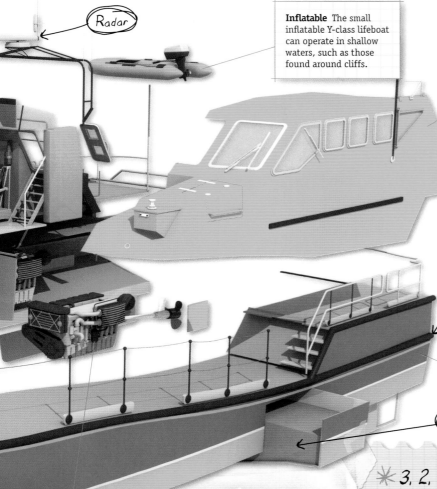

Radar

Inflatable The small inflatable Y-class lifeboat can operate in shallow waters, such as those found around cliffs.

Superstructure All of the doors, windows and hatches have watertight seals to prevent crashing waves and spray from soaking the interior.

Lifeboats are fast for their size. The Trent Class can travel at 46 km/h and smaller inflatable RIB types (see next page) exceed 55 km/h.

Rubbing strips

Hull The hull material is the latest fibre-reinforced composite, able to withstand impact from huge waves.

Ballast tanks

Powerful engines The propellers are spun by marine diesel engines of more than 1000 horsepower each.

✴ 3, 2, 1, SPLASH!

How offshore lifeboats launch depends partly on the type of coastline. If the shore angles steeply into the sea, the lifeboat can slide down a slipway or ramp straight into fairly deep water. If the beach slopes very gently, the lifeboat may be towed across it and into water that is deep enough to float in by a tractor and trailor. In places where there are harbour walls, piers or other suitable places, the lifeboat may be left in the water, tied up safely until a call-out.

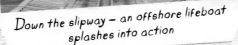

Down the slipway – an offshore lifeboat splashes into action

COASTGUARD PATROL BOAT

Bad weather does not stop coastguards responding to an emergency. Their roles vary from country to country, but most will rush to help craft and people in trouble, often assisting the lifeboats. In some countries the coastguards enforce the law too, as they tackle smugglers, illegal fishing and modern-day pirates.

Eureka!

Coastguards are sometimes called the 'fourth emergency service' after police, ambulance and firefighting. National coastguards were set up from about 1800, chiefly to control the boom in smuggling.

Whatever next?

Some coastguard forces have tested underwater pursuit craft such as small submarines, which can follow illegal craft, video their crimes and catch them red-handed.

Speakers It's often noisy at sea, with whooshing winds and crashing waves. But the powerful loudspeakers allow the crew to 'hail' or call to people on nearby vessels.

The USA has more than 70 Marine Protector Class patrol boats. Each is 27 m long, 5.9 m wide and travels at a top speed of 46 km/h.

The 90-tonne Marine Protector patrols have enough supplies for the ten crew to stay at sea for five days. The boat can travel more than 1000 km before needing to refuel.

Berths (bunk beds)

M2 machine gun

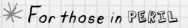
A patrol boat endures high seas

Gun mounts Machine guns on swivel mountings allow trained crew members to fire at enemies that threaten the patrol boat – either warning shots or real shoot-to-kill.

✳ For those in PERIL

Most national coastguards do SAR – search and rescue. They respond to emergency calls from stricken vessels that have run aground or lost engine power. Or perhaps a person has been swept overboard. In these cases the coastguard may have its own aircraft and helicopters to help, or perhaps it calls on the local air force, as it coordinates with the lifeboat service. Some nations limit their coastguards to SAR and watch-only patrols. If a patrol spots something suspicious, such as possible terrorists trying to land, at once they contact a branch of the military, usually the navy.

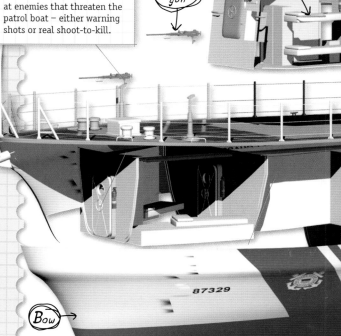

Bow

87329

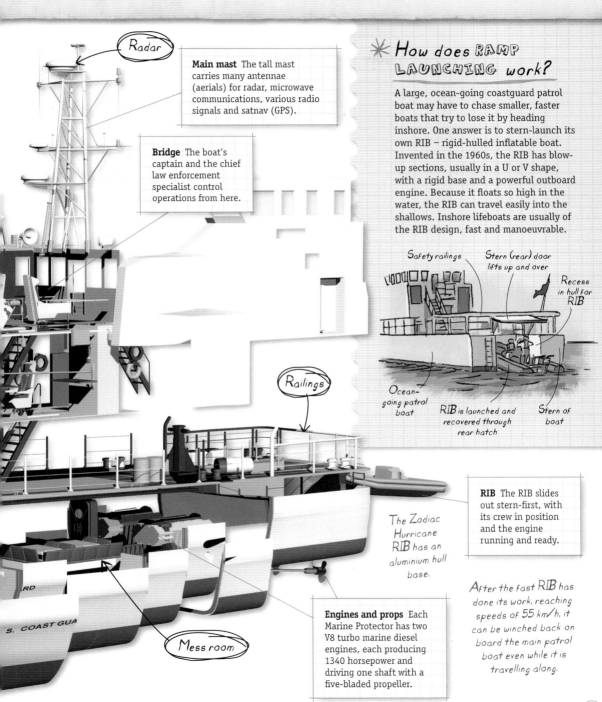

Radar

Main mast The tall mast carries many antennae (aerials) for radar, microwave communications, various radio signals and satnav (GPS).

Bridge The boat's captain and the chief law enforcement specialist control operations from here.

How does RAMP LAUNCHING work?

A large, ocean-going coastguard patrol boat may have to chase smaller, faster boats that try to lose it by heading inshore. One answer is to stern-launch its own RIB – rigid-hulled inflatable boat. Invented in the 1960s, the RIB has blow-up sections, usually in a U or V shape, with a rigid base and a powerful outboard engine. Because it floats so high in the water, the RIB can travel easily into the shallows. Inshore lifeboats are usually of the RIB design, fast and manoeuvrable.

Safety railings

Stern (rear) door lifts up and over

Recess in hull for RIB

Ocean-going patrol boat

RIB is launched and recovered through rear hatch

Stern of boat

Railings

RIB The RIB slides out stern-first, with its crew in position and the engine running and ready.

The Zodiac Hurricane RIB has an aluminium hull base.

After the fast RIB has done its work, reaching speeds of 55 km/h, it can be winched back on board the main patrol boat even while it is travelling along.

Engines and props Each Marine Protector has two V8 turbo marine diesel engines, each producing 1340 horsepower and driving one shaft with a five-bladed propeller.

S. COAST GUA

RD

Mess room

UNDERWATER RESCUE SUBMERSIBLE

Rescue missions are dangerous enough, but when they are in deep water, the risks multiply. The enormous water pressure brings great hazards since it crushes anything not built to withstand its huge pressing force – including human lungs. Most underwater rescue sites are also very cold and dark. And there is a time limit as the air supply runs lower and lower.

Eureka!

A forerunner of the rescue sub, the diving bell is a bell-shaped chamber lowered into water, trapping air inside. Divers can enter it for a few breaths. In use for more than 2000 years, the 16th century saw greatly improved versions.

Whatever next?

Personal survival suits are common for people exposed to risk at the water's surface. Underwater pressurized versions have been tested to depths of 100 metres.

The LR5 submersible rescue vessel has a maximum working depth of about 400 m.

The world record dive for crewed submersibles is 10,911 m, set in 1960 by Trieste.

Safety cage A metal cage surrounds the front windows to protect against rocks and other objects.

Pressure dome windows A spherical or domed shape is very good at resisting pressure, spreading out the force evently. So curved surfaces are used wherever possible for the sub's design.

A rescue sub being prepared for transportation

✳ To the RESCUE

The rescue submersible is a very specialized vessel, designed for careful manoeuvring at slow speeds. It cannot get to a rescue site under its own power, so it is transported by various means, as quickly as possible. Methods include a low-loader truck, a flatbed railway wagon, or even a cargo aircraft, and then the final stage by a 'mother ship' to the surface above the rescue site. The mother ship stays in position, or on station, ready to receive the rescued people who may need medical care.

Remote arm A manipulator arm can grab, move and cut objects such as cables, rocks or weeds. There is also a powerful cutting or grinding disc.

The LR5 is 9.2 m long and 3 m wide, with a hull height of 2.75 m.

Crew The standard crew of three is pilot, co-pilot and systems officer. They can be joined by up to 16 people at 'cram capacity' in the rescue chamber.

Rescue hatch

The LR5 travels at only 4 km/h, but it can position itself very precisely.

Before it has to recharge its batteries, the LR5 can carry out up to eight diving missions.

LR5 SUBMERSIBLE

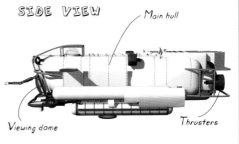

SIDE VIEW

Main hull

Viewing dome

Thrusters

The Russian nuclear submarine Kursk sank in 2000 with the loss of all 118 crew.

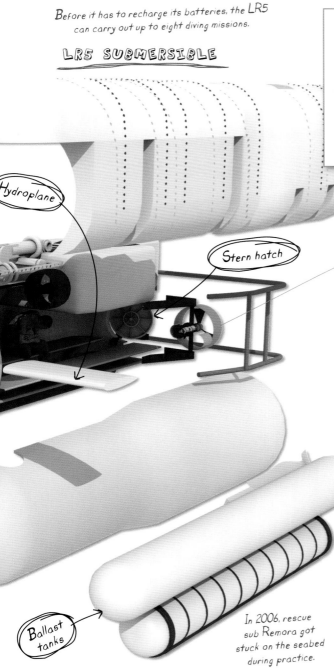

Hydroplane

Stern hatch

Ballast tanks

In 2006, rescue sub Remora got stuck on the seabed during practice.

Rear thrusters Three-bladed thruster propellers, each controlled seperately and driven by an electric motor, push or thrust the submersible in almost any direction. They are reversible for fast braking and manoeuvring backwards.

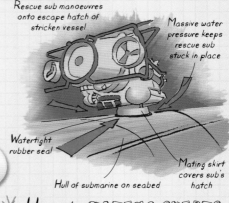

Rescue sub manoeuvres onto escape hatch of stricken vessel

Massive water pressure keeps rescue sub stuck in place

Watertight rubber seal

Mating skirt covers sub's hatch

Hull of submarine on seabed

✳ How do MATING SKIRTS and AIRLOCKS work?

A mating skirt is a rubber-edged collar placed against one of the submarine's trapdoor-like hatches. Water is pumped out of it so that the surrounding water pressure squeezes it onto the sub's hull. Then both subs' hatches are opened and people can pass through. Another method is to have a separate in-between airlock chamber, as found on spacecraft.

AIR AMBULANCE HELICOPTER

Blocked roads, flooded fields and broken bridges are no barriers to the air ambulance – a helicopter with life-saving equipment and a doctor or other trained medical staff. All it needs is a small patch of ground, such as a cleared roadway or farmer's field, for landing. Air ambulances also rush critical patients from one hospital to another more specialized centre, and carry donated body parts such as kidneys or hearts.

Eureka!

The first 'flying doctor' organization was set up in Australia in the 1920s. It was the brainchild of religious minister and keen pilot John Flynn (1880–1951). It used aircraft to take sick people to the nearest hospital, which could be hundreds of kilometres away.

Whatever next?

Helicopters are excellent at vertical take-off and landing, but forward speed is relatively slow. Tilt-wing aircraft, where wings and engines swivel through 90°, may take over.

Crew The highly trained pilot may be joined by a co-pilot or a helicopter-based paramedic, depending on the flying distance and conditions.

✳ How is a HELICOPTER controlled?

Flying a helicopter is different to flying an ordinary aircraft. The helicopter pilot has three sets of controls. The rudder foot pedals control yaw, or swivelling around left and right. The collective lever, which looks like a car handbrake, controls the rate of climb – going up or down – and also has the engine speed throttle. The cyclic lever, positioned like a plane's control column or 'joystick', adjusts the flight direction – forwards, back or sideways.

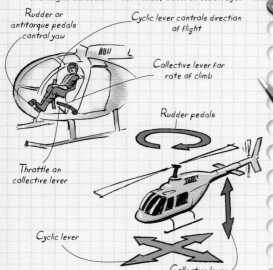

Rudder or antitorque pedals control yaw

Cyclic lever controls direction of flight

Collective lever for rate of climb

Rudder pedals

Throttle on collective lever

Cyclic lever

Collective lever

Emergency supplies First aid equipment includes drugs and medicines, oxygen masks, splints and bandages, and a defibrillator to restart a heart that has stopped or is fibrillating (beating with an abnormal rate and rhythm).

Stretcher The patient usually lies on the stretcher, strapped down in case of turbulence, where the medical staff can give mid-air care.

Tail boom The rear rotor or stabilizer is driven by a spinning shaft inside the boom.

Tail rotor blades This rotor counteracts the tendency of the helicopter's fuselage (body) to spin in the opposite direction to the main rotor.

Blade

A casualty is airlifted from a road accident in central London, UK

✳ The best way to get OUT is to go UP

The air ambulance helicopter's great advantage is VTOL – vertical take-off and landing. It can set down in an area not much bigger than a tennis court. However this area must be cleared first. In a traffic accident, police and other emergency services often have to supervise drivers, moving their vehicles closer together, to make space for the landing. Most major hospitals have a dedicated landing site or helipad, which is always kept free.

Step

Sliding windows

DartMouth-H Medical Cente

Left door The large doors must allow stretchers and big pieces of medical equipment to pass through. Equipment may include a portable X-ray machine to check the patient for broken bones or fractures. The medical staff then radio ahead the patient's condition to specialists at the waiting hospital.

In some countries an air ambulance does other jobs when not needed for emergencies, such as checking electricity power lines or pipelines.

Landing skids Skids offer the best all-round landing ability. They are less likely to sink into soft ground than wheels and can cope with an uneven surface such as a ploughed field.

Treating a patient in mid air is very different from on the ground. A bumpy flight means that delicate procedures such as putting a needle into a vein become more difficult. Also the medic cannot hear the patient's heartbeat or breathing sounds due to the helicopter's noise.

SAR HELICOPTER

Search and rescue, SAR, saves thousands of lives daily around the world. Its workhorses are helicopters or 'choppers', usually air force types modified for rescue work. For people stranded up mountains, on cliffs, in remote canyons, in quicksand or out at sea, and perhaps injured too, the 'chop-chop-chop' of rotating blades means help has arrived. For rough-weather rescue, pilots need to be the best.

Eureka!

The first helicopter hoist rescue was in 1945. Two men were lifted by a Sikorsky R-5 from a stranded oil barge near Fairfield, Connecticut, USA. The violent storm meant no other method was possible.

Whatever next?

Helicopters continue to improve their performance, especially in high winds, when new electronic aids and advanced computer programs help the pilot.

Drive shaft

Radome

✳ Hold it STEADY!

High winds and crashing waves demand the highest piloting skills. One of the many difficulties is downdraft, where the downwards rush of air from the rotors causes spray, waves and wind at the water's surface. This can soak, blow sideways or even capsize (tip over) small vessels such as rowing boats. The pilot must hover high enough to minimize this problem. But greater height means a greater length of hoist cable, which makes it less controllable as it sways or swings in the downdraft and wind.

NAVY RESCUE
HS-12

Winch A powerful electric winch lowers and raises a hook, harness or other attachment on a long steel cable. The winch operator trains closely with the pilot.

A chopper lifts a casualty from a lifeboat, for the dash to hospital

The SAR version of the Sea King has a top speed of 267 km/h and a total range of 1000 km.

Rescue crew The winchman (winchperson) uses a combination of hand signals and spoken radio messages to communicate with the winch operator and pilot, to be placed onto the right spot and then winched up when all is ready.

The UK's new S-92 SAR helicopters reached their 500th mission in just two years.

Rotor head (hub) This complex piece of engineering makes the rotor blades twist or angle by different amounts as they turn around, according to the flight direction.

Turboshaft engines Twin engines deliver their spinning power to the main rotor. If one engine fails, the 'copter can still fly using the other, but with reduced ability.

Eurocopter Super Puma SARs have rescued more than 10,000 people since going into service in the 1980s.

Cowling

Main rotor blades The blades are made of flexible 'high tensile' composite material, able to withstand enormous stresses.

Pilot

Co-pilot

Seaworthy hull The lower fuselage has a boat's hull-like shape and is watertight. If the chopper suffers its own emergency it can land or 'ditch' in a lake or the sea and stay afloat for a time.

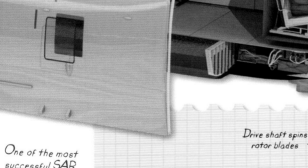

One of the most successful SAR helicopters is the Sikorsky S-61, also called the Sea King. It is 17 m long, weighs 9.5 tonnes when fully loaded, and has a rotor span of 18.9 m. The S-61 first flew in 1961.

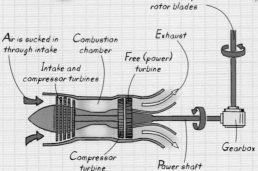

Drive shaft spins rotor blades

Air is sucked in through intake

Combustion chamber

Exhaust

Intake and compressor turbines

Free (power) turbine

Compressor turbine

Power shaft

Gearbox

✳ How do TURBOSHAFT ENGINES work?

A turboshaft works in a similar way to other jet engines. Fast-spinning fan-like turbine blades suck in and squeeze air. The air mixes with fuel vapour, burns fiercely and forms a blast or 'jet' of hot expanding gases. In a standard engine this jet gives thrust for forward movement. In a turboshaft engine the jet gases spin another turbine as they leave. This power turbine spins its own shaft, which connects to the rotor blades through a gearbox.

SPEED
MACHINES

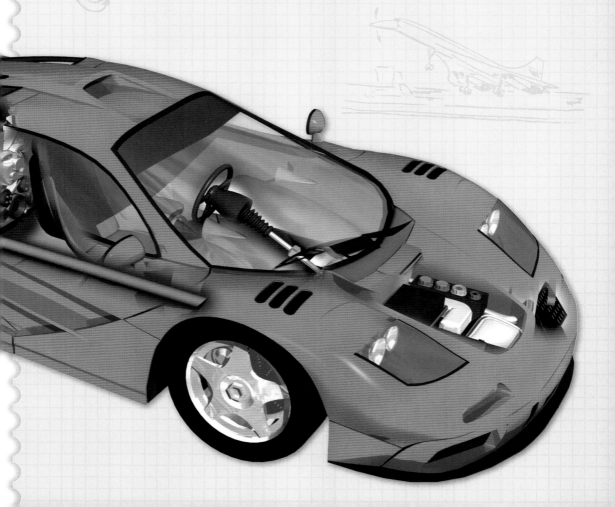

INTRODUCTION

People have always wanted to travel faster, higher and further. In Greece more than 2500 years ago, ancient Olympians celebrated human achievements by staging athletic events. As new ways of travelling were invented, people competed using these too. Horses and chariots, then sailboats, trains, bicycles, cars, speedboats, planes and rockets, created many new kinds of speed records. To be the fastest resulted in fame, status, respect, your name in history – and maybe a big money prize.

In the 1920s, cars such as this *Bentley* reached then-amazing speeds of 200 km/h.

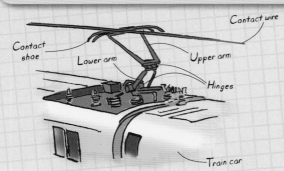
Contact wire
Contact shoe
Lower arm
Upper arm
Hinges
Train car
Electric trains are fast, but they need specialized equipment to pick up the current.

PICKING UP SPEED

As each new wave of technology and engineering came along, people applied it to speed machines. For example, steam trains battled each other for the rail record during the first half of the last century. Then along came electric trains, which travelled almost twice as fast as their steam cousins. Recently, maglev trains have taken the rail record, nudging 600 kilometres per hour.

JUST RIGHT

Attempts at speed records are a huge gamble. For example, it takes months to get a boat ready for a record-breaking venture. Then, on the day, the wind may die away for a sailboat, or it could be too strong for a powerboat. Some jet-powered water speed records have failed because ducks and geese got in the way, bobbing on the surface or almost flying into the jet engine.

Sail records continue to be set. In 2009, the trimaran *Hydroptere* reached a speed of 95 km/h.

THE SPEED TEAM

Extreme speed machines need lots of dedicated back-up. Teams of engineers, mechanics and other helpers push technology to the limits, with constant delicate adjustments, plenty of fuel and spare parts, and complicated equipment to make sure everything runs smoothly. Everyone must pay huge attention to each tiny detail. A few specks of dirt in the fuel could make the engine cut out at a critical moment and cause disaster.

Spinning turbine impeller sucks in fuel from the fuel tank

Electric drive motor is situated inside the pump

Fuel is pumped out at high pressure along a pipe towards the engine

Fuel enters

Pump casing

Fuel flows past motor

More power requires more fuel, so fuel pump design continually improves.

THE NEED FOR SPEED

Speed aces are brave. Drivers, riders and pilots put their lives on the line. Some records are tremendously difficult to break – the water speed record was set more than 30 years and shows little sign of being broken. In the meantime, progress brings fresh challenges for new types of vehicles and craft. Today, many of these are kinder to the environment, using solar power or fuel cells. Speed machines are becoming clean machines.

Bloodhound SSC aims to break the magic 1500 km/h land speed record.

Russia's Tu-144 resembled Concorde. But the era of supersonic airliners is over.

The future may see speed records for hover-cars, personal jet-packs, human-powered aircraft and even a return trip into orbit – a race into space.

115

YAMAHA R1 SUPERBIKE

Ever since people started to add engines to their two-wheeled cycles, they have raced against each other and the clock. Travelling at speed on two wheels is dangerous because the rider must stay perfectly balanced and in firm contact with the ground. A sideways gust of wind, a pebble on the track or dabbing the brake at the wrong time could spell disaster – a rider has no bodywork protection on a motorcycle.

Eureka!

The biggest championship in motorcycle racing is MotoGP, which started in 1949. It grew out of unofficial races on ordinary roads in the 1930s. These were exceptionally dangerous because normal traffic was often using the roads at the same time.

Some racing bike engines run at 18,000 rpm (revolutions per minute) – 300 times per second.

Whatever next?

Small hovercraft-type motorbikes and jet-propelled bikes have been tested over the years, but they are too tricky to steer and slow down.

Lights

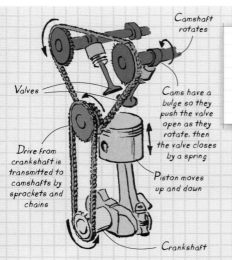

Camshaft rotates

Valves

Cams have a bulge so they push the valve open as they rotate, then the valve closes by a spring

Drive from crankshaft is transmitted to camshafts by sprockets and chains

Piston moves up and down

Crankshaft

Forks Hydraulic dampers and springs (shock absorbers) absorb road bumps and sudden steering manoeuvres.

✳ How do DOHC ENGINES work?

A petrol or diesel engine has mushroom-shaped valves at the top of each cylinder. The inlet valve opens to let in fresh air and fuel mixture. When this mix has exploded, the exhaust valve opens to let out the stale gases. The valves open by being pushed downwards. In the double overhead camshaft (DOHC) each valve is pushed by a collar-like part with a bulge on one side, the 'cam'. This turns on an 'overhead' shaft spinning above the engine. There are two shafts, hence the word 'double'.

Brake disc Special metal alloys and plenty of ventilation holes prevent the disc overheating.

Spokes As few spokes as possible decrease wheel weight and air resistance as the wheel spins.

Handlebars The handlebars are set low down, so the rider crouches over them for less air resistance, rather than sitting more upright.

In a MotoGP race the rider who finishes first gains 25 points, the second rider receives 20, third place is 16, and so on – all the way down to the rider who comes in fifteenth, who gains one point!

Cleland rides into the record books on his electric superbike

Low-profile seat

☀ Going ELECTRIC

The problem with electric motorbikes is the great weight of the batteries. Not only do they slow down the vehicle and make it less efficient, they also cause difficulties with balance, since leaning over slightly means shifting their heavy weight and making the bike less steady. However record-breaking electric motorcycles only need enough current for a few runs. In 2009 Jeremy Cleland set a new electric motorbike top speed of 240 kilometres per hour.

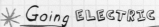

Rear drive sprocket

MotoGP has several classes, including 125 cc and Moto2 (600 cc) for smaller-engined motorbikes, and the MotoGP class for bigger engines.

Tyres Different tyre patterns and treads are used depending on conditions, with smooth 'slicks' in the dry and grooved treads when it is wet.

Engine The R1 has four cylinders in a line across the bike (left to right), each parallel to the others. The cylinders are forward-inclined, or leaning to the front. The total engine size is 998 cc (almost one litre).

Suspension arms The suspension design is known as swingarm. It has a long bar on each side that pivots at its front end, with the wheel at its rear end.

Until 1987, riders were allowed to push-start their MotoGP bikes and jump on when the engine was going!

The fastest speed for a MotoGP bike was set in 2009 at 349.3 km/h by Dani Pedrosa on his Repsol Honda, during practise at the Italian Grand Prix.

NASCAR STOCK CAR

Stock racing cars are based on cars that anyone can buy from a normal supply or 'stock'. Of course the rules say that they can be souped up with more powerful engines, tougher suspension and better safety equipment. The world's biggest stock car races are organized by the US National Association for Stock Car Auto Racing, NASCAR, and draw giant crowds of 200,000 or more.

Eureka!

Racing 'modded' or modified ordinary cars on normal roads might seem cool. However over the years it's caused many tragedies. NASCAR had its origins in the first organized races during the 1930s and was founded in 1948.

Whatever next?

Most stock cars race on giant oval tracks called speedways, raceways or bowls. Speeds are limited not so much by the cars themselves, but by how tightly the track curves at the bends and other safety factors.

The longest NASCAR track is Talladega in Alabama, USA at 4.3 km.

V8 Engine The main NASCAR events specify an 8-cylinder engine of 5860 cc with pushrod valves (see below left).

Radiator The 'rad' is a very vulnerable part of the car. If damaged, its engine-cooling water leaks and the engine may overheat and even seize up completely.

✳ How do OHV ENGINES work?

The mushroom-shaped valves of a petrol or diesel engine open to allow fresh fuel-air mixture into the cylinder, and let out stale gases after the mixture has burned or combusted (see page 116). In the OHV or overhead valve design, the valves are in the top of the cylinder. Each one is opened by a see-saw rocker that is tilted from below by a long push rod. This is pushed up by a cam, which is like a ring with a bulge on one side. The cam turns on a spinning camshaft low down, beside the main engine.

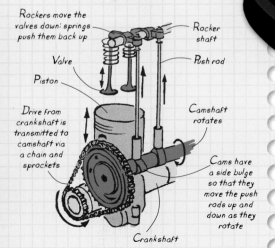

Rockers move the valves down: springs push them back up

Rocker shaft

Valve

Push rod

Piston

Drive from crankshaft is transmitted to camshaft via a chain and sprockets

Camshaft rotates

Cams have a side bulge so that they move the push rods up and down as they rotate

Crankshaft

Fan belt

Front skirt

Radiator

Sponsors Several sponsors provide money or equipment for the race teams. In return they gain publicity with their names and logos displayed on the cars and trackside.

Racing tyres To even out car performance, NASCAR entries use Goodyear slick tyres – that is, smooth, with no tread.

NASCAR drivers must wear a collar-like HANS (Head And Neck Support) to prevent neck injuries in high-speed impact.

NASCAR is a family concern. It was founded by Bill France Snr in 1948. In 2003 his grandson Brian France became chief of the organization.

Roll cage A strong cage of welded metal tubes stops the car and driver being crushed if the car rolls over in a serious crash. The tubes and weld joints must exceed a certain level of strength.

Of the World Top 20 crowds for single-day sports events, *NASCAR* draws more than 15 of the biggest.

Shatterproof windows The windows are made from special impact-resistant clear plastic.

Spoiler This angled surface 'spoils' the airflow at the rear of the car, giving a downward force that keeps the wheels pressed against the track.

Jimmie Johnston won his fourth successive *NASCAR* Sprint Cup title in 2009. No other driver has won four in a row.

Side skirt

Odd tyres The tyres can be different sizes depending on the direction and tightness of the track's bends.

NASCAR oval speedways evolved from races at Daytona Beach, Florida, with straight sections along the sand and the beachfront highway joined by two tight bends.

On the raceway, car 07 is trashed in a high-speed bump

✳ Rough 'n' TOUGH

Stock car racing is not just about speed. Drivers can swerve in front of each other, brake to slow down the car behind, and even nudge other cars out of the way, although all of the action is controlled by strict laws. Sometimes cars smash into the outer barrier around the track or get pushed onto the grassy infield at its centre. With speeds reaching 300-plus kilometres per hour, drivers need nerves of steel, and also plenty of aggression to force their way to the front and stay there.

MCLAREN F1 SUPERCAR

People who love fast cars like to think they are driving a vehicle that's just one step away from the very best on the track – Formula One Grand Prix. The McLaren F1 was produced during the 1990s as the ultimate road car, based on the McLaren team's fantastic record of Formula One successes. The driver has that 'F1' feel because unlike in other super sports cars, the two passenger seats on either side are set slightly behind the driver.

Eureka!

McLaren's aim was a car with very low weight, extremely high power, and high-tech parts and components 'borrowed' from Formula One. Only 106 F1s were built. They rarely come up for sale.

Whatever next?

In 1998, the F1 set a record 391 kilometres per hour for a production road car. Since then others have gone faster, more than 410 kilometres per hour.

The F1 has a six-speed manual gearbox – not automatic.

Butterfly doors The doors move both out and up as they open, so that people do not have to stoop down too low to get in.

Radiator

✳ How does ABS work?

Anti-lock braking system, ABS, stops the road wheels 'locking' or stopping suddenly when the driver brakes too hard. It's safer if the wheels keep their grip on the road, rather than locking and skidding. Electronic sensors check the spinning speed of each wheel. If one starts to turn slower than the others, this indicates it could lock. So a valve in the brake pipe to that wheel reduces the brake pressure. This happens many times very fast, as a series of clicks or pulses.

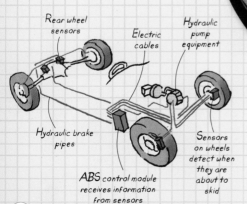

Rear wheel sensors

Electric cables

Hydraulic pump equipment

Hydraulic brake pipes

Sensors on wheels detect when they are about to skid

ABS control module receives information from sensors

Battery

The F1 is 4.29 m long, 1.82 m wide and just 1.14 m high. Its fully fuelled weight is 1.14 tonnes.

Central driving position The driver sits in the centre of the vehicle, which gives much better weight distribution and stability than being to one side.

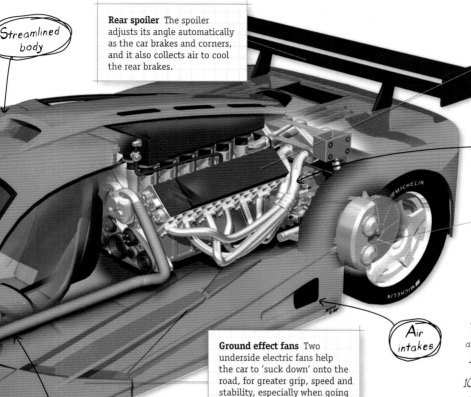

Streamlined body

Rear spoiler The spoiler adjusts its angle automatically as the car brakes and corners, and it also collects air to cool the rear brakes.

BMW V12 engine The 12-cylinder, 6.1-litre S70/2 engine produces 672 horsepower – over five times more than a typical family car.

Exhaust

Powerful brakes On the original F1 design the brakes were not power-assisted and there was no ABS (see left), but some of the cars have since been converted.

Air intakes

Ground effect fans Two underside electric fans help the car to 'suck down' onto the road, for greater grip, speed and stability, especially when going around corners.

The F1 accelerates from a standstill to 100 km/h in just over three seconds. It can then brake from 100 km/h to zero in slightly under three seconds and less than 40 m.

Engine cooling system

Two self-build kit cars called Edward and Albert were used as testbeds or 'mules' for various parts of the F1.

Although designed for the road, the F1 still triumphed on the track

✷ BACK on the TRACK

The McLaren F1 was designed as a 'street legal' road car. It has indicator lights, side lights and other features needed by law for normal roads, that track cars do not have. Yet it still managed to win several track races, including the world-famous gruelling Le Mans 24-Hour in France in 1995. The race-ready F1 was slightly changed from the normal road version, as it had to compete against cars purpose-designed and specially built for that particular race at the Le Mans circuit.

TESLA ROADSTER

Electric cars are nothing new. They have been around for more than 100 years. In fact in 1899 the world land speed record was held by an electric car (see below). With modern worries about the energy crisis, exhaust pollution and global warming, electric cars are making a comeback. There are some people at the traffic lights who always want to speed away faster than everyone else. The all-electric Tesla Roadster is ideal for them.

Eureka!

In the 1970s–80s, partly because of political problems around the world, there were worries about the supply of oil (petroleum) to make petrol and diesel. Coupled with new air pollution laws, people went back to the old idea of electric cars.

Whatever next?

The key to success with electric cars is better batteries that charge faster and power the vehicle for longer. Several new kinds of batteries offer hope for the future.

Lotus windscreen

Sports styling
Typically low, sleek sports-car styling based on the Lotus Elise gives the Roadster very low air resistance.

Body panels All body panels are made from carbon fibre composites, helping to keep the car's weight down to about 1.23 tonnes.

In a special endurance race a Roadster covered 511 km on a single charge.

✳ When VOLTS ruled

During the later 1800s, the newly invented petrol and diesel engines were still noisy and unreliable. Electric motors had been around for many years, and they powered various kinds of cars and wagons. In 1899 Belgian race ace Camille Jenatzy set a new land speed record in his electric car *La Jamais Contente* (meaning 'Never Satisfied'). On a straight road near Paris, France, it sped along at 105.9 kilometres per hour – the first land vehicle to go past 100 kilometres per hour.

Jenatzy celebrates his record in the electric *La Jamais Contente*

The Roadster is very economical, covering about 50 km on the electrical energy equivalent of one litre of petrol.

Lithium-ion batteries
The battery packs or 'ESS' (Energy Storage System) contain more than 6800 Li-ion cells arranged in separate sheets, which are cooled by a circulating fluid.

The Roadster's battery packs take about 3.5 hours for a full charge.

The Roadster is the first production electric car to travel more than 300 km on a single charge of electricity. In fact, driven carefully it can cover almost 400 km.

Electric circuits
Computerized electronics keep a check on the battery packs, motor and other circuits, and lessen power to the motor if there are problems.

The Roadster has excellent acceleration, going from zero to just under 100 km/h in 3.7 seconds. However some drivers say that it is too quiet. They like a car to roar as they speed away.

How do Li-ion cells work?

Lithium-ion rechargeable batteries are found in all kinds of gadgets, from mp3 players and mobile phones to laptops. The Li-ion battery is a group of individual Li-ion cells. When the battery is charged, particles called lithium ions, which are positive, are forced to move from the negative contact (cathode) to the positive one (anode). When in use (see diagram below), the ions naturally go back, attracted to the negative contact, and their movement forms an electric current.

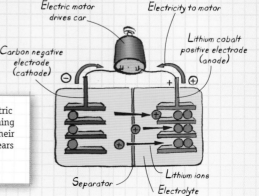

Electric motor drives car

Electricity to motor

Carbon negative electrode (cathode)

Lithium cobalt positive electrode (anode)

Separator

Lithium ions

Electrolyte

Electric motor The single electric motor weighs just 32 kilograms, yet in the Sports version of the Roadster it produces almost 290 horsepower. It spins more than 10,000 times each minute at high speed.

Transmission Because electric motors have a powerful turning force (torque) throughout their speed range, there are no gears to change – the gearbox is single-speed.

BLUEBIRD CN7

Some people say that speed and risk-taking run in the family. This was certainly true of Malcolm Campbell and his son Donald. The father set 13 world speed records in cars and boats during the 1920s–30s, and son Donald continued the tradition in the 1950s–60s (see page 130). The name *Bluebird* was used for many of their vehicles. In *Bluebird CN7* Donald took the land speed record in 1964 at 648.7 kilometres per hour.

Eureka!

At first, world speed records had no official rules or independent timekeepers. In 1904 the FIA (Fédération Internationale de Automobile) formed in Paris, to oversee all kinds of car racing and also land speed record attempts.

The first version of *Bluebird CN7* lacked a vertical stabilizer or tail fin. This unusual design could have contributed to its crash at Bonneville in 1960.

The 'C' in CN7 refers to Donald Campbell. The 'N' is for the Norris brothers, Ken and Lew, who carried out most of the design work on Campbell's cars and boats.

Aeroweb bodywork The smoothly curved body had outer and inner skins of very thin metal alloy separated by a sponge-like layer of 20-mm-thick metal 'honeycomb'.

Cockpit The driver's cockpit was smoothed into the front of the car, The steering wheel in the cockpit was linked to the steering mechanism between the front wheels by two chains.

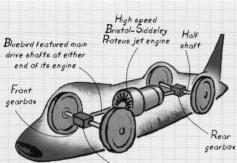

Bluebird featured main drive shafts at either end of its engine

Front gearbox

High speed Bristol-Siddeley Proteus jet engine

Half shaft

Rear gearbox

Gearboxes change the direction of the drive from the main shaft, at right angles out to the wheels

✳ How do GEARBOXES work?

A gearbox has two or more wheels with teeth, called cogs, that fit or mesh together. A bigger cog turning a smaller cog makes the smaller cog spin much faster, but with less turning force or torque. A small cog meshing with a big one spins the big one more slowly but with more torque (turning force). The comparison between the cog sizes is called the gear ratio. The trick is to get the best ratio for each gearbox. *Bluebird CN7*'s designers did many calculations and experiments to get the best ratio between the spinning speed of the engine and the road wheels.

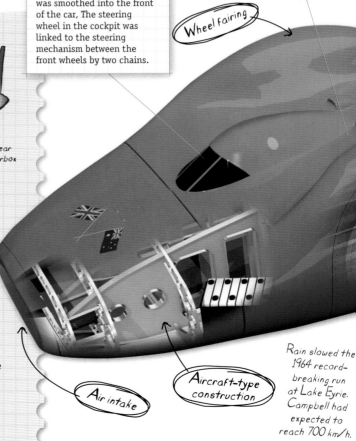

Wheel fairing

Air intake

Aircraft-type construction

Rain slowed the 1964 record-breaking run at Lake Eyrie. Campbell had expected to reach 700 km/h.

In the 1960 Bonneville crash, CN7 took off for more than 300 m and bounced three times.

Chassis The main chassis (framework) was constructed of aluminium-based alloys for strength and extreme lightness, with a hoop-like design similar to an aircraft fuselage.

Fin (vertical stabilizer) This upright surface helped to prevent the CN7 swerving from side to side or 'snaking' at high speed.

Bristol-Siddeley Proteus engine Designed for aircraft use, this 5000-horsepower jet engine delivered its power by spinning a drive shaft, rather than by blasting a thrust of hot gases from the rear exhaust.

Four Proteus engines were also used to drive the propellers on the huge Bristol Britannia airliner of the 1950s–60s.

Dunlop tyres Specially made tyres with an outer diameter of 1.32 metres and width of 20 centimetres were fitted to the lightweight alloy metal disc wheels.

Fuel tanks

Oxygen bottles

Brakes The CN7 had three separate braking systems, including disc brakes on the inner sides of the wheel and air brakes at the rear.

☀ *Always in* DANGER

Speed record attempts are always dangerous. On land, you need the longest, flattest place on Earth. This is usually the dried-up bottom of a salt lake, where the slowly drying water leaves behind a hard, flat sheet or bed of salt crystals. The first *Bluebird CN7* was wrecked in 1960 in a crash at Bonneville Salt Flats in the USA. The next version went to Lake Eyrie in Australia but its 1963 attempt was washed out by the first rain there in 20 years.

The wrecked first Bluebird CN7 after its high-speed crash

125

THRUST SSC

In 1997 at Black Rock Desert, Nevada, USA, there was a huge roaring noise and then an eerie thunder-like boom. It was the first land vehicle to go faster than sound and break the 'sound barrier' – jet-powered *Thrust* SSC (SuperSonic Car). Driven by jet fighter pilot Andy Green, it clocked an average speed over two runs of 1228 kilometres per hour.

Eureka!

The land speed record shift from petrol engines to jets began in the 1960s. At first the official rules did not recognize jet cars. But after much argument they agreed that there should be several types of record. The 'absolute' one has been held by jets ever since.

Whatever next?

Several teams are building cars to break *Thrust* SSC's record, including the UK's *Bloodhound* project and the US-Canada *North American Eagle*.

Driver Andy Green kept in touch with the pit crew, who informed him when to hit maximum power in order to pass the timing equipment at top speed.

Thrust SSCs two jet engines had a power output of 110,000 horsepower.

More than 100 electronic sensors sent information by radio to the pit crew.

Thrust SSC makes its record-breaking run

Air intake

Girder chassis

The total length of Thrust's run track was almost 20 km.

✳ Rules RULE!

The official land speed record rules say that a vehicle must be timed as it goes between two points a certain distance apart, twice – usually on one day and then the next. The two runs or passes can be in the same direction. Formerly they had to be in opposite directions, within an hour of each other – this is how *Thrust SSC* gained its record. The rules mean the vehicle needs several kilometres to get up speed. Then the driver must get to top speed and stay there as the vehicle passes the timing equipment. There should also be enough distance after the measurement to slow down safely.

Nose cone The streamlining of SSC included an almost needle-sharp nose, which contained a crash sensor that set off the automatic fire extinguisher.

Engine pod Each engine was about 5.2 metres long and one metre in diameter, with a weight of almost two tonnes.

The two engines would burn the amount of jet fuel equivalent to a family car's full tank of petrol in three seconds.

Steering The two offset rear wheels, one in front and slightly to the side of the other, steered the vehicle.

Fuel tank More than 1000 litres of jet fuel were used for each run, contained in the specially constructed fireproof tank.

Tailplane

✳ How does PARACHUTE BRAKING work?

The fastest land vehicles go so quickly that when they try to slow down, even special brakes would glow red hot within a second or two. Instead the driver releases a small umbrella-shaped parachute from the rear. This is the drogue, which catches the air and pulls out the much bigger main parachute for greater air resistance. Once the speed has dropped enough, the driver can then apply the brakes.

'Bullet' is fired and pulls out the drogue chute

Drogue chute

Drogue chute opens and pulls out the main braking parachute

Cables

Main parahute

Rolls-Royce Spey jet engines After early tests with the Spey 202, the engines were updated to the Spey 205 version. These engines have powered many aircraft, from Buccaneer and Phantom fighters to the BAC 111 jetliner and Nimrod military reconnaissance craft.

Formers Each engine was encased in a metal tube with a framework of hoop-like formers.

Engine cowl

Thrust had six carbon wheel brakes, two for each front wheel and one for each rear wheel.

Front wheels Since SSC was driven by thrust from the jet engines, the front and rear wheels simply rotated by themselves. All wheels are solid aluminium discs without tyres.

Thrust SSC is 16.5 m long and weighs more than 10 tonnes when ready to go. This compares to a length of just over 9 m and a weight of 4.2 tonnes for its record-holding predecessor from 1964, Bluebird CN7 (see page 124).

TGV BULLET TRAIN

The speediest trains are long, slim and extra-streamlined, with a rounded front, similar to a bullet. They travel almost as fast as real bullets fired from guns. One type is the French TGV, *Train a Grande Vitesse* ('Big Speed Train'). The locomotive or pulling part has huge electric motors that are powered by electric current gathered from overhead wires. On a special test run in 2007 a TGV took the world rail speed record at 574.8 kilometres per hour.

Eureka!

There are many kinds of passenger-carrying electric trains, from subway types in tunnels below cities, to specialized services in big airports and shopping malls. The first ones operated in 1879 at the Berlin Trade Fair, Germany.

Whatever next?

Train speeds continue to increase. A recent record for the fastest regular passenger service was set by the Harmony Express in China. at speeds of more than 310 kilometres per hour.

'Shinkansen' means 'New Main Line' in Japanese.

Cooling The electrical equipment in the power or traction car has its own cooling systems and hot-air vents.

Driver's cab The driver keeps in touch by radio with other on-board staff as well as with signallers and track controllers.

Polarized glass

SNCF

Power car

Motorized bogie The front bogies have wheels turned by powerful electric motors next to them.

✳ JAPANESE BULLETS

The original 'bullet trains' were Japanese Shinkansens, which came into service in 1964. Every few years newer, faster versions or series are introduced. They take many years of design and testing so that they are safe and reliable. The Shinkansen E5 series trains are designed to travel at speeds of up to 320 kilometres per hour. They could probably go faster still. But there are other limitations such as wear on the overhead lines, too much noise outside and inside, and trains taking too long to slow down.

A Japanese Shinkansen streaks past Mount Fuji near Tokyo

The first Japanese bullet trains reached speeds of 200 km/h. Newer test versions have reached 440 km/h. Several countries now have high-speed networks, such as AVE in Spain and THSR in Taiwan.

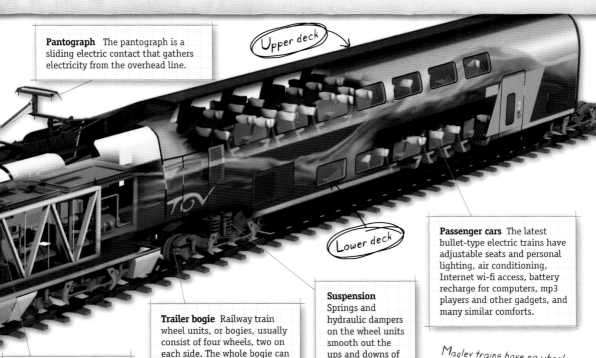

Pantograph The pantograph is a sliding electric contact that gathers electricity from the overhead line.

Upper deck

Lower deck

Passenger cars The latest bullet-type electric trains have adjustable seats and personal lighting, air conditioning, Internet wi-fi access, battery recharge for computers, mp3 players and other gadgets, and many similar comforts.

Suspension Springs and hydraulic dampers on the wheel units smooth out the ups and downs of the track.

Trailer bogie Railway train wheel units, or bogies, usually consist of four wheels, two on each side. The whole bogie can swing or steer to the left or right as the track curves. The trailer bogies are unpowered, with no electric motors.

Electrics The power car is mostly filled with huge power packs and transformers to change the very high voltage of the overhead current into a voltage suitable for the wheel motors.

Maglev trains have no wheels or any other contact with the track. The cars are held up and moved by very strong magnetic forces. Manned maglev trains in Japan have exceeded 580 km/h on the Yamanashi Test Track near Kofu.

Compared to more than 500 km/h for electric trains, the fastest steam locomotive was Mallard, reaching 202 km/h in 1938.

The fastest ever rail speed was set by a rocket-powered 'sledge' that reached more than 10,000 km/h – with no person on board. This happened as part of weapons safety testing in 2003 at Holloman Air Force Base in New Mexico, USA.

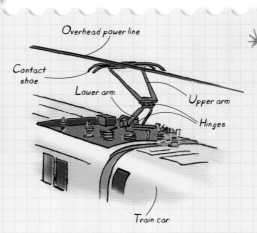

Overhead power line

Contact shoe

Lower arm

Upper arm

Hinges

Train car

✳ How does a PANTOGRAPH work?

The pantograph is a hinged arm that holds up an electrical contact against the overhead wire or cable, for an electric train, tram or trolleybus. It is spring-loaded, or it has hydraulic or pneumatic pistons, to keep it pressed against the wire with the right amount of force. Too little pressure means that the contact shoe flops and bounces, causing sparks and loss of power. Too much pressure and the shoe and wire wear away fast.

BLUEBIRD K7

In 1964 British speed expert Donald Campbell set both the world land and water speed records (see page 124). This itself is a record – no one else has achieved the double. Campbell's watercraft, like his cars, were called *Bluebird*. Between 1955 and 1964 in the jet-powered *Bluebird K7* he set the water speed record seven times. After a new jet engine was fitted, he tried to go even faster in 1967. But the craft crashed at great speed and Campbell was killed.

Eureka!

Bluebird K7 was one of the first of a new breed of jet-powered speedboats. Before the mid 1950s, most record-holders were propeller-driven craft with petrol or diesel engines. Recently there have also been rocket-powered boats, but jet power still rules (see page 132).

Whatever next?

A major problem for speedboats is waves. Even the smallest ripple can cause the craft to flip over. Special environmentally-safe chemicals on the water could make it smoother.

Stabilizing fin The upright fin helped to keep the craft aiming straight. It was adapted from the same aircraft that the engine comes from, the Folland Gnat jet trainer.

Transparent sponson fin

Bristol Siddeley Orpheus jet engine After six records with a Metropolitan Vickers Beryl engine, K7 was fitted with a more powerful Orpheus that was 2.4 metres long and weighed 440 kilograms.

Water rudders At first the rudder area was too large, causing the craft to swerve violently at speed. The design was 'offset' – not based on the centreline along the middle of the boat but slightly to one side.

✳ Back to the SURFACE

Campbell's final water record attempt was at Coniston Water in the Lake District, northwest England. After the crash at more than 480 kilometres per hour, many people thought that Campbell's body and craft should be left on the lake bed, as a silent memorial. During 2000–01 divers recovered them, so that Campbell could be given a suitable burial and the craft could be examined to see what went wrong. There was still fuel in the pipe to the engine, so the idea that the fuel ran out may not be correct.

After more than 30 years underwater, *Bluebird K7* is recovered

Sub-sponson fin

K7 was 8 m long, 1.4 m high and weighed 2.5 tonnes.

Campbell set his final water speed record in 1964, reaching 444.7km/h on Dumbleyung Lake, a 13-km long salt lake in Western Australia.

Radio aerial

✳ How does HYDROPLANING work?

Ordinary boats float in, not on, the water and so have to push through it as they move. Water is heavy and moving through it needs massive energy. In hydroplaning (see page 132) the craft makes its own lifting force at speed and skims across the surface, which uses far less energy. The underside surfaces are specially shaped and spaced out to cause the craft to bounce back slightly each time it comes into contact with the water.

Aerodynamic stabilizing fin helps boat to 'track' straight

Sponson

Hull

Struts work like wings to generate lift

As Bluebird travels at high speed only three points are in contact the water - the rear tips of the sponsons and the rear of the main hull

Cockpit The pilot needed good all-round frontal vision in order to avoid areas of ripples or waves. The see-through upright fin on each sponson allowed a clear view to the side.

Instrument panel

K7 is the code for the type of insurance policy on the craft, arranged with Lloyds of London. K6 was the insurance code for Crusader, the boat of speed ace John Cobb, who died attempting the water record in 1952.

Bluebird K7 was designed by Campbell's chief design team, brothers Ken and Lew Norris.

In 2009, K7's rescue team announced that the restored craft would race one more time on Coniston Water, as a tribute to Donald Campbell, before being put on museum display.

Sponsons These are like mini hulls on the side of the main hull, added to make the craft more stable and also to help it reach higher speed. Most very fast watercraft have a sponson design.

Main hull The main hull had a framework of high-strength steel tubes covered with body panels constructed of 'Birmabright' aluminium-magnesium lightweight alloy sheets.

The jet engine drank almost one litre of kerosene fuel per second and also sucked in 50 kg of air each second to burn it.

SPIRIT OF AUSTRALIA

No speed record has remained unbroken for so long as the fastest manned craft on water. It was set back in 1978 on Blowering Dam in southeast Australia. Boat pilot Ken Warby steered his jet-powered *Spirit of Australia* to an amazing 511 kilometres per hour. Everything was just right: the craft itself, its engine, the wind, the water surface and the pilot's skill. No other speed record has had so many failed attempts ending in tragedy, either. Several people have died trying to go faster than Warby.

Eureka!

Hydroplaning was discovered in the 1950s by speedboat designers tryng to improve their craft. They used ideas from aircraft design to make their craft 'fly' across the surface of the water rather than push through it (see page 131). The basic planing method has hardly changed since.

Whatever next?

Despite the dangers and warnings, speed-lovers still attempt the water speed record. Some are designing rocket-powered boats rather than using a jet engine.

Hull cross-section

Fuel tank *Spirit's* weight varied according to the fuel load, but was on average 1.5 tonnes in total. On slightly rippled water, more fuel was added to keep the craft down on the surface.

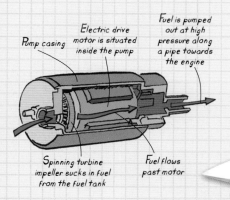

Electric drive motor is situated inside the pump

Fuel is pumped out at high pressure along a pipe towards the engine

Pump casing

Spinning turbine impeller sucks in fuel from the fuel tank

Fuel flows past motor

KW2N

✳ How do FUEL PUMPS work?

Powerful jet engines need massive amounts of fuel. If the fuel pump fails, the engine suffers fuel starvation and this could cause a disaster. There are several designs for fuel pumps, including piston-based ones that squirt out fuel with each push of the piston. In another type an electric motor is actually inside the pump casing. It spins an impeller, like a rotating electric cooling fan with angled blades. The impeller sucks in fuel from the tank and pushes it at high speed and pressure into the engine.

Main hull Spirit was just 8.2 metres long – tiny in comparison to many other rivals for the water speed record. Its hull was built not of complex metal alloys, but from a timber frame of spruce and Douglas fir trees, covered by plywood and fibreglass sheets.

Sponsons *Spirit of Australia* was of forward three-point design. It had the sponsons on either side at the front, with the hull touching the water at the rear.

Spirit, like many ultimate speed machines, is now in a museum – in this case the Australian National Maritime Museum in Darling Harbour, Sydney, Australia. The Museum also has one of Warby's balsawood models of Spirit, vital for testing in a wind tunnel.

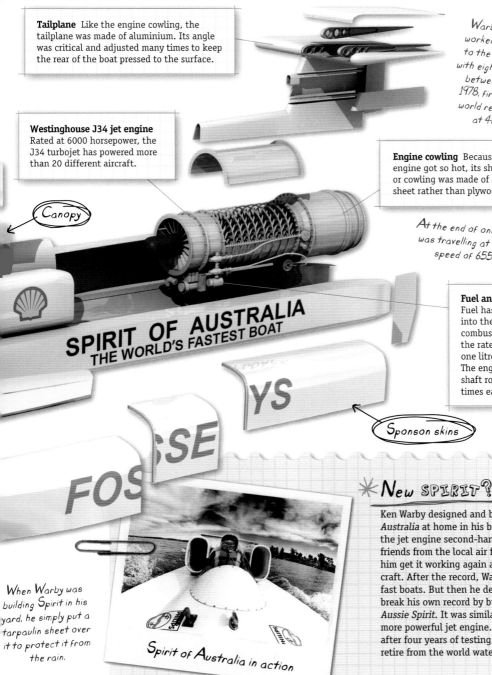

Tailplane Like the engine cowling, the tailplane was made of aluminium. Its angle was critical and adjusted many times to keep the rear of the boat pressed to the surface.

Warby and Spirit worked their way up to the world record with eight sets of runs between 1974 and 1978, first taking the world record in 1977 at 464 km/h.

Westinghouse J34 jet engine Rated at 6000 horsepower, the J34 turbojet has powered more than 20 different aircraft.

Engine cowling Because the jet engine got so hot, its shaped cover or cowling was made of aluminium sheet rather than plywood.

Canopy

At the end of one run Spirit was travelling at a maximum speed of 655 km/h.

Fuel and turbine Fuel has to be forced into the jet engine's combustion chamber at the rate of more than one litre every second. The engine's turbine shaft rotated 12,500 times each minute.

SHELL

SPIRIT OF AUSTRALIA
THE WORLD'S FASTEST BOAT

YS

Sponson skins

SSE

FOS

When Warby was building Spirit in his yard, he simply put a tarpaulin sheet over it to protect it from the rain.

Spirit of Australia in action

✳ New Spirit?

Ken Warby designed and built *Spirit of Australia* at home in his backyard. He bought the jet engine second-hand and got engineer friends from the local air force base to help him get it working again and install it in the craft. After the record, Warby took a rest from fast boats. But then he decided to try and break his own record by building another one, *Aussie Spirit*. It was similar to *Spirit* with a more powerful jet engine. However in 2007, after four years of testing, Warby decided to retire from the world water speed quest.

B-29 SUPERFORTRESS

Today, jet- and rocket-powered planes are the fastest craft in the air. But before jets were invented, designers pushed propeller power to its limits. One of the speediest and biggest 'prop' planes was the Boeing B-29 Superfortress, a heavy bomber in the US Air Force. Despite its huge weight of up to 60 tonnes, it could power along at top speeds of more than 570 kilometres per hour.

Eureka!

The B-29 had many high-tech features for its time. One was a pressurized cabin (see below). This idea was suggested in the 1920s. In 1931 the German Ju 49, a two-person, single-engined plane successfully tested the technology.

Whatever next?

In some ways, military aircraft no longer need to go faster and faster. They cannot easily outrun the fastest rocket missiles. More important is stealth – staying undetected by the enemy.

Pressurized tunnel A long tunnel linked the pressurized flight deck and nose section with the tail section. The main bomb bays could not be pressurized since their doors had to open.

Gun aimer's dome

Flight deck Up to six people were on the flight deck, including the pilot, co-pilot and flight engineer.

Norden bomb sight

LUCKY LADY

Bomb bays The standard payload carried in the two huge bomb bays was 9 tonnes of various high explosives.

Hamilton propellers Built by the famous Hamilton engineering company, the four-bladed propellers were 5 metres across and when taxiing cleared the ground by only 36 centimetres.

✳ How does PRESSURIZATION work?

The higher you go, the colder it gets. Also there is less air, and so less oxygen for breathing. So early aircraft had to stay low, otherwise the people inside them would freeze and suffocate. However greater height takes an aircraft 'above the weather' and the thin air means it can go faster with less fuel. So a modern aircraft cabin is sealed and filled with warm air to keep people comfortable, known as cabin pressurization. The first passenger planes with this feature were the Boeing 307 (1938) and Lockheed Constellation (1943).

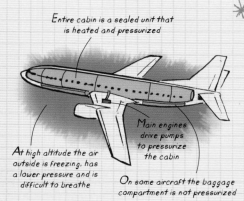

Entire cabin is a sealed unit that is heated and pressurized

Main engines drive pumps to pressurize the cabin

At high altitude the air outside is freezing, has a lower pressure and is difficult to breathe

On some aircraft the baggage compartment is not pressurized

Remote controlled turrets
The four remote turrets were aimed and fired by gunners in the nose and tail pressurized sections, using an early form of computerized remote control. Each turret had two M2 .50 calibre machine guns.

Fin

Rudder

Once airborne, the B-29 could fly and land with just two working engines.

224863

Because of its pressurized conditions, the B-29 could fly at heights above 10,000 m – too high for most enemy fighter planes and anti-aircraft guns.

Tail gunner The gunner in the rear turret was helped by an early form of radar-assisted aiming.

Tail skid

The B-29 was 30.1 m long, 8.5 m high and had a wingspan of 43 m. Its cruising speed was 350 km/h. Fully loaded with weapons its range was more than 5000 km.

Bunks

Engines In early B-29s the Wright R-3350 engines struggled for power and sometimes overheated. They were replaced by Pratt & Whitney R-4360s, each with 28 cylinders, producing 4300 horsepower.

Wing ribs

The name 'Superfortress' came about because the B-29 was developed from the earlier Boeing B-17 bomber nicknamed the 'Flying Fortress' because of its many defensive guns and weapons.

B-29s empty their deadly payload over Japan

✳ An end to the WAR

B-29s were designed for long-range bombing raids, at first by day, and then at night too. After World War II (1939–45) finished in Europe, the battle against Japan continued. In the end the USA, Britain and other Allied Nations decided to use the ultimate weapon – the atomic bomb. The first was dropped over the city of Hiroshima, Japan on 6 August 1945, by a B-29 code-named *Enola Gay*. Three days later another bomb was dopped on the city of Nagasaki by the B-29 *Bockscar*. World War II ended soon afterwards.

LYNX HELICOPTER

Helicopters are not really built for speed. They have other special features, such as being able to take off and land straight up and down, hover in mid-air and even fly backwards. But speed comes in useful now and again, such as when rushing sick people to hospital in an air ambulance. In 1986 a Lynx helicopter set the world record for the fastest helicopter, at 401 kilometres per hour. The record still stands today.

Eureka!

Early helicopters were rattling machines that flew slowly and unsteadily. During the 1950s more powerful engines and better controls made them more agile in the air. One of the most successful was the Bell UH-1 (utility helicopter 1), called the 'Huey'.

Whatever next?

Helicopter racing is very skilled. Pilots race between one landing site and the next, land on a small target and even fly through hoops. Luckily these are small remote-controlled helicopters – at present.

Engines Power comes from two Rolls Royce Gem turboshaft engines, each producing 1000 horsepower.

Tail rotor The tail rotor steers the helicopter by counteracting the tendency of the main body to spin in the opposite direction to the main rotors.

The Westland Lynx first flew in 1971. After many trials it entered active military service in 1978. About 30 years later it is still in production, as the Agusta-Westland Lynx.

Fin

The Lynx and the improved Super Lynx are in service with almost 20 countries around the world, mainly as naval aircraft.

Tail skid

Tail boom The tail boom is lightweight and hollow, containing only the control and electrical cables for the tail rotor.

Two Lynx helicopters give an amazing display of airborne agility

✳ Aerial BALLET

Fast, agile helicopters like the Lynx work at the edge of their abilities. Turning sharply puts enormous stress on the mechanical parts, especially the whirling rotor blades and the rotor hub where they meet, because there are no fixed wings to take most of the strain. Even so, pilots have learnt to do all kinds of amazing aerobatics. In helicopters such as the Lynx and Apache they can even fly up and over in a circle or loop.

British forces have more than 200 Lynxes in service.

The Super Lynx, introduced in the 1990s, has a top speed of 325 km/h and can fly for 520 km unless equipped with extra fuel tanks. The craft is 15.24 m long and 3.7 m high at the rotor hub.

✳ How does FLIRS work?

Forward-looking infra-red (FLIRS) is a way of sensing infra-red rays – heat. Infra-red is similar to light rays but the waves are longer and carry heat energy. Like night vision goggles, FLIRS looks in front of a helicopter, plane, ship or vehicle to detect heat sources ahead. These might include the engines of other vehicles and craft, missiles, buildings, fires and even human bodies. FLIRS works by day or night and is not affected by rain or hazy conditions. The best systems can 'see' many kilometres in front, to help pilots and drivers steer the best course and avoid crashes.

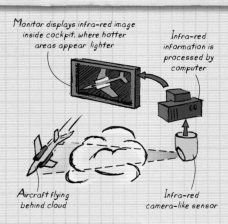

Monitor displays infra-red image inside cockpit, where hotter areas appear lighter

Infra-red information is processed by computer

Aircraft flying behind cloud

Infra-red camera-like sensor

Rotor hub

Main rotor The rotor design is termed semi-rigid, which gives good speed and agility. The rotor diameter is 12.8 metres.

Roof window

Flight deck and crew Pilot and co-pilot sit side by side at the front. The rear compartment has room for up to nine combat-ready troops, or a range of other people such as paramedics and wounded. Total payload is 750 kilograms.

In development is the Future Lynx, also called the Lynx Wildcat. It will not be quite as fast as the Lynx, but it will carry heavier loads and have a greater range.

The speed record-holding Lynx of 1986 had modified extra-powerful Gem engines and notched rotor blades.

Torpedo

Electronics Like most combat aircraft the Lynx has an array of radar and infra-red equipment in its nose section. Some Lynxes can tow sonar sounders to detect submarines in the water.

BELL X-1

As aircraft got faster and faster, their builders and pilots began to worry about the 'sound barrier'. They knew from general science that going above a certain speed causes a sonic boom (shock wave) – this is how lightning makes thunderclaps. Would an aircraft that went supersonic (faster than sound) shake to bits or even explode? On 14 October 1947 they found the answer was no, as the Bell X-1 broke the sound barrier.

Eureka!

The Bell X-1 was the first of the US X-plane programme. 'X' is for experimental and also for unknown or secret. The Xs are a mix of strange aircraft, missiles and rockets designed to test various kinds of new technology. Another famous X, the X-15, is on page 144.

Whatever next?

The newest aircraft designs are hypersonic, which is five times faster than the speed of sound, more than 5000 kilometres per hour (see page 144). Much above this, scientists are not sure what will happen.

X-1 test pilot 'Slick' Goodlin asked for a bonus of $150,000 to break the sound barrier. He was not chosen for the task.

All-moving tailplane

6062

Ethyl alcohol tank
The fuel or propellant was the substance ethyl alcohol – the same alcohol that is in beers, wines and spirits.

The Bell X-1 in front of its B-29 'mothership'

Rocket engine The Reaction Motors XLR11-RM3 rocket engine had four combustion chambers where fuel and oxidizer burned, producing almost 6000 pounds of thrust.

High-visibility paint

✳ Into the UNKNOWN

Experts were unsure if the Bell X-1 could take off under its own power. Its wings were designed for enormous speed, and were too small to give enough lifting force at low speed. For the record attempt, the craft was carried into the air inside the altered bomb bay of a B-29 Superfortress (see page 134). The X-1 dropped and fell like a stone. Then pilot Chuck Yeager switched on the rocket engine to blast it higher and higher and go supersonic. Its rocket fuel finished, the plane glided down to land at Murdoc (now Edwards) Air Force Base. In 1949 Yeager managed to take off from an ordinary runway – the only time the X-1 did so.

Wings Unlike a normal aircraft wing, the X-1's wings were the same shape on the upper and lower surface, for 'laminar flow' – to generate no lift for a smooth, straight ride.

Sensor

In 1953 Chuck Yeager went twice the speed of sound in a follow-up aircraft, the X-1A.

The X-1 was designed as a 'bullet with wings', following the same shape as the bullets from the famous Browning .50 calibre machine gun.

Aneroid hollow discs or wafers contain air at ground pressure

Altimeter casing

Pointer

Altitude indication dial

Wafers expand as aircraft gains altitude due to lower outside air pressure

Gears, rods and levers transmit movement of wafers to the pointer

✳ How do ALTIMETERS work?

The altimeter is a device that measures altitude – how high it is. There is less air with height, giving less pressing force or air pressure. This lower air pressure allows a set of small chambers in the altimeter, which are filled with air at ordinary pressure, to get larger or expand. The expansion moves a series of levers and gears that register on a dial or display (see page 145). Heights are measured not from the ground, which goes up and down far too much, but from sea level.

LOX tank The X-1 needed no air intake for oxygen to burn its fuel. It carried its own supply as super-cooled liquid oxygen, LOX. This got around the problem of thin air with too little oxygen at great height.

The sound barrier was broken as the X-1 hurtled over the Mojave Desert of California, USA, at a height of 13,000 m.

Pilot Several test pilots flew the three X-1s. The record-breaking sound barrier flight was in the hands of US Air Force Captain Charles 'Chuck' Yeager. The tiny cockpit was smoothly contoured into the nose, with no bulge.

Data transmitter

Fuel pipe fairing

Explosive straps

Pitot to measure air pressure

GLAMOROUS GLENNIS

Bullet shaped fuselage The fuselage had almost no projections or side extensions, which would cause turbulence or swirling in the air flow at such high speed. The nitrogen spheres (right) provided pressure to push fuel into the rocket engine, rather than using a fuel pump.

Nitrogen gas spheres

The X-1 was small – just 9.45 m long and 3.3 m high, with wings 8.5 m across. Its take-off weight was about 6 tonnes – carried by a mothership (see page 138).

Glamorous Glennis For the sound barrier attempt the authorities allowed the X-1 to be named Glamorous Glennis after the wife of pilot Chuck Yeager.

The flow of air into the pitot (see page 145) showed that the Bell X-1 reached a top speed of 1127 km/h.

CONCORDE

The only supersonic passenger plane to go into full service was Concorde. There were 20 Concordes, built during the 1960s-70s by a partnership between Britain and France. The first test flight was from Toulouse in France in March 1969. Only two airlines, British Airways and Air France, bought them. The last official landings occurred in 2003 and most Concordes are now in museums.

Eureka!

The idea for SST, SuperSonic Transport, goes back to the early 1950s. While Concorde was being tested, the US started their own version, the Boeing 2707. But it was cancelled in 1971 due to cost and environmental worries.

Whatever next?

It's doubtful that there will be another superfast jetliner. Fuel costs, pollution and noise problems mean modern aircraft are slower but quieter and cleaner.

Concorde could cruise at an altitude of 18,000 m, which is twice as high as most passenger jetliners.

Concorde's cruising speed was about 2100 km/h. It had a top speed of 2330 km/h, which was 2.2 times faster than the speed of sound.

Visor After take-off, when the nose had been raised, a heat-resistant visor slid over the flight deck windows for extra safety and streamlining. At full speed the cockpit windows became too hot to touch.

Cabin doors Because of Concorde's crusing height, the specially designed doors had to cope with much greater pressure difference between inside and outside than on other passenger aircraft.

Radio antenna

Nose The nose cone was 'drooped' by 5 degrees for take-off, raised for level flight, then lowered again by 12.5 degrees for landing (see opposite).

BRITISH AIRWAYS

Narrow fuselage During the 1960s when Concorde was being developed, most airlines had a narrow body or fuselage. Wide-bodied jets arrived in the 1970s.

Concorde's fuselage was narrow compared to modern airliners

Faster than a BULLET

People who travelled on Concorde rarely forgot the experience. But it was a small plane with a narrow body and only four seats in each row. It carried just 120 passengers (the latest Airbus A380 holds up to 800), with no modern features such as in-flight movies. The ride was also noisy and shaky compared to today's quiet jetliners. However there was luxury service with the best food and drink. But the tickets were amazingly expensive. Gradually people decided that they would rather pay much less and arrive at their destination a couple of hours later.

Concorde could fly from London or Paris to New York in just 3.5 hours. With the time difference across the Atlantic, this meant that going by local time, passengers arrived before they took off!

Fin

Concorde's landing speed was about 300 km/h – almost three times the UK motorway speed limit.

Elevons The two-part elevons at the rear of the delta wings controlled going up or down, or pitch. Only the inner part was used at high speed.

At take-off, when fully loaded for a long flight, Concorde weighed almost 190 tonnes. About half of this weight was fuel.

Engines Concorde was powered by four Rolls Royce-SNECMA Olympus 593 afterburning turbojets, each weighing more than 3 tonnes. By today's standards they were extremely noisy.

Engine intake

Leading edge

Delta wing The delta shape is stronger than a normal wing design and cuts through the air better at great speed.

Windows The passenger windows were small. This was partly for strength, and also to reduce the rate of air pressure loss in the cabin in the event of one breaking.

Fuel tanks To keep the aircraft properly balanced, pumps moved the fuel between various tanks to shift the weight distribution as Concorde sped up and slowed down.

As Concorde heated up from the intense air friction at full speed, its overall length increased by about 30 cm.

In July 2000 a Concorde crashed in flames near Paris, France, killing 113 people. The airlines later decided to retire the jetliner. The last three British flights landed one after the other at Heathrow Airport, London in October 2003.

✳ How do DROOP-SNOOTS work?

Concorde had to have the best in streamlining, with a very long, sharp nose, and small flight deck windows to cope with the intense heat and pressure at full speed. But this meant that as the plane came down with its nose angled up, ready to land, the pilots could not see the runway. The answer was the 'droop-snoot'. The nose tilted down on the approach to landing, to allow the pilots a clear view.

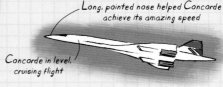
Long, pointed nose helped Concorde achieve its amazing speed

Concorde in level, cruising flight

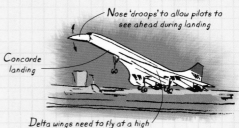
Nose 'droops' to allow pilots to see ahead during landing

Concorde landing

Delta wings need to fly at a high 'angle of attack' at low speeds

SR-71 BLACKBIRD

Few shapes suggest sheer speed and power as much as the Lockheed SR-71A Blackbird. It was designed as a spy plane for the USA to keep an eye on Russia and nearby countries during the 'Cold War' of the 1960s–70s. At this time the two powerful nations, with their huge amounts of nuclear weapons, argued greatly. The Blackbird first flew in 1964. Its specialities were long-range, very high-flying reconnaissance (spying) – and breaking records.

Eureka!

The very first aircraft used in warfare, in the early 1900s, were spy planes. They droned slowly over the enemy army, so that observers could count troop numbers and positions. Soldiers below tried to shoot them down.

Whatever next?

It's possible that Blackbird's air speed record will never be broken. Instead of superfast planes, we now have all kinds of satellites to spy on each other. Or we use remote-controlled aircraft called drones, which are usually quite slow.

In total, 32 Blackbirds were built and 20 remain. The other 12 were lost in non-combat accidents.

Star-tracking The navigation systems included a star-tracker that could detect pinpoints of starlight even during daytime.

Crew The incredible speed and altitude meant that crew had to wear pressure suits to survive ejecting in an emergency (see opposite).

Paintwork The very dark blue colour reduced the chance of the aircraft being seen against a background of the night sky.

Radar

Blackbirds served the US military for 34 years up until 1998.

Pitot

Fuselage The titanium metal panels covering the fuselage only fitted loosely when the Blackbird was on the ground. At speed they heated up and expanded by several centimetres to give a tight fit.

Small chines were also fitted to the sides of the engine pods

Section through forward fuselage

Chines shown in yellow

Chines act like 'low-drag' wings, producing extra lift

✳ How do CHINES work?

The Blackbird's main fuselage had sharp ridges along the sides at the front, which merged into the main wings behind. These ridges are called chines. Some of the plane's designers suggested the idea, but others were not impressed. So they built many wind tunnel models and found that chines were very helpful. They gave extra lift to keep the plane up, and they made it more steady at low speeds. Many modern fast aircraft have similar features, although smaller.

Like the fuselage, the fuel tanks of the Blackbird had tiny gaps when cool. So they leaked JP-7 jet fuel until the aircraft had heated to working temperature.

The Blackbird was 32.7 m long and had a wingspan of 16.94 m.

Exhaust nozzle

Twin fins Two smaller fins (vertical stabilizers) give less overall air resistance and better control at both low and high speeds compared to one large fin.

17974

In 1974 a Blackbird flew from New York to London in less than two hours, compared to Concorde's 3.5 hours (see page 140).

Elevon

Wheels (retracted)

Engines Two Pratt & Whitney J58 turbojets with afterburners, each weighing 2.7 tonnes, produced a total output of more than one million horsepower.

Massive fuel tanks The Blackbird had a full-tank range of 5400 kilometres but it was often fuelled several times in mid air, after coming down a few thousand metres.

Spike The sharp, cone-shaped 'spike' at the engine air intake was positioned forwards for take-off and slow flight. Then it slid backwards by 66 centimetres to reduce shock waves at high speed.

Loaded and ready to take off, the Blackbird weighed 78 tonnes – the same as an Airbus A320 180-seater short-medium airliner.

In 1976 the Blackbird set two world records. One was the fastest speed of any non-rocket manned aircraft, at 3530 km/h. The second was for aircraft height with an altitude of 25,929 m.

✳ Almost ASTRONAUTS

For low-level missions the Blackbird's cockpit could be pressurized and air-conditioned like a normal aircraft. So the two crew members wore standard jet fighter pilot helmets, oxygen masks and flying suits. For high-altitude missions they wore full pressure suits, similar to spacesuits. These supplied air and kept them cool – even with cockpit air conditioning, the inside of the windscreen got hotter than boiling water. Improved designs of the pressure suit became standard wear for space shuttle crew.

The crew of the Blackbird looked like they were heading into space

NORTH AMERICAN X-15

In 1967 US pilot Pete Knight took the record for the fastest speed of all aircraft, in the X-15 rocket plane. The X-15 already held the record for the highest flight of any aircraft, achieved in 1963 with pilot Joe Walker. As part of the X-plane's programme (see page 138), this amazing flying machine did almost everything except actually going into orbit.

Eureka!

The X-15 was designed to research how aircraft handle at higher altitudes where there is little or no air. It last flew in 1968.

Whatever next?

Rocket planes have now merged with spacecraft. In 2004 SpaceShipOne went up into space, more than 100 kilometres high, and landed safely.

Wedge section fin

Anhydrous ammonia fuel The substance burnt by the on-board oxygen was greatly cooled and pressurized anhydrous ammonia, a form of the chemical ammonia (NH_3) that usually exists as a horrible-smelling, suffocating gas.

XLR99 throttled rocket engine Most rocket engines gain full power within a few seconds of start and then stay fully on. The Reaction Motor XLR99 was throttled, meaning the pilot could adjust its thrust between half and full power. The engine's 'burn time' was between 80 and 150 seconds.

NASA
66671

FUEL VENT
FUEL JETT

USAF

Pete Knight's manned aircraft speed record is 7274 km/h, set in 1967.

Jettison-ready lower fin

The X-15 landed on rear skids – there was no room for rear wheels

✳ Rocket-powered SKID

Like the Bell X-1, the North American X-15 (built by the company North American Aviation) was not intended to take off under its own power. It could never carry enough fuel to go from ground level all the way to the edge of space. So it was carried aloft under the wing of a giant B-52 bomber. Before landing the lower part of the rear fin came away, or jettisoned, otherwise it would slice into the ground.

Only three X-15s were built, each slightly different from the others. They made 199 flights with 12 test pilots. One pilot was Neil Armstrong – the first person to walk on the Moon.

In 1963, Joe Walker set an altitude record is 107.8 km in an X-15. He reached space briefly. Officially, space starts at a height of 100 km.

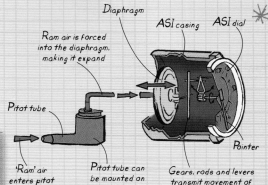

Diaphragm

Ram air is forced into the diaphragm, making it expand

ASI casing   ASI dial

Pitot tube

'Ram' air enters pitot tube

Pitot tube can be mounted on wing or nose of aircraft

Gears, rods and levers transmit movement of diaphragm to the pointer

Pointer

※ How does an ASI work?

To show their speed, fast machines need an ASI (air speed indicator). The simplest versions work by sensing the pressure of air in a small pipe, the pitot tube. If you run faster, the wind feels stronger on your face. The faster an aircraft goes, the more air tries to force its way into the pitot tube. It raises the air pressure inside and pushes on a flexible sheet, the diaphragm, which bends inwards. The bending moves a series of levers and gears linked to a dial. Air speed equipment is often combined with altitude-sensing devices to form a pitot-static system.

Wings Stubby wings gave the X-15 just enough stability and control to fly straight at top speed and then land safely.

Sharp leading edge

LOX (liquid oxygen oxidizer) Like the Bell X-1 (see page 138), the North American X-15 had to take its own supply of oxygen in liquid form to burn its fuel. There is almost no air, and so no oxygen, at the edge of space. At full power the engine consumed more than 70 kilograms of fuel and oxidizer per second.

The X-15 was 15.45 m long and 4.12 m high. Its wingspan was only 6.8 m – less than half the length. The modified second aircraft, the X-15A-2, was 0.5 m longer.

Helium tank

Controls Apart from the usual aircraft controls, the pilot could also squirt small puffs of hydrogen peroxide gas from small nozzles in the nose and wings, for precise control at high altitudes.

S. AIR FORCE

Ejector seat

Drop-off fuel tanks The second-built craft, X-15-2, was damaged when landing. It was rebuilt slightly longer and with extra fuel tanks that could fall away, and renamed the X-15A-2. This was the plane that took the ultimate air speed record. But heat damage meant it had to be retired.

Heat-proof paint

After mid-air launch and the rocket 'burn', the X-15's flight lasted about ten minutes. It ended with a landing at over 300 km/h.

Retracted nose wheel The nose wheel could not be steered. So the X-15 had to land on a long, wide dry lake bed rather than on an ordinary runway, which would be too narrow.

MILITARY MACHINES

INTRODUCTION

Since history was first recorded, people have waged war on each other. Some want to take power and rule, while others just wish to defend their homelands and citizens. The end result often depends on military technology. Through the ages, new inventions such as gunpowder, cannons, tanks, submarines, bomber planes and missiles have been the difference between defeat and success. Developments in warfare also have spin-offs for ordinary life, from warmer clothes to the latest electronic gadgets.

The Romans conquered dozens of nations with the latest siege engines and catapults.

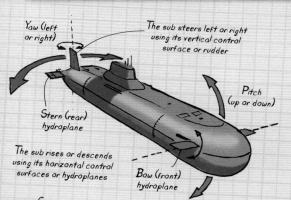

Yaw (left or right)

The sub steers left or right using its vertical control surface or rudder

Pitch (up or down)

Stern (rear) hydroplane

The sub rises or descends using its horizontal control surfaces or hydroplanes

Bow (front) hydroplane

Submarines were the sneaky new weapons of World War II, and were nicknamed 'The Secret Service'.

LET BATTLE BEGIN

Military machines are born from the technology of their time – and then they push it to the limit. In ancient times, wood and stone were naturally the first weapons. The Iron Age brought heavier hammers and sharper blades. Archimedes of ancient Greece invented a massive lever-crane to grab enemy ships and shake them to bits. Medieval scientists came up with catapults and rams to knock down the strongest castle walls.

WORLD AT WAR

In 1914 the first of two World Wars began. Early cars, trucks and aircraft broke down on a regular basis. However, by the time World War I ended in 1918 there were powerful tanks, huge guns on railway wagons, off-road vehicles, and many kinds of planes including fighters and bombers. The most powerful war machines were battleships. Not many years later, World War II (1939–45) attacks combined huge forces on land, at sea and in the air.

Douglas Dauntless dive-bombers fly over the US aircraft carrier Enterprise, ready for a decisive World War II battle.

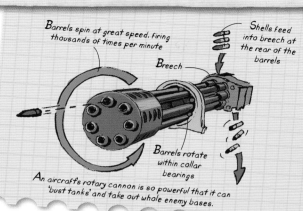

Barrels spin at great speed, firing thousands of times per minute

Shells feed into breech at the rear of the barrels

Breech

Barrels rotate within collar bearings

An aircraft's rotary cannon is so powerful that it can 'bust tanks' and take out whole enemy bases.

TOP GUNS

By the 1950s, air forces had come into their own. One long-range bomber could carry enough nuclear weapons to destroy a whole country. Fighters rode 'shotgun' to protect it, while reconnaissance (spy) aircraft went ahead to check the route. On the ground, tanks were faster and better armoured, so bigger, more powerful guns were invented to smash them to bits. The first ship-launched missiles appeared – unmanned machines took over from people.

UNSEEN ENEMY

In recent years, it's no longer a show of strength that wins battles. It's no show at all. Stealth is the latest trend. Planes, ships and ground forces must stay hidden from the enemy's radar, heat-seeking missiles and microwave messages. There is a need for less explosives and more electronics. In the future, military power will continue to change. So what's the next big thing in the arms race?

Ships carrying massive missile firepower can speed to anywhere in the world.

Heavily armed Land Rovers patrol local conflict in Helmand Province, Afghanistan.

However complicated war machinery becomes, in the end it's still down to people to decide how and when to attack and defend.

M3M 50-CAL MACHINE GUN

The Browning M3M is a modern variant of John Browning's tried and tested M2 .50 Calibre heavy machine gun, which came into service more than 90 years ago after World War I (1914–18). Used by forces the world over, the M2 has been the model for many rapid-fire variants since. The M3M fires more than 1000 rounds per minute – that's 18 bullets each second.

Eureka!

John Browning (1855–1926) was just a boy when he built a rifle from scrap metal. His idea for automatic weapons (weapons that rapidly reloaded themselves as they fired) came from the hand-cranked Gatling gun of the era (see page 162).

Whatever next?

Experiments with high-power laser 'ray guns' show they can carry enough energy to explode munitions half a kilometre away.

Front sight

Rear sight

Cocking handle

Spade grip

Recoil mechanism Energy from the 'kick' or recoil of the fired bullet is used to eject the empty, or spent, cartridge casing and load the next cartridge into position, ready to fire.

Spent cartridge

✳ How do BULLETS work?

Bullets are usually solid metal or plastic and do their damage by smashing into the target. (Shells are similar but contain explosives that blow up when they hit an object.) A typical machine gun bullet is packaged into a unit called a cartridge along with its casing, explosive and primer. The primer is a small amount of explosive that ignites easily when the firing pin bangs into it. In turn, it sets off the main explosive propellant, which blasts the bullet from its casing and along the barrel.

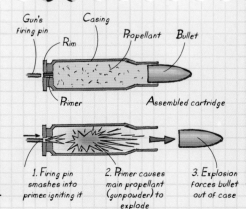

Gun's firing pin

Casing

Rim

Propellant

Bullet

Primer

Assembled cartridge

1. Firing pin smashes into primer, igniting it

2. Primer causes main propellant (gunpowder) to explode

3. Explosion forces bullet out of case

Pintle mount A metal pin holds the gun in a U-shaped bracket, allowing it to tilt up and down. The cylindrical base under the bracket slots into a hole in a tripod, or in a bracket on a vehicle, so the gun can swivel. The whole assembly is known as a pintle mount.

The Browning M2 is the USA's longest serving weapon. Troops call it by the nickname 'Ma Deuce'.

Some medium and heavy machine guns are water-cooled so they can fire longer bursts. Otherwise they may overheat and 'cook-off' or misfire a bullet even though the trigger is not pulled.

The M3M was developed mainly for use on US Navy helicopters, with the code name GAU-21. It is also now deployed on several other vehicles and craft, from Humvee jeeps and armoured cars to tanks and spy planes.

Barrel thermal cover Machine guns get very hot with the continual explosions inside, and this may limit the time that they can fire in short bursts. Various metal parts such as the barrel thermal cover, or dissipator, disperse as much of this heat as possible to the air around.

Barrel In most guns the inside of the barrel has spiral grooves, called rifling, which make the bullet twist or spin as it passes along and out. This causes the bullet to fly much straighter through the air due to the gyroscope effect.

The M3M's effective range (where its bullets can still cause damage) is almost 2000 m.

Exchangeable barrel

.50 Calibre or 'c 50-cal' means the gun's barrel has an internal diameter, or calibre, of half an inch – 0.5 in. The metric equivalent of 12.7 Calibre (12.7 mm) doesn't sound quite so cool.

Muzzle The speed at which the bullet exits the end of the barrel, or muzzle, depends on the ammunition fired. In some versions of the M2 and M3 it can be more than 800 metres per second.

The M3M began tests in 2001 and went into full service in 2004. It is 152 cm long and weighs 36 kg. The barrel length is 91 cm, of which 80 cm have eight rifling grooves.

The F-86 Sabre was one of many M2-equipped aircraft

✳ *Airborne* FIREPOWER

More than 100 versions of the Browning M2 have been fired in over 50 wars and major conflicts. Some of the most highly modified were fitted to fighter and bomber aircraft. The US F-86 Sabre of the 1950s had six AN/M3 guns, angled so their armour-piercing bullets converged at one spot about 300 metres in front of the plane. Every sixth round (bullet) was a tracer that glowed brightly so the pilot could see and aim the stream of ammunition.

TOMAHAWK AND GRANIT MISSILES

Guided missiles are basically bombs that fly under their own power with some kind of onboard or ground-control guidance. The US's Tomahawk launches from ships or submarines and can strike to within a few metres of targets up to 2500 kilometres away. The larger Russian Granit is also sea-launched but much faster, so its range is limited to less than 1000 kilometres.

Eureka!

The V-1 Flying Bomb of World War II (1939–45), also known as the 'buzz-bomb' or 'doodlebug' from its droning noise, was in effect an early type of cruise missile. It had two small wings and a tail like an aircraft, with a pulse-jet engine at the tail's top.

Whatever next?

Upgrades to the GPS (satellite navigation) set-up may mean that future missiles can be guided to an accuracy of a few centimetres.

TOMAHAWK MISSILE

The first Tomahawks entered service in 1983 and they are still on standby today.

Munitions Various kinds of 'bomblets' and other weapons can be carried in up to 24 pre-loaded canisters.

Gyro

Nose cone

Radar and guidance Different types of radar detect the surroundings and steer the missile.

Skin

✳ How do CRUISE MISSILES work?

The 'cruise' of a guided cruise missile is the phase of its flight under its own power, usually from some kind of jet engine, assisted by small wings or fins that provide lift and control direction. Once launched, cruise missiles head towards their target, but they may take detours – either from their on-board computer guidance, or underground control – to avoid problems such as enemy aircraft anti-missile missiles.

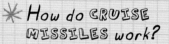

Stage 1
Missile takes off from launch tube

Stage 2
Missile converts to 'fly' like an aircraft

Tail fins fold out

Wings fold out to supply stability and lift, thereby saving fuel

Launch booster jettisons (falls away)

Scoop air intake folds out

Rocket booster or compressed air used for launch

The Tomahawk is about 5.6 m long and weighs almost 1.5 tonnes. It is subsonic, which means it flies slower than the speed of sound, at about 880 km/h.

Older Tomahawks flew at a fixed speed, but improved versions have a throttle to go faster or slower.

Fin

Engine

Tailplane

Swept wings

At 10 m and 7 tonnes, the Granit is supersonic, reaching over 4000 km/h.

GRANIT MISSILE

Engine The small Williams F107 turbofan jet engine was developed specially for cruise missiles. It is only 126 centimetres long, 33 centimetres across, and weighs just 66 kilograms.

Air intake After launch in folded-up mode, the scoop-like air intake flips out of the main body, to gather air for the turbojet engine.

Munitions The P-700 Granit's main warhead chamber can hold up to 750 kilograms of high explosives, or a nuclear weapon with the explosive power of 500 kt (half a million tonnes) of TNT (trinitrotoluene).

Tomahawks can take off vertically, as well as horizontally, from a submarine's torpedo tubes.

A sub-launched missile booster ignites

✳ Underwater LAUNCH

A submarine-launched missile is blasted from its launch tube, which is also its protective canister during transport, by a sudden burst of extremely high gas or water pressure. After the missile breaks the surface, the solid-fuel rocket booster switches on like a giant firework to gain height and speed as fast as possible. After a preset burn time the booster falls away, then the jet engine fires up and takes over propulsion.

M2 BRADLEY IFV

Part armoured car, part troop transport and part light tank, the M2 Bradley is termed an IFV (Infantry Fighting Vehicle). Its role is to take troops under armoured protection to a particular area of the battlefield, support them by providing covering fire and shelter, and repel attacks against itself. Its cousin the M3 is a scout version to survey and gather information.

Eureka!

Battle-ready soldiers need all their stamina and strength when they get to the front line, rather than having to march there. Early troop carriers were horse-drawn carts and even oxen-pulled wagons.

Whatever next?

Several armies are testing robot-type soldiers. These are not so much human-shaped warriors as very small armoured tanks, some no larger than a pet dog – but with tremendous weaponry.

The Bradley is named after US General Omar Bradley, one of the main commanders in Europe during World War II. It is one of several types of armoured troop carriers known as 'battle taxis'.

Main gun Most M2 Bradleys are equipped with the M242 Bushmaster chain gun. It has a calibre of 2.5 centimetres and fires shells more than 3 kilometres.

Engine The Cummins VTA-903T turbo diesel engine is almost 15 litres – ten times the size of a smallish family car. On full tanks of 660 litres, the M2's range is around 400 kilometres.

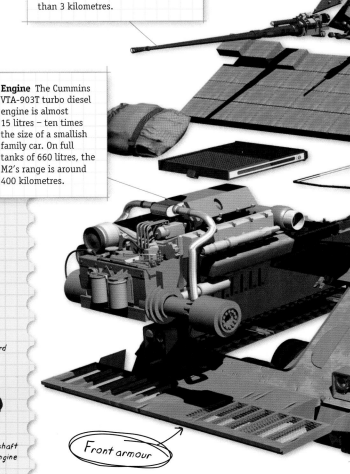

Front armour

✳ How do CATERPILLAR TRACKS work?

Also called crawler tracks or endless belt loops, caterpillar tracks have many rectangular plates linked by hinged joints. Long, ridged gear-type teeth on the drive wheel, which is turned by the engine, fit into gaps between the plates and pull the track round and round. The other wheels are toothless and undriven – return rollers that support the track along the top, and road wheels, which take the vehicle's weight along the base.

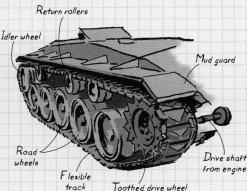

Return rollers

Idler wheel

Mud guard

Road wheels

Flexible track

Toothed drive wheel

Drive shaft from engine

An M2 Bradley roars into action

Sighting unit

Night vision

Turret The gunner sits in the left of the turret. The commander is to the right and can take over gun firing if necessary.

Smoke grenade launchers

Troop compartment In the rear of the Bradley's main body, or hull, is room for up to seven combat-ready soldiers. They enter and leave through the rear hydraulic ramp.

* Ready for BATTLE

The M2 Bradley's 600-horsepower diesel engine gives a top speed of 65 kilometres per hour, which is enough to outrun tanks and many other armoured vehicles. The tracks can cross most obstacles including ditches and fallen trees. The M6 Linebacker variant carries four Stinger anti-aircraft missiles, while the M7 moves to forward positions and helps direct the firepower of tanks and other attackers.

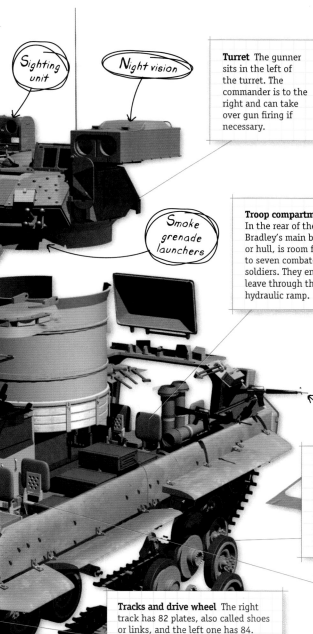

Machine guns

The basic model of the M2 Bradley is 6.5 m long, 3.3 m wide, and almost 3 m to the top of the turret. When fully equipped and ready for action it weighs about 33 tonnes.

Road wheels The six road wheels on each side have rubber tyres. Each one has its own suspension system known as a torsion bar, where a springy metal bar cushions the wheel's movements.

Bradleys have been modified into supply carriers, mobile medical centres, and even mobile generators using their own engines or an additional engine-powered electrical generator.

Driver's station This is at the front left, next to the engine. Foot pedals control the engine speed.

Tracks and drive wheel The right track has 82 plates, also called shoes or links, and the left one has 84. The drive wheel at the front bears 11 teeth or sprockets.

M270 ROCKET LAUNCHER

Warhead-carrying rockets and missiles are among the most destructive in battle. The M270 MRLS (Mobile Rocket Launch System) is a speedy tracked launcher based on the M2 Bradley shown on the previous page. Its speciality is 'shoot and scoot' – get into position fast, launch its load of up to 12 rockets, and move on before the enemy can pinpoint its position and fire back at it.

Eureka!

Rockets were first used in warfare more than 1000 years ago in China. They were called 'fire arrows' and driven by 'black powder', an early form of gunpowder. They caused few casualties, being mainly intended to scare the enemy.

Whatever next?

The M270 will gradually be replaced by the HIMARS (High Mobility Artillery Rocket System). Known as 'Six-Pack', it carries half the load but is faster and more accurate.

Crew area The standard crew of three consists of the commander on the right, the gunner in the middle and the driver on the left.

Armour All parts of the M270 are made of armoured aluminium-based metal alloys. The sheets are welded for extra strength and to prevent splintering under impact.

The M270 weighs over 24 tonnes but still has a relatively fast top speed of 64 km/h.

More than 400 years ago in Korea, large arrrows with gunpowder tips were launched by more gunpowder, like big exploding fireworks. More than 150 could be let off from a cart pulled by people (or very scared oxen).

Armoured roof panel

Blast shutters The front viewing windows are made of specially toughened glass. When under fire, strong shutters fold down over them for extra protection.

✳ Rocket ATTACK

In general warfare, a rocket is self-powered but unguided, while a missile is self-powered and guided. The M270 'family' of ammunition includes the M26, a basic rocket (unguided) that releases grenade-type 'submunitions' in mid air, to shower down and explode on impact. Its range is about 32 kilometres. The MGM-140 is a missile (guided) with a range of over 300 kilometres, armed with submunitions or one large warhead.

Drive wheel

A rocket blasts away from its M270

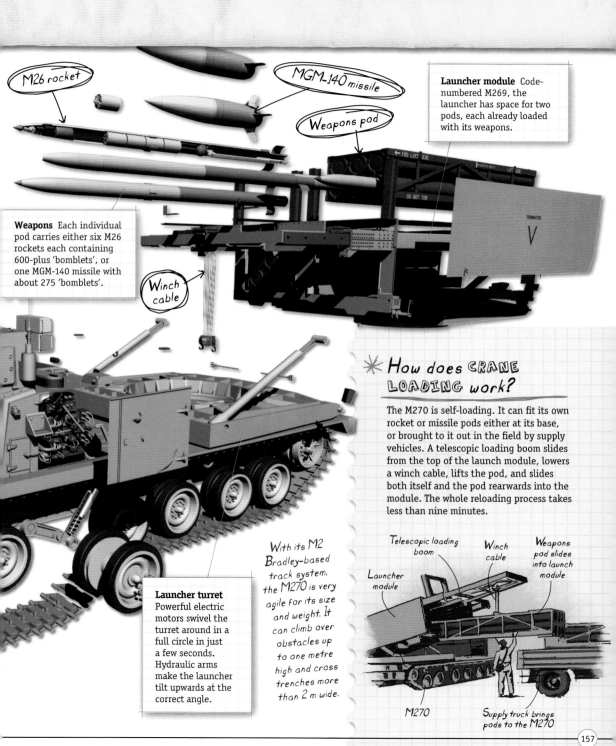

M26 rocket

MGM-140 missile

Weapons pod

Launcher module Code-numbered M269, the launcher has space for two pods, each already loaded with its weapons.

Weapons Each individual pod carries either six M26 rockets each containing 600-plus 'bomblets', or one MGM-140 missile with about 275 'bomblets'.

Winch cable

Launcher turret Powerful electric motors swivel the turret around in a full circle in just a few seconds. Hydraulic arms make the launcher tilt upwards at the correct angle.

With its M2 Bradley-based track system, the M270 is very agile for its size and weight. It can climb over obstacles up to one metre high and cross trenches more than 2 m wide.

✳ How does CRANE LOADING work?

The M270 is self-loading. It can fit its own rocket or missile pods either at its base, or brought to it out in the field by supply vehicles. A telescopic loading boom slides from the top of the launch module, lowers a winch cable, lifts the pod, and slides both itself and the pod rearwards into the module. The whole reloading process takes less than nine minutes.

Telescopic loading boom

Winch cable

Weapons pod slides into launch module

Launcher module

M270

Supply truck brings pods to the M270

157

M1 ABRAMS TANK

One of the world's most powerful mobile weapons, the M1 Abrams MBT (Main Battle Tank) packs a massive punch, and is also protected against almost all kinds of return fire. Its ammunition is stored in a 'blowout' compartment so that if it explodes, the force of the blast directs to the outside, rather than within the tank, which would kill the crew at once.

Eureka!

The first tanks went into action in 1916, in the midst of World War I. To keep their function secret from the enemy while they were transported, they were said to be large storage tanks for fresh water. The name stuck.

Whatever next?

Armoured protection continually improves. Reactive armour has an explosive layer that detonates when hit, deflecting the incoming force.

Turret The traverse or swivelling of the turret is carried out by electric motors, but it can be traversed by a hand-cranked handle in an emergency.

Engine The Honeywell AGT 1500C turbine engine is similar to an aircraft jet engine. It produces more than 1500 horsepower and can run on several types of fuel.

Shells

Armour skirt

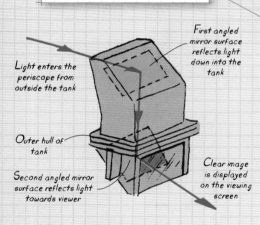

First angled mirror surface reflects light down into the tank

Light enters the periscope from outside the tank

Outer hull of tank

Second angled mirror surface reflects light towards viewer

Clear image is displayed on the viewing screen

✳ How do PERISCOPES work?

When the M1 goes into battle, all hatches are closed. The driver and crew have electronic screens to see outside, but the old technology of the periscope is still essential. The M1 has nine periscopes, also known as vision blocks. Incoming light bounces, or reflects, off two mirror surfaces, each at an angle of about 45°, through a gap in the tank's main outer body covering or hull. The periscope unit can be replaced by a night-vision version using electronics to detect and display infra-red (heat) rays.

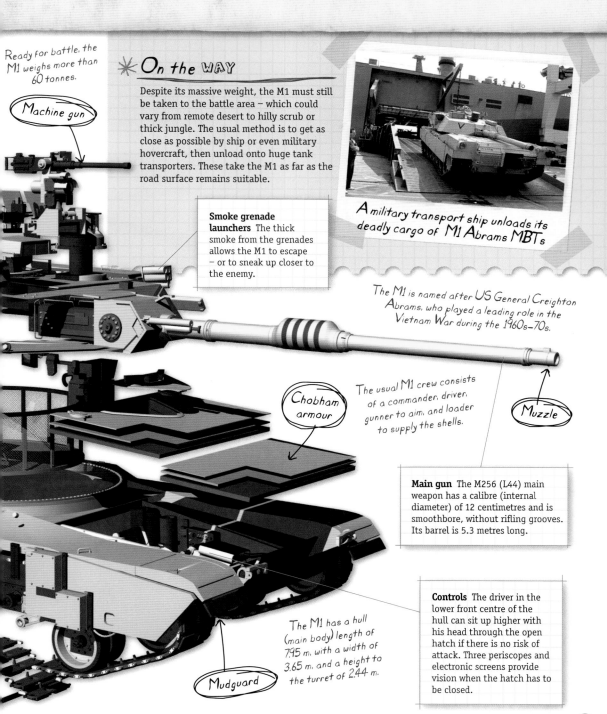

Ready for battle, the M1 weighs more than 60 tonnes.

Machine gun

✳ On the WAY

Despite its massive weight, the M1 must still be taken to the battle area – which could vary from remote desert to hilly scrub or thick jungle. The usual method is to get as close as possible by ship or even military hovercraft, then unload onto huge tank transporters. These take the M1 as far as the road surface remains suitable.

A military transport ship unloads its deadly cargo of M1 Abrams MBTs

Smoke grenade launchers The thick smoke from the grenades allows the M1 to escape – or to sneak up closer to the enemy.

The M1 is named after US General Creighton Abrams, who played a leading role in the Vietnam War during the 1960s–70s.

Chobham armour

The usual M1 crew consists of a commander, driver, gunner to aim, and loader to supply the shells.

Muzzle

Main gun The M256 (L44) main weapon has a calibre (internal diameter) of 12 centimetres and is smoothbore, without rifling grooves. Its barrel is 5.3 metres long.

The M1 has a hull (main body) length of 7.95 m, with a width of 3.65 m, and a height to the turret of 2.44 m.

Mudguard

Controls The driver in the lower front centre of the hull can sit up higher with his head through the open hatch if there is no risk of attack. Three periscopes and electronic screens provide vision when the hatch has to be closed.

AH-64 APACHE HELICOPTER

Helicopters are among the most versatile military machines. The Apache is chiefly an attack 'helicopter gunship', fitted with guns, rockets, missiles and other weaponry for use against ground targets. But at a pinch, this fast and agile chopper can carry out surveillance, transport emergency equipment, carry the sick or wounded, and even attend natural disasters to rescue trapped people or bring urgent relief supplies.

Eureka!

A relatively recent addition to military hardware, helicopters first saw action in World War II with the US's Sikorsky X/R-4. This was also the first helicopter to enter mass production, with 130 made.

Whatever next?

Tiny helicopters no larger than a dragonfly are becoming 'spies in the skies'. Remote controlled, their cameras take pictures to send by radio or deliver back to base.

Canopy The canopy windows, made of specially strengthened glass composite, allow a very wide view, including above.

Radar dome

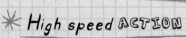
An Apache banks into a tight turn

Sights

✳ High speed ACTION

The Apache has a top speed of almost 300 kilometres per hour and climbs at a stomach-churning rate of 12 metres per second. It is also one of the few helicopters that can 'loop the loop', flying up and right over onto its back before diving to become horizontal again in a complete circle. This puts huge strain on the craft, especially its rotor blades. However this happens mainly as a result of the helicopter's moving energy or momentum. It cannot fly upside down in a sustained way, as some aerobatic planes can.

The Apache's all-up weight is 8 tonnes. It can carry a weapons load of an extra 2-plus tonnes.

Gun The M230 chain gun has a calibre of 30 millimetres. It can be 'locked' to point the way the helicopter faces, or aimed independently via the co-pilot-gunner's head-up helmet display.

Crew The co-pilot-gunner sits in the lower front position, with the main sights and weapon controls, with the pilot above and behind.

The Apache's standard range of about 400 km can be increased by fitting external fuel tanks to the stub wings instead of missiles or rockets.

Fin and tailplane The upright fin or vertical stabilizer, and the small rear wings – the tailplane – are control surfaces found on most aircraft but not all helicopters. They allow exceptional control even at high speeds.

Rotor blades New advanced composite rotor blades were fitted to Apaches from 2004, giving better performance. The four blades have a total diameter of 14.6 metres.

The Aapche first flew in 1975 but took another nine years to enter service.

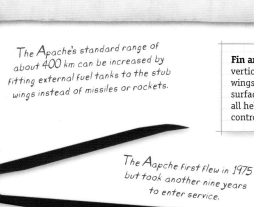

Drive shaft to tail rotor

Tailplane

✳ How does a TAIL ROTOR work?

A basic law of science says that every action has an equal and opposite reaction. With a helicopter's fast-spinning main rotors pushing through the air as the action, the reaction is a turning force or torque that tries to make the helicopter's body, or fuselage, rotate the other way. The tail rotor spins like an aircraft propeller and produces exactly the right amount of thrust to counteract this tendency and keep the helicopter steady.

Stub wing

Engines Twin T700-GE-701 turboshaft engines power the rotors, but the Apache can fly on only one if necessary.

Weapons A mix of Hellfire, Stinger and Sidewinder missiles and Hydra rockets can be clipped to the stub-wings.

1. Main rotor blades spin clockwise, generating lift

2. Torque reaction causes the fuselage to spin the opposite way, anti-clockwise

3. Tail rotor counteracts the torque reaction so the fuselage remains stable

4. Adjusting tail rotor speed allows helicopter to turn while hovering

A-10 THUNDERBOLT

Some of the affectionate names given to the A-10 by its pilots and engineers are 'Wart-hog', 'Hog' and 'Tankbuster'. This relatively slow but exceptionally tough, well-armoured aircraft offers CAS (Close Air Support). It is called in to attack enemy troops and ground vehicles near to its own forces. Despite its limited speed, the A-10 is extremely agile, twisting and turning to evade anti-aircraft guns and missiles.

The A-10 has a very long service history. It first flew in 1972 and it may still be around 50 years later.

Eureka!

The A-10's GAU/8A Avenger Gatling gun, or rotary canon, is one of the most powerful guns ever fitted to an aircraft. The original version was invented in 1861 by Richard Gatling (1818–1903) at the start of the American Civil War (1861–65).

Whatever next?

The 'good old A-10' is near the end of its life. In the 2020s it should be replaced by the F-35 Lightning, which first flew in 2006.

Ejector seat

Dash

Main gun

Nose cone

✳ Nice 'n' SIMPLE

The A-10 is not fitted with the latest complicated machinery and features – and that is part of its success. It is designed to still be able to fly with just one engine, as well as with one tailplane plus part of a main wing missing. The jet engines are mounted on stub pylons rather than being built into the wings or fuselage. This means their covers can be removed for fast, easy servicing and repair.

Armoured bathtub
The pilot sits in a protective container made of lightweight but super-tough titanium metal known as the 'bathtub'.

The exposed engines of the A-10 are easy to work on or replace

Bearing

Rotary cannon The massive cannon fires a standard mix of armour-piercing and high-explosive shells. They leave at a speed of almost 1000 metres per second.

Ammunition drum The drum holds more than 1150 rounds. Each round, or shell, is almost 30 centimetres long.

The recoil or 'kick' of the rotary cannon at the instant each shell fires is about the same as the aircraft's two engines.

Only one two-seater A-10 was built, as a test aircraft for night-time and bad-weather work.

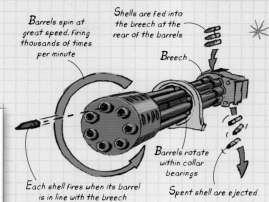

Barrels spin at great speed, firing thousands of times per minute

Shells are fed into the breech at the rear of the barrels

Breech

Each shell fires when its barrel is in line with the breech

Barrels rotate within collar bearings

Spent shell are ejected

How does a ROTARY CANNON work?

A Gatling-type gun reloads itself rapidly but not under its own power. It must be cranked, or turned, by an external force such as a person, an electric motor, or a hydraulic (pressurized liquid) or pneumatic (pressurized air) mechanism. The A-10's Avenger gun has seven barrels, measures nearly 6 metres in length and fires 65 times per second. With its full load of ammunition, it weighs almost 2 tonnes.

Engines The twin TF34-GE-100 turbofan jet engines give the A-10 a top speed of 700 kilometres per hour.

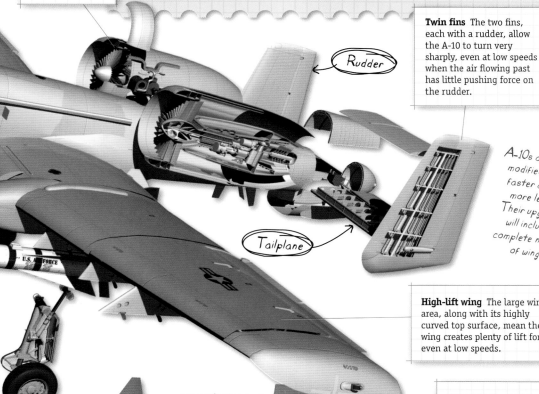

Rudder

Twin fins The two fins, each with a rudder, allow the A-10 to turn very sharply, even at low speeds when the air flowing past has little pushing force on the rudder.

A-10s are being modified to go faster and be more lethal. Their upgrades will include a complete new set of wings!

Tailplane

High-lift wing The large wing area, along with its highly curved top surface, mean the wing creates plenty of lift force even at low speeds.

U.S. AIR FORCE

Weapons The A-10 is armed with Sidewinder and Maverick missiles plus a range of bombs attached to its 11 clip-on 'hardpoints'.

The name 'Thunderbolt' honours the P-47 Thunderbolt propeller-driven fighter of World War II.

V-22 OSPREY TILTROTOR

For many years, inventors have tried to build an aircraft with the benefits of both a standard fixed-wing plane and a helicopter. The V-22 Osprey is one of the more successful ones. The engine-and-rotor assembly at each wingtip swivels so the rotor faces up for vertical take-off or landing, then forwards for normal flight. Ospreys can carry cargoes of more than 6 tonnes for hundreds of kilometres, which no helicopter can match.

Eureka!

Tiltrotor designs were sketched in the 1930s but never built. A German prototype, the FA-269 'Heliplane', was partly built in the 1940s but never flew. The Osprey was developed from the Bell XV-15, which first flew in 1977.

Whatever next?

The HTR (Hybrid Tandem Rotor) is a planned combination of tiltrotor and helicopter – a tiltwing. Its whole wing swivels by 25°, but only on the drawing board. Construction has not yet started.

The Osprey's wingspan is 14 m but the rotors increase its width to almost 26 m.

Stub wing The wing must be much stiffer and stronger than in an ordinary plane, to carry the weight of the engine and rotor and withstand their pulling force.

Nacelle

✳ How do TILTROTORS work?

Helicopters have amazing flight abilities, especially hovering. However they lack wings to give them lift as they move forwards. Without this lift, they have to use much more fuel to stay airborne. The V-22 Osprey solves this by having aircraft wings, and also rotors that can be tilted and controlled like those of a helicopter. However, in helicopter mode the wing gets in the way of the air downflow from the rotors, reducing their effectiveness.

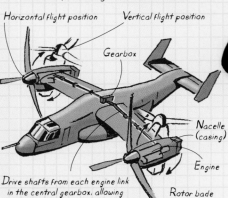

Horizontal flight position   Vertical flight position

Gearbox

Nacelle (casing)

Engine

Rotor bade

Drive shafts from each engine link in the central gearbox, allowing emergency flight on one engine

Crew and controls The flight deck crew of two are the usual pilot in the left seat and co-pilot in the right. The controls are less usual, including rotor tilt angle, but computers do much of the work automatically.

In the main fuselage there is room for up to 32 troops. A hook beneath allows the Osprey to airlift vehicles.

Rotor hub This complicated device, as found on a helicopter, adjusts the angle of the rotor blades while hovering, depending on the amount of lift needed.

The early development of the Osprey was marred by several crashes and the loss of more than 30 lives, needing much redesign. By the time the aircraft got to test flight stage, its cost had increased ten times.

Rotor blades A combination of aircraft propeller and helicopter rotor, the rotor blades are called proprotors. Each has three blades and an overall diameter of 11.6 metres. Because of the two jobs they do, the blades are not especially efficient at either.

Airframe The very light structural framework and cladding mean the Osprey has a range of some 1600 kilometres, increasing to more than 4000 kilometres with mid-air refuelling.

✳ Pack-up PLANE

If there's no rush, it's far more fuel-efficient to take a V-22 long distances by ship. To stow away the craft, the whole wing and engine-rotor assemblies swivel around by 90° so the wing is in line with the fuselage. At each wing tip, two of the rotor blades can also fold to line up with the third.

Engine Each Rolls Royce TT406/AE 1107 turboshaft engine puts out more than 6000 horsepower. The pumps for the fuel and other flowing liquids must work whether the engine is vertical or horizontal, counteracting the effects of gravity.

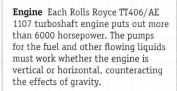

The Osprey folds up for easy storage

F-22 RAPTOR

Some of the meanings for the term 'raptor' are 'thief', 'hunter' and 'raider' – and the F-22 is all of these. A very rapid and adaptable aircraft, it uses stealth design to sneak into enemy air space, gather survey information, listen to enemy radio messages, jam radar, carry out a missile strike, and blast away again using its afterburners before even being detected. All for just $143 million, plus the cost of the pilot and fuel.

Eureka!

Stealth technology began in the late 1950s with aircraft designed not to reflect, or bounce back, the radio waves of radar. It has since spread to lessen a craft's noise levels, heat production, radio messages and even visible shape.

Whatever next?

In active camouflage or active stealth, an object 'bends' light from the background around itself and on towards the observer, and so becomes invisible.

Canopy

Lt Col. Gary Jeffrey

Fly-by-wire Like most modern jets, the side-stick control is linked to computers that send instructions as electrical signals along wires, to move parts such as the rudder and elevators. This replaces the old metal cables that physically pulled these parts.

Radar A special type of stealth radar known as AESA (Active Electronically Scanned Array) makes the F-22 difficult to detect.

Probe

Engine air intake

✳ BURST of speed

Afterburning, also called reheat, greatly increases a jet engine's pushing force, or thrust. However this uses huge amounts of extra fuel. It also produces a lot of extra heat that the engine and surrounding structure cannot withstand for long. So it's used only when necessary. One situation is during take-off, to reach lift-off speed as quickly as possible. In combat, afterburners allow the craft to accelerate away from danger.

Afterburners glow as a Raptor heads away and goes supersonic

The Raptor first took to the air in 1997. However some of its roles can be partly carried out by other aircraft, such as the F-35. The cost of each F-22 also rose to $143 million. By the late 2000s its future was uncertain.

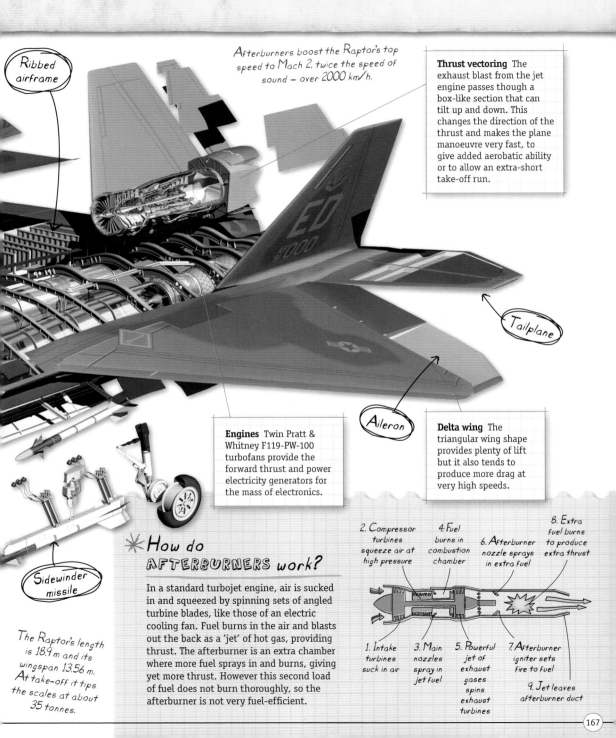

Ribbed airframe

Afterburners boost the Raptor's top speed to Mach 2, twice the speed of sound – over 2000 km/h.

Thrust vectoring The exhaust blast from the jet engine passes though a box-like section that can tilt up and down. This changes the direction of the thrust and makes the plane manoeuvre very fast, to give added aerobatic ability or to allow an extra-short take-off run.

Tailplane

Aileron

Engines Twin Pratt & Whitney F119-PW-100 turbofans provide the forward thrust and power electricity generators for the mass of electronics.

Delta wing The triangular wing shape provides plenty of lift but it also tends to produce more drag at very high speeds.

Sidewinder missile

The Raptor's length is 18.9 m and its wingspan 13.56 m. At take-off it tips the scales at about 35 tonnes.

✳How do AFTERBURNERS work?

In a standard turbojet engine, air is sucked in and squeezed by spinning sets of angled turbine blades, like those of an electric cooling fan. Fuel burns in the air and blasts out the back as a 'jet' of hot gas, providing thrust. The afterburner is an extra chamber where more fuel sprays in and burns, giving yet more thrust. However this second load of fuel does not burn thoroughly, so the afterburner is not very fuel-efficient.

2. Compressor turbines squeeze air at high pressure

4. Fuel burns in combustion chamber

6. Afterburner nozzle sprays in extra fuel

8. Extra fuel burns to produce extra thrust

1. Intake turbines suck in air

3. Main nozzles spray in jet fuel

5. Powerful jet of exhaust gases spins exhaust turbines

7. Afterburner igniter sets fire to fuel

9. Jet leaves afterburner duct

E-3 SENTRY AWACS

Modern military conflicts are partly about hardware, such as tanks, battleships, planes and missiles – and partly about electronics. Radio and microwave communications, radar and satellite systems are vital tools. Airborne Warning And Control Systems (AWACS) such as the Sentry keep watch for suspicious activity and also command and coordinate their own forces.

Eureka!

In radar (see opposite), radio waves can detect an object's direction, distance and perhaps its identity – aircraft, ship, missile or rocket. Radar was explored by several inventors in the 1930s. The first working systems were devised by an Allied team led by Robert Watson-Watt in World War II.

Whatever next?

Satellite radar and madar (based on microwaves rather than radio) may one day track almost every single military vehicle and craft.

The Sentry is 46 m long, 12.5 m high to the fin tip, and has a wingspan of almost 44 m.

The Sentry can stay in the air for more than eight hours without refuelling. Its best cruising speed, with greatest fuel economy, is about 570 km/h.

Computer stations Up to 19 mission crew operate monitor stations, each with screens and displays. These show the multitude of invisible radio, radar and microwave signals always present in the atmosphere.

Radar operators study their screens during an AWACS trip

Navigation The Sentry has six main navigation systems including ground-mapping radar, GPS (or satnav) – and the old-fashioned magnetic compass in case of emergency.

✳ EYE in the SKY

The E-3 Sentry is based on one of the first and longest-serving passenger jets, the Boeing 707. Sentries patrol the skies around the clock, monitoring air activity with their amazingly powerful radar. They also 'listen in' to radio and microwave signals used by other nations. All of these signals are screened by computers programmed to alert the operators to anything unusual.

Airframe formers

Flight deck

NATO ✛ OTAN

Onboard electronics Vast amounts of electronic and computing equipment mean that a significant amount of jet engine power is used to generate electricity.

Main landing gear

Flight radar

Rotodome The rotating radar turns around six times each minute. It is 9.1 metres across, 1.8 metres deep and held 4 metres above the main fuselage on two metal struts.

In 1995, a Sentry crashed in Alaska. The cause was traced to a flock of Canada geese that were sucked into two of the engines.

'Lookdown' radar The immensely powerful million-watt pulse doppler radar detects low-flying aircraft, ships and similar objects more than 300 kilometres away. Its range is even farther for high-flying planes – and spacecraft.

✳ How does PULSE DOPPLER RADAR work?

Radar bounces radio signals off an object and detects the echoes, to work out its direction and distance. With short signals or pulses, if the object moves towards them, it gets slightly nearer for each pulse, so the reflected pulses are closer together. Similarly if the object moves away, the pulses are more spaced out. This doppler effect allows fast-pulse radar to measure an object's speed.

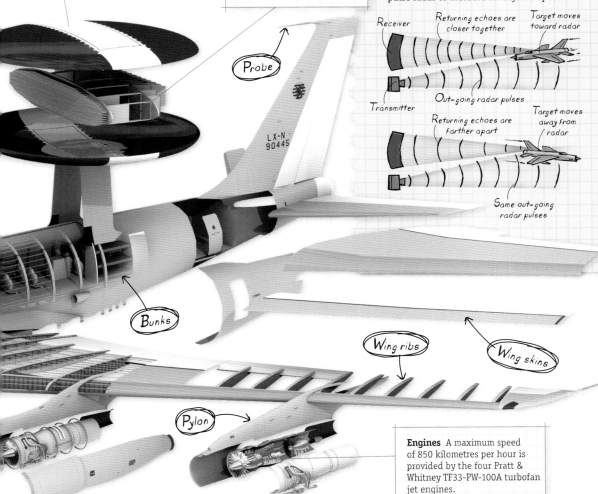

Receiver

Returning echoes are closer together

Target moves toward radar

Transmitter

Out-going radar pulses

Returning echoes are farther apart

Target moves away from radar

Same out-going radar pulses

Probe

LX-N 90445

Bunks

Wing ribs

Wing skins

Pylon

Engines A maximum speed of 850 kilometres per hour is provided by the four Pratt & Whitney TF33-PW-100A turbofan jet engines.

B-52 STRATOFORTRESS

Stalwart of the US Air Force for more than 50 years, the B-52 heavy bomber was designed for the Cold War era of the 1950s–70s. At this time the superpowers of the USA and former USSR (Russia and its allies) paraded their nuclear weapons with unspoken but clear threats. The B-52 not only carries a massive weapons load, it can deliver to targets 8000 kilometres away and return with ease.

Eureka!

The first purpose-designed large aircraft to drop bombs saw action in World War I. For their heavy loads they needed multiple engines, from two to four or more, compared to the small, light, single-engined fighters.

Whatever next?

Solar-powered, remote-controlled aircraft can stay up for days, and may be used to drop small, powerful, lightweight explosives.

Massive wing The enormous wings give plenty of lift so that less fuel is needed to keep the B-52 airborne.

Weapons bay The total weight of weapons can be up to 32 tonnes, depending on the fuel load. The bombs, rockets, missiles and mines are mixed and matched according to the mission.

Crew The basic crew of five are headed by the captain-pilot, along with the co-pilot, navigator, bombardier or 'target acquisition officer', and an electronics warfare specialist.

Twin engine pods

A B-52 takes a high-altitude 'drink'

✳ Topping-UP up TOP

Mid-air (aerial or in-flight) refuelling was first achieved in 1923 in the USA, between two DH-4B aircraft. By 1930 records of more than 500 hours in the air were being set by teams of pilots and flight crew. For a truly long-distance mission the refuelling plane, or tanker, is itself refuelled by a second tanker, and this can extend to a third tanker, in a relay system with carefully timed flights to meeting points or rendezvous locations.

The B-52 is not especially fast compared to modern aircraft, with a top speed of 1000 km/h. Its advantages are its long range and great destructive load.

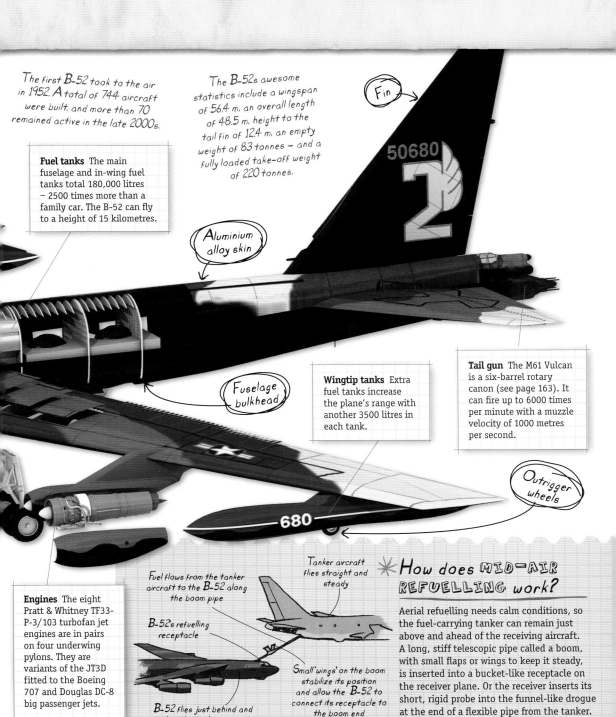

The first B-52 took to the air in 1952. A total of 744 aircraft were built, and more than 70 remained active in the late 2000s.

The B-52's awesome statistics include a wingspan of 56.4 m, an overall length of 48.5 m, height to the tail fin of 12.4 m, an empty weight of 83 tonnes – and a fully loaded take-off weight of 220 tonnes.

Fin

50680

Fuel tanks The main fuselage and in-wing fuel tanks total 180,000 litres – 2500 times more than a family car. The B-52 can fly to a height of 15 kilometres.

Aluminium alloy skin

Fuselage bulkhead

Wingtip tanks Extra fuel tanks increase the plane's range with another 3500 litres in each tank.

Tail gun The M61 Vulcan is a six-barrel rotary canon (see page 163). It can fire up to 6000 times per minute with a muzzle velocity of 1000 metres per second.

Outrigger wheels

680

Engines The eight Pratt & Whitney TF33-P-3/103 turbofan jet engines are in pairs on four underwing pylons. They are variants of the JT3D fitted to the Boeing 707 and Douglas DC-8 big passenger jets.

Fuel flows from the tanker aircraft to the B-52 along the boom pipe

B-52's refuelling receptacle

Tanker aircraft flies straight and steady

B-52 flies just behind and below the tanker aircraft

Small 'wings' on the boom stabilize its position and allow the B-52 to connect its receptacle to the boom end

✳ How does MID-AIR REFUELLING work?

Aerial refuelling needs calm conditions, so the fuel-carrying tanker can remain just above and ahead of the receiving aircraft. A long, stiff telescopic pipe called a boom, with small flaps or wings to keep it steady, is inserted into a bucket-like receptacle on the receiver plane. Or the receiver inserts its short, rigid probe into the funnel-like drogue at the end of a flexible pipe from the tanker.

AVENGER MINEHUNTER

Naval mines are floating or seabed bombs that explode when another craft comes near or touches them. They are cheap to make and release or 'lay', and remain a threat for months or even years to ships and boats in the area. Minehunters like the Avenger patrol an area, detect mines using sonar equipment and destroy them.

All 14 of the the US's Avenger-class vessels are named after the first one built. They are relatively small, at 68 m long and with a beam (maximum width) of 12 m. Ready-for-action weight is 1300 tonnes.

Eureka!

The first sonar or echo-sounding systems came into use in 1914. They followed the terrible tragedy of the sinking of the *Titanic* in 1912, when sonar could have warned the liner about the iceberg.

Whatever next?

Dolphins and some whales use a natural form of sonar to find their way. Dolphin military 'recruits' can be trained to detect mines and may carry out this role in the future.

Mast Apart from radar to detect aircraft, other ships and perhaps mines, the mast carries several types of antennae (aerials) for radio and microwave communications.

Hull The main hull structure is wood – chiefly oak, fir and cypress – covered with a skin of glass-fibre plastic. Lack of metal means a low 'magnetic signature', which is much less likely to set off magnetic mines.

Sonar pods are readied for underwater action

✳ Seeing with SOUND

Mines and other objects in the water can be detected by active sonar on the minehunter vessel, usually mounted on its hull. The returning echoes are analyzed and displayed by computers on screens. Several transmitters and receivers spaced apart on the hull, known as a sonar array, give a more accurate view, because echoes returning from a particular direction reach the nearest receivers first. Or sonar equipment can be towed on long lines behind a vessel, to lessen interference from its own engines and other noises.

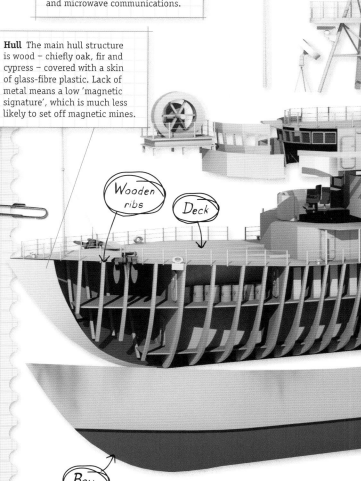

Wooden ribs

Deck

Bow

USS Avenger began construction in 1983, was launched in 1985, and received its commission into service in 1987.

✳ How does SONAR work?

Sonar (Sound Navigation And Ranging) is the sound version of radar. In active sonar, a vessel sends out ping-like pulses of sound, which travel well and far through water. The vessel's underwater microphones, called hydrophones, detect any returning echoes and a computer works out the size, distance and direction of the object. In passive sonar the vessel simply 'listens' for noises in the water – from whales to enemy subs.

Active Sonar

Hydrophone receiver 'hears' the echoes

Transmitter sends out sound pulses

Sound pulses hit objects and bounce back or reflect as echoes

Passive Sonar

Hydrophone on a long line is clear of noise produced by its own ship's engines

Objects such as submarine engines produce noise and vibrations that pass easily through water

Funnel

Display screens

Sonar pod Each towed submersible pod contains two sonar systems. The ship also has ROVs (Remote-Operated Vehicles) such as underwater robots.

RIBs

Towing winch The sonar pods are let out and then hauled in by a large-drum winch powered by an electric motor.

Engines Four Waukesha diesel engines each produce 600 horsepower, for a maximum speed of 26 kilometres per hour. The engines are specially designed using metal alloys with low 'magnetic signature'.

Propulsion Apart from the main propellers driven by the diesel engines, Avengers also have smaller propellers powered by electric motors. These allow it to 'keep station' – stay in the same place above the seabed despite winds, waves and currents.

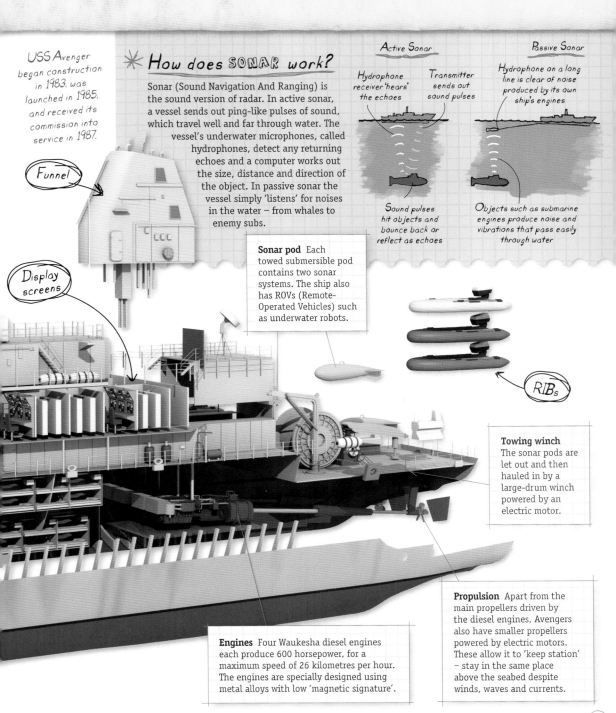

TYPE 45 DESTROYER

Destroyers are medium-sized, fast, manoeuvrable, long-distance warships that often escort larger vessels such as aircraft carriers or transporters. They protect these bigger ships against attack from enemy surface vessels, submarines, aircraft, missiles and other threats. The UK's Type 45 Class destroyers are also known as D Class after the first of their kind, HMS *Daring*, launched in 2006.

Eureka!

All warships were wooden until the arrival of ironclads, the first being France's *La Gloire* (1859), the wooden hull of which was covered in metal sheets. Fully metal hulls came in about ten years later.

Whatever next?

The same features used in stealth aircraft such as the F-22 Raptor are being extended to ships, with shapes and materials that lessen reflection of radar's radio waves.

Radar

Engines Two Rolls Royce WR21 gas turbines provide turning power, not for propellers, but for electricity generators.

Drive shafts The engines produce electricity for two massive electric motors that turn drive shafts with propellers at the ends.

HMS Daring was launched in 2006, went into sea trials and entered service in 2009.

HELI-PAD

Rear deck

Bulkeads

Outer hull

✳ How do GAS TURBINES work?

The gas turbine is similar to the turbojet engine shown on page 167. However the propelling force is not the exhaust jet of hot gases. It is the inner shaft in the middle of the engine, which is turned by the compressor turbines. A series of gears slows the rotation speed to spin the ship's propellers with great power.

Exhaust turbines connect to intake turbines via tube-like outer shaft

Exhaust gases led away

Intake turbines

Exhaust turbines

Air intake

Compressor turbines

Compressor turbines spin on inner shaft that is connected to gearbox and propellers

Superstructure The 'clean' outline has smooth panels with anti-radar coatings, few right angles and sharp edges, and other stealth features. These reduce the chances of being detected by radar.

HMS Daring honours the destroyer of the same name launched in 1949 – and five previous 'Darings' in the UK's Royal Navy.

Funnel The funnel has several cooling systems for the hot exhausts from the gas turbines. This lowers the ship's 'infra-red signature', where others can locate it using heat-sensitive or infra-red-detecting equipment.

Radar

PLAN VIEW

Type 45s are sizeable craft, with a length of 152 m, a width of 21.2 m, and a total weight of 7350 tonnes when fully equipped for a lengthy voyage.

Bridge

Armament The front gun is a 4.5 Mark 8 (calibre 4.5 inches or 113 millimetres). However the main weapons are a variety of missiles.

T45

Anchor

Type 45s are built at three separate shipyards, two in Glasgow and one in Portsmouth, with final fitting in Glasgow.

Lifeboats Even the lifeboats are hidden behind quick-release panels, so the radio waves of radar cannot bounce off them in a characteristic pattern.

The standard Type 45 has a crew of 190, with room for an extra 40 people if necessary.

✳ SHIP SHAPE

Most ships and boats are built on dry land. Some are constructed on the shore, then launched by sliding down a ramp or slipway into the water. Another method is the dry dock, which is an area that can be closed off with watertight gates and then emptied by pumps or drains. The vessel is launched by flooding the dock – allowing water back in through gaps or pipes – and then opening the gates. Ships and boats also come into dry dock for repairs and refits.

The latest destroyer nears completion on the slipway

TYPE 212 SUBMARINE

Nuclear reactors do not need air to burn their fuel, unlike jet, diesel or petrol engines. So nuclear-powered submarines can stay underwater and on the move for weeks, even months. The German Type 212 submarine is non-nuclear and has a diesel engine. However it can also travel submerged for weeks using a second source of energy – electricity made by its hydrogen-oxygen-powered fuel cells.

Eureka!

A sub's chief weapons include its torpedoes – underwater missiles like self-propelled bombs. The first torpedoes were tested in the 1860s. Some were powered by jets of compressed air from a high-pressure cylinder. Others had wind-up clockwork motors!

Whatever next?

Sneaky submarines can come and go undetected, apart from by sonar, as shown previously. Strung-out automatic sonar arrays may form 'listening walls' around ports, naval centres and other important bases.

The Type 212 can stay under the surface for three weeks. This time is extended to 12 weeks if it comes near the surface to 'snorkel' air.

Type 212s have been tested to depths of 700 m, which is deeper than many other submarines.

Sail The fin or sail runs with gentle, smooth curves into the main hull. This reduces the sub's 'sonar signature'.

Hatches A sub's 'doors', or hatches, are normally kept closed underwater. To allow divers out, the diver goes through the inner hatch door into the hatch compartment. The inner door is sealed, the compartment is flooded, and the outer door opens.

Open hatch

✳ How do HYDROPLANES work?

Submarine controls are similar to those of an aircraft. The vessel turns left or right, called yaw, by angling its vertical control surfaces – rudders – to the opposite side. They press against the water flowing past and are pushed sideways, as in a surface ship. A sub tilts up or down, known as pitch, using horizontal control surfaces known as hydroplanes or diving planes.

Moving the rudder to the left (or right) pushes the rear of the sub to the right (or left) for steering

Yaw (left or right)

Stern (rear) hydroplane

Tilting the hydroplanes causes the sub to angle up or down, helping it to rise or dive

Bow (front) hydroplane

Pitch (up or down)

Torpedoes There are six torpedo tubes in two groups of three, and 12 torpedoes ready to fire. The advanced DM2A4 torpedo is 6.6 metres long and driven by an electric motor and batteries, with a range of 50 kilometres.

Bathroom

Before refuelling, the Type 212 can sail for a distance of more than 670 km. Its maximum submerged speed is 37 km/h.

☀ Prepare to DIVE!

Periscope The sub's slide-up periscope tube allows a view above the surface of the water.

The control centre of a ship is usually known as the bridge. On surface vessels it has wide windows for a panoramic view. Underwater, submarines 'see' what's around using sonar, as shown previously, as well as other sensors, such as magnetic detectors for metal parts of nearby ships. If the sub is just below the surface, the crew can raise or hoist the extendable periscope so that its upper end is just above the water. This gives an all-round or 360° view.

On the submarine's bridge, the captain keeps an eye on his vessel and his crew

Drogue

Oxygen tanks

Propeller

Prop drive shaft

Hydrogen tanks

Bulkhead

Control room The nerve centre of the craft contains navigation equipment, sonar stations and communcations. It also has controls for sailing depth, direction and speed, as well as weapons.

Fuel cells and diesel-engined generator The fuel cell system, with either nine smaller or two larger cells, is just in front of the diesel engine. The fuel cells combine oxygen and hydrogen to make water and generate an electric current.

Electric drive motor The Permasyn 1.7-MW (1.7 million watts) electric propulsion motor can switch between electricity from the fuel cells or the diesel generator.

The overall length of the 212 is 56 m, with a beam (width) of 7 m. Its weight is 1450 tonnes.

The first Type 212, known as the U-31, took to the water in 2002 and entered commission in 2005. Running with its quiet electric motor, it is very difficult to detect by passive sonar.

NIMITZ SUPERCARRIER

A floating, self-powered city designed for warfare, the supersized aircraft carrier is the world's largest mobile military base. These giant vessels are nuclear-powered, using uranium fuel pellets smaller than suitcases. If they had to carry liquid fuel for diesel or gas turbine engines, this would take up vast amounts of space inside and severely limit the craft's time at sea.

Eureka!

The first successful nuclear-powered ship was not an aircraft carrier but a submarine, USS *Nautilus*, launched in 1955. It was followed by the Russian icebreaker *Lenin* in 1957. In 1958, *Nautilus* sailed under the Arctic ice cap to the North Pole.

Whatever next?

Replacing the Nimitz carriers will be the Gerald R Ford class, of similar size but with advanced reactors and electronics. Building work started in 2007 and the first ship should be ready by 2016.

Radar

Island The bridge and other main control rooms are located here. Observers constantly watch aircraft, on radar and by eye, to avoid collisions.

The position of the island on the right of a carrier's deck dates back to when propeller-driven aircraft took off and landed. The direction of the prop's rotation meant these planes were more likely to veer to the left than the right.

68

Reactors and propulsion Two A4W nuclear reactors are heavily shielded by thick metal to prevent radioactivity leaks. They boil water into steam to drive the four steam turbines that turn the propellers.

Props

✳ All HOOKED UP!

As well as having to accelerate very quickly at take-off, aircraft landing on a carrier must slow down, or decelerate, just as rapidly. The usual method is a long bar with a U-shaped claw at the end, the tailhook or arrestor hook, that lowers from under the aircraft's tail as it prepares to land. At touchdown this catches on one of several steel cables or wires strung across the deck. As the cable run outs, more and more braking force is applied to slow it down or arrest it. So the aircraft stops quickly but smoothly.

With an all-up weight of more than 100,000 tonnes, the Nimitz class are the largest military ships in the world. However the cruise liner *Oasis of the Seas*, launched in 2008, is 225,000 tonnes.

A fighter 'catches a wire' on the deck of an aircraft carrier

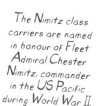

The Nimitz class carriers are named in honour of Fleet Admiral Chester Nimitz, commander in the US Pacific during World War II.

Jet blast deflector

F-18 Hornet fighter ready for take-off

Catapult shuttle engages in the aircraft's nose gear

Catapult control pod

Catapult officer

Flight deck crew

Catapult track set into deck

✳ How do STEAM CATAPULTS work?

Despite a supercarrier's size, it has a relatively short deck from which aircraft take off. So a steam-powered catapult system hidden under the deck boosts a plane's speed at the start of its take-off run. A bullet-shaped shuttle slides in a long hollow track in the deck, and attaches to a quick-release catch at the plane's nose wheel. A blast of high-pressure steam piped from the ship's boilers then pushes a cylinder that pulls along the shuttle, to accelerate the plane before its own engines take over.

Angled flight deck
The total flight deck length is more than 330 metres. Planes can both take off and land within seconds of each other using the additional angled side deck.

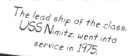

The lead ship of the class, USS Nimitz, went into service in 1975.

Take-off ramp Aircraft need different take-off runs according to their type and their weapons and fuel loads. The angled bow ramp (at the front) gives them an added uplift.

The reactors of Nimitz carriers do not need refuelling for 20 years. However the refuelling process must be done with great caution and is only possible at certain ports.

Hangars Aircraft are folded up for storage on the main hangar deck, which is 208 metres long, 33 metres wide and 8 metres high.

Accommodation More than 5000 people take it in shifts to eat, relax, sleep and go on active duty.

The carrier has enough aircraft fuel for 13 days of non-stop action.

GIANT MACHINES

INTRODUCTION

Is bigger always better? Yes – and no. Giant machines do more work more quickly than small ones, saving time and effort. They are often more efficient, using less fuel to carry out more work. Also, sheer size is impressive. It encourages people to buy or hire massive machinery, and it may cause concern for their business rivals. There are drawbacks, however. Mobile giants are difficult to move along small roads, through narrow tunnels and over weak bridges. And if a giant breaks down, its parts are more expensive to buy and bring to the site.

This steam tractor from 1890, loaded with coal and water, was too big and heavy to catch on.

METAL TAKES OVER

In ancient Greece and Rome, early big machines were large cranes, levers, and catapults for warfare. They were mostly made from wood with a few small metal parts. During the 1700s, as the Industrial Revolution got under way, engineers developed ways of making huge metal parts from iron, and later from steel.

Immense excavators gobble up thousands of tonnes of rocks daily.

SUPER POWERS

People and animals powered the first large machines and vehicles. But you need far more force to power something as big as a house. The Industrial Revolution, which took place in the late 18th and early 19th centuries, was based on steam engines. By 1900, petrol and diesel engines were taking over. Then enormous electric motors began to be used. The biggest trucks, construction machines and railway locomotives are powered by diesel-electric systems.

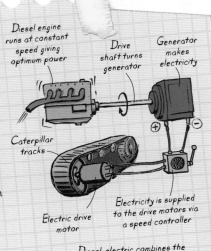

Diesel engine runs at constant speed giving optimum power

Drive shaft turns generator

Generator makes electricity

Caterpillar tracks

Electric drive motor

Electricity is supplied to the drive motors via a speed controller

Diesel-electric combines the best of both systems.

AGE OF GIANTS

The world needs coal and oil for energy, as well as metals and other raw materials. People want bigger houses, shops and places to work, and more food. All of this means that machines such as excavators, dump trucks, bulldozers, cranes and harvesters become even more colossal. To build and maintain these mammoths needs new factories, service centres and delivery trucks for parts – which, in turn, means more giant machines.

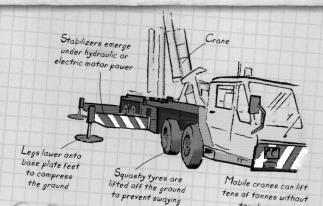

Stabilizers emerge under hydraulic or electric motor power

Crane

Legs lower onto base plate feet to compress the ground

Squashy tyres are lifted off the ground to prevent swaying

Mobile cranes can lift tens of tonnes without toppling over.

How many wheels? Lots, as a multi-trailer truck delivers a vast grain silo (storage container).

ARE THERE LIMITS?

Just how big can machines and vehicles get? In the future our planet may suffer from energy shortages, pollution, climate change and other problems. This may affect the size of future machines.

Even space shuttles need a lift – from huge transport planes.

Perhaps the giant machines of today will one day give way to smaller, smarter versions.

BIGFOOT TRUCK

The 'Bigfoots' and similar monster trucks have been thrilling crowds since the 1970s. They are combinations, or hybrids, of a standard pick-up truck body such as the Ford F-250, with the suspension, drive shafts and axles from huge cargo or military vehicles. The giant 'flotation' tyres, such as those used on tractors and harvesters, are taller than a person, so the driver rides some 3 metres above the ground.

Eureka!

The original Bigfoot was built in 1975 by construction worker Bob Chandler, who liked to go off-roading at weekends. More trucks followed over the years. Some are for display, others are specialized for racing, jumps or stunts such as somersaults.

Whatever next?

Almost 20 official Bigfoot trucks have been built, and even bigger vehicles with massive mining dump-truck tyres are planned.

The Bigfoot Fastrax is based on a US Army M48 troop carrier with two 7.5-litre engines.

Exhaust manifold The tubes of the manifold collect exhaust gases from each cylinder and channel them to the exhaust pipes, one on each side.

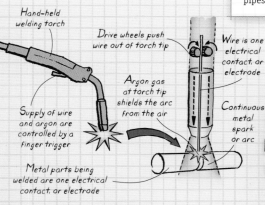

Hand-held welding torch

Drive wheels push wire out of torch tip

Wire is one electrical contact, or electrode

Argon gas at torch tip shields the arc from the air

Supply of wire and argon are controlled by a finger trigger

Continuous metal spark or arc

Metal parts being welded are one electrical contact, or electrode

✳ How does WELDING work?

Welding joins metal parts by heating them to a very high temperature so that their edges almost melt and fuse. In gas welding, the heat is an incredibly hot flame from burning gas. In arc welding, the parts being welded are in an electrical pathway, along with a length of flexible filler wire that emerges slowly and steadily from the tip of the welding torch. When the wire touches the parts, it completes an electrical circuit and the electric current jumps across in the form of a very hot continuous spark called an arc. This melts the filler wire into the part edges like superhot glue.

Brakes The body of the Bigfoot does not weigh much, but when the heavy wheels and tyres spin, they need disc brakes to slow them.

Differential When steering around corners, this set of gears, the 'diff', allows the wheel on the outside of the curve to turn faster (see page 195).

The original Bigfoot series goes from 1 to 14. There is no Bigfoot 13 – due to the unlucky nature of this number!

In 1999, Bigfoot 14 made a long jump of more than 61 m – over a Boeing 727 passenger jet.

Body Some Bigfoot-type trucks have the original steel body. Others have bodywork moulded from light, flexible, non-rusting GRP (glass-reinforced plastic) also known as fibre-glass.

A monster truck leaps over a school bus at its action-packed display

✳ It's the HIGH JUMP!

Bigfoots, monster trucks and similar huge vehicles put on special displays at race tracks and exhibition grounds. They compete against each other, sometimes with a handicap or drawback such as pulling a heavy trailer. They also have high-jump and long-jump competitions, or drive through hoops of fire. Emergency services, including an ambulance and fire appliance with cutting gear, stand by in case one of the trucks is crashed or crushed.

Rear diff

Tyre tread The tread grooves are usually cleaned of sand, mud, leaves and other debris with pressure-washers, to ensure a good grip.

Flotation tyres These massive tyres 'float' or stay on the surface of soft ground, rather than digging in like traction tyres. This allows them to maintain better grip – a traction tyre slips if it turns too fast.

Suspension Rows of shock absorbers (hydraulic dampers) allow the axles to tilt, jolt and vibrate, while keeping the body relatively stable so the driver can keep control.

The Grave Digger series of monster trucks is based on the 1950 Chevrolet Panel van. They have ghoulish scenes painted on the sides and the red headlights glow like a demon's eyes.

Bigfoot's stunt of crushing old cars started as a joke in 1981.

TRACTOR

The giant tractor is the endlessly adaptable 'workhorse' of the modern industrial farm. It pulls trailers loaded with all kinds of items, from hay bales to cattle or sheep. Its power take-off or PTO (see below), can connect to dozens of kinds of machines. Its huge diesel engine is heavy and noisy, but it is also reliable, powerful at low speeds and easy to adjust, service and repair.

Eureka!

From the 1850s, working animals such as horses, oxen and buffalo were replaced by steam-driven traction engines, adapted from railway locomotives. Diesel- and petrol-engined tractors became popular from the 1900s.

Whatever next?

Simpler farming methods that are 'greener', causing less damage to the environment, are constantly being tested. Some farmers no longer plough fields, preferring to plant seeds straight into last year's surface.

Tractors have between three and six main gears, and also a range changer to alter these, so they can have more than 18 gear combinations.

The power of a big tractor engine is more than 750 horsepower – about the same as a Formula One racing car.

The power take-off system was introduced in 1918, partly as a result of engineering research during World War I.

Power take-off The take-off coupling is usually at the rear of the tractor. But some types have a front coupling too, and even one to the side. However the tractor can only work one of these at a time.

✳ How does PTO work?

Power take-off (PTO) supplies a rotary or turning force from the tractor at a special joint, or coupling, usually at the vehicle's rear. All kinds of machines can be connected such as seed drills (planters), cutters, mowers, balers and spreaders for fertilizers or pesticides – meaning these machines do not need their own engines. The tractor tows the machine by a separate drawbar or hitch. The PTO is controlled by the driver through the gearbox, separately from the tractor's own wheels. So the tractor can be stationary while still supplying PTO. Most tractors also have connections to supply electricity and a hydraulic link.

Mudguard

Steps

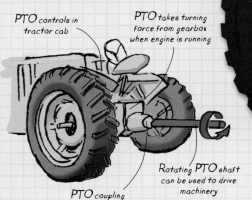

PTO controls in tractor cab

PTO takes turning force from gearbox when engine is running

Rotating PTO shaft can be used to drive machinery

PTO coupling

Multi-wheels An extra outer wheel can be bolted to the inner wheel for very soft surfaces, then taken off to make the tractor narrower for road travel.

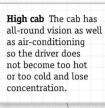

High cab The cab has all-round vision as well as air-conditioning so the driver does not become too hot or too cold and lose concentration.

High exhaust

Multiple wheels damage soil less

Taking CARE

Farmers are careful to protect the soil that provides their living. One problem is compaction, when the soil is squeezed or compacted into a hard mass. This presses out the tiny air and water-filled spaces that plants need to grow well, and makes the lumps too hard for plant roots to penetrate. Very large, low-pressure tyres, or several sets of smaller tyres, mean a larger tyre surface in contact with the soil. This reduces the pressure caused by the tractor's weight.

Articulated steering The rear section of this tractor is articulated – linked to the front section by an adjustable joint. It steers by changing the angle between the front and rear sections (see page 198).

Radiator

In 2005, a Case Steiger STX500 Quadtrac tractor ploughed 321 hectares in 24 hours, that's equivalent to a square with each side 1.8 km long.

Engine Many big tractors have V-8 or even V-12 turbocharged diesel engines. These start well even when very cold and resist knocks and rough treatment better than petrol engines.

Crankshaft The pistons are joined by connecting rods to the main crankshaft that runs along the bottom of the engine. This has important main bearings at each end.

Wheel electric motor This tractor is diesel-electric. The diesel engine powers a generator that makes electricity for the wheel motors.

COMBINE HARVESTER

The combine harvester combines the separate tasks of harvesting – cutting the crop and separating the valuable seeds or grains from less valuable parts, such as the straw (stalks) and chaff (dry cases around the grains). A modern combine harvester is the biggest and most expensive vehicle on the farm, doing the jobs of 100 people with its 10,000-plus moving parts, all driven by the big diesel engine.

Eureka!

During the 1800s, separate harvesting machines such as reapers and threshers were powered by animals, then steam engines, then tractors. The first self-powered combine harvesters were produced in the 1950s.

Whatever next?

Day by day, satellite photographs show farmers which parts of which fields are ready to harvest. The instructions are fed into the harvester's satnav or GPS so that it almost drives itself during its work.

Big combines measure more than 10 m long, 5 m wide and 4 m high. They weigh over 20 tonnes – and that's without their load of grain inside.

Advanced combines not only have satnav (GPS) but also autopilot systems, like those on aircraft, to help the driver keep the machine straight on vast prairie-like fields.

Forward cab The latest cabs are full of controls and displays, showing which parts of the combine are wearing and may need replacing.

Cutter bar The very sharp cutter works like a hedge-trimmer to slice off the crop plant cleanly near to the ground, leaving a row of short stalks called stubble.

Controls

Tinted glass

Conveyor

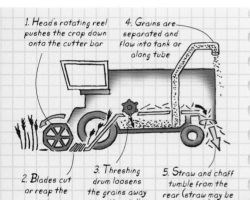

1. Head's rotating reel pushes the crop down onto the cutter bar

4. Grains are separated and flow into tank or along tube

2. Blades cut or reap the crop

3. Threshing drum loosens the grains away from the stalks

5. Straw and chaff tumble from the rear (straw may be baled)

✳ How do COMBINE HARVESTERS work?

For most grain crops, harvesting begins with reaping (cutting off the plants), which is carried out by the combine's reel-and-blade head. Next is threshing, when the seed grains are loosened from the unwanted parts, followed by winnowing, when the dry, light seed cases are blown away from the grains. The grains may be stored in the harvester's tank or blown along a pipe to a trailer pulled alongside by a tractor.

Reel Different reels or heads are used for different crops. These are usually various types of grain grasses, such as wheat, barley and rye.

Combine harvesters are expensive. For smaller farms, or those with few crop fields, it may be best to hire a combine and its driver, or to club together into a cooperative and buy one to share.

✳ Mechanized
FARMING

Modern highly productive or 'intensive' farms rely on massive machines such as tractors, combine harvesters and spreaders. These use up vast resources of energy and materials to manufacture and run. However they harvest crops very quickly compared to simpler, less mechanical methods. Less of the crop is unripe or overripe and so less is wasted.

Vast fields are harvested by combine 'armies' when the grains are ripest

Unloader pipe The grains are blown by high-pressure air from a powerful fan out of the unloader pipe into a trailer.

Spreader This ejects and spreads the straw behind the combine.

Straw walkers These conveyors move the straw and other unwanted parts to the rear of the combine, for spreading or baling.

Steps

Threshing drums The rotating drums shake and rattle the grains away from the stems, chaff and other bits of the crop plant.

Sieves The grains fall through the holes in the sieves to the base of the combine, where they are stored or moved into the combine's own storage tank.

Laser beams allow the combine to harvest on sloping fields, by sensing the tilt necessary for the reel at the front by up to 5 degrees to either side.

BACKHOE LOADER

No building site is complete without at least one digger, otherwise known as the backhoe loader. The 'loader' refers to the front bucket, which scoops big items from ground level up to the top of its reach. The 'backhoe' is the longer rear arm, which not only reaches up but also down below ground level. It can dig trenches with a selection of narrow buckets or hoes.

Eureka!

In the 1950s, the backhoe loader was an early success for UK engineering company J C Bamforth, which expanded into the US and worldwide from the 1960s. This is why these machines are also known as JCBs.

Whatever next?

Pushing a digger blade into earth takes lots of force. Engineers are testing blades that vibrate to shake the soil and loosen its particles, letting the blade cut in more easily.

Joseph Cyril Bamforth founded his company in 1945, at the end of World War II, to take advantage of the rebuilding boom after the war.

Hydraulic rams Hydraulic liquid pumped into one side of the piston moves it one way, then liquid pumped into the other side forces it back again the opposite way.

In 1948 JCB employed six people. Today they have more than 8000 workers.

Loader bucket There are two main controls, one to raise and lower the bucket on its arms, and one to tilt its angle.

Engine

435 B

Three diggers show some fancy bucket work in their dance routine

✳ Diggers on HOLIDAY

It's not all hard, dirty work for backhoe loaders, earth scrapers, tipper trucks and other construction giants. Some makers show off their vehicles in a light-hearted way to gain feelgood publicity. JCB's 'Dancing Diggers' formation team demonstrate skills such as lifting the main vehicle off the ground by its buckets, spinning around on the spot and climbing a steep slope using the backhoe as a long-reach grasping claw. This also showcases the machine's power, abilities and safety aspects.

Teeth

The world's largest backhoe loader factory is at Ballabgarh, in northern India. This town is also home to India's Cement Research Institute.

Loader arms The loader bucket cannot be lowered much below ground level (see page 198). If it is set at 'zero' height and driven forwards, it works as a simple ground leveller.

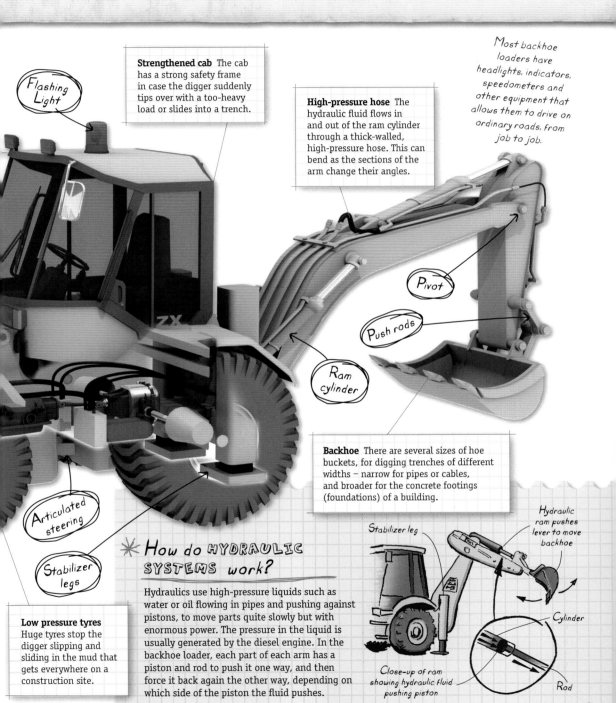

Flashing Light

Strengthened cab The cab has a strong safety frame in case the digger suddenly tips over with a too-heavy load or slides into a trench.

High-pressure hose The hydraulic fluid flows in and out of the ram cylinder through a thick-walled, high-pressure hose. This can bend as the sections of the arm change their angles.

Most backhoe loaders have headlights, indicators, speedometers and other equipment that allows them to drive on ordinary roads, from job to job.

Pivot

Push rods

Ram cylinder

Backhoe There are several sizes of hoe buckets, for digging trenches of different widths – narrow for pipes or cables, and broader for the concrete footings (foundations) of a building.

Articulated steering

Stabilizer legs

✳ How do HYDRAULIC SYSTEMS work?

Hydraulics use high-pressure liquids such as water or oil flowing in pipes and pushing against pistons, to move parts quite slowly but with enormous power. The pressure in the liquid is usually generated by the diesel engine. In the backhoe loader, each part of each arm has a piston and rod to push it one way, and then force it back again the other way, depending on which side of the piston the fluid pushes.

Low pressure tyres Huge tyres stop the digger slipping and sliding in the mud that gets everywhere on a construction site.

Stabilizer leg

Hydraulic ram pushes lever to move backhoe

Cylinder

Close-up of ram showing hydraulic fluid pushing piston

Rod

CONCRETE TRUCK

Thanks to the concrete truck there is no need for construction sites to store cement, sand, coarse aggregate (gravel-like stones), water and mixing machinery – all the components needed to make concrete. The ready-mix truck can carry several tonnes of concrete made to an exact recipe. Then it has to transport the mix to where it is needed within an hour or two, before the mix 'goes off' – sets as hard as rock.

If a concrete truck breaks down, or gets stuck in a traffic jam, its load hardens. Then it must be cleared out using road drills or even explosives.

Eureka!

Deliveries of already-mixed mortar and concrete began in the UK in the 1930s. The business expanded from the 1960s as more mixing centres meant that more customers could be reached before the mix hardened.

Whatever next?

Experiments are happening with concrete-type mixtures that stay softer for longer, hardening when exposed to powerful laser beams.

Drum The drum or barrel is turned by the truck's main engine, so the driver needs to keep on the move with little engine idling.

Loading chute The truck is loaded, or charged, with ingredients for the mix through this opening. The mix falls in from a tall container called a hopper at the concrete depot.

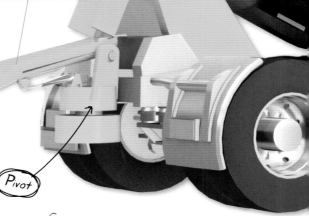

Discharge chute The mix flows out of this lower chute into whatever is waiting – a trench or hole, a concrete pump, or even wheelbarrows.

Pivot

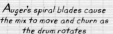
Auger's spiral blades cause the mix to move and churn as the drum rotates

With clockwise rotation the mix is pushed forwards into the base of the drum and keeps churning around

Anti-clockwise turning screws the mix rearwards, up and out of the drum, ready for use

✳How do AUGERS work?

An auger is a screw-like spiral or twisted structure that, when turned, drills into an object or material, or moves it along. Its basic design is like the Archimedes screw, used since ancient times to raise water from rivers into ditches. Big augers drill holes in the ground, raising the soil up and out. Another simple auger design is the corkscrew. The ready-mix drum has an auger, either a helical (coiled) blade on a central shaft, or spiral curved blades along the inside. As the drum spins, the blades mix and move the contents.

Concrete is measured in cubic metres, with a typical single measure weighing 2.5 tonnes.

The first concrete trucks were developed in 1916 by Stephen Stepanian of Columbus, Ohio, USA.

✳ In the MIX

All concrete may look similar, but it is not. There are hundreds of ingredients, chemical additives and recipes for specialized mixes. These include recipes for very low or very high temperatures, enduring great weight or lots of vibrations, or for exposure to fresh or salty water. Concrete does not set by drying and losing water, but by a chemical reaction that depends on temperature. Keeping it cool helps to slow the hardening process.

Ready-mix pours from the chute into a footings trench for a building

Concrete mix

Blades In this truck, sets of blades keep the mixture churning as the drum turns, to stop the mixture setting.

Water tank

Engine A powerful diesel engine turns the drum and/or the road wheels. An empty truck is less than half the weight of a full one, so the driver must adapt to the change.

Multi-axles Several sets of wheels spread the huge weight, to stay within axle weight limits on ordinary roads and bridges.

Gearbox The engine can be disconnected from the road wheels so that it only drives the drum.

Big mixer trucks weigh 10–15 tonnes empty, and their loads are 10–20 tonnes.

DUMP TRUCK

On the building site, dumpers or tippers carry all kinds of objects – not only loose materials such as earth or rubble, but also huge pipes, girders and other heavy items. The dump truck needs a loader (see page 198), conveyor or similar machine to fill it up. But it can unload at the rear simply by raising, or tipping, its hinged body, called the bed or box.

Eureka!

The first dump trucks, modified from standard flat-bed trucks, were built in the 1920s in New Brunswick, Canada. The front end of the box was lifted by a winch and cable just behind the cab. By the 1930s they were spreading across North America and Europe.

The giant tipper trucks called 'centipedes' have a series of seven axles, rather than the usual two or three.

Diesel-electric dump trucks use powerful electric motors, like diesel-electric trains. This is more efficient than a diesel engine driving the road wheels through a complex system of gears, when much energy is lost.

A massive dumper takes on a load

Tailgate lip

✳ MONSTER dumpers

The biggest, roughest, toughest dumpers are used in mining and quarrying. They carry ores (rocks containing valuable substances such as metals) and similar loads away from the mine or quarry face, to long conveyors for loading onto road trucks or railway wagons. The latest robot dumpers use satnav (GPS) to follow their regular route within the mine or quarry site. Some can fit a whole house into the box, and cope with loads of 400-plus tonnes, making them among the largest of all vehicles.

Hydraulic rams
These produce incredible force to lift the fully loaded box upwards as it tilts at the rear pivot. They work using high-pressure oil (see page 191).

Traction motor This diesel-electric truck has an enormously powerful electric motor for each road wheel. The motor turns very powerfully throughout its speed range (see page 209).

Chassis

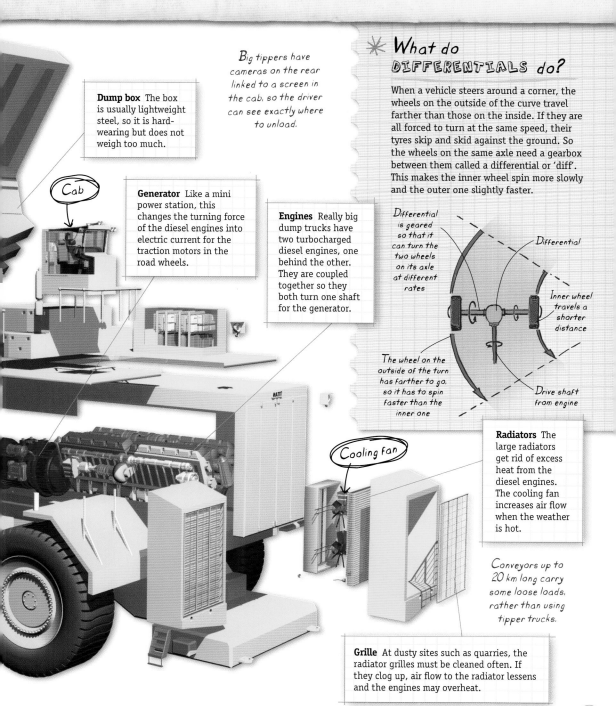

Dump box The box is usually lightweight steel, so it is hard-wearing but does not weigh too much.

Big tippers have cameras on the rear linked to a screen in the cab, so the driver can see exactly where to unload.

Cab

Generator Like a mini power station, this changes the turning force of the diesel engines into electric current for the traction motors in the road wheels.

Engines Really big dump trucks have two turbocharged diesel engines, one behind the other. They are coupled together so they both turn one shaft for the generator.

What do DIFFERENTIALS do?

When a vehicle steers around a corner, the wheels on the outside of the curve travel farther than those on the inside. If they are all forced to turn at the same speed, their tyres skip and skid against the ground. So the wheels on the same axle need a gearbox between them called a differential or 'diff'. This makes the inner wheel spin more slowly and the outer one slightly faster.

Differential is geared so that it can turn the two wheels on its axle at different rates

Differential

Inner wheel travels a shorter distance

The wheel on the outside of the turn has farther to go, so it has to spin faster than the inner one

Drive shaft from engine

Cooling fan

Radiators The large radiators get rid of excess heat from the diesel engines. The cooling fan increases air flow when the weather is hot.

Conveyors up to 20 km long carry some loose loads, rather than using tipper trucks.

Grille At dusty sites such as quarries, the radiator grilles must be cleaned often. If they clog up, air flow to the radiator lessens and the engines may overheat.

BULLDOZER

Often the biggest machine on the building site, and probably the heaviest, is the bulldozer or 'dozer. Its main task is to push loose material such as earth, sand or gravel, in order to spread it out and level the surface. Its crawler or caterpillar tracks spread its weight and prevent it slipping or sticking. The 'dozer's extraordinary push-pull power means that it can be called on for many tasks, including towing logs or rescuing vehicles that get stuck in the mud.

Eureka!

The first bulldozers were built in the 1920s in Kansas, USA. The term 'bull-dose' meant a large amount of very strong medicine to subdue a bull or similar large animal. It came into use for several big, powerful machines.

Whatever next?

Smaller, lighter bulldozers known as calfdozers are becoming more common for small building sites and to smooth snow for skiers.

Rear lights

Caterpillar's best-selling big D9 bulldozer weighs about 50 tonnes, while the giant D11 tips the scales at 100 tonnes.

✳ RIP it UP!

Very hard compacted soil or rubble, tarmac roads, concrete parking areas – none of these stand a chance against the bulldozer's ripper. Most 'dozers have one or more claw-like rippers at the rear that can be raised, lowered and angled like the blade. The ripper is pushed down through the hard surface, perhaps into a hole made by a road drill. Then the bulldozer uses its vast strength and tremendous weight to move along slowly, tearing up the material behind so it can be loosened further and collected or worked by other machines.

Caterpillar tracks These are usually made of very hard rubber or metal. They consist of many linked parts called shoes or plates, or one long rubber belt with crosswise ridges.

FD14E TURBO

The ripper claw tears up the ground for smoothing or clearing

Drive axle The axle turns the rear drive wheel for each track. The track's front wheel may not be driven and just rotates with the track.

Rear gearbox (diff) The fast rotation from the front gearbox is greatly slowed here, for the drive axles to move the tracks. In the process, the turning force (torque) increases hundreds of times, giving the bulldozer its tremendous power.

✳ How does the 'DOZER BLADE work?

Some bulldozers have a blade worked by strong steel cables that winch it up or down. But most use hydraulic arms to raise or lower the blade. Advanced bulldozers have a laser levelling system (see page 200) that measures the height of the blade and the 'dozer's body above a set point in the ground. The system automatically moves the blade to scrape the required surface perfectly flat or at a particular angle of slope.

Blade in raised position

Hydraulic ram

Caterpillar tracks grip well and spread the 'dozer's weight so it does not sink in

Depressing blade below ground level scoops out material

Reversing the 'dozer with blade lowered smooths the ground

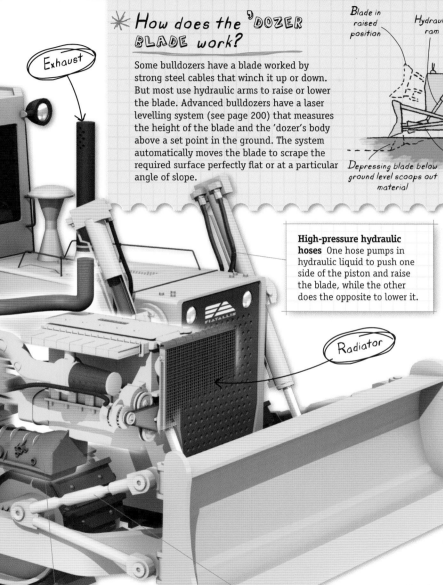

Exhaust

High-pressure hydraulic hoses One hose pumps in hydraulic liquid to push one side of the piston and raise the blade, while the other does the opposite to lower it.

In a typical bulldozer the left-hand joystick controls direction while the right-hand one controls the blade.

Radiator

Blade There are many blade designs, depending on the job and the material. Open-sided blades allow the material to spill out sideways, while side flanges (shown here) keep the material within the blade's width.

The biggest bulldozer is a one-off made in 1980 by Acco. It weighs more than 180 tonnes and its blade is 7 m wide and almost 3 m tall. Its two engines produce over 1300 horsepower.

Gearbox The main gearbox has 15 or more gear combinations, or ratios, for all tasks and ground conditions.

Blade pivots The blade ends pivot or swivel on V-shaped bars attached to the main chassis, to keep the blade angle steady.

BUCKET LOADER

Loading power is vital in mining, construction and other heavy industries – and the front-end loader provides this. Its bucket can lift many tonnes of loose material in one go and tip it where needed – into a trench or dump truck (see page 194), or onto a conveyor belt. Loader buckets are also useful for carrying items such as stacks of building bricks or bundles of timber and lifting them, for example, up onto scaffolding walkways.

Eureka!

Like dumpers and bulldozers, front-end bucket loaders were developed in the 1920s in the USA. The first types were based on farm tractors with a system of cables and winches to raise and tilt the bucket. The first purpose-built version was the Hough HS in 1939.

Whatever next?

Like many giant machines, loaders get bigger and stronger almost every year. There are plans for buckets so big that they could hold more than 300 people.

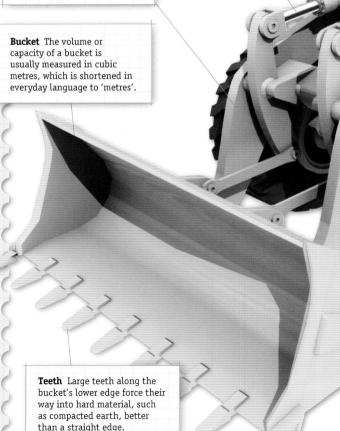

Bucket ram This hydraulic pusher-puller tilts the bucket, making it face upwards, level or downwards.

Arm The bucket arm alters the height of the bucket between preset limits, so it cannot go too high and make the loader topple over.

Bucket The volume or capacity of a bucket is usually measured in cubic metres, which is shortened in everyday language to 'metres'.

Teeth Large teeth along the bucket's lower edge force their way into hard material, such as compacted earth, better than a straight edge.

Giant wheeled loaders (as distinct from caterpillar tracked ones) have tyres more than 4 m tall that weigh 8 tonnes each.

How does ARTICULATED STEERING work?

A long, rigid, one-piece loader chassis is difficult to steer and manoeuvre in restricted places. The articulated loader has a joint between the front bucket and front wheels, and the main body with the engine and rear wheels. This replaces the usual steering system where the wheels themselves turn at an angle. It allows the loader to bend itself into tight corners and line up its bucket neatly with the material it will lift.

Front unit

Flexible pipes carry electrics and hydraulic oil

Main hinge joins front and rear units

Rear unit

Wheels of front (bucket) unit

Left and right hydraulic rams alter the angle between the two units, allowing the whole vehicle to steer and turn

Wheels of rear (cab-engine) unit

High-level exhaust Like most big machines with diesel or petrol engines, the exhaust outlet is above the level of the driver, to prevent fumes around the cab.

Le Tourneau's L2350 wheeled loader can lift almost 75 tonnes in one bucket to a height of more than 13 m, with a forward reach of 3.8 m.

Engine housing

Engine

FR130

Floodlights and spotlights Most giant machines have plenty of powerful lights all around, partly for emergency work that has to be done in darkness, as well as to be seen.

Fuel tank

The log grab closes its claws on another load of future paper

Articulated steering This articulated system (see opposite) allows the loader to wriggle in and out of narrow spaces. It is one of more than 12 separate hydraulic systems all over the machine.

Arm ram This hydraulic unit lifts or lowers the arm on which the bucket is mounted. A system of pivoted links between the arm and bucket means that the bucket stays at a constant angle as the arm goes up or comes down.

The 16-cylinder, 65-litre diesel engine in the biggest loaders produces 2300 horsepower.

✳ Lots of LOADING

A key feature of most loaders is the interchangeable front end. The ordinary bucket can be removed at its standard-sized fitting brackets or lugs, and replaced with any one of a huge variety of sand scoops, bale spikes, log grabs, hooks, pallet forks and similar 'handling' devices. The hydraulic power that controls the tipping bucket is then linked in to work the device, such as opening and closing the arms or claws of the log grab.

EARTH SCRAPER

Bulldozers can do some of the work to level an area. But they are slow and their strength may be needed elsewhere on site. So along comes the earth scraper, also called the land plane. It doesn't have the huge pushing power of the bulldozer, so it cannot cope with too many big lumps and bumps. But it is more efficient at earth-moving. One common task is cut-and-fill, which is scraping earth from a high area, leaving it flat, and taking the load to a lower area that needs building up.

Eureka!

Earth scrapers were the brainchild of US engineer-inventor Robert Gilmore LeTourneau, in the 1930s. He was responsible for more than half of the machines and gadgets still in use today in the earth-moving industry.

Whatever next?

As robot drivers, laser systems and satnav (GPS) improve, earth scrapers may become almost entirely automatic. However a human might always be needed in case the robot goes wrong.

The biggest self-powered scrapers have an extra second engine to drive the rear wheels.

Air conditioning The cab's air con unit is on the roof, where the air is least dusty.

Tractor unit The front section pulls along the scraper or hopper. The weight of the engine and cab in front of the wheels balances the load of the hopper to the rear.

Air filter

Engine A big diesel engine drives the front wheels with a large selection of very slow gears for different terrains.

Off-set cab The driver's cab is next to the engine, with a clear view all along one side of the vehicle for precise steering.

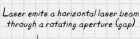

Laser emits a horizontal laser beam through a rotating aperture (gap)

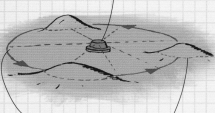

Hollows or low areas of ground are built up or filled to the level of the laser beam

Bumps or high areas of ground are cut down down by several passes of the earth scraper

✳ How does LASER LEVELLING work?

Lasers are high-energy, powerful beams of light that shine perfectly straight and do not spread out. They are used more and more in heavy engineering and earth-moving, for measuring and checking surfaces. On a large site the laser source is set to exactly the right height and then sends out light pulses that are horizontal and rotate like a lighthouse. Laser sensors on earth scrapers, bulldozers and other earth-movers tell the driver whether each small patch of ground needs to be lower or higher.

Arm

Hopper Huge amounts of earth can scrape into the hopper, and the blade can be adjusted up or down.

The original invention on which most earth scrapers are based is the Fresno scraper of 1883 from California. It was developed by James Porteous to help dig drainage canals and ditches in the local vineyards.

Blade

Rear wheels The massive rear wheels take the weight of the full hopper. Tyre pressure must be checked because it affects the height of the blade above the ground.

Robert Gilmore LeTourneau's first job was levelling and grading a 16-acre field with a tractor and towed scraper belonging to the local agricultural engineer boss. He opened his first tractor workshop in 1921.

CAT

CATERPILLAR 631D

Apron Earth or other material slides into the hopper through the forward-facing gate or apron opening. To unload, a rear hydraulic pusher bar forces it back out again through the gate to the required depth.

Hydraulic steering The hopper is joined to the tractor unit by an articulated steering link (see page 199).

A typical large scraper is 12–15 m long and weighs 40–60 tonnes when fully loaded.

An earth scraper runs to and fro on its cut-and-fill route

✳ SMOOTHLY does it

Scrapers and planers are sometimes known as 'graders'. This means they prepare the surface to a certain quality or grade of flatness and slope. Bulldozers and scrapers tend to the rougher or coarser end of grading, although scrapers in particular can cover enormous areas rapidly. For fine grading, with the smoothest finish, the ideal machine is well named – the grader. It is a tractor with a slim, wide blade set low down between the front and rear wheels. This gives the final 'polish' to areas such as sports pitches.

MOBILE CRANE

Cranes are the big lifters among giant machines. Tower cranes stay in one spot, floating cranes are used at sea, while on land, mobile cranes can be transported to where they're needed. Most cranes are carried on huge trucks and weigh more than 100 tonnes. When they hoist a load, the combined weight can be over 500 tonnes. Crane drivers make sure the vehicle is steady and secure before attempting a big lift – and that includes checking the ground underneath.

Eureka!

Simple cranes date back more than 2500 years to ancient Greece. By the time of the Roman Empire they were lifting stone blocks of more than 100 tonnes. Mobile cranes had to wait for the invention of steam engines from the 1800s, and then diesel engines.

Whatever next?

The world's tallest buildings approach 1000 metres in height, but no tower crane can reach that high. The newest methods allow smaller side cranes to 'piggyback' off the main building.

The longest crane booms extend more than 100 m, but their loads and also the hoisting speed are strictly limited.

Boom base The main 'arm' of the crane is called the boom or jib, depending on the design. If it can move up and down, as here, it's called a luffing boom.

The farther a crane boom reaches outwards, the less load it is allowed to lift. A 60-tonne load at 12 m would reduce to 40 tonnes at 15 m.

Swivel joint To traverse, or move the boom to the side, the whole base section of the crane swivels on a rotating platform or turntable.

✳ How do STABILIZERS work?

Most mobile cranes travel on normal highways and so the carrying truck has a limited size. Before the crane starts work, it extends outriggers or stabilizers with legs and feet, to make itself wider at the base. This means the crane cannot topple to the side, especially when it lifts or swings loads in that direction. The truck itself is usually long and heavy enough to prevent toppling in the front-back direction. Gravity and movement sensors warn if the crane starts to lean too much in any direction.

Crane engine

Drive engines

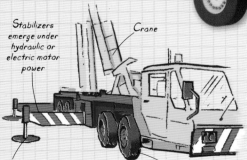

Stabilizers emerge under hydraulic or electric motor power

Crane

Legs lower onto base plate feet to compress the ground

Squashy tyres are lifted off the ground to prevent swaying

Hydraulics Several separate hydraulic systems are used to swivel and luff the crane. If one fails, the machinery locks in a failsafe position to prevent a terrible accident.

Stabilizer legs (retracted)

Multi-wheels Many axles spread the crane's load, which helps to even out the different soft and hard spots in the ground.

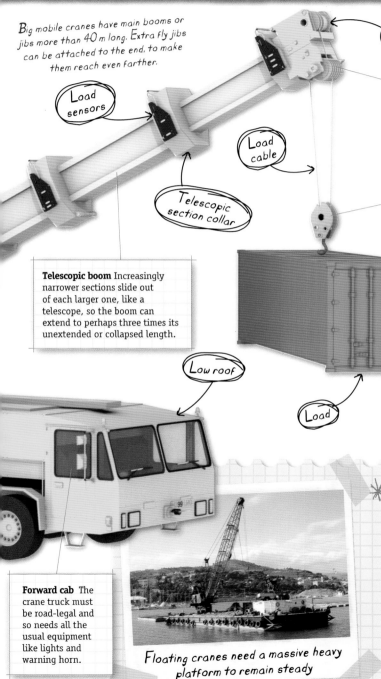

Big mobile cranes have main booms or jibs more than 40 m long. Extra fly jibs can be attached to the end, to make them reach even farther.

Electric winch

Load sensors

Upper load sheaves The sheaves are a row or block of pulleys around which the load cable winds. The upper set is usually called the fixed block.

Load cable

Telescopic section collar

Lower load sheaves The moving block is the lower row of pulleys or sheaves, with the hook or similar attachment below. The more pulleys and turns of cable, the lower the tension or pulling force in the cable, although the total load remains the same.

Telescopic boom Increasingly narrower sections slide out of each larger one, like a telescope, so the boom can extend to perhaps three times its unextended or collapsed length.

The pulley block or block-and-tackle system is the rope equivalent of a lever. You reduce the force needed to move a large load, but the load moves less distance. It makes big objects easier to shift, but in the end, the total work done is the same.

Low roof

Load

Forward cab The crane truck must be road-legal and so needs all the usual equipment like lights and warning horn.

Floating cranes need a massive heavy platform to remain steady

⚹ CRANES to the RESCUE

The biggest mobile cranes are on the water. Smaller floating cranes usually consist of a standard land-based crane mounted on a large floating raft-like platform called a pontoon. The biggest floating cranes are purpose-designed using similar engineering to oil rigs or platforms. They lift weights of more than 14,000 tonnes. These cranes are called out to raise sunken ships or barges, to unload vast cargo vessels, and to dredge or scoop up mud and other seabed materials, for instance, when making a shallow channel deeper.

CAR TRANSPORTER

Delivering 10 or 12 cars to the showroom or dealership would be costly if every car had a driver and its own fuel. The transporter packs as many vehicles as possible into its every available corner, with just one driver, and one diesel engine using fuel. The cars arrive fairly clean and with their odometers – the dials or readouts that record mileage travelled – still close to zero.

Eureka!

Multi-vehicle transporters for long-distance travel arrived when mass production by Ford and other car companies took off in the USA in the 1910s. However the most expensive, exclusive car makers still deliver their new products one at a time on a small transporter.

Whatever next?

People who can afford to can now have their new car delievered direct no matter where they are, even on a mountain top. They call a drop-in helicopter service that lowers the vehicle on a cable.

Upper deck After the upper deck is loaded, its rear is raised by the hydraulic struts, and then cars can be driven onto the lower deck.

New vehicles

Hydraulic strut This lowers the rear of the upper deck onto the rear of the lower deck, for loading the upper cars first.

✳ How does the CV JOINT work?

In most vehicles, turning power must be transmitted from the engine in the main body, to the axles and wheels, which move up and down with the suspension. The CV or constant-velocity joint allows this to happen. The drive shaft spun by the engine is connected through the flexible joint to the driven shaft to the wheel. It carries the turning action at the same constant speed (velocity).

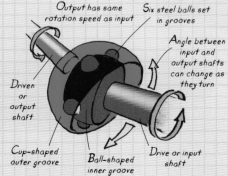

Output has same rotation speed as input

Six steel balls set in grooves

Angle between input and output shafts can change as they turn

Driven or output shaft

Cup-shaped outer groove

Ball-shaped inner groove

Drive or input shaft

Each load of vehicles presents different problems. Vans are tall and need plenty of headroom, while sports cars are low so an extra deck may be fitted.

Apart from delivering new vehicles, transporters also collect them for service or repairs, such as a steering fault recall, that can only be done at a properly equipped factory workshop.

✳ All FULL up

The latest transporters are very adaptable, with decks and ramps that alter length, height and angle. For each delivery, all the vehicle makes and models are fed into a computer program, which calculates their sizes and works out the deck and ramp set-up and loading order. The system also plots the most effective route between several drop-off sites, to save time and fuel.

Every inch of space is used when loading a big transporter

Chocks Small wedges called chocks stop the cars rolling, and they are also tied down using ratchet straps.

Car hire companies use transporters to take cars from a common drop-off point, such as an airport, back to the various pick-up locations.

Tractor unit Various types of tractor unit – cab plus engine – can pull the trailer, provided they have the correct electrical and hydraulic connections.

Fifth wheel The articulated link between the tractor unit and the transporter trailer is known as the 'fifth wheel'. It allows the trailer to manoeuvre easily from side to side.

Sump The oil that lubricates the inside of the engine drains to the sump or oil pan at the base, and is then pumped back around by the oil pump.

Alternator The alternator is driven by the diesel engine and generates electricity for the lights, displays, power steering, servo brakes, hydraulics and other systems.

A transporter's height and width are fed into a route planner that advises the best way to the destination, avoiding low bridges and narrow lanes due to roadworks.

TUNNEL BORING MACHINE

The tunnel boring machine (TBM) is like a giant mechanical worm that drills and scrapes its way through solid rock. It not only cuts into the rock but also sends away the resulting bits and pieces, called spoil, on a conveyor belt or rail wagons. TBMs are controlled by laser guides and other hi-tech systems. This is to ensure that they come out at the other end at exactly the right place.

Eureka!

TBMs were first used in the mid 1800s to cut under the Alps in Europe and make railway tunnels in eastern North America. They were based on lots of small drills, spikes or hammers and were not reliable. The first TBM with a rotary cutting head saw successful action in the 1950s.

Whatever next?

Adding micro-explosive capsules or pellets to the rotary cutting head can help to soften and shake apart the hardest rock by thousands of tiny blasts every second – provided the cutting head itself can cope.

The Channel Tunnel between England and France is 50.5 km in length and drops to a maximum depth of 75 m beneath the Channel.

Japan's Seikan Tunnel, 54 km long and completed in 1988, is the world's longest railway tunnel.

Conveyer belts Conveyors take the spoil away to the tunnel opening, or to secondary shafts that are dug down from the surface.

Rock

Each of the Channel Tunnel's two main bores is 7.6 m wide.

A massive TBM breaks through to finish off a new tunnel.

Services Electricity cables, hydraulic and pneumatic pipes, ventilation pipes and other supplies trail along behind the TBM.

✳ WORM or MOLE?

A TBM has features in common with a burrowing earthworm and a digging mole. It extends itself using propulsion jacks to force its way along a small distance, then shortens and moves bodily forwards, like a worm. The cutting head has ultra-hard teeth that scratch and scrape like a mole's front claws. Behind the TBM, more machines add ready-made curved lining sections onto the tunnel walls, or spray concrete-like mixtures that soon harden, to prevent collapse and cave-ins.

Linings Prefabricated (already made) sections of collar-like rings are installed as soon as it is practically possible, to stop the tunnel walls breaking.

The Channel Tunnel's TBMs were drilled into a side tunnel and left behind when the tunnel was complete.

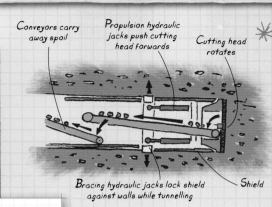

Conveyors carry away spoil

Propulsion hydraulic jacks push cutting head forwards

Cutting head rotates

Bracing hydraulic jacks lock shield against walls while tunnelling

Shield

✳ How do TBMs and CUTTING HEADS work?

The TMB's shield is a metal cylinder with the cutting head at the front. The head's one or more toothed wheels turn or rotate slowly with enormous power to grind the rock. Loosened spoil falls onto a collecting conveyor for removal. The shield is held against the walls by bracing hydraulic jacks so that propulsion jacks can push the cutting head into the rock. After a time, the bracing jacks loosen, the propulsion jacks shorten, the whole TBM moves forwards and the process starts again.

Bracing jacks These push sideways against the tunnel wall, so that as the propulsion jacks press the cutting head forwards, the shield does not slide backwards.

Shield The main boring machinery is housed in this large casing, which helps to keep most particles of rock away from the moving parts.

Cutting head The head or wheel turns at a slow and steady rate, perhaps once every few seconds. Its size determines the diameter or width of the tunnel.

Propulsion jacks These are hydraulic rams that force the cutting head forwards against the rock. They respond and adjust their pressure to the rock's varying hardness.

Rock Different types of rock have very different hardness and consistency. Narrow test drills in front of the main bore help to warn engineers about conditions ahead.

NASA CRAWLER TRANSPORTER

The world's largest self-powered tracked vehicles are two crawler-transporters at the USA's Kennedy Space Centre, Florida. They carry mobile launch platforms with rockets or space shuttles on top, from the vast assembly building where they are put together and prepared, out to the launch area. The crawler moves away before the rocket or shuttle blasts from the platform on its immense journey.

Eureka!

Early in its space programme the US decided to assemble its rockets in an upright position and move them like this to the launch area. This got around the problem of putting together a huge rocket lying down and then having to tip it upright.

Whatever next?

The crawlers have been on duty since the 1960s. They have many more missions to come as the US readies its replacements for the shuttles, known as Ares rockets.

The crawlers come back from the launch area with their empty platforms at just over 3 km/hour, which is twice as fast as they travel on the outward trip.

✳ SNAIL'S pace

The crawler-transporter must travel very slowly with its tall, weighty and possibly wobby load. The whole shuttle set-up with the white orbiter spaceplane, the huge bullet-shaped brown fuel tank (empty) and two white rocket boosters weighs more than 1200 tonnes, and the mobile launch platform it sits on is 3700 tonnes! The crawler's top speed loaded is just 1.5 kilometres per hour. So the average trip from the assembly building to the launch area takes more than five hours.

Generators The two Alco propulsion diesel engines turn four generators, each producing 1000 kilowatts, for the total of 16 electrical traction engines.

Laser-controlled hydraulic jacks alter the angle of the launch platform.

Gantry

Traction motor

The massive crawler slowly makes its way to the launch site

The whole crawler vehicle is 40 m wide and 35 m long and weighs 2400 tonnes.

Shoes Each shoe weighs almost one tonne and there are 57 in each crawler track.

Launch platform The crawler moves from under the mobile launch platform for blast-off, then carries the empty platform back to the assembly building.

The crawlers have travelled more than 4000 km since they began work. They carried the Saturn V rockets that lifted the Apollo moon missions into space.

Cooling fans

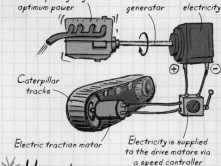

Diesel engines runs at constant speed giving optimum power

Drive shaft turns generator

Generator makes electricity

Caterpillar tracks

Electric traction motor

Electricity is supplied to the drive motors via a speed controller

Alco diesels The two massive propulsion diesel engines were adapted from diesel-electric railway locomotives.

✳ How does DIESEL-ELECTRIC PROPULSION work?

Petrol and diesel engines run best in a narrow range of turning speeds. Too fast or too slow and they are less efficient with fuel, and also their turning force, or torque, is weaker. These problems are reduced by the use of electric motors. In diesel-electric propulsion, a diesel engine stays running at its best speed and spins a generator, which produces electricity for very powerful electric traction motors to drive the wheels.

Radiators Because the crawler moves so slowly, the natural air flow over it is too small to keep the engines cool, so it has huge radiators and fans.

Fan motor

Control cabs There are two cabs, one on each side. The drivers talk to each other by radio and keep an eye on each other's displays and controls.

Tracks The eight crawler tracks were adapted from tank designs. Each track is 12 metres long and 3 metres tall. The tracks run in trenches 2 metres deep.

Apart from the propulsion diesel engines, each rated at 2750 horsepower, there are also two 1065 horsepower engines driving two generators for the hydraulics, cooling and other systems.

BUCKET WHEEL EXCAVATOR

Our modern world is hungry for energy and materials such as metals and chemicals. Most of these come from the Earth itself. Coal and valuable metal- and mineral-bearing rocks are mined, quarried, drilled, dug and excavated from the surface by massive machines. The bucket-wheel excavator is the most gigantic of all. It crawls along and 'eats' into the soil and rocks, moving hundreds of tonnes with just one turn of its big wheel.

Really big excavators take four years to build and need a crew of five or six operators. They can dig out more than 200,000 tonnes of coal or ore every day.

Eureka!

Mining went mechanical hundreds of years ago, with stone or iron hammers on wooden levers smashing into the area being mined. As the Industrial Revolution got under way in the 1700s it brought steam-powered excavators fuelled by the coal they were digging out.

Whatever next?

Already the biggest vehicles ever made, bucket-wheel excavators may grow even larger to cope with demands from today's industry. But they will probably be built and moved to the site as separate parts, then fitted together.

Frame The main frame is made of massive steel beams and girders welded together. The design basics are a combination of oil rigs and huge cranes.

Counterweight The long arm with the bucket wheel at its end puts enormous strain on the main vehicle. It is balanced or countered by a large container or hopper filled with spoil.

Cooling fans

Secondary unit The secondary crawler at the end of the second conveyor can be positioned to tip its material into waiting dump trucks, train wagons, another conveyor or onto a storage pile.

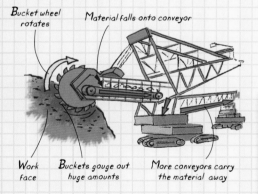

Bucket wheel rotates

Material falls onto conveyor

Work face

Buckets gouge out huge amounts

More conveyors carry the material away

* How do BUCKET WHEELS work?

The excavator's wheel rotates slowly as it moves into the rock, carried on the vast arm which swivels on the main vehicle. The sharp-edged buckets gnaw and nibble into the work face (see above), loosening and collecting pieces. As the buckets turn up and over, the material falls onto the conveyor. After one arm swivel, the whole machine moves along on its crawler tracks and repeats the action.

✳ Enormous APPETITES

Huge excavators work tirelessly day and night, scraping away ever-deeper layers as they creep across the landscape. They remove entire habitats of plants and animals, leaving behind bare soil or rocks. Modern quarrying and mining methods aim to replace the natural scenery by covering with earth, planting new trees and flowers, and bringing back the original creatures. This may happen after the empty area is filled with unwanted material, or spoil, from mines elswehere.

A giant excavator gulps up huge loads leaving the area bare

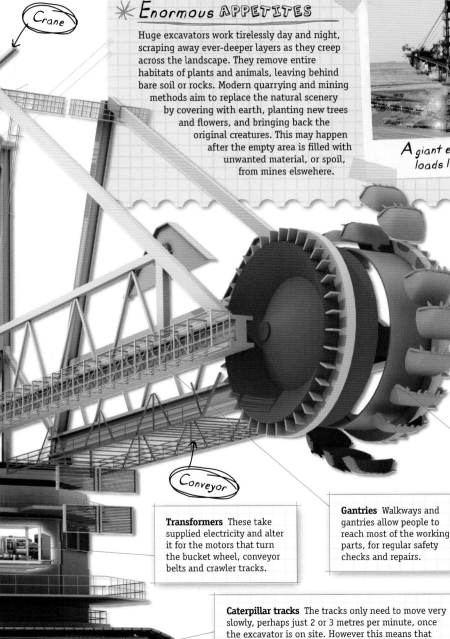

Crane

Conveyor

The German Takraf Bagger 293 holds the record as the largest-ever land vehicle. It is 200 m long and 96 m tall, and weighs 14,000 tonnes.

Buckets The bucket teeth and edges are made of ultra-hard metals such as titanium alloys, but even so, they need replacing often.

The largest bucket wheels measure more than 20 m across. Each bucket holds up to 15 cubic m – about the same amount as 100 bathtubs.

Transformers These take supplied electricity and alter it for the motors that turn the bucket wheel, conveyor belts and crawler tracks.

Gantries Walkways and gantries allow people to reach most of the working parts, for regular safety checks and repairs.

Caterpillar tracks The tracks only need to move very slowly, perhaps just 2 or 3 metres per minute, once the excavator is on site. However this means that travelling to new areas might take several weeks.

LONDON EYE

The UK's most popular paying tourist attraction is the London Eye, also known as the Millennium Wheel, on the south bank of the river Thames in central London. Built to mark the Millennium celebrations, and opened to the public in the year 2000, it is Europe's biggest 'entertainment wheel' and third-largest in the world. To emphasize the high up-and-over action of the trips or rides, they are known as 'flights'.

Eureka!

Theme park wheels or 'big wheels' are often known as ferris wheels after bridge designer George Ferris. He built the first working version in Chicago, USA in the 1890s for the World's Columbian Exposition. It was 80 metres tall.

Whatever next?

Since its opening the London Eye has been overtaken by taller wheels, first in Nanchang, China, then Singapore. The soon-to-be opened Beijing Great Wheel, also in China, will be bigger too, and opens in 2010.

Each flight or rotation takes about 30 minutes, with up to 800 passengers if all the capsules are full.

Peak times for London Eye trips are booked many weeks in advance. You can just turn up, but you might have a wait of several hours!

Spoke cables These 64 cables work by tension, or pull, only. They have little pushing strength, like the spokes of a bicycle wheel.

✳ What a FLIGHT!

Apart from St Paul's Cathedral towards the eastern side of central London, the city had no high-level observation areas for the public. This was one of the main ideas behind the London Eye. Passengers can see all the major landmarks including the Houses of Parliament, Buckingham Palace, Tower Bridge, and the skyscrapers of the City of London including the 'Gherkin', and beyond into Docklands. On a clear day the view extends for 40 kilometres, far beyond the city to the North Downs towards the south.

Hub and spindle The spindle is 23 metres long and the hub turns on it using massive bearings. The spindle and hub together weigh 330 tonnes, and the whole London Eye, with capsules, has a total weight of 2100 tonnes.

Around 3.5 million people 'fly the Eye' every year.

Stairs

Tourists enjoy a view of the Big Ben clock tower at the top of a flight

Drive wheels The wheel is rim-driven by friction, or rubbing. Lorry tyres turned by electric motors press onto the rim and make it move along.

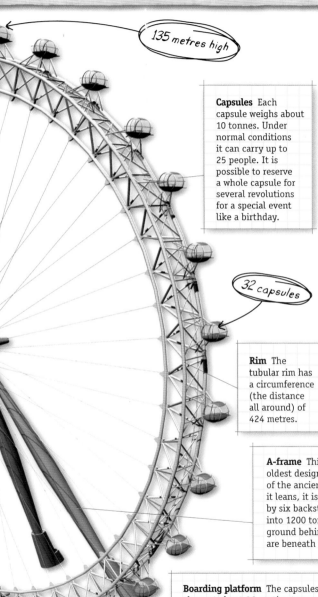

135 metres high

Capsules Each capsule weighs about 10 tonnes. Under normal conditions it can carry up to 25 people. It is possible to reserve a whole capsule for several revolutions for a special event like a birthday.

32 capsules

Rim The tubular rim has a circumference (the distance all around) of 424 metres.

A-frame This one of construction's oldest designs, used since the time of the ancient Romans. Although it leans, it is held securely in place by six backstay cables anchored into 1200 tonnes of concrete in the ground behind. Another 2200 tonnes are beneath the A-frame.

Boarding platform The capsules move along at about 26 centimetres per second, so the wheel does not usually have to stop as people get on or off.

Control room

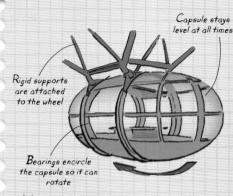

Capsule stays level at all times

Rigid supports are attached to the wheel

Bearings encircle the capsule so it can rotate

✳ How do the CAPSULES work?

Each pod or capsule is fitted into two sets of circular bearings or mounting rings that allow it to spin around or rotate. As the wheel turns, the capsule also turns within its bearings so that it stays horizontal – otherwise, at the top of the flight, the floor would become the ceiling! Movement sensors warn if a capsule gets stuck and starts to tilt as the wheel lifts it higher. Then the wheel can be reversed to bring the problem capsule back to the ground.

The capsules (also known as pods or gondolas) have all-round windows as well as emergency buttons and an intercom system to speak or listen to the staff.

The London Eye was first sponsored by British Airways. In 2005 the main sponsors changed in a complicated business deal. It then became Merlin Entertainments London Eye.

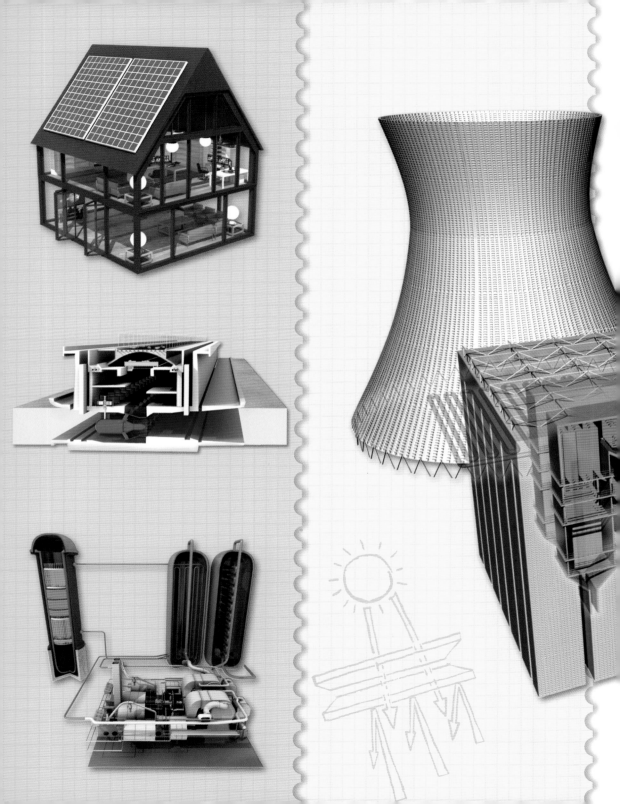

ENERGY
AND POWER

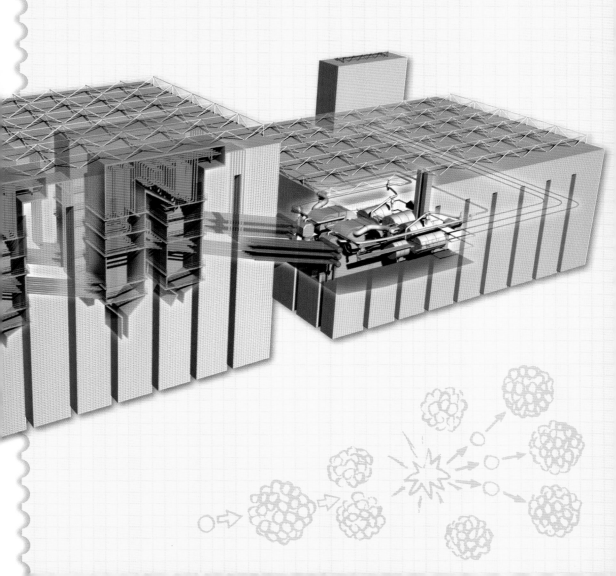

INTRODUCTION

Energy comes in many forms – movement, heat, light, sound, chemical substances in fuels, electrical and magnetic forces, and radioactivity. We use energy when we flick on a light switch, cook a meal or travel in a plane. Energy is never created or destroyed – it changes from one form to another. For example, a car's fuel energy changes into heat, sound and movement. In a television, electrical energy becomes tiny dots of coloured light.

Energy from fast-flowing water is used to generate electricity at a hydroelectric power station.

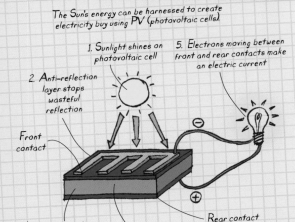
The Sun's energy can be harnessed to create electricity buy using PV (photovoltaic cells).

1. Sunlight shines on photovoltaic cell

5. Electrons moving between front and rear contacts make an electric current

2. Anti-reflection layer stops wasteful reflection

Front contact

3. Light hits junction between P-type and N-type silicon layers

4. Electrons jump from N- to P-layer

Rear contact

SUN POWER

Our world runs on energy changes. It started when ancient people burned wood, turning its chemical fuel energy into heat for cooking and warmth. Next came movement or kinetic energy – air blowing on a windmill's sails, and flowing water pushing a watermill's paddles, to grind grain or lift water from wells. These forms of energy can all be traced back to the Sun. Its light is captured by trees to grow wood. Its heat warms air to cause winds, and turns water into rising water vapour, which turns back into water droplets in clouds, falls as rain and flows downhill into rivers.

FOSSIL ENERGY

Giant oil platforms satisfy our fossil fuel needs – for now.

Our major energy sources today also come from the Sun – or rather, they did. Coal, oil and gas are fossil fuels. Coal is the preserved remains of plants from millions of years ago. Petroleum oil and natural gas come from preserved tiny sea plants and animals. These fuels provide five-sixths of all energy worldwide, especially for industry, vehicles, heating and electricity-generating power stations.

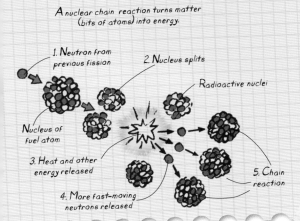

A nuclear chain reaction turns matter (bits of atoms) into energy.

1. Neutron from previous fission

2. Nucleus splits

Radioactive nuclei

Nucleus of fuel atom

3. Heat and other energy released

4. More fast-moving neutrons released

5. Chain reaction

ENERGY CRISIS

If we continue using fossil fuels at today's rate, they will probably run out in less than 200 years. Also, burning them makes greenhouse gases that speed up global warming and worsen climate change. The same goes for burning biofuels from plants such as wood, straw and oil, and biogas from rotting decay. There is little effect on global warming from a nuclear power station, once it's up and running. However it has other hazards, such as the risk of accidents and radioactive products that no one can make truly safe.

LOW-E-FUTURE

There are solutions to the energy crisis. We can reduce energy needs with more efficient transport, heating systems, lighting and insulation. Cleaner, greener, sustainable and renewable energy sources – hydro (flowing water), solar (Sun), wind, tides, waves and geothermal (heat from deep underground) can also be used.

The solar stove goes back to basics, focusing light from the Sun to boil water and cook food.

Fifty years from now people may look back at our energy waste and wonder: 'Didn't they care?'

The eco-friendly Subaru G4e has almost zero emissions and runs on electricity – G4e stands for 'Great for Earth'.

COAL MINE

About 250 years ago, coal was the main fuel driving the steam engines of the Industrial Revolution. Today it is the main fuel burned worldwide to generate electricity. Over the years, new sources of coal were discovered, mined in quantity and gradually used up. So mines and coal-burning power stations shifted around the world, and still do.

Eureka!

Small-scale coal mining dates back more than 2000 years to Roman times. Early large-scale mining began in the north-east of England, around Durham and Newcastle, from the 1700s.

Whatever next?

There is enough coal in the world to last for about 150 years. But coal-burning power stations are a major cause of global warming.

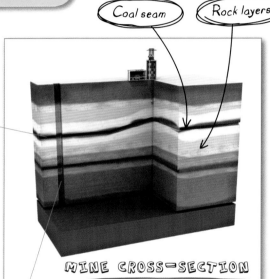

Coal seam

Rock layers

Tunnels The excavated tunnels follow the layers or seams of coal, angling up or down as necessary.

MINE CROSS-SECTION

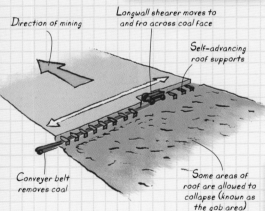

Direction of mining

Longwall shearer moves to and fro across coal face

Self-advancing roof supports

Conveyer belt removes coal

Some areas of roof are allowed to collapse (known as the gob area)

Ventilation Shafts to the surface and powerful fans remove dangerous explosive gases and heat from the tunnels and replace them with fresh air.

The world's greatest coal producer is China, closely followed by Russia, then India, Australia and South Africa.

✳ How do COAL FACE CUTTERS work?

About half of underground coal is cut by longwall mining. A machine called a longwall shearer moves to and fro across a wide face or wall of coal. Its rotating drum and sharp metal teeth scrape and loosen the coal into lumps. These fall onto a conveyor belt or a chain of large bucket- or pan-like containers. The belt or buckets carry the raw cut coal to the vertical conveyor or coal elevator. As the shearer eats its way forwards, supports or props hold up the ceiling of rock behind it for as long as needed. Then the ceiling is allowed to fall in or collapse.

Winding room The large reel or drum, driven by electric motors, winds in the cables to raise the elevator cages. It lets out the cables in a safe, controlled manner to lower the cages.

Headframe Also called the winding tower, this is usually built of steel girders or concrete beams to hold up the pulley gear.

Over the centuries a belief grew up that carrying a small lump of coal brings good luck — you will always have something to keep you warm.

Pulley axle bearings

Lifting cables Strong steel cables, hundreds or even thousands of metres long, lift the elevator cages for the miners and equipment.

Blasting coal from a surface mine

✳ SURFACE STRIP MINING

Coal is usually removed from open-cast or open-cut (surface) mines by the strip method. A long strip is drilled and the holes filled with explosives. A loud siren warns of the blast, which blows up the coal into small lumps. These are removed by excavators, draglines, dump-trucks or conveyors. Some coal conveyor belts are more than 15 kilometres long.

Headgear pulleys The cables run over a set of large pulleys (winding wheels) to raise and lower the cages from the pithead to the tunnels far below. Bigger pulleys mean easier winding and less bending strain on the cable.

About two-thirds of the world's coal is mined underground. The rest comes from open-cast mining of exposed seams at the surface, or those easily uncovered by removing a thin overlying rock layer known as overburden.

Elevator shaft

The oldest, hardest and most energy-packed type of coal is anthracite, formed up to 400 million years ago. Lignite is much softer, burns cooler, and may be less than two million years old.

OIL AND GAS PLATFORM

Some of the biggest structures in the world are oil and gas platforms. They are used anywhere there's petroleum oil or gas below – these two energy-packed fossil fuels often occur together. The principle of drilling is simple, as the toothed bit grinds its way deep into rocks. But it's a rough, tough process with constant dangers including fires, explosions and high-pressure blowouts.

Eureka!

The most famous early oil strike was by Edwin Drake near Titusville, Pennsylvania, USA in 1859. However other oil boreholes were drilled before this, such as the Bibi-Eibat well of 1848 near the city of Baku, Azerbaijan, by Russian engineer FN Semyenov.

At sea, exploratory oil rigs or platforms make the first boreholes to see if the area has any oil or gas. After this early work, a production platform may be brought to the site to extract the oil or gas over many years.

One of the world's tallest structures is the Petronius oil platform in the Gulf of Mexico. It stands 610 m above the ocean floor.

Crane Large onboard cranes unload food, water, scientific equipment and other stores from supply ships that moor alongside the platform. The rig must have enough supplies to last out several weeks of stormy weather when ships cannot reach it.

Accommodation block Like a small town, the platform has many amenities for the workers including bedrooms, kitchens, canteen, gymnasium, cinema and other leisure areas. There are also workshops for maintenance and repair jobs, and laboratories for scientific testing of rock, oil and gas samples.

✳ How does the DRILL BIT work?

Few machines have such a hard-wearing time as the oil drill bit. Its three toothed wheels interlock or mesh so that they rasp and bite through solid rock as the drill string spins. A specially made fluid 'mud' is pumped down the hollow inside of the drill string. It cools and lubricates the bit wheels, and flows back up around the drill string, carrying pieces or cuttings of rock. At the surface the expensive 'mud' is filtered and pumped down again.

Decks The busiest areas are the wide, flat main decks, which have the rotary table (turntable) and its electric motors.

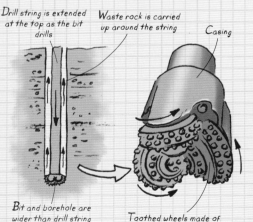

Drill string is extended at the top as the bit drills

Waste rock is carried up around the string

Casing

Bit and borehole are wider than drill string

Toothed wheels made of toughened metal rotate to scrape off and crush rock

Legs Some rigs are fixed, with legs that are flooded with water to stand on the ocean floor. Others have hollow legs and partially float, kept in position by cables or stays anchored to the seabed.

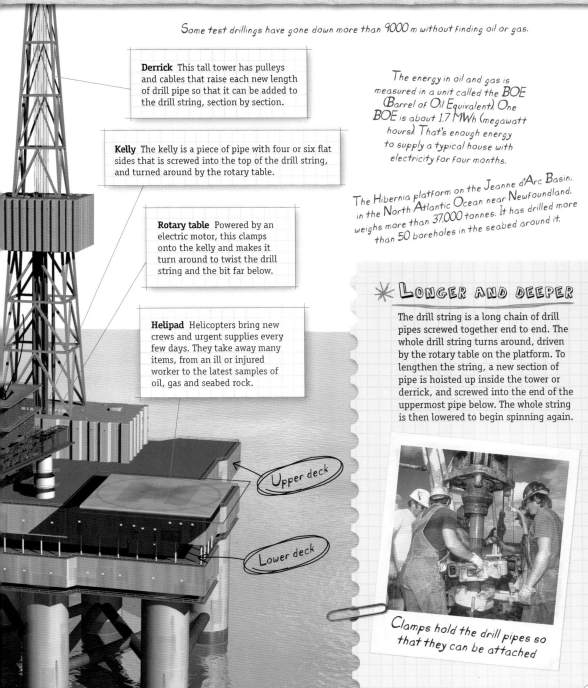

Some test drillings have gone down more than 9000 m without finding oil or gas.

Derrick This tall tower has pulleys and cables that raise each new length of drill pipe so that it can be added to the drill string, section by section.

Kelly The kelly is a piece of pipe with four or six flat sides that is screwed into the top of the drill string, and turned around by the rotary table.

Rotary table Powered by an electric motor, this clamps onto the kelly and makes it turn around to twist the drill string and the bit far below.

Helipad Helicopters bring new crews and urgent supplies every few days. They take away many items, from an ill or injured worker to the latest samples of oil, gas and seabed rock.

The energy in oil and gas is measured in a unit called the BOE (Barrel of Oil Equivalent). One BOE is about 1.7 MWh (megawatt hours). That's enough energy to supply a typical house with electricity for four months.

The Hibernia platform on the Jeanne d'Arc Basin, in the North Atlantic Ocean near Newfoundland, weighs more than 37,000 tonnes. It has drilled more than 50 boreholes in the seabed around it.

Upper deck

Lower deck

☀ LONGER AND DEEPER

The drill string is a long chain of drill pipes screwed together end to end. The whole drill string turns around, driven by the rotary table on the platform. To lengthen the string, a new section of pipe is hoisted up inside the tower or derrick, and screwed into the end of the uppermost pipe below. The whole string is then lowered to begin spinning again.

Clamps hold the drill pipes so that they can be attached

POWER STATION

There are about ten main kinds of power (electricity-generating) stations. They all convert or transform one source of energy into another – which is electricity. In fossil fuel power stations the energy source is coal, oil or gas. It is burned to make heat energy, which is converted using high-pressure steam and turbines into movement (kinetic) or mechanical energy, which spins the generators to make electricity (see page 224).

Eureka!

The first large-scale power generator for paying customers was the Pearl Street Station in New York City, USA. Built by the Edison Electric Light Company, it used coal as fuel and started in 1882 with about 85 customers.

Cooling tower Excess heat is removed in these giant towers. Newer power stations often lack cooling towers. Instead the heat is used to warm nearby buildings and to provide hot water.

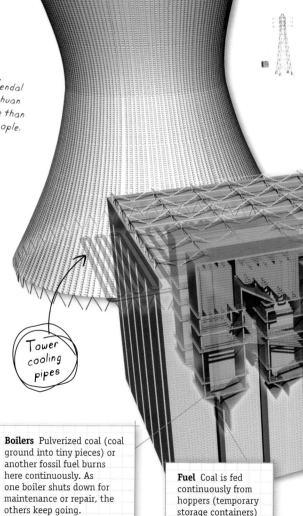

The world's biggest coal-fuelled power stations include the Kendal Power Station near Johannesburg, South Africa, and the Yuhuan Power Station in Zhejiang Province, China. They produce more than 4000 MW (megawatts), enough electricity for half a million people.

Each set of turbine blades is specially shaped and angled to get the most energy from the steam at that position

Steam leaves at much lower speed and pressure

Spinning shaft is connected to generator

High-pressure steam blasts into turbine intake

Tower cooling pipes

✳ How do TURBINES work?

A turbine is a device that converts the flow of a fluid, such as superheated steam or water, into a spinning motion. It has long, slim blades fixed onto a central shaft in a radial pattern, like the spokes of a wheel. Most turbines have several sets of blades. Their sizes and angles are carefully designed to extract the most energy from the steam, which loses speed and pressure as it moves past each set of blades.

Boilers Pulverized coal (coal ground into tiny pieces) or another fossil fuel burns here continuously. As one boiler shuts down for maintenance or repair, the others keep going.

Fuel Coal is fed continuously from hoppers (temporary storage containers) and ash is removed.

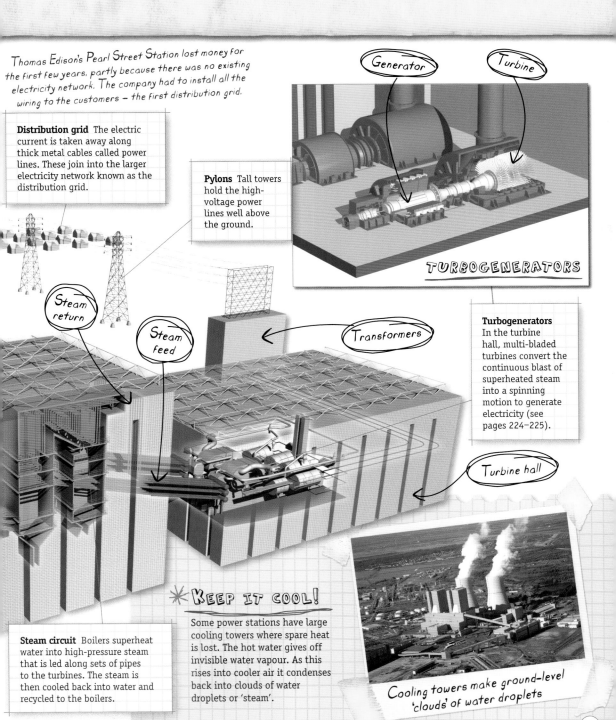

Thomas Edison's Pearl Street Station lost money for the first few years, partly because there was no existing electricity network. The company had to install all the wiring to the customers – the first distribution grid.

Distribution grid The electric current is taken away along thick metal cables called power lines. These join into the larger electricity network known as the distribution grid.

Pylons Tall towers hold the high-voltage power lines well above the ground.

Generator

Turbine

TURBOGENERATORS

Steam return

Steam feed

Transformers

Turbogenerators In the turbine hall, multi-bladed turbines convert the continuous blast of superheated steam into a spinning motion to generate electricity (see pages 224–225).

Turbine hall

Steam circuit Boilers superheat water into high-pressure steam that is led along sets of pipes to the turbines. The steam is then cooled back into water and recycled to the boilers.

✳ KEEP IT COOL!

Some power stations have large cooling towers where spare heat is lost. The hot water gives off invisible water vapour. As this rises into cooler air it condenses back into clouds of water droplets or 'steam'.

Cooling towers make ground-level 'clouds' of water droplets

ELECTRICITY GENERATOR

The heart of a power station is the generator, which changes mechanical or kinetic energy (the energy of movement) into electrical energy. The mechanical energy is usually in the form of a rotary or spinning motion. This is harnessed directly from moving wind or water, or from the superheated steam produced by burning fossil fuels such as coal, oil and gas, or biofuels like wood – even animal droppings!

Eureka!

Generators depend on an effect called electromagnetic induction. This was discovered in about 1831 by English scientist and experimenter Michael Faraday, and at around the same time, but separately, by US scientist and engineer Joseph Henry.

Whatever next?

The working temperature of a generator affects how much electricity it produces. Supercooled materials of the future could make the process more efficient, giving more electricity for less fuel.

Current take-off contacts

Casing

Some power station transformers deal with half a million volts

✳ TRANSFORM IT!

An electric current's pushing strength is measured in volts. Most power station generators make currents of a few thousand volts. But electricity travels best over long distances in power lines at hundreds of thousands of volts, because it loses less energy as heat and in other ways. Power station step-up transformers increase the voltage from the generators to 400,000 volts or more for the power lines. At the other end, step-down transformers reduce it for daily use, for example, to 240 volts in Britain.

Small generators driven by petrol engines can provide electricity at the normal household voltage almost anywhere in the world. There are even underwater models!

Stator The outer sets of wire coils (which stay still) make up the stator. Electricity fed into them from the grid makes a magnetic field around them by the electromagnetic effect.

Main shaft The rotor spins on a long shaft between high-precision bearings. It must keep turning at a steady speed to make sure the voltage output stays constant.

Most generators make AC, (alternating current). The electricity flows one way and then the other many times each second (for example, 50 times per second in Britain).

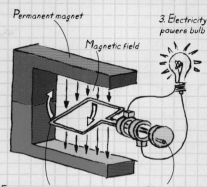

Permanent magnet

Magnetic field

3. Electricity powers bulb

2. Electricity is induced in wire coil rotor spinning in magnetic field

1. Mechanical energy turns wire coil rotor

Rotor The inner sets of wire coils that spin around are known as the rotor. As they turn within the magnetic field made by the stator, electricity is induced to flow through them.

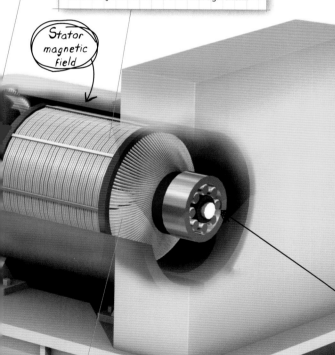

Stator magnetic field

Main shaft ball bearings

✳ How do GENERATORS work?

Electricity and magnetism make up one of the Universe's four basic forces – electromagnetism. If a wire moves near a magnet, electricity flows along it – this is electromagnetic induction. In a simple generator, a wire coil (the rotor) spins within the magnetic field of a permanent magnet made of iron. In a power station generator, the permanent magnet is replaced by another set of wire coils, the stator. As electricity passes through them they make a magnetic field by the electromagnetic effect. This is when a flowing electric current produces a magnetic field around itself. It's the 'opposite' of electromagnetic induction.

Windings Each of the rotor and stator coils has thousands of turns of wire, to produce as much electricity as possible. The windings are carefully designed so that their individual magnetic fields add together and do not interfere or cancel out, which would waste energy.

Because of the spinning motion of the generator, it produces AC rather than DC (direct current) which flows steadily one way only.

Hungarian scientist and priest Anyos Jedlik started experimenting with early generators in the 1820s. He made a small working version in the 1850s. Jedlik also invented carbonated or fizzy drinks.

NUCLEAR POWER STATION

Like most power stations, the nuclear generating plant has steam turbines, electricity generators and transformers. Its special feature is the way it produces the heat energy to boil the water for the turbines. It has a nuclear reactor where heat is made by splitting apart nuclei – the central parts of atoms. Atoms are the smallest pieces or particles of ordinary substance or matter.

Eureka!

The first nuclear chain reaction was made at the University of Chicago, USA in 1942. The team, led by Enrico Fermi, built the reactor, called a 'pile', in a converted racket court under the university's sport grandstand.

Whatever next?

In the USA, radioactive nuclear waste was due to be buried deep underground at a site called Yucca Mountain, Nevada. However in 2009, after 22 years of planning, the idea was dropped.

Fuel rods The nuclear fuel is usually made in the shape of long rods, which can be lowered into the main part of the reactor, surrounded by the moderator.

Containment The reactor vessel itself, shown here, is housed in an outer casing designed to keep in, or contain, any radioactive gases and other substances accidentally released.

Primary circuit feed

Primary circuit return

What is NUCLEAR FISSION?

A typical nuclear power station uses nuclear fission – the nuclei are broken apart (as opposed to nuclear fusion, see page 228). The fuel is usually a metal such as uranium or plutonium, whose huge atoms come apart easily. External energy starts the reaction, breaking up the nucleus of a fuel atom. This gives off fast-moving particles called neutrons, and these do the same to nearby nuclei, producing heat, radioactivity and other forms of energy as they go. The key is to control the chain reaction so it does not get out of hand and explode.

Control rods These rods take in, or absorb, excess neutron particles to make sure the chain reaction does not get out of hand. They can be raised or lowered to adjust the progress of the reaction.

Moderators The moderator substance slows down the neutron particles so that they produce continual heat rather than a sudden explosion. Moderators include water, graphite (a form of carbon) and, more rarely, the metal-like substance beryllium.

1. Neutron from previous fission smashes into nucleus

2. Nucleus splits

Radioactive nuclei

4. More fast-moving neutrons released

Nucleus of fuel atom

3. Heat and other energy is released

5. Neutrons smash into more fuel atom nuclei

A nuclear chain reaction

Secondary circuit return

✳ RADIOACTIVE WASTE

Primary circuit
Fluid circulates
between the
reactor and the
heat exchangers
inside this sealed
circuit or loop.

Nuclear reactions produce radioactive waste
of used or spent fuel, fluids, pipes and other
equipment. These give off harmful rays and
particles known as radiation. Some of this
waste will be dangerous for thousands of years.
For now, the waste is stored in deep ponds or
concrete containers. Some of the fuel is moved to
reprocessing plants to be treated and used again.

These giant radioactive waste tanks will
be encased in concrete and earth

Secondary circuit Heat from
the reactor is brought here
by the primary circuit. It
boils water into superheated
steam that flows through the
secondary circuit pipes to the
turbines and back.

The biggest nuclear
accident was at Chernobyl,
Ukraine, in 1986. Reactor
Number 4 exploded
and released clouds of
radioactive gases and dust.

The world's biggest nuclear power station is
Japan's Kashiwazaki-Kariwa Nuclear Power
Plant. Its seven reactors generate
8000-plus MW (megawatts).

Heat exchangers Heat
energy passes from the
primary circuit to the
secondary circuit in
these numerous loops
of pipes, keeping any
radioactivity in the
primary circuit.

Secondary
circuit
feed

At Chernobyl, about
50 people died at
the scene. More than
4000 died over the
following years from
the after-effects,
as gases and dust
spread across Europe
and exposed millions
of people to low-level
radiation. In some
areas even cows' milk
was too radioactive
to drink.

Steam turbogenerators The
high-pressure steam from the
secondary circuit spins turbines
that turn generators, as in most
other thermal (heat-based)
power stations.

FUSION POWER

Most nuclear power stations generate electricity from heat made by breaking apart big nuclei, known as nuclear fission. Experimental reactors are testing fusion power, where small nuclei are brought together and joined or fused into bigger ones, giving off heat in the process.

Eureka!

Fusion power is well known in nature. The Sun and other stars make their immense amounts of light and heat using it. The idea for a fusion reactor to generate electricity was suggested by George Thompson and Moses Blackman as long ago as the 1940s.

Whatever next?

So far, fusion experiments have used up more energy than they produced. ITER, an international reactor being built in Cadarache, France, should produce more energy than it uses when it starts up around 2015–2020.

The Sun's natural fusion power happens in its centre or core, where the temperature is 15 million degrees Celsius. Here, hydrogen nuclei fuse together in the gigantic heat and pressure to make helium.

Experimental fusion reactors include JET, the Joint European Torus (a torus is a doughnut-shaped ring) at Culham, England, and KSTAR in Korea. KSTAR's magnets weigh 300 tonnes.

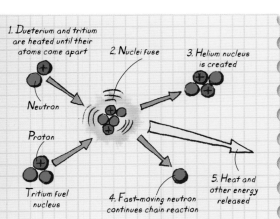

1. Dueterium and tritium are heated until their atoms come apart

2. Nuclei fuse

3. Helium nucleus is created

Neutron

Proton

Tritium fuel nucleus

4. Fast-moving neutron continues chain reaction

5. Heat and other energy released

Toroidal magnets The incredibly hot plasma inside the reactor is kept trapped or confined by magnetic fields from several sets of electromagnets. The outer toroidal magnets make a doughnut-shaped field.

☀ How does FUSION work?

Fusion fuel is deuterium or tritium or a combination of both. These substances are naturally occurring heavier forms of hydrogen, the lightest substance with the smallest, simplest atoms. The fuel is heated to millions of degrees, into a form or state of matter called plasma. Its atoms come apart and two of their nuclei join or fuse to make a bigger nucleus of the substance helium. As this happens, a fast-moving neutron is given off and fuses two more nuclei, and so on, in a chain reaction. The plasma is so hot it would melt any substance it touches. So it must be held in place in the reactor by intense magnetic fields.

Tokomak The main part of the reactor is a doughnut-shaped vessel called a tokomak. Sets of huge wire coils around it work as electromagnets.

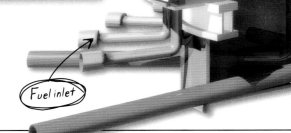

Fuel inlet

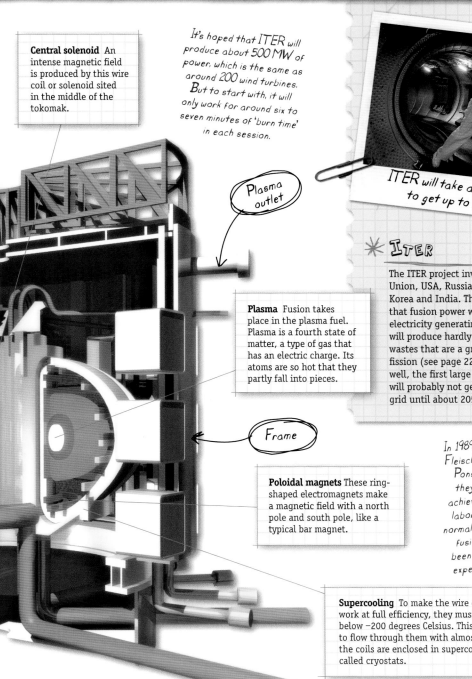

Central solenoid An intense magnetic field is produced by this wire coil or solenoid sited in the middle of the tokomak.

It's hoped that ITER will produce about 500 MW of power, which is the same as around 200 wind turbines. But to start with, it will only work for around six to seven minutes of 'burn time' in each session.

Plasma outlet

ITER will take about 20 years to get up to full power

Plasma Fusion takes place in the plasma fuel. Plasma is a fourth state of matter, a type of gas that has an electric charge. Its atoms are so hot that they partly fall into pieces.

Frame

Poloidal magnets These ring-shaped electromagnets make a magnetic field with a north pole and south pole, like a typical bar magnet.

✳ ITER

The ITER project involves the European Union, USA, Russia, Japan, China, South Korea and India. The eventual hope is that fusion power will generate heat for an electricity generating station, and that it will produce hardly any of the radioactive wastes that are a great problem for nuclear fission (see page 227). Even if ITER works well, the first large fusion power stations will probably not generate electricity for the grid until about 2050.

In 1989 scientists Martin Fleischmann and Stanley Pons announced that they had managed to achieve fusion power in a laboratory test tube at normal temperatures – 'cold fusion'. But no one has been able to repeat their experiments successfully.

Supercooling To make the wire coil electromagnets work at full efficiency, they must be supercooled to below −200 degrees Celsius. This allows electricity to flow through them with almost no resistance. So the coils are enclosed in supercooling containers called cryostats.

HYDROELECTRIC POWER STATION

Unlike fossil fuel and nuclear power stations, the hydroelectric generating plant does not have a direct heat source. Its energy comes from water flowing along a river. The water runs downhill under the force of gravity, having fallen as rain far upstream. That rain was once water in clouds, and it was originally evaporated from the sea and lakes by the heat of the Sun. So a hydroelectric power station is, in effect, Sun-powered.

Eureka!

An early use of flowing water for energy was the waterwheel. This was common in ancient Greece, more than 2000 years ago, to turn millstones and grind grain into flour, and to raise river water up into ditches for crops.

Whatever next?

Hydroelectricity is increasing around the world since it does not involve burning fuels that contribute to global warming. Norway produces 99 percent of its electricity in this way.

The Itaipu Complex of dams on the Parana River between Brazil and Paraguay is 7.2 km long and produces 14,000 MW.

Sluice gates and spillways If the river floods and too much water builds up behind the dam, sluice gates or flood gates are opened to let some of it flow away downstream.

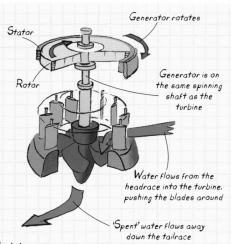

Stator

Generator rotates

Rotor

Generator is on the same spinning shaft as the turbine

Water flows from the headrace into the turbine, pushing the blades around

'Spent' water flows away down the tailrace

Dam The dam is in effect a wall across the river, holding back the water on the upstream side. It is thicker at the base to cope with increased water pressure at depth.

✳ How does HYDROELECTRICITY work?

The hydroelectric turbine has angled blades that are spun by the force of water pushing past them. The water is made to build up behind the dam to give it increased pressure or pushing force, known as the height or 'head' of water. This body of water is also a store or reserve for times when it rains less and the river level falls, giving it the name reservoir.

Tailrace This pipe or duct carries the water away from the turbine, through the base of the dam to the downstream section of the river.

Downstream flow

The first hydroelectric power station was built in 1882 on the Fox River in Wisconsin, USA – just after the Pearl Street Station, New York.

Reservoir Water trapped behind the dam builds up into an artificial lake called a reservoir. This can be very useful for supplying water to farmers' fields – and for swimming, sailing, fishing and other leisure pursuits.

Control vanes The angle of these vanes or slats is adjusted to keep the flow of water steady, depending on its pressure, which in turn depends on the surface level of the reservoir.

Shaft

Generator The whole turbine set-up must be in a waterproof casing to keep water away from the generator just above.

Thrust bearing This huge ball-bearing takes up the stresses and pressure of the water so that they do not affect the electricity generator.

Headrace (penstock) This pipe or duct takes the water from the inlets to the turbines. Grilles or meshes over the inlets keep out large objects.

Blades The turbine blades are shaped to take as much movement energy as possible from the water as it flows past.

TURBINE

Inlet

Turbines

The world's largest power stations are hydroelectric. The Three Gorges Complex on the Chang-Jiang (Yangtze) River in China generates 22,000 MW.

✳ DAM BYPASS

Hydroelectric plants do not produce greenhouse gases or radioactive wastes. But they do alter a river's flow, flood the upstream area with a reservoir and take water away from downstream regions, all of which greatly alters local wildlife. The dam also blocks the way for animals that journey or migrate along the river. Some dams have a series of pools at the side. Fish such as salmon can jump from one pool to the next, a small distance each time, to get past the dam.

The 'fish ladder' acts as a dam bypass

GEOTHERMAL ENERGY

At its centre or core, the Earth is exceedingly hot – probably more than 5000 degrees Celsius. It gradually cools to an average of just 15 degrees Celsius at the surface. Even though we cannot drill very deep, we can still get down to the hot rocks and bring their heat energy to the surface, to warm our buildings and water, and to generate electricity.

Eureka!

The first geothermal energy plants to provide heating for homes and buildings began in the 1890s, in places as far apart as Paris, France and Boise, Idaho, USA. The earliest attempts to generate electricity from naturally heated steam were made at Larderello, Italy, in the 1900s. Japan followed in 1919 and California, USA in 1921.

Whatever next?

Experiments are taking place to see if it is possible to 'tap' runny lava, the red-hot molten (liquid) rock from volcanoes, and use its heat to produce electricity.

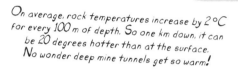

On average, rock temperatures increase by 2 °C for every 100 m of depth. So one km down, it can be 20 degrees hotter than at the surface. No wonder deep mine tunnels get so warm!

Production (extraction) boreholes Pipes carry up very hot, high-pressure water and steam from deep underground.

Cool crust rocks

Geothermal plant

Injection boreholes Water is pumped down at great pressure to replenish the water and steam taken up the production boreholes, otherwise the deep rock layers would gradually dry out.

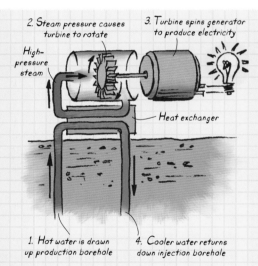

2. Steam pressure causes turbine to rotate

3. Turbine spins generator to produce electricity

High-pressure steam

Heat exchanger

1. Hot water is drawn up production borehole

4. Cooler water returns down injection borehole

✳ How does GEOTHERMAL ENERGY work?

Heat from inside the Earth is carried up to the surface by a liquid substance or medium, commonly water, in the primary circuit. As the water warms, it rises naturally, gets to the surface, passes its heat energy to water in the secondary circuit, cools and is pumped back down again. In the secondary circuit, water or a similar 'flash vapour' liquid boils and drives the turbogenerators.

In parts of Iceland, New Zealand and Japan, hot rocks are just below the surface. These regions are best for development of geothermal energy.

Hot water and steam blast from a natural geyser

Rock strata (layers)
The boreholes or wells pass through many layers of rock until they get to heat-bearing strata.

✳ THE GEYSER BLOWS!

We can see the Earth's natural heat energy at work when a geyser erupts. Deep below the geyser is a network of narrow holes and cracks in the hot rocks. Water trickles into them from the rocks around and becomes heated. Its pressure and temperature build up until they are high enough to make the water spurt up to the surface. The pressure is released, then more water starts to trickle in, and the whole process repeats, usually at regular intervals.

Cooling exhausts
Excess heat is lost or vented to the air through cooling towers.

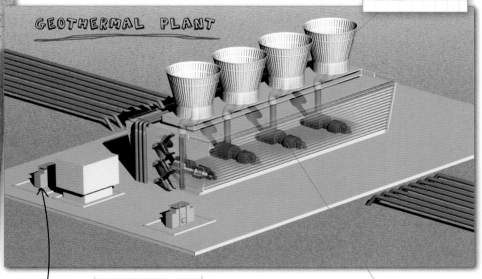

GEOTHERMAL PLANT

Pumping station

Production well base

Magma Far below the surface the rock is so hot and pressurized that it is partly melted and known as magma. This is what erupts from volcanoes as red-hot runny lava.

Much of the heat inside the Earth is left over from when the planet formed out of a gas cloud. The cloud squeezed together under its own gravity, about 4600 million years ago.

Generators The turbines spin generators as in other types of power stations. The biggest geothermal plants produce up to 1000 MW.

TIDAL BARRAGE

As the Earth spins around every 24 hours, the Moon pulls with its force of gravity on the seas and oceans. The Moon causes the water to 'bulge' towards it, and as the Earth slowly turns beneath, the bulge travels around the planet. We see the bulge as the raised sea level of a high tide, followed by a low tide as that part of the Earth carries on spinning away from the Moon. The energy in this vast and predictable water movement can be harnessed as tidal power for electricity.

Whatever next?

Waves are caused by winds, due to the Sun's heating effect on the atmosphere (see page 236). But capturing wave power is difficult since big storms can easily destroy even the toughest equipment.

A tidal barrage and its machinery must be cleaned regularly to avoid build-up of seaweeds and encrusting animals such as mussels, barnacles and limpets.

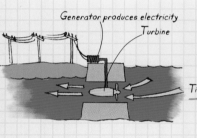

Generator produces electricity
Turbine
Tide comes in

Drive shaft and gearing from turbine to generator
Tide goes out

Blades are spun by water and work in either direction

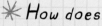

Inspection walkway

Gantry crane

✳ How does TIDAL POWER work?

Some tidal turbines are bi-directional. This means the blades spin one way as the tide comes in and water forces its way past the blades, from the open sea into the bay or estuary (river mouth). Then as the tide goes out and the sea level falls, the flow reverses and the blades spin the other way. Electrical circuits make sure the electricity current stays the same.

Generators The electricity generators (see page 224) convert the spinning motion of the turbines into electric current.

Turbines The turbines are in ducts that channel the water with greatest force over their blades.

Shrouded turbines, with the blades inside a collar-like shroud, are being tested on Australia's Gold Coast and Canada's west coast. The shrouds increase the speed of the water through the turbine.

Road crossing The barrage works as a bridge to allow road traffic and perhaps a railway to cross the water.

Barrage The barrage is a wall-like barrier or dam across the narrow part of a river or bay. The site is chosen for its high tidal range (difference in sea levels between low and high tide).

Tidal power stations only make electricity for 6–12 hours in every 24, when the water flows fastest. They do not generate as the tidal flow slows down around the high and low water marks.

Sluice gates The water flow past the turbines is controlled by raising or lowering huge sluice gates, for example, to carry out repairs.

Sluice gate recess

The river Rance tidal barrage and power station in north-west France began producing electricity in 1967. The generating part is 333 m long and the whole barrage measures 755 m in length.

✳ SUPER-BARRAGE

There have been plans for a giant tidal barrage power station across the estuary of the river Severn between south-west England and south Wales. In one design the barrage would be over 15 kilometres long and produce about six percent of all electricity used in England. However the effects on fish, shellfish, wading birds and other wildlife would be enormous. The way sand and silt are carried away by the river would also be disrupted.

The river Rance tidal power station has a peak output of 240 MW

WIND TURBINES

L ike hydroelectricity and solar power, wind energy comes from the Sun. Its heat warms different parts of the land, sea and air by varying amounts. As hotter air rises, cooler air moves along to take its place – and this moving air is the wind blowing.

Eureka!

Wind power is not new. More than 1200 years ago windmills in the Middle East turned millstones to grind grains into flour, and lifted water out of rivers up into the irrigation ditches for crops.

A huge wind turbine in Emden, Germany has rotor blades 126 m across and produces 7 MW of electricity.

Spinner

Blade

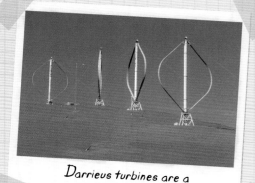

Darrieus turbines are a vertical axis design

✳ NEW DESIGNS

Engineers test new wind turbine designs to see if they work better in very light or strong winds. In the Darrieus version the main shaft or axis of the turbine is upright. This vertical axis design reduces strain on the bearings compared to the design where the rotor shaft is parallel with the ground, known as horizontal axis.

Pylon The tall tower holds the rotor blades high above ground level, so that they can rotate safely where the wind is stronger. Steps inside the tower allow engineers to get up to the machinery in the pod.

✳ How does VARIABLE PITCH work?

To produce a regular flow and voltage of electricity, and avoid wind damage, the generator should turn at a constant speed. So the rotor blades change their angle or pitch. In high wind they swivel more edge-on to the moving air. The pushing force on them is less, which prevents their spin speed rising. In weak wind the blades twist more flat-on to the wind, for more turning force, to prevent their spin speed reducing.

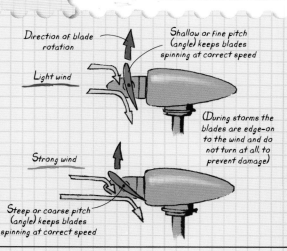

Direction of blade rotation

Shallow or fine pitch (angle) keeps blades spinning at correct speed

Light wind

(During storms the blades are edge-on to the wind and do not turn at all, to prevent damage)

Strong wind

Steep or coarse pitch (angle) keeps blades spinning at correct speed

Whatever next?

A gyromill is a wind turbine on a long cable. Its whirling rotor blades generate electricity that comes down the cable, and the blades also work like helicopter rotors to keep the gyromill up.

Wind turbines are also called aerogenerators or wind power units. Lots of them in a windy place are known as a wind farm.

Pod casing (nacelle)

Once built and installed, wind turbines do not produce greenhouse gases. However they can be noisy and a hazard to birds, and spoil the view in beautiful scenery.

Gearbox The gearing system changes the slow rotation of the rotor blades to a faster spinning motion suitable for the generator.

Pitch control The angle or pitch of the rotor blades changes according to the speed of the wind.

Hub Strong bearings cope with enormous stresses as they allow the rotor shaft to spin in the hub.

Generator The mechanical spinning movement from the rotor is changed into electrical energy (see page 224) which travels along cables, down the pylon and away underground.

Some turbines have to be stopped at certain times because the sunlight flashing rapidly off their shiny blades can affect people nearby, causing headaches and even fits or convulsions.

In most wind turbines the blades are designed to spin about once every three to four seconds.

Blade The rotor blades are usually made of combined fibreglass-reinforced plastic (GRP) or a similar light, strong composite material.

Yaw control The pod swings around or yaws on a swivel bearing, to keep the rotor blades pointing into the wind.

Blade shape The blade surface moves through the air much more slowly near the hub compared to the tip. So the blade shape alters along its length, with the best angle and curve to get the most energy from the wind at that place.

Wind-generated electricity is far from constant, so other forms of generation will always be needed – or giant batteries to store the electricity.

BIOMASS ENERGY

Material from living things is known as biomass. Many types of biomass can be used as fuel for energy, either directly or indirectly. Wood, straw and other plant products are burned directly for warmth, cooking and to generate electricity. Rotting plants, animal bodies, droppings and other biomass decay to produce biogases such as methane, which can also be burned to provide heat or electricity.

Some power stations are designed to burn chicken droppings – plentiful where chickens are raised in huge sheds for eggs and meat.

Eureka!

Simple biogas digesters or fermenters were used in ancient times in the Middle East, India and China. They were built from stone slabs and covered by wooden poles, branches, twigs and soil. The basic design is still the same in modern versions, although the building materials have changed.

Whatever next?

More and more waste disposal landfill sites have pipes to collect the methane given off by rotting leftover food, vegetable peelings, garden cuttings and similar materials. This is partly for energy and partly for safety, to prevent the methane exploding!

Inlet Leftover food, plant matter from cooking and gardening, animal wastes and effluent – all together known as the feedstock – are added through the inlet. There is usually a 'gas-trap' to prevent smells escaping.

Fixed dome The strong dome-shaped cover is rigid enough to prevent anything that moves over it above ground from falling into the tank below.

✳ INCINERATORS

Incineration, or burning thoroughly at very high temperatures, is one way to get rid of rubbish that might otherwise go to landfill sites. It also produces great amounts of heat, typically burning at more than 800 degrees Celsius, to warm buildings or generate electricity. This technology is known as WtE, waste-to-energy. However incinerating mixed rubbish usually gives off poisonous fumes and leaves behind toxic ash waste. Cleaning the fumes before they go out into the air, and disposing of the ashes, can cause considerable problems.

BIOGAS DIGESTER

Biogas Most biomass rots anaerobically (without oxygen) to give off a mix of methane (about two-thirds), also carbon dioxide and small traces of nitrogen, ammonia, sulphur dioxide and hydrogen sulphide. This last gas gives a 'rotten eggs' smell.

Incinerators are heat sources for generating electricity

For thousands of years, people in country areas burned the dried dung or droppings of animals as fuel, including dung from horses, cows and chickens.

How do BIOMASS AND BIOGAS burners work?

Biomass can be burned in solid form for hot water, like coal or similar fuel, by adding it in small amounts from a storage container called a hopper. Biogas is burned in the same way as natural gas (see page 220) – the two are similar in many ways, both containing mostly methane. The size of the gas jet or nozzle is important, and so is the air flow for the flame. The methane must mix with the correct amount of air to burn steadily, otherwise it might go out – or explode.

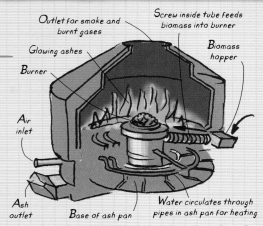

Outlet for smoke and burnt gases

Screw inside tube feeds biomass into burner

Glowing ashes

Biomass hopper

Burner

Air inlet

Ash outlet

Base of ash pan

Water circulates through pipes in ash pan for heating

Cap The cap is sealed to keep out air, but it can be removed when the tank is emptied, cleaned or repaired.

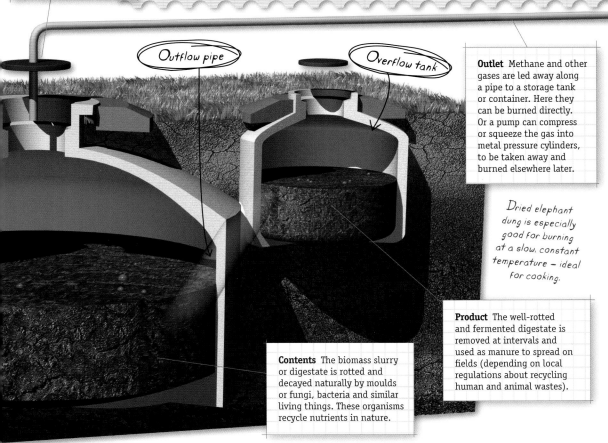

Outflow pipe

Overflow tank

Outlet Methane and other gases are led away along a pipe to a storage tank or container. Here they can be burned directly. Or a pump can compress or squeeze the gas into metal pressure cylinders, to be taken away and burned elsewhere later.

Dried elephant dung is especially good for burning at a slow, constant temperature – ideal for cooking.

Contents The biomass slurry or digestate is rotted and decayed naturally by moulds or fungi, bacteria and similar living things. These organisms recycle nutrients in nature.

Product The well-rotted and fermented digestate is removed at intervals and used as manure to spread on fields (depending on local regulations about recycling human and animal wastes).

SOLAR PANELS

Many forms of energy we rely on every day come from our nearest star, the Sun. They include its light to see by, its warmth and the wind turbines and hydroelectric dams that generate electricity. Another way to produce electricity is to harness sunlight directly by the electronic devices known as photovoltaic or PV cells. These are grouped together on sheets and usually known as 'solar panels'.

Eureka!

The first solar cell was made in 1883 by Charles Fritts. It converted only about one-hundredth of the light energy falling on it into electrical energy.

The latest ATF (advanced thin film) photovoltaic cells are 25 percent efficient, which means they convert one-quarter of the light energy hitting them into electrical energy.

A typical photovoltaic cell produces about 14 milliwatts of electricity. This is enough for a small electronic device such as a calculator.

✳ How do SOLAR (PV) CELLS work?

In a photovoltaic cell are two layers of silicon. In one layer, mixing or 'doping' with tiny amounts of boron gives the silicon 'holes' where negative electrons should be, making the layer positive, the P-type layer. In the N-type layer the silicon is doped with small quantities of phosphorus, which make it negative, with extra electrons. When light energy hits the boundary between the two layers, it knocks the negative electrons from the N to the P side. This happens to millions of electrons every second and the moving electrons set up the electric current.

1. Sunlight shines on photovoltaic cell

2. Anti-reflection layer stops wasteful reflection

Front contact

3. Light hits junction between P-type and N-type silicon layers

5. Electrons moving between front and rear contacts make an electric current

Rear contact

4. Electrons jump from N- to P-layer

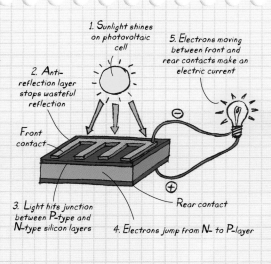

Sunlight

Electron jumps to next atom

Nucleus

Electron

✳ What is ELECTRIC CURRENT?

Electricity is a flow of electrons. These are particles that make up the outer parts of atoms. They whizz around the central nucleus of the atom in layers or 'shells' at different distances from the nucleus. In some substances, mainly metals, the outermost electrons are easily knocked from one nucleus to the next, causing a current to flow.

Whatever next?

New materials and substances for solar cells, and mass producing them in greater numbers, will make solar power cheaper. But it will probably never become economical in cloudy places.

If the Sahara Desert was covered in solar panels, it would provide about 40 times the amount of electricity used by the whole world.

Frame The small, individual photovoltaic cells are protected by an outer frame and joined together in a grid network as a photovoltaic array or 'solar panel'. Several panels connected together make bigger, more useable quantities of electricity.

A planned 32-hectare solar park in Germany, with 57,000 photovoltaic panels, should provide enough electricity for 3000 homes.

The 1 MW 'solar furnace' thermal power station at Odeillo, France

✳ THERMAL SOLAR POWER

In addition to light, another way of using the Sun directly as an energy source is to trap its thermal or heat energy, by the clever design of houses and other buildings (see page 244). Another option is the thermal power station. Here the Sun's infrared or heat rays are reflected and concentrated by many curved mirrors into one small collecting area, producing a temperature of 3000 degrees Celsius. This is more than hot enough to boil water into steam for turbines and generators.

FUEL CELL AND ELECTRIC MOTOR

Will 'clean' electric cars ever take over from petrol and diesel ones with their dangerous greenhouse gas exhaust fumes? One problem is that the batteries needed to store enough electricity to power a car for a day are bulky and heavy. The fuel cell is a portable generating device small and light enough for use in cars. It has no moving parts to wear out and makes a continual flow of electricity from the simplest substance known – hydrogen gas.

Eureka!

Scientist and lawyer William Grove developed the idea of the fuel cell in the 1830s. He called it the 'gas voltaic battery'. Grove also invented a new kind of chemical battery that produced a much higher voltage than others of the time. But it gave off harmful fumes and was soon abandoned.

The first practical use of fuel cells was in the US Gemini spacecraft in the mid 1960s.

Whatever next?

If fuel cells catch on in cars, then we will no longer fill up with petrol or diesel, but with hydrogen gas. However changing all the refuelling stations to hydrogen would probably take at least 20 years.

Most fuel cells run on hydrogen as fuel, with oxygen from the air. But there are versions that use alcohol as fuel, or natural gas, or even the poisonous gas chlorine.

✳ How do FUEL CELLS work?

Pass an electric current through water, between a positive contact or anode and a negative cathode, and the particles of water (H_2O) split into hydrogen and oxygen. This is electrolysis of water. A fuel cell does the reverse, combining hydrogen and oxygen to make water and produce electricity. The anode and cathode are separated by a PEM (proton exchange membrane). As hydrogen flows in, the electrons in its atoms (see page 241) separate at the anode and flow away along a wire as the electric current, finally returning to the fuel cell cathode.

1. Hydrogen fuel flows past anode (+ contact)

6. Electrons flow out along wire as electric current

2. Oxygen from air flows past cathode (– contact)

PEM separates anode and cathode

5. Electrons return to cathode and join with protons to make water, a waste product

3. Hydrogen splits into positive protons and negative electrons

4. Protons can pass across PEM to cathode (but electrons cannot)

MEA The membrane electrode assembly houses one PEM (see left) unit of the 'stack'. Many units are butted end to end for more electric current.

Gas flow plate Hydrogen and oxygen flow easily to the exchange membrane along these grooves.

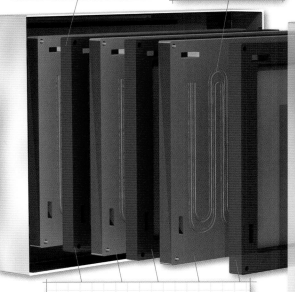

Stack A single fuel cell produces only about 0.6 volts of electric current. So many of them are linked together, as with photovoltaic cells, into a fuel cell stack that generates useable amounts of electricity.

Brushes Smooth carbon-based pads called brushes press on the commutator and pass electricity to it.

Permanent magnet north pole

Magnet A powerful permanent magnet around the armature produces a non-changing magnetic field, inside which the armature rotates.

Shaft

Permanent magnet south pole

ELECTRIC MOTOR

Commutator This set of contacts spins around with the armature. It receives electricity from the brushes and feeds it through the wire coils, changing the direction of electricity in the coils as they turn.

Armature Many separate sets of wire coils make up the armature. Their magnetic fields alternately push or pull against the stationary field of the permanent magnet to make the armature spin.

MOTORS EVERYWHERE!

The most effective way to turn electrical energy into moving or kinetic energy is the electric motor. It works in the reverse way to an electric generator, using the electromagnetic effect (see page 225). The wire coils are electromagnets that interact with the magnetic field of the permanent magnet around them, causing the coils to spin on a shaft. Electric motors have thousands of applications, from huge electric trains to electric toothbrushes and computer hard disc drives.

An electric motor is very efficient. It turns more than 80 percent of the energy put into it, as electricity, into movement energy. This compares with . . .

. . . less than 25 percent efficiency in a typical petrol engine.

Casing

FUEL CELL

Many everyday tools and appliances rely on electric motors

ENERGY-SAVING BUILDING

Burning coal, oil and other fuels is causing great changes to our world. The greenhouse gases produced mean global warming and climate change. To reduce the damage, we must design buildings that use natural, sustainable forms of energy, and use them more efficiently. This includes heat, light, electricity, and saving water and other resources.

Eureka!

The solar stove uses a dish-shaped shiny metal reflector to concentrate the Sun's heat onto a pot, pan or oven. The first solar box oven was invented in 1767. Modern versions produce temperatures of more than 400 degrees Celsius.

A bathful of drinking water takes the same amount of energy to treat and purify as a flat-screen television left on for about 24 hours.

A typical house loses about one-quarter of its heat through the roof, one-third through the walls, one-fifth through the windows, one-tenth through the doors and the rest into the ground below.

Large triple-glazed windows facing the midday Sun are one of the best ways of saving energy in a house.

Pipe loops of a ground source heating system are ready to be buried

❋ HEAT FROM THE GROUND

Every day the Sun shines on the ground and its heat soaks into the soil, plants and rocks. Ground source heating systems gather this heat and carry it into a building, to help warm rooms and produce hot water. The system has loops of pipes buried in the ground around, through which water circulates. It takes in warmth from the ground, which is extracted by a heat pump in the building. The heat pump works in a similar but opposite way to a fridge, moving heat one way and cold the other way.

Chimney Internal ducts from the chimney carry warm air around the dwelling to heat the other rooms. In hot weather they work as cooling ducts.

Sun-trap windows Windows that face the Sun allow in its rays, which are then converted into heat, as in a greenhouse. This means even the winter Sun has a warming effect.

Wind turbine Extra electricity produced by a domestic wind turbine, and not needed by the house, can be fed into the main distribution grid.

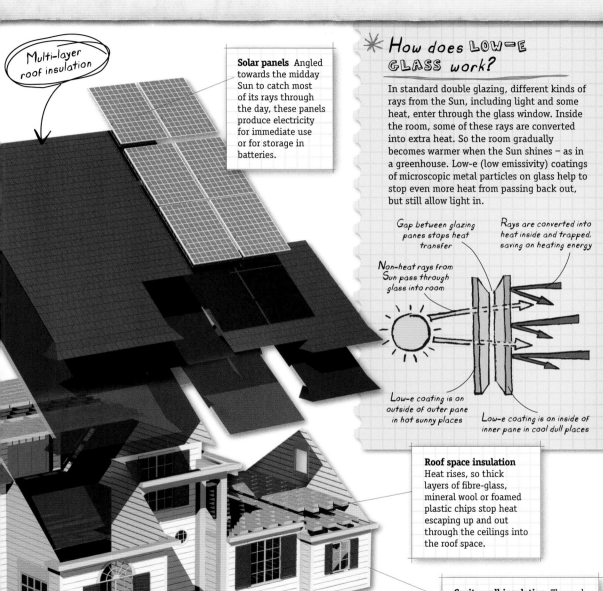

Multi-layer roof insulation

Solar panels Angled towards the midday Sun to catch most of its rays through the day, these panels produce electricity for immediate use or for storage in batteries.

✳ How does LOW-E GLASS work?

In standard double glazing, different kinds of rays from the Sun, including light and some heat, enter through the glass window. Inside the room, some of these rays are converted into extra heat. So the room gradually becomes warmer when the Sun shines – as in a greenhouse. Low-e (low emissivity) coatings of microscopic metal particles on glass help to stop even more heat from passing back out, but still allow light in.

Gap between glazing panes stops heat transfer

Rays are converted into heat inside and trapped, saving on heating energy

Non-heat rays from Sun pass through glass into room

Low-e coating is on outside of outer pane in hot sunny places

Low-e coating is on inside of inner pane in cool dull places

Roof space insulation Heat rises, so thick layers of fibre-glass, mineral wool or foamed plastic chips stop heat escaping up and out through the ceilings into the roof space.

Cavity wall insulation Thermal insulation such as mineral wool, fibre-glass sheets or foam is sandwiched between two wall layers. This prevents heat loss in winter and also reduces overheating in summer.

Double or triple glazing Two or three panes or sheets of glass with air gaps between them stop heat passing, so the rooms stay warm in winter and cool in summer (see panel, above).

LOW-ENERGY TRANSPORT

Cars are common for going to school and the shops, fun trips and holidays. But they use up fast-disappearing fossil fuels and they give out dangerous exhaust fumes and greenhouse gases. To save both energy and the environment, we need cleaner, greener ways to travel, such as public transport like buses and trains, also electric vehicles, bicycles and our own feet.

Eureka!

The first maglev train service to carry passengers ran in Hamburg, Germany in 1979 at an international transport exhibition. The track was 900 metres long and more than 50,000 passengers took the trip.

Whatever next?

Sadly hover-cars are still in the realm of science fiction. No known power source could make them small, safe and powerful enough, until perhaps scientists discover some kind of anti-gravity drive.

Magnetic levitation means the train uses magnetic forces to levitate – float or hover just above the track, without touching it.

Even the best-designed wheeled train has friction or rubbing due to its wheels, axles and other mechanical moving parts. Maglev trains do not suffer friction and so can reach greater speeds. A planned Japanese maglev railway line should have trains swishing along at 500 km/h.

✳ ELECTRIC VEHICLES

Several types of more energy-efficient, less polluting vehicles are finding their way onto the roads. Electric vehicles (EVs) have only an electric motor to drive the road wheels. They store their electrical energy in rechargeable batteries that need to be plugged into an electricity supply when discharged. A fuel-cell car makes electricity for its electric motor as it goes along (see page 242). Hybrid vehicles run on an electric motor and batteries, and also have a small petrol engine that can drive the road wheels when the batteries run down. The engine may also recharge the batteries while the car is on the move.

Electric taxis are quiet and make no exhaust fumes

Propulsion coils These wire coils (blue) carry changing electric currents. So their magnetic fields change and interact with the magnetic fields of the train's propulsion coils, pulling the train along from the front and pushing it from behind.

Levitation coils A second set of coils (red) in the guideway sides provide the magnetic forces that interact with the train's levitation coils, to make the train rise above the guideway by a few centimetres.

Supply rail The central rail supplies electricity to the train by means of sliding contacts on the train's underside.

Guideway surface The surface of the track or guideway on either side of the central supply rail is kept clear and smooth, in case the auxiliary wheels need to be used.

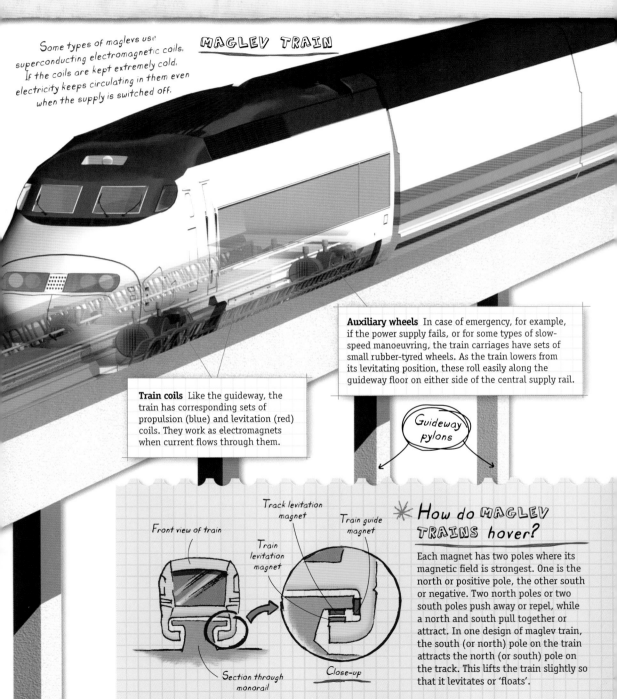

Some types of maglevs use superconducting electromagnetic coils. If the coils are kept extremely cold, electricity keeps circulating in them even when the supply is switched off.

MAGLEV TRAIN

Auxiliary wheels In case of emergency, for example, if the power supply fails, or for some types of slow-speed manoeuvring, the train carriages have sets of small rubber-tyred wheels. As the train lowers from its levitating position, these roll easily along the guideway floor on either side of the central supply rail.

Train coils Like the guideway, the train has corresponding sets of propulsion (blue) and levitation (red) coils. They work as electromagnets when current flows through them.

Guideway pylons

Front view of train

Track levitation magnet

Train guide magnet

Train levitation magnet

Section through monorail

Close-up

✳ How do MAGLEV TRAINS hover?

Each magnet has two poles where its magnetic field is strongest. One is the north or positive pole, the other south or negative. Two north poles or two south poles push away or repel, while a north and south pull together or attract. In one design of maglev train, the south (or north) pole on the train attracts the north (or south) pole on the track. This lifts the train slightly so that it levitates or 'floats'.

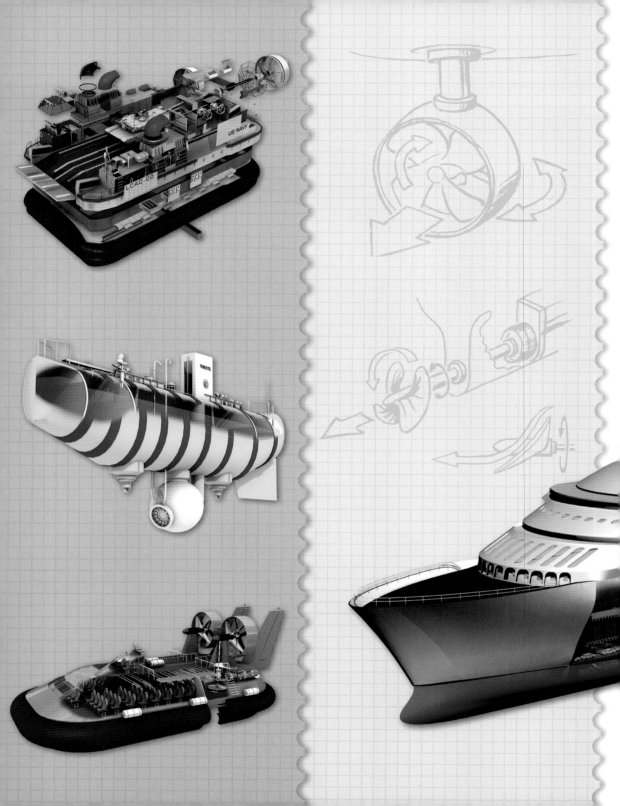

SHIPS AND SUBMARINES

INTRODUCTION

The first people who sat on a floating fallen tree, then tied a few trimmed tree trunks together as a raft, and then hollowed out one log as a canoe – started something incredible. Thousands of years before cars and aircraft, early traders transported valuable cargoes along rivers and coasts, while explorers crossed oceans to settle new lands. Towns grew up along shorelines, and water became the the most important way to travel.

Kayakers use a double-ended paddle to propel, steer and stop, for complete craft control.

PADDLES AND SAILS

To sail where you want, you need propulsion. Push against water and it partly pushes back, and human hands were the first true paddles. Larger surfaces for pushing came with paddles and oars, but they were tiring to use. Sails appeared more than 5000 years ago to catch wind power. Oars were still needed because the sail design for travelling into the wind, or tacking, did not arrive for another 4000 years.

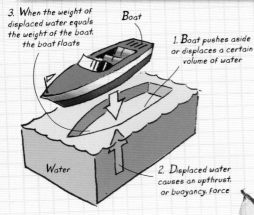

3. When the weight of displaced water equals the weight of the boat, the boat floats

Boat

1. Boat pushes aside or displaces a certain volume of water

Water

2. Displaced water causes an upthrust, or buoyancy, force

SINK OR FLOAT?

The scientific reason why boats float was worked out by Archimedes of ancient Greece. An object lowered into water pushes aside, or displaces, a volume of water. The water pushes back with a force, upthrust, equal to the weight of water displaced. When the object is low enough, the upthrust of the displaced water equals its own weight, and it floats. A heavy stone's weight is always more than the weight of water it displaces, so stones sink.

Tall ships are traditionally rigged sailing vessels that are still hugely popular today.

PROPS ARE TOPS

Steam engines that powered the Industrial Revolution in the late 18th and early 19th centuries soon found their way onto ships. The paddlewheels of early steamers were adapted from the waterwheel familiar at the time. Several inventors experimented with designs of propellers, also called water-screws, which were a reverse version of the Archimedes screw used for moving water. In 1845 the British Navy raced the paddlewheeler *Alecto* against the screw-driven *Rattler*. The latter won easily, and from that time, props were tops.

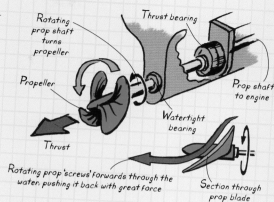

Rotating prop shaft turns propeller

Thrust bearing

Propeller

Prop shaft to engine

Watertight bearing

Thrust

Rotating prop 'screws' forwards through the water, pushing it back with great force

Section through prop blade

The helmsperson may steer a ship, but the captain is in complete command on the bridge.

Motorcruisers are travelling personal hotels with all mod cons.

BIGGER AND FASTER

Many new kinds of watercraft continued to develop, such as commercial oil supertankers from the 1860s and military aircraft carriers from the 1920s. For fun we have luxury motorcruisers and offshore powerboats for the rich, and jetskis and sailing dinghies for the not-so-rich. Seafaring is easier when a ship's control room, or bridge, bristles with the latest gadgets such as radar, sonar, satellite weather maps and GPS satnav.

As fuel prices rise, sail power could return in earnest – but heavy seas, high tides, and unpredictable currents and storms will still challenge the most experienced sailors well into the future.

YACHT

For more than 5000 years, starting along the river Nile in ancient Egypt, people used the wind to push their ships and boats along. Boats propelled by oars go back farther still, but sailing is easier than rowing – provided there is some wind. Yachts are mainly fairly small, light sailing craft. They are used for fun and pleasure, or for racing, rather than for carrying big loads of cargo.

One of the world's largest sailing yachts is Maltese Falcon, with masts 58 m tall, 15 sails and a length of 88 m – as long as a soccer pitch.

Eureka!

Until about 1100 years ago sailing ships had mainly square sails that could only be pushed by the wind. Then the lanteen, or triangular sail, was invented, which could be swung around to catch the wind from any angle.

Whatever next?

Modern energy costs are high, but wind power is free. Boat designers are testing big cargo-carrying ships with both engines and sails.

Mast Tall upright poles, or spars, are masts. They hold up the tops of the sails and keep the vertical sides straight.

✳ How do SAILS work?

The boom holds the sail at an angle to the wind so that the wind pushes it along, partly forwards and partly sideways. The boat does not slide sideways because of its hull shape and the large surface area of the keel or centreboard, which both resist sideways movement. The sail also forms a curved shape, like an aircraft wing. Air passes over the curve more quickly than under it (see page 263) to 'suck' the boat along.

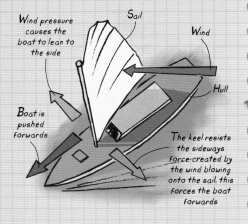

Wind pressure causes the boat to lean to the side

Sail

Wind

Hull

Boat is pushed forwards

The keel resists the sideways force created by the wind blowing onto the sail, this forces the boat forwards

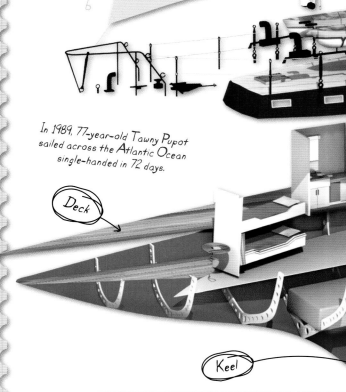

Jib

In 1989, 77-year-old Tawny Pupot sailed across the Atlantic Ocean single-handed in 72 days.

Deck

Keel

Sails Some yachts have one sail, others 20 or more. They are made from very strong tear-proof fabric, either natural fibres such as cotton or flax (linen), or artificial fibres like nylon and polyester.

The ships with the biggest sails were 'clippers' bringing tea and spices from East Asia to Europe and North America. The famous Cutty Sark was launched in 1869. It had more than 30 sails with a total area of almost 3000 square metres – bigger than ten tennis courts.

Boom The pole or tube forming the boom is attached along the bottom, or foot, of the sail. It can swing the sail around according to the wind direction.

Main sail

Rigging Various kinds of ropes, or lines, hold up the mast (standing rigging) and move the sails (running rigging). They are made from strong, smooth-running, rot-proof fibres and steel rope.

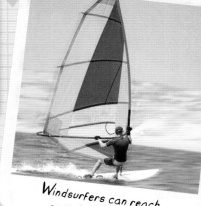

Windsurfers can reach speeds of 90 km/h

SAILBOARDING

In 1948 Newman Darby fixed a sail and a mast mounted on a swivel joint onto a small, flat-bottomed boat and invented the sailboard. The rider holds a double-sided boom and tilts the sail to catch the wind, moving along the board and leaning back so that it does not flip over.

Frames and bulkheads U-shaped frames give the hull (the main body of the boat) its strength and form, and have holes to save weight. Bulkheads are like dividing walls inside the hull.

RACING CATAMARAN

The 'cat' is a boat with two hulls (main bodies) usually of equal size. It has several advantages over the usual single hull or monohull. For example, it is so wide that it is much more difficult to capsize – tip over onto its side in the water. The hulls, called vakas, are connected by one or more decks, or akas, that hold the masts. Catamarans were used in South Asia for centuries but only became accepted for official racing in the 1970s.

Eureka!

In the 1690s, part-time pirate William Dampier described catamaran-style double-canoes in the Bay of Bengal, in the Indian Ocean. However boat-builders did not start to use the design until Nathanael Herreshoff made a 'cat' in 1876/77.

Since the 1970s, huge engine-powered catamarans have become popular as high-speed ferries carrying people and vehicles, and even huge trucks. They are smoother and safer in rough seas than hydrofoils.

Sails 'Cats' can have a bigger sail area than a monohull boat because they are more steady and stable in the water.

✳ How do HULLS AND MULTI-HULLS work?

A monohull may tip over if it has heavy loads on deck and tall sails. The deep-keeled monohull is more stable since the keel adds weight low down and its surface area resists tipping. 'Cats' and trimarans (three-hulled craft) have wider bases with a larger deck area for cabins, people and equipment.

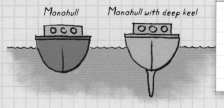

Monohull   Monohull with deep keel

Multi-hull Trimaran   Multi-hull Catamaran

Boom

Rails

Wheel

Stern This is the rear or 'aft' end of the boat, which usually has the rudder for steering.

Rudder

Keel The keel resists sideways pressure and forces the boat to move forwards.

Alloy mast The mast is made from alloys, or mixtures of metals and other substances, especially aluminium. It is a hollow tube, lighter and stronger than a solid rod.

One of the newest, largest catamarans is Hemisphere, 44 m long and 500 tonnes in weight, with a 52-m-tall mast. It carries 12 guests on luxury cruises around the Caribbean, manned by a crew of eight.

The fastest round-the-world sailing trip was in 2004 by legendary adventurer Steve Fossett and a crew of 12. In their catamaran Cheyenne they took 58 days and nine hours. The record was broken a year later by Bruno Peyron in Orange II, taking 50 days 16 hours.

A catamaran race, with spinnakers rigged

✳ What are SPINNAKERS?

The spinnaker is a large sail that blows out like a balloon. It works like a normal sail when moving in the direction of the wind, or at an angle downwind. However unlike a normal sail, the spinnaker cannot sail into the wind. This means that racing sailors put up, or rig, the spinnaker for the downwind parts of their course, then roll or furl it and use the normal sails for the upwind parts of the race.

Bow This is the front or 'forward' end of the boat, which is sharp and streamlined to slice through the water easily.

Lightweight hull Modern 'cats' have hulls made of very light but strong materials such as fibre-glass or carbon-fibre composites.

JET SKI

The PWC, personal watercraft, is often called a 'jet ski' or 'aquabike'. It's a combination of motorcycle and speedboat, powered by a 'jet' of water that makes the hull 'ski' across the surface. Jet skis are mainly for fun, racing and stunt-riding. However they are also useful for emergencies, such as rescuing a swimmer swept away by strong water currents.

Eureka!

The first jet skis were invented by bank official and off-road motorbike enthusiast Clayton Jacobson in the early 1970s. They were built by Kawasaki, which also makes fast, powerful motorcycles.

Whatever next?

Some jet skis are fitted with a small parachute so that the rider can take off at speed over the crest of a wave, open the parachute to float back down, reel in the parachute quickly, and start all over again.

In 2002, Count Álvaro de Marichalar y Sáenz de Tejada of Spain took four months, riding 12 hours each day, to travel from Rome, Italy across the Mediterranean Sea to Gibraltar and then across the Atlantic Ocean to Miami, USA – all on a jet ski.

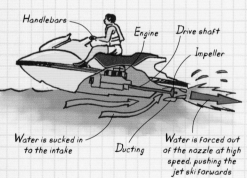

Handlebars | Engine | Drive shaft | Impeller | Water is sucked in to the intake | Ducting | Water is forced out of the nozzle at high speed, pushing the jet ski forwards

✳ How does WATERJET PROPULSION work?

The impeller sucks in water from below the craft and forces it out rearwards at high pressure through the nozzle. The force of the water blasting backwards pushes the craft forwards. The nozzle is connected by cables to the handlebars. Turning the handlebars to the left makes the nozzle swing to the left, so the craft steers left. The rider can also steer by 'leaning' the craft as on a motorbike.

Engine Some jet skis have four-stroke petrol engines, others are two-stroke (see page 258). The engine is low down to make the craft stable so it does not tip over.

Front fairing

Rub strip

Hull

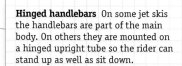

Hinged handlebars On some jet skis the handlebars are part of the main body. On others they are mounted on a hinged upright tube so the rider can stand up as well as sit down.

Seat

A jet ski stunt rider gets some 'big air'

Some jet skis reach speeds of more than 100 km/h, and riders have travelled 1000 km in 24 hours.

✳ AQUABATICS!

Jet ski riders don't just race. They also have freestyle competitions for tricks and stunts such as somersaults, backflips, mid-air spins and barrel rolls, and even diving under the surface and surging back up again into the air. The riders earn points for each manoeuvre as well as speed as they race around a track marked by floating buoys.

GL-X900

GL-X

In freeriding, jet ski riders use waves and surf as jump ramps to take off and reach amazing heights.

Drive shaft A long spinning shaft from the engine turns the impeller. The drive shaft has watertight seals around it so water cannot leak into the engine compartment.

The jet ski rider has an ignition key on a rope or line tied to the wrist or lifejacket. The key slots into the ignition switch before the engine can start. If the rider falls off the key comes out and the engine stops.

Impeller Shaped like a fan or propeller, the impeller spins quickly inside its duct (curved tube).

Jet nozzle The jet of water blasts out of a tube-like nozzle to push the jet ski along.

Impeller duct Water is sucked in for the impeller through an opening or inlet. This has a mesh-like grate or screen to keep out larger objects such as seaweed, driftwood and fish.

OUTBOARD SPEEDBOAT

A speedboat has a long, streamlined hull with a sharp front or bow. The lower surface is designed to 'plane' or skim over the surface at high speed. This is faster than a hull that is partially submerged and tries to push or carve through the water. An outboard engine is one mounted outside the main hull, rather than inboard or within the hull.

Eureka!

The hydroplane is a special design of speedboat devised in the 1950s. It has two sponsons, or short projections, one on each side at the front of the hull. These give stability and lift the craft clear of the water except for its propeller.

Whatever next?

In 1978 Ken Warby reached a speed of 510 kilometres per hour in his hydroplane *Spirit of Australia*. Several people have since died trying to break this record.

Dash The dash or control board has dials for information such as engine temperature and fuel level.

Controls The steering wheel is linked by cables to the outboard motor and makes it swivel from side to side.

Until 1911 the world water speed record was held by steam-powered boats.

Fuel tank Fuel for a two-stroke engine has special lubrication oil mixed with the petrol.

Planing shape The hydroplaning hull is almost flat-bottomed or shaped like a shallow V. It lifts nearly clear of the water at high speed, to avoid the water pushing back to cause resistance or drag.

✳ How does a TWO-STROKE ENGINE work?

A two-stroke engine produces power every two strokes of the piston inside the cylinder. The upstroke squashes a mixture of fuel and air in the cylinder above the piston, while sucking fresh fuel-air mixture into the crankcase below the piston. The mixture burns or combusts and forces the piston down. This transfers the fresh fuel-air mixture from below the piston to above, where the fresh mixture also pushes out the burnt mixture.

1. Fuel mixture is compressed and ignited
Spark plug
3. Combustion forces piston down
4. Compressed fuel mixture is pushed from crankcase to cylinder
5. Burnt mixture is pushed out (exhaust)
Cylinder
Piston
Con-rod
Side port
2. Fresh fuel mixture is sucked into crankcase
Crankcase
Crankshaft
Upstroke
Downstroke
Con rod turns crankshaft

Carbon fibre hull The hull must be extremely strong and rigid, for slamming into waves at great speed.

World water speed ace Ken Warby built his craft *Spirit of Australia* at home. He set the world water speed record in 1978 at Blowering Dam, on the Tumut River in the Snowy Mountains of southeast Australia.

A powerboat 'guns' its engines

✳ LUXURY POWER

Motorcruisers, motoryachts and similar powerboats are not built for out-and-out speed. However they are great for travelling relatively fast, more than 60 kilometres per hour, and in comfort. Larger versions are equipped with berths (beds), a saloon (living area) and a galley (kitchen). The main control area is the cockpit, and on top of this may be an open area, the flybridge, with a second set of controls for use in good weather.

Seat The pilot's seat is well padded since even small ripples on the surface cause sudden jolts and knocks at speed.

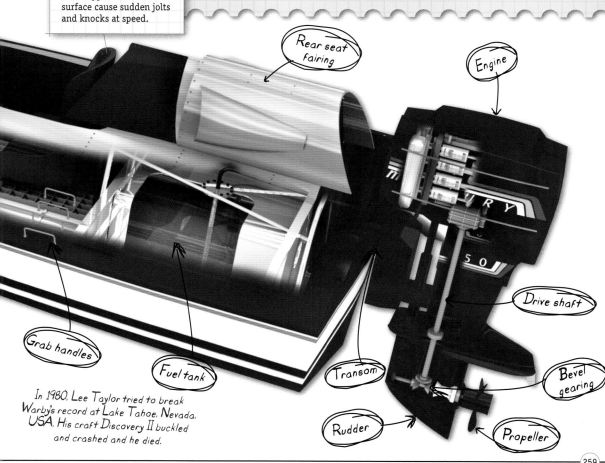

Rear seat fairing

Engine

Drive shaft

Bevel gearing

Grab handles

Fuel tank

Transom

Rudder

Propeller

In 1980, Lee Taylor tried to break Warby's record at Lake Tahoe, Nevada, USA. His craft *Discovery II* buckled and crashed and he died.

OFFSHORE POWERBOAT

Offshore powerboats are built to withstand waves, wind and weather away from the shore, out in the open ocean. Slamming into a wave at 160 kilometres per hour is almost like hitting a brick wall. Powerboats have to be enormously tough, strong and rigid. They are usually powered by twin marine diesel or petrol engines. In World Championship P1 races, the diesels can be up to 13 litres – six times the size of a family car engine.

Eureka!

The diesel engine was invented by Rudolf Diesel in the early 1890s. It is heavier than a petrol engine but a useful design where much power is needed, as in powerboats, trucks and tractors.

Whatever next?

Electric powerboats have been around since 1880. The latest models can travel faster than 100 kilometres per hour, are quiet and do not produce polluting fumes.

One of the longest offshore powerboat races is the Round Britain competition, which covers 2500 km at average speeds of more than 100 km/h.

Fuel tanks Some powerboats hold well over 1000 litres of fuel, enough for cruising for most of the day.

Hull shape Powerboats 'plane' or skim with only the propellers and rudders under the surface. The hull is made from aluminium-based metal alloys or carbon-fibre composites.

Rails

Cleat

Inner structure Apart from fuel tanks, inside the watertight hull is mostly air, so the boat is very light. The framework of metal alloy keeps the hull shape rigid.

✳ High speed ACTION

Powerboat racing is extremely expensive – a top team needs to spend tens of millions of pounds. However it's not just pure speed that wins. The boats must be reliable and economical with fuel. The pilots, or drivers, have to take into account waves, tides, currents and wind, and keep a constant lookout for dangers such as driftwood. Crashing through the waves is physically demanding, even when strapped into well-padded seats.

A 'full-on' offshore powerboat race

Some powerboat meetings consist of several races, such as a sprint of less than 50 km and an endurance of more than 150 km.

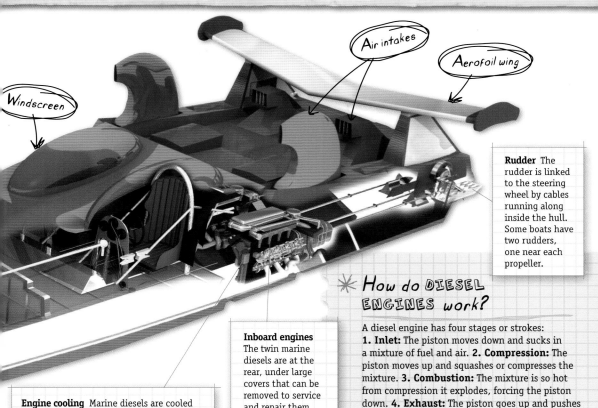

Air intakes

Aerofoil wing

Windscreen

Rudder The rudder is linked to the steering wheel by cables running along inside the hull. Some boats have two rudders, one near each propeller.

Inboard engines The twin marine diesels are at the rear, under large covers that can be removed to service and repair them.

Engine cooling Marine diesels are cooled by sea water taken in continuously through an inlet and expelled through an outlet, rather than water circulating through a radiator as in a car.

✳ How do DIESEL ENGINES work?

A diesel engine has four stages or strokes:
1. Inlet: The piston moves down and sucks in a mixture of fuel and air. **2. Compression:** The piston moves up and squashes or compresses the mixture. **3. Combustion:** The mixture is so hot from compression it explodes, forcing the piston down. **4. Exhaust:** The piston goes up and pushes out the burnt mixture. The piston's up-down movements turn the engine's main shaft, the crankshaft, by a connecting rod.

Depending on conditions, some powerboats race at more than 250 km/h. However in some events, if the weather is bad, they are kept to lower speeds by a device called a limiter fixed to the engine.

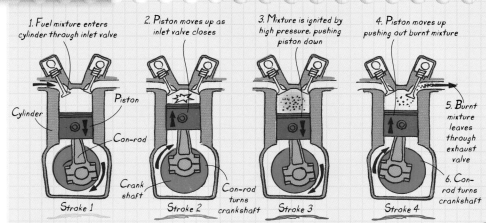

1. Fuel mixture enters cylinder through inlet valve

2. Piston moves up as inlet valve closes

3. Mixture is ignited by high pressure, pushing piston down

4. Piston moves up pushing out burnt mixture

Cylinder

Piston

Con-rod

Crank shaft

Con-rod turns crankshaft

5. Burnt mixture leaves through exhaust valve

6. Con-rod turns crankshaft

Stroke 1

Stroke 2

Stroke 3

Stroke 4

HYDROFOIL

Hydrofoil watercraft 'fly' above the surface on wing-like foils fixed to struts beneath the hull. The foil works like an aircraft wing to generate a lifting force at speed, which raises the foil so the craft above it is above the surface. This greatly reduces the drag or resistance of the craft moving through the water. It also means the hull is held clear of rough water and waves.

Eureka!

Hydrofoils were developed in stages by several scientists and engineers, including John Thornycroft around 1900, Alexander Graham Bell (inventor of the telephone) from about 1906 and Enrico Forlanini in 1910.

Whatever next?

Engineers are always working on new foil designs, including 'smart' foils that can alter their curved shape according to their speed.

The sit-down hydrofoil is like a chair on a large water ski that 'flies' over the water, towed behind a speedboat.

Rails

Bulkheads

Propellers One prop turns faster than the other to steer the craft.

Drive shafts The long drive or propeller shafts extend deep below the boat, so the propellers remain in the water when the hull is lifted clear.

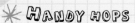

A hydrofoil lifts well clear of the water

✳ HANDY HOPS

Commercial hydrofoils run as fast ferries in many areas, especially South and East Asia. They provide a quick smooth ride, handy for hops across lakes, rivers, bays and sheltered inshore waters. However they may have trouble with large waves and high winds.

Struts The struts are thin with sharp front and rear edges to produce as little water resistance as possible. On some hydrofoils they can swivel left or right to work as rudders.

Some surfers have boards fitted with foils to cope with really big waves away from the shore.

Water flow is faster over the foil, resulting in lower pressure

Hydrofoil is sucked upwards, supporting the weight of the hull

Strut

Foil shape with curved upper surface

Sea

Trailing edge

Leading edge

Direction of travel

Water flow is slower under the foil, resulting in higher pressure

✳ How do HYDROFOILS work?

A foil's shape is curved when seen edge-on, known as an aerofoil (see page 252). The curve is greater on the upper surface than the lower. Water flowing past the foil must go faster over the top than beneath. Faster water means less water pressure. So the lower pressure above the foil sucks it upwards with a force called lift, raising the hull out of the water.

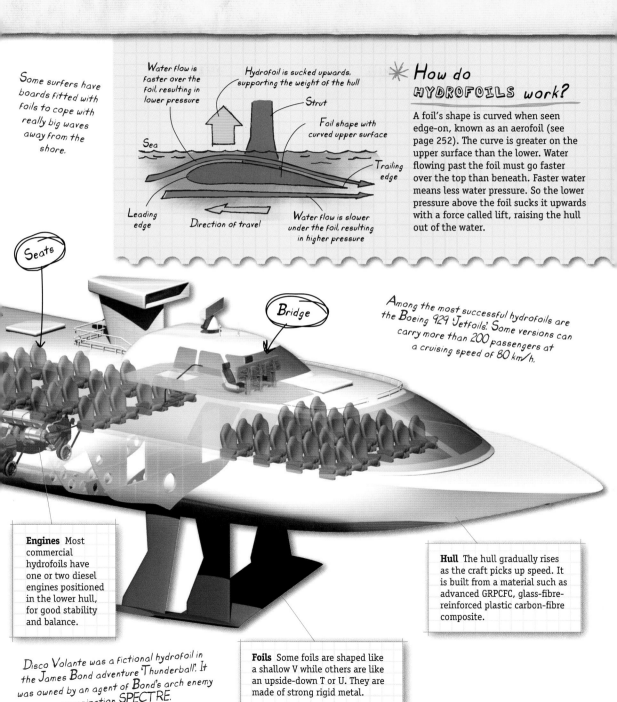

Seats

Bridge

Among the most successful hydrofoils are the Boeing 929 'Jetfoils'. Some versions can carry more than 200 passengers at a cruising speed of 80 km/h.

Engines Most commercial hydrofoils have one or two diesel engines positioned in the lower hull, for good stability and balance.

Hull The hull gradually rises as the craft picks up speed. It is built from a material such as advanced GRPCFC, glass-fibre-reinforced plastic carbon-fibre composite.

Disco Volante was a fictional hydrofoil in the James Bond adventure 'Thunderball'. It was owned by an agent of Bond's arch enemy organization SPECTRE.

Foils Some foils are shaped like a shallow V while others are like an upside-down T or U. They are made of strong rigid metal.

MILITARY HOVERCRAFT

Hovercrafts fly rather than sail, floating just above the surface. They are also known as ACVs, Air Cushion Vehicles. Their great benefit is that they can travel across smooth ground as well as water. The giant LCAC, Landing Craft Air Cushion, is the US military's combined boat, low-altitude aircraft and load-carrier. It can take troops, vehicles and equipment from a larger transport ship to the shore and even up onto the land.

Eureka!

The first full-sized working hovercraft, SRN-1, was built in 1959 by Christopher Cockerell and his team from the Saunders Roe aircraft makers. It hovered at a height of about 25 centimetres.

Whatever next?

Personal hovercraft are gaining popularity, but mainly for fun and racing. They are not allowed to travel on roads and are awkward to steer in high winds.

LCACs carry a load of 70 tonnes – the weight of an Abrams M1 battle tank.

Bow thruster This tube carries some of the air from the lift fans and can be turned to blow it in any direction to help with manoeuvring and steering.

Control station

Ramp

✳ How do HOVERCRAFTS work?

A hovercraft floats on a high-pressure 'cushion' of air. Its lift fans (impellers) have large angled blades and are driven by an engine such as a gas turbine (as used in helicopters). The lift fan blows air downwards with great speed and force. The air collects in the skirt area below and builds up enough pressure to lift the craft. As the skirt rises, air begins to escape from under its edge but the pressure remains high enough for the craft to hover.

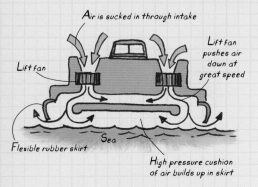

Air is sucked in through intake

Lift fan pushes air down at great speed

Lift fan

Flexible rubber skirt

Sea

High pressure cushion of air builds up in skirt

The US LCAC is almost 25 m long, 14 m wide and 7.2 m high when hovering.

LIFT FAN

Bow thruster

Front lift fan

Rear lift fan

Air outlet ducting

The British Griffon 2000 TD hovercraft is in service with more than seven military forces around the world.

Propeller The large aircraft-type propeller is housed in a collar-like shroud with the rudder just behind.

Rudder

Prop shaft Each propeller spins on a shaft driven by a gas turbine engine, which produces more than 4500 horsepower.

Engine housing

US NAVY

-00

Outlets

Skirt The flexible rubberized skirt hangs down around the hull. It traps air to raise the air pressure and lift the craft and passes easily over waves.

✳ Get the BALANCE right

A hovercraft must be balanced or trimmed so that the weight of the craft plus its load is evenly spread. If not, it it might hover nose-down rather than level, or lean to one side and veer around. The loadmaster's job is to put all parts of the load into the correct places and secure them for stable balance.

Loading a military hovercraft

PASSENGER HOVERCRAFT

Hovercraft that carry passengers and vehicles have been used in many parts of the world, although they are less common today. They can fly off the water up onto a ramp to load and unload. They are also fast, cruising at more than 100 kilometres per hour, and the trip is smooth in calm weather. However the ride is noisy and big waves make the craft sway and rock making some passengers sick.

Eureka!

Early types of hovercraft had no skirts and tipped over easily. The flexible multi-section skirt was developed in 1962 by Denys Bliss, a colleague of Christopher Cockerell, and helped rectify the stability problem.

Whatever next?

A new breed of hovercrafts are exploring remote swamps. They cause little disturbance to wildlife as they switch off their engines and observe rare animals.

The largest commercial hovercraft included the French N500 Naviplane and the British SR-N4. They weighed about 250 tonnes, were 50 m long and could carry 400 passengers and more than 50 cars.

The Russian ZUBR are the largest hovercraft in the world, weighing 550 tonnes – 150 tonnes more than a fully loaded jumbo jet.

Controls A hovercraft's main controls are the lift throttle or lever to adjust hovering height, main throttle for speed and the steering wheel for the rudders.

Bridge The bridge is the control centre of a large ship, where the captain and pilot or helmsperson keep watch and steer.

Radar

Seats

Skirt

Life raft containers

Hovercraft steers left

Propellers push hovercraft forwards

Fast-moving air from the propeller pushes past the rudders

Rudder

Rudders deflect air to the left

✳ How does a HOVERCRAFT STEER?

Like a propeller aircraft, a hovercraft is pushed along by its props. In some versions the propellers swivel left or right on their pylons to blow air at an angle for steering around corners. Other types have rudders that push the air to the side and make the hovercraft turn. Control is tricky in high winds.

The giant SR-N4 hovercraft went into service in 1968 but was phased out by 2000 due to increasing fuel costs.

Propeller pylon

Propeller The propellers or thrust fans are usually made from advanced composite materials and can spin more than 50 times each second.

Rudder The rudder is directly behind the propeller, where it has most effect in the stream of very fast-moving air.

Engine Smaller hovercraft can be powered by turbocharged diesels, and larger ones by gas turbine engines.

Steps

Lift fan

In the mid-1950s, British engineer Christopher Cockerell built a number of ground-effect machine test models.

In 1716, Emanuel Swedenborg drew the first hovercraft design, but he had no suitable engine so he suggested human-powered oars. It would never have worked!

An artist's impression of the Boeing GEV

✳ SEA MONSTERS?

A Ground-Effect Vehicle, or ekranoplan, has wings like an aircraft and a hull-shaped body like a boat. As it picks up speed on the water, the angled wings create an air cushion between themselves and the water below that lifts the craft just above the surface. It cannot rise higher because without the ground effect the wings do not produce enough lift. GEVs weighing more than 500 tonnes and cruising at more than 500 kilometres per hour, powered by turbojet engines, have been tested for military use on large lakes and inland seas.

CRUISE LINER

It's a luxury hotel with every comfort, from swimming pools to cinemas, restaurants and gyms – all travelling smoothly across the ocean. Cruise liners are holiday homes to thousands of passengers as they visit famous ports and sightseeing locations. When a liner docks, passengers go off to visit the sights as the crew work fast to restock the ship with food, water, fuel and other essentials.

Eureka!

The first purpose-built cruise liner was *Prinzessin Victoria Louise*, launched in 1900. It weighed 4400 tonnes and travelled across the Atlantic and Caribbean, as well as the Mediterranean and Black seas. When it ran aground in 1906, the captain felt so guilty that he shot himself.

Whatever next?

Vast cruise ships planned for the future may have a grassy central area like a city park with paths, flower borders and trees.

Radar mast

One of the largest cruise ships is Queen Mary 2, launched in 2003. At 150,000 tonnes in weight, it is 344 m in length – longer than three soccer pitches.

Bridge

Bow

Cargo hold Stores such as fresh water and food are kept towards the bottom of the hull. They must be tied or lashed down to prevent rolling about or falling over in rough seas. Their weight is ballast to increase the ship's stability.

A powerful tug helps a cruise liner into port

✳ Give us a TOW!

It takes several kilometres for a massive ship to slow down and stop. During this time it can be blown off course by winds or carried along by tides and currents. Tugs are small, powerful boats that tow big ships using strong cables called hawsers. They may even 'nudge' the bigger ships. The tug captain knows local conditions well and inches the ship into the correct position. Two or more tugs may work together for extra control.

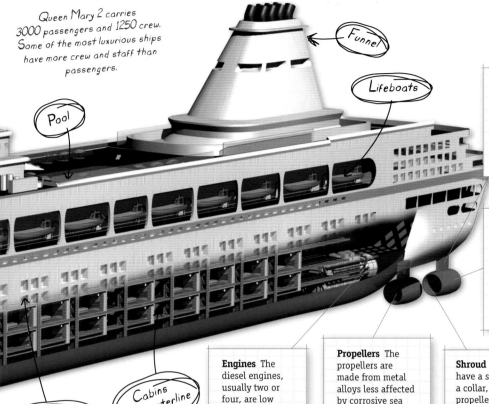

Queen Mary 2 carries 3000 passengers and 1250 crew. Some of the most luxurious ships have more crew and staff than passengers.

Funnel

Lifeboats

Pool

Cabin windows

Cabins below waterline

Column The drive shaft for the propeller in the thruster passes down inside the column or stalk, connected to the engine by gears.

Azimuth thrusters These thrusters push the boat along and also swivel to give it sideways thrust for manoeuvring, so there is no need for a rudder.

Engines The diesel engines, usually two or four, are low down in the ship for stability.

Propellers The propellers are made from metal alloys less affected by corrosive sea water.

Shroud The thrusters have a shroud, like a collar, around the propeller for protection and to direct the water for extra pushing force. Some thruster designs have an open propeller, lacking the shroud.

A ship called The World has apartments you can buy. You can stay in them for a time or live there permanently as the ship travels slowly round and round the globe.

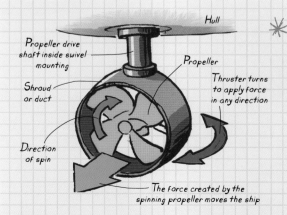

Hull

Propeller drive shaft inside swivel mounting

Propeller

Shroud or duct

Thruster turns to apply force in any direction

Direction of spin

The force created by the spinning propeller moves the ship

✳ How do BOW THRUSTERS work?

Giant cruise liners often have to enter small ports or harbours. The main rudders do not work at low speed, so there are bow thrusters – as main propellers, or as small extra props at the bow (front) and perhaps stern (rear). They swivel around to produce a push or thrust in any direction. The liner can move sideways, diagonally or backwards.

FREIGHTER

Cargo ships, freighters and other similar ships are the hard-working 'trucks' of the ocean. They criss-cross seas around the world carrying all manner of freight and cargo, from cars and televisions to food and flowers. As soon as they reach a port they unload quickly, fill up with another load and set off once more. Global trade is big business where time is money and cannot be wasted.

Eureka!

Cranes were loading and unloading ships in ancient Greece, more than 2500 years ago. Mathematician and scientist Archimedes (287–212 BC) designed one so huge that it could lift enemy ships out of the water!

Mast

Coasters are ships with a small draught — that is, the hull does not extend very far down into the water. They can travel through shallow water and over rocks and reefs where ocean-going ships with much deeper hulls would run aground.

Bridge The ship is controlled from the bridge, with the wheel for steering, speed controls and displays showing information such as engine temperature, fuel levels and much more.

In 2008, a Japanese cargo ship, able to carry 6400 cars, set sail, powered partly by electricity from more than 320 solar panels.

Rudder

Propeller

Rotating prop shaft turns propeller

Thrust bearing

Propeller

Prop shaft to engine

Watertight bearing

Thrust

As prop rotates, it 'screws' forwards, blasting back water with great thrust

Section through prop blade

*How do WATER SCREWS work?

A water screw or ship's propeller has angled blades that spin around to push the water backwards and so thrust the ship forwards. They are designed with a foil-type shape so that they are sucked forwards as well as pushing backwards (see page 263). The drive shaft or prop shaft from the engine passes through several sets of bearings that transfer the force of thrust from the prop to the ship's hull.

Hull Most working cargo ships have hulls made of steel plates welded together for long-lasting strength and toughness. They can also be repaired easily.

Hook Different-sized hooks can be fitted to the cranes, depending on the loads being lifted.

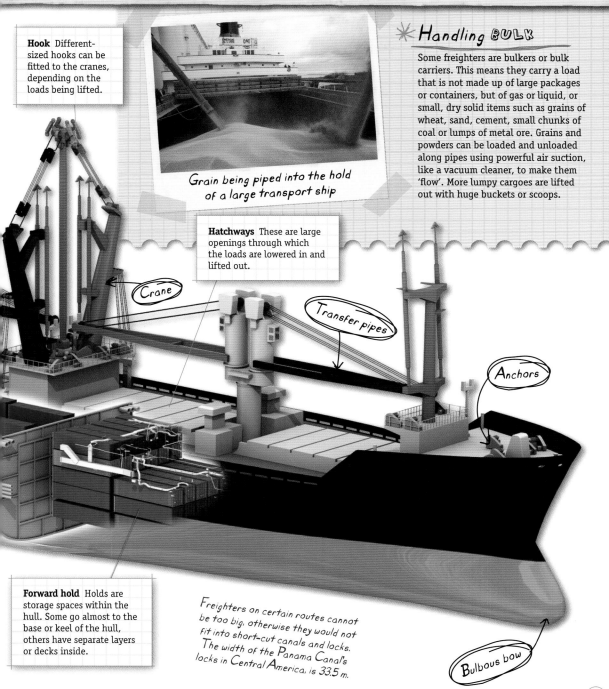

Grain being piped into the hold of a large transport ship

✳ Handling BULK

Some freighters are bulkers or bulk carriers. This means they carry a load that is not made up of large packages or containers, but of gas or liquid, or small, dry solid items such as grains of wheat, sand, cement, small chunks of coal or lumps of metal ore. Grains and powders can be loaded and unloaded along pipes using powerful air suction, like a vacuum cleaner, to make them 'flow'. More lumpy cargoes are lifted out with huge buckets or scoops.

Hatchways These are large openings through which the loads are lowered in and lifted out.

Crane

Transfer pipes

Anchors

Forward hold Holds are storage spaces within the hull. Some go almost to the base or keel of the hull, others have separate layers or decks inside.

Freighters on certain routes cannot be too big, otherwise they would not fit into short-cut canals and locks. The width of the Panama Canal's locks in Central America, is 33.5 m.

Bulbous bow

CONTAINER SHIP

The container ship or 'box boat' carries hundreds of containers in its hold and also stacked in piles on its deck. Standard containers are enormous metal boxes, mostly 12.2 metres long by 2.44 metres wide by 2.59 metres high. They are filled with all kinds of goods and materials, and then transported by road, rail – and ship.

Eureka!

Container ships were first used in the 1950s. The earliest ones were made from converted oil tankers that were built during World War II (1939–1945).

Whatever next?

Containers made out of modern composite materials are more expensive to build, but they are lighter to transport and could pay for themselves in five years.

Dockside cranes Many container ships only have small cranes. They rely mainly on huge purpose-built overhanging cranes that run along rails on the dockside to load and unload their containers.

Bulkheads The strong steel hull has partitions called bulkheads that separate it into watertight compartments. If one is damaged and leaks, the others keep the ship afloat.

Up to 10,000 containers are probably lost at sea each year. Most slip overboard during high winds or storms, while others sink with their ship.

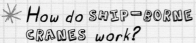
Winch

✳ How do SHIP-BORNE CRANES work?

Many cranes on ships are hydraulic, worked by high-pressure oil. The oil is pumped into a cylinder and pushes along a piston linked by a connecting rod to the crane's 'arm' – the jib or boom. The jib lowers to extend the reach of the crane, and the whole crane swivels around on its base. The cable goes around pulleys or sheaves and is reeled in slowly but powerfully by an electric winch.

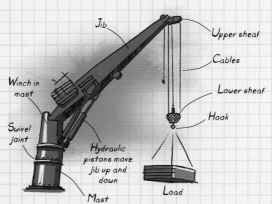

Jib
Upper sheaf
Cables
Winch in mast
Lower sheaf
Swivel joint
Hook
Hydraulic pistons move jib up and down
Mast
Load

Cargo too large to carry in containers can be handled using flat racks, open top containers and platforms.

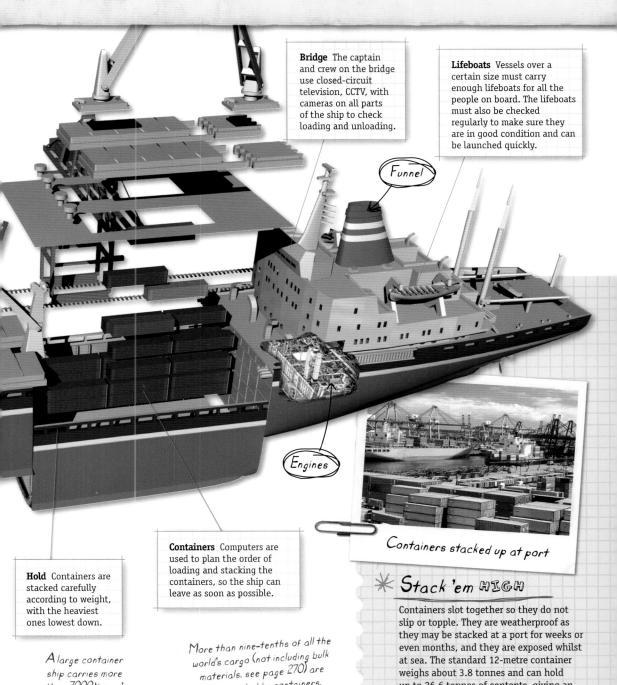

Bridge The captain and crew on the bridge use closed-circuit television, CCTV, with cameras on all parts of the ship to check loading and unloading.

Lifeboats Vessels over a certain size must carry enough lifeboats for all the people on board. The lifeboats must also be checked regularly to make sure they are in good condition and can be launched quickly.

Funnel

Engines

Containers stacked up at port

Hold Containers are stacked carefully according to weight, with the heaviest ones lowest down.

Containers Computers are used to plan the order of loading and stacking the containers, so the ship can leave as soon as possible.

A large container ship carries more than 7000 'boxes'.

More than nine-tenths of all the world's cargo (not including bulk materials, see page 270) are transported by containers.

* Stack 'em HIGH

Containers slot together so they do not slip or topple. They are weatherproof as they may be stacked at a port for weeks or even months, and they are exposed whilst at sea. The standard 12-metre container weighs about 3.8 tonnes and can hold up to 26.6 tonnes of contents, giving an overall weight of 30.4 tonnes.

OIL SUPERTANKER

The world's biggest ships are the bulk carriers known as oil tankers. Crude carriers transport crude oil, or petroleum, from oilfields such as those in the Middle East to countries all around the world. Product carriers convey the substances made from crude oil at refineries, such as fuels like petrol, diesel and kerosene, lubricating oils, alcohols and chemical solvents.

Eureka!

Oil tankers were first used in the 1860s in eastern Asia, sailing across the Caspian Sea and along the rivers of northern Europe. By the 1890s, tankers were crossing all major oceans.

Whatever next?

The biggest oil tankers are 'sitting duck' targets for pirates, enemies in war, terrorists and other dangers. Some shipbuilders now use smaller, faster carriers to avoid these risks.

A cofferdam is a small space left open between two bulkheads to give protection from heat, fire, or collision. Tankers generally have cofferdams forward and aft of the cargo tanks, and sometimes between individual tanks.

Loading pipes Flexible hoses and rigid pipes carry the pumped oil in and out, and also transfer it between tanks to spread the load for good balance.

Supertankers are more accurately known as ULCCs, Ultra Large Crude Carriers, carrying more than 320,000 tonnes of cargo.

Waterline mark

Hull Most modern tankers are double-hulled, with two layers of 'skins' in case one is damaged and leaks. The hard hull surface forms a huge area for reflecting sonar pulses, so other ships can detect the supertanker even at night or in thick fog by sonar as well as radar.

✳ How does SONAR work?

Sonar, Sound Navigation And Ranging, detects nearby objects in water using sound waves. A transmitter sends out pulses or 'pings' that travel far and fast through the water. These bounce off objects as echoes that are detected by a receiver. The direction and timing of the echoes shows the position and distance (range) of the object. Sonar is like a sound version of radar (see page 277).

5. Ship's computer displays information

1. Ship emits sound waves or tows sonar probe

2. Probe emits sound waves

4. Echoes (reflected waves) detected by probe

3. Sound waves bounce off surfaces such as sea bed

Pumping control station
Huge pumps driven by electric motors force oil into the hold tanks when loading, and out again at the destination. They are usually sited all together in the pump room.

A large oil tanker starts to slow down at least one hour and 20 km before it needs to stop. In an emergency, it can stop in about 15 minutes and 3 km.

Bridge

Crane

Propeller

Cofferdam

Long hull

Oil tanks As the oil is unloaded and the tanks empty, they are filled with inert gases that do not combine or react with other substances. Otherwise the oil fumes might catch fire and explode.

Bulkheads One vast tank inside the hull would allow oil to slosh around and upset the ship's balance. So bulkhead walls divide it into many compartments.

By weight, oil tankers form more than one-third of all cargo carried at sea.

Oil pollutes the sea from 'Braer' oil tanker off the Scottish coast in 1993

The world's largest supertanker was Seawise Giant, built in 1979. It was extended, damaged by enemy attack, altered again, and had names including Happy Giant and Jahre Viking. Finally it became the 458-m-long floating oil storage tank Knock Nevis, moored off Qatar in the Middle East.

✳ Environmental DISASTERS

Oil tanker accidents have caused some of the greatest environmental disasters of modern times. The oil leaks out as a floating slick that smothers the water's surface and kills fish, seabirds, seals, corals and other marine life. One of the worst spills was in 1991 when the ABT Summer leaked more than a quarter of a million tonnes of oil off Angola, Africa.

AIRCRAFT CARRIER

Some of the largest ships in the world are floating air bases designed to go to anywhere for war – or hopefully, to guard the peace. In addition to carrying jet aircraft and helicopters, these giant vessels have other weapons such as guided missiles, torpedoes and mines. They also act as command, control and communications centres for other seacraft in their fleet such as battleships and destroyers.

Eureka!

In 1910 Eugene Ely was the first pilot to take off from a ship, the US armoured cruiser *Birmingham*. The next year he was first to land on a ship, the USS *Pennsylvania*, another cruiser with a specially built platform.

Whatever next?

Stealth planes scatter radar signals with their angled surfaces, edged shapes and radio-absorbing paint. Stealth ships with similar features have also been tested and will become more common.

Nimitz class carriers have two nuclear reactors powering four steam turbines and can cruise at more than 50 km/h.

Fuel tanks Huge tanks store jet fuel for the aircraft. Many carriers are nuclear-powered so their plutonium fuel pellets could fit into a small truck.

Flight deck Longer than three soccer pitches, the flight deck is 76 metres wide at its broadest part.

Catapult rail

✳ How do carriers store AIRCRAFT?

Carriers have huge flat elevators or lifts – platforms that rise up and down between the lower decks and flight deck, transporting aircraft and equipment. Nimitz carriers have four of these along the sides, called upper-stage elevators. They only go down two decks. Then their loads have to be moved sideways to lower-stage elevators inside the hull, which take them down further.

Island

Flight deck   Crane

Hanger entrance

Aircraft have folding wings to take up less space

Upper stage elevator forms part of flight deck when raised

Anchor

Air defence guns

The flight deck of an aircraft carrier is one of the world's most dangerous places to work.

Hull The steel alloy hull on a US Nimitz class carrier is more than 300 metres long, with a flight deck about 20 metres above the water.

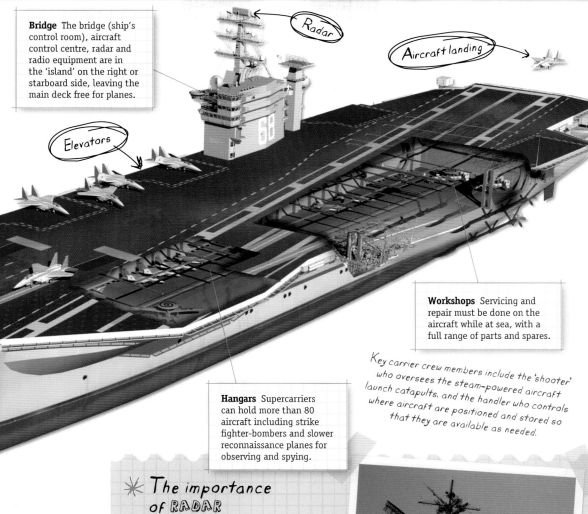

Radar

Aircraft landing

Bridge The bridge (ship's control room), aircraft control centre, radar and radio equipment are in the 'island' on the right or starboard side, leaving the main deck free for planes.

Elevators

68

Workshops Servicing and repair must be done on the aircraft while at sea, with a full range of parts and spares.

Key carrier crew members include the 'shooter' who oversees the steam-powered aircraft launch catapults, and the handler who controls where aircraft are positioned and stored so that they are available as needed.

Hangars Supercarriers can hold more than 80 aircraft including strike fighter-bombers and slower reconnaissance planes for observing and spying.

Big carriers have a ship's crew of up to 3000 people, and another 3000 aircraft crew including pilots and maintenance engineers.

✳ The importance of RADAR

Radar (Radio Direction And Ranging) works like sonar (see page 274) but uses radio waves instead of sound. Radar can detect nearby ships, shorelines and hazards such as icebergs showing above the surface, and also aircraft or other objects in the sky many hundreds of kilometres away. Radar cannot be used beneath the surface because radio waves travel very poorly underwater.

A complex array of radar and radio masts on a modern carrier

SUBMARINE

A submarine is designed to travel underwater for long distances. (Submersibles go deeper but not long distances, see page 280.) Most large subs are military craft, known as the 'silent service' because they can remain hidden under the surface and undetected for weeks or even months. To do this they must carry all their fuel, food and other stores, although they can make fresh water to drink and also vital oxygen to breathe, both from sea water.

Eureka!

The first submarines were built in the 1620s by Cornelius Drebbel. Powered by oars, they were rowed along the river Thames to impress King James I. In 1776 David Bushnell built the *Turtle*, the first military submarine, to attack British ships in the American War of Independence (1775–1783).

Whatever next?

One of the strangest sports is submarine racing. Spectators try to spot the positions of the submarines by the bubbles they release, or their periscopes – if it ever happens, that is!

Periscope The periscope is a vertical telescope that extends from the tower when the sub is 'below' (submerged), to see around at the surface.

Ballistic missile

Tower The fin, sail or conning (control) tower is where people enter and leave through hatches, and where the crew can keep watch when the sub is at the surface.

Bridge

☀ UNDERSEA WORLD

Many coastal areas now have tourist submarines where visitors can travel beneath the surface to watch fish, corals and other underwater life. It's easier than scuba-diving! The latest versions are 20 metres long, carry 50 passengers down to 100 metres, and stay under for more than an hour. They are powered by electric motors driven by rechargeable batteries so they are quiet and cause almost no pollution.

Bunks

Tourists enjoy an all-round view

Sonar sphere

In 1958 the US submarine Nautilus sailed past the North Pole – under the floating raft of ice that covers most of the Arctic Ocean.

Most submarines can only descend a few hundred metres at the most. American Seawolf subs would probably be crushed below 500 m. The Russian Komsomlets sub could reach 1200 m.

Nuclear reactor
The nuclear reactor is contained in a radiation-proof casing. In many subs it only needs refuelling every 12–15 years.

Turbines Heat from the nuclear reactor boils water that pushes at huge pressure past the angled blades of a turbine, making it spin to turn the propellers.

Propeller The prop is designed to work very quietly, without forming too many swirls or bubbles, so that other boats cannot hear or see the sub approaching.

Galley

Mess room

726

Planes Hydroplanes tilt to make the submarine rise or fall, and the rudders steer it left or right.

Ballast tanks These chambers are between the outer waterproof hull and the inner pressure hull that withstands the incredible pressure at depth.

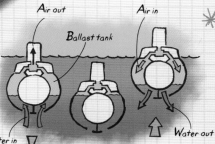

Air out

Ballast tank

Air in

Water in

Going down

Water out

Coming up

Some submarines can stay underwater for more than six months. The limit is not so much fuel, drinking water or oxygen but food for the crew.

✳ How do subs WORK?

A sub goes up or down using the ballast tanks between its inner and outer hulls. To sink, it allows air out of the tanks and water in. This makes the sub heavier than the water around it, so it descends. To rise, compressed air made from sea water is forced at high pressure into the tanks. Here the air expands, and although it weighs the same as when compressed, it takes up more space – which was formerly occupied by much heavier water. The sub is now lighter, so it ascends.

DEEP-SEA SUBMERSIBLE

Submersibles are specialized to dive very deep but not travel too far (unlike submarines). They are used mainly for scientific research, surveys and exploring wrecks. Crewed submersibles must have air inside, and the pressure of the water around would crush an ordinary submarine like paper. The best shape to withstand all-around pressure is all round – like the sphere of *Trieste*. In 1960 it descended to Earth's lowest point, the Challenger Deep in the northwest Pacific. No craft or people have ever been nearer to the centre of the Earth.

Eureka!

In 1985 in the north-west Atlantic Ocean the remote submersible Argo, a sled-like design with cameras, located the wreck of the massive liner *Titanic*. It had sunk in 1912 and rested 3800 metres down on the seabed.

Whatever next?

An 'undersea town' where people live and work will allow scientists to study ocean wildlife. They would not have to keep coming up to the surface, which involves slow depressurization to avoid the dangerous condition known as the 'bends'.

Piccard and Walsh spent 20 minutes on the Challenger Deep seabed, eating chocolate for extra energy.

ROVs (Remote Operated Vehicles) are uncrewed submersibles controlled by a long cable, the umbilical or tether. Some have TV cameras and mechanical hands so the operator at the surface can see and hold items.

Propeller

Water ballast tanks
The water tanks were positioned at the front and rear of the upper float part.

Gasoline tanks Filling most of the upper float part, these tanks contained 85 cubic metres of gasoline (petrol).

✳ How did TRIESTE work?

The crew sphere had to withstand pressures of more than one tonne on a fingernail-sized area. Made of 13-centimetre thick steel, it weighed 8 tonnes in water and would sink like a stone. So it was made buoyant by the upper float part containing lighter-than-water gasoline (petrol). The water ballast tanks were adjusted so the craft descended slowly. At the end of the dive, release magnets allowed iron ballast to fall out of the ballast hoppers, making the whole craft lighter so it could rise.

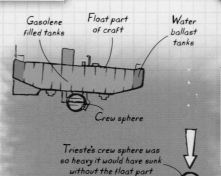

Gasolene filled tanks

Float part of craft

Water ballast tanks

Crew sphere

Trieste's crew sphere was so heavy it would have sunk without the float part

Seabed

Ballast hopper
Nine tonnes of ballast or weight in these two chambers was in the form of small iron pellets.

Release magnets

In 1996 the remote submersible Kaiko dived to 10,895 m in the Challenger Deep – not quite as far as Trieste.

Entrance hatch The hatch opened into a tunnel that went through the middle of the upper float part of the craft to the crew sphere below.

The crew on Trieste's record-breaking dive were Jacques Piccard, son of the craft's designer Auguste, and Don Walsh.

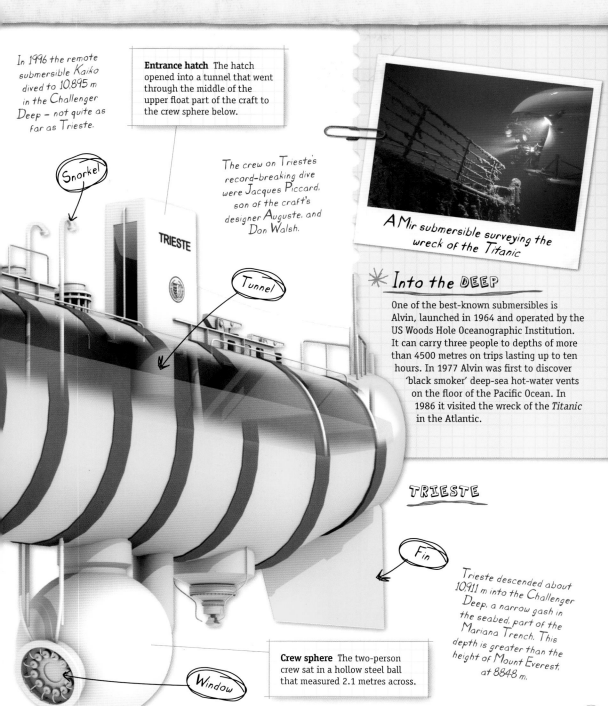

Snorkel

TRIESTE

Tunnel

A Mir submersible surveying the wreck of the Titanic

❋ Into the DEEP

One of the best-known submersibles is Alvin, launched in 1964 and operated by the US Woods Hole Oceanographic Institution. It can carry three people to depths of more than 4500 metres on trips lasting up to ten hours. In 1977 Alvin was first to discover 'black smoker' deep-sea hot-water vents on the floor of the Pacific Ocean. In 1986 it visited the wreck of the *Titanic* in the Atlantic.

TRIESTE

Fin

Trieste descended about 10,911 m into the Challenger Deep, a narrow gash in the seabed, part of the Mariana Trench. This depth is greater than the height of Mount Everest, at 8848 m.

Crew sphere The two-person crew sat in a hollow steel ball that measured 2.1 metres across.

Window

AIRCRAFT

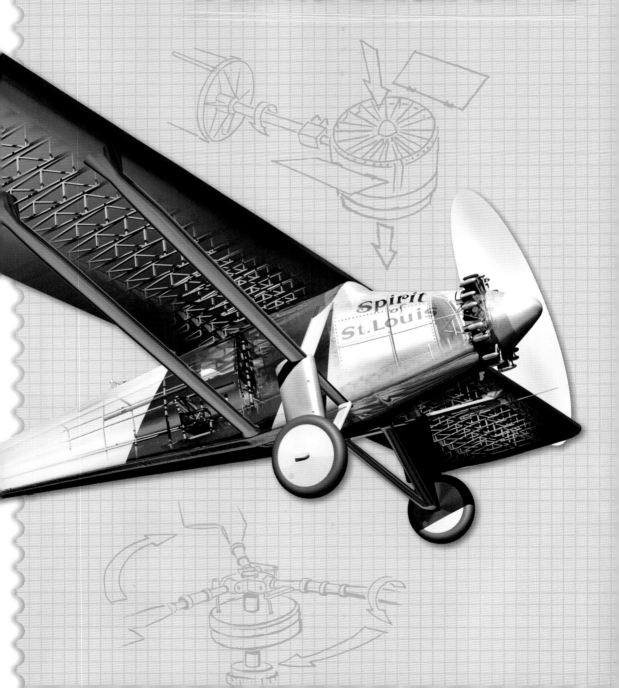

Spirit of St.Louis

INTRODUCTION

It's an age-old dream to fly like the birds. People once strapped wings of feathers or cloth to their arms, jumped off cliffs and church towers and flapped as hard as they could. No one flew, and several plunged to their deaths. Gradually, people realized that human muscles are too weak for the body to fly on its own, even with wings. It needs help from machinery and technology.

Birds inspired early human fliers.

Aerofoil shape with curved upper surface

Curved shape of wing gives LIFT

Airflow is faster over the wing, resulting in lower pressure

Air resistance causes DRAG

Forward force of engine gives THRUST

Craft is pulled down by GRAVITY

An aircraft's movements are the result of the balance of four forces – lift and gravity and thrust and drag.

LIFT-OFF

More than 200 years ago the first people left the ground. They were balloonists and they stayed airborne for hours, even days. However they could only go where the wind took them. Over 100 years ago, pioneer pilots built wood-and-cloth craft – the first gliders or sailplanes. They copied the curved 'aerofoil' shape of bird wings to give lift. They saw how wings twist, or warp, to give a balance of forces that controls speed and direction. But without power they couldn't stay airborne for long.

PLANES TAKE OFF

In 1903 the Wright Brothers from Dayton, Ohio, USA added a small, light, home-made petrol engine to their carefully tested glider. The engine turned propellers to provide a forward force called thrust. The craft's wings twisted to control its direction. The brother's spindly machine not only flew, but began a new era of travel, leisure and danger – the Age of Aircraft.

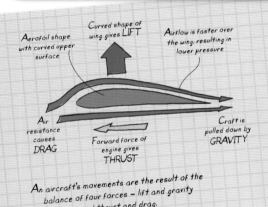

The Wrights' Flyer and other early aircraft were light, delicate and easily blown around by the wind – flying was limited to dry, calm days.

ADVANCES IN WAR

During World War I (1914–1918) planes became bigger, stronger, more controllable and more reliable. After the conflict, more people took up flying and set all kinds of aerial records. World War II (1939–1945) brought more progress, especially a new design of engine to produce the forward force of thrust. It was named after the hot blast of gases from its rear end – the jet.

World War II was the first major conflict where aircraft, like the Supermarine Spitfire, played leading roles.

YAW
controlled by rudder

ROLL
controlled by
ailerons

Rudder

Ailerons

Elevator

PITCH
controlled by
elevators

Three sets of control
surfaces steer an aircraft
through the sky.

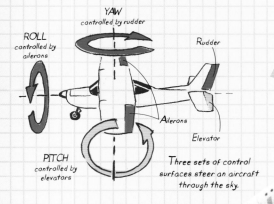

The Airbus A380 Super Jumbo is the latest and biggest in a long line of passenger aircraft.

TOWARDS TOMORROW

As more peaceful times arrived during the 1950s, air travel really took off. Jumbo-sized passenger jets now carry people around the world for business meetings and exotic holidays. Military planes have become faster and sleeker, with stealth technology to avoid radar and heat-seeking missiles. Some craft take off and land straight up and down, with hovering jets or whirling helicopter rotors. Like everything else, computers get in on the act, as 'fly-by-wire' helps pilots and their planes to stay safer.

The world of aircraft never stands still. Aviation is still hardly more than one century old. What will the next 100 years bring?

HOT-AIR BALLOON

Balloons do not truly fly – they float. A hot-air balloon contains air that is heated by a burner. The heat makes the tiny particles (molecules) of air spread out so there are fewer of them in the same space. This makes the air inside the balloon lighter than the air around it, so the balloon rises. The pilot can control the balloon's height by turning up the flame, but its direction depends entirely on the wind.

Eureka!

The first people to make a flight in a hot-air balloon were Pîlatre de Rozier and Francois Laurent, Marquis d'Arlandes. In 1783 in France, they travelled 9 kilometres across the city of Paris, at a height of about 25 metres, in a balloon made by brothers Joseph and Jacques Montgolfier.

Whatever next?

Scientists have tested a personal helium balloon attached to a backpack with an electric motor and propeller. The idea is that people can fly where they want.

Turning vent

Balloon safaris over the African plains are a good way for tourists to see wildlife.

Envelope The balloon's main part is the tough outer casing, the envelope. It's made of long curved strips, called gores, of non-tear fabric such as nylon. The part near the burner – the throat – is made of heat-proof material such as Nomex.

In 2007 David Hempleman-Adams soared to a record height for a hot-air balloon – 9.7 km.

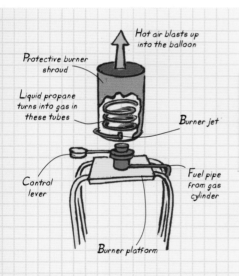

Hot air blasts up into the balloon

Protective burner shroud

Liquid propane turns into gas in these tubes

Burner jet

Control lever

Fuel pipe from gas cylinder

Burner platform

Load ropes Strong cords sewn into the seams between the panels extend down to the skirt. They spread the weight of the basket around the envelope, like a giant net.

✳ How do BURNERS work?

Most balloons have a burner that uses propane gas as fuel. The propane is compressed (squeezed) into a liquid inside a metal cylinder. It flows to the burner along a coiled tube where it's heated by the flame nearby. Then it squirts out of a jet (hole) as a gas where it mixes with air and catches fire to make the flame.

Old airships used the very light gas hydrogen, but this can catch fire. The Hindenburg went up in flames in 1937, killing 36 people and ending the airship era.

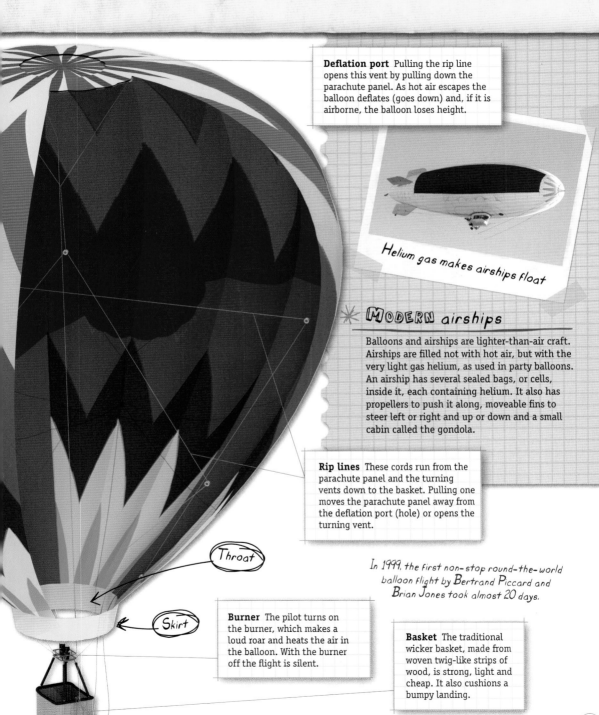

Deflation port Pulling the rip line opens this vent by pulling down the parachute panel. As hot air escapes the balloon deflates (goes down) and, if it is airborne, the balloon loses height.

Helium gas makes airships float

✳ MODERN airships

Balloons and airships are lighter-than-air craft. Airships are filled not with hot air, but with the very light gas helium, as used in party balloons. An airship has several sealed bags, or cells, inside it, each containing helium. It also has propellers to push it along, moveable fins to steer left or right and up or down and a small cabin called the gondola.

Rip lines These cords run from the parachute panel and the turning vents down to the basket. Pulling one moves the parachute panel away from the deflation port (hole) or opens the turning vent.

Throat

In 1999, the first non-stop round-the-world balloon flight by Bertrand Piccard and Brian Jones took almost 20 days.

Skirt

Burner The pilot turns on the burner, which makes a loud roar and heats the air in the balloon. With the burner off the flight is silent.

Basket The traditional wicker basket, made from woven twig-like strips of wood, is strong, light and cheap. It also cushions a bumpy landing.

HANG-GLIDER

A glider is an aircraft without an engine. A hang-glider is a fabric wing stretched over a rigid frame from which the pilot hangs by straps. It can be steered left and right and go fast or slow. However it cannot climb unaided (unless carried by rising air) so it gradually descends through the air around it.

Eureka!

Hang-gliding was pioneered over a century ago by Otto Lilienthal near Berlin, Germany. He built his own hill and 20 of his own-design gliders and made more than 2500 flights. Sadly, in 1896 he crash-landed and died.

Leading edge tubes Strong tubes along the wing's front give it the correct shape. Like all parts of the frame, they are made of light but strong aluminium metal or carbon-fibre composite.

Bracing wires Thin, strong metal wires join many sections of the hang-glider frame. They strengthen it and help it keep its shape even in high winds and during fast turns.

Nose

✳ How do HANG-GLIDER controls work?

The pilot lies in a harness inside a bag, or cocoon, with body weight directly below the main wing for straight, level flight. Moving the control bar shifts the body weight from this central position and tips the wing at an angle.

A-frame

Pushing the control bar forwards moves the body weight back and makes the craft rise

Swinging the control bar right shifts body weight to the left and the craft turns left

Swinging the control bar left shifts body weight to the right and the craft turns right

Pulling the control bar moves body weight forwards and the craft tilts nose-down to descend faster

A-frame This metal frame is fixed by a firm, rigid joint at its top end to the hang-glider's main lengthways pole, the keel.

Control bar Part of the A-frame, the pilot holds the control bar by the non-slip grips and pushes or pulls it to make the hang-glider fly in different directions.

In 2002 in Texas, USA, Michael Barber flew a hang-glider more than 700 km.

Whatever next?

A powered hang-glider has a small, lightweight motorcycle-type engine just behind the pilot, which turns a small propeller. It's the closest machine that most of us can get to a personal aircraft.

Crossbar

Plastic battens Long, thin strips called battens slide into pockets in the wing. These keep the wing straight and rigid in the right places, so it slips easily through the air without flapping.

Wing (sail) The shape of a hang-glider is based on a design called the Rogallo wing. It's also made of very strong, tear-proof, material such as nylon or Kevlar.

The fastest hang-gliders can exceed speeds of 140 km/h.

Keel

In the best conditions with lots of rising air, hang-glider pilots can reach heights of more than 5000 m.

✳ FLY like a bird!

Gliders cannot climb under their own power – they have none. They slowly descend through the air. However, if the pilot can find air that's rising – like wind blowing up a hill or hot air rising from sun-warmed rocks – this will carry the glider higher. After swooping down the pilot can do the same again and in favourable conditions stay up in the air for hours.

Air rising over mountains lifts a hang-glider higher

SAILPLANE

Like any type of glider, the sailplane cannot rise through the air under its own power since it has no motor or engine. However, the modern high-performance sailplane is so light and streamlined that it loses height very, very slowly as it glides. If it finds rising air – such as wind blowing up a hill – it soon climbs up near the clouds.

Eureka!

Most sailplanes have a skin of light, smooth, strong glass-fibre (GRP, glass-reinforced plastic resin). This was first used in the German Akaflieg FS-24 glider in 1957.

Whatever next?

The newest gliders use carbon, aramid and polyethylene fibres for construction and have detachable upturned wing ends or 'twisted winglets' as found on passenger jets.

Retractable undercarriage The single wheel folds up into the body after take-off and until landing to reduce air resistance, or drag.

Construction Sailplanes make use of the strongest, lightest materials such as carbon-fibre composites and alloys (mixtures of metals).

Cockpit The pilot has fewer controls and displays than a powered plane since there are no levers or dials for engine speed, fuel level and similar readings.

Tow point

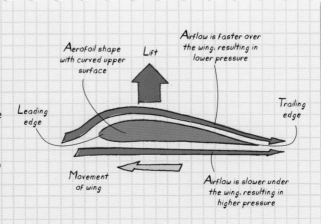

✳ How do WINGS work?

An aircraft's wing is not a flat sheet. It is curved when seen edge-on, a shape called an aerofoil. The curve is greater on the upper surface than the lower. Air flowing past the wing must go faster over the top than beneath, and faster air means less air pressure. So the lower air pressure above the wing sucks it upwards with a force called lift.

Aerofoil shape with curved upper surface

Lift

Airflow is faster over the wing, resulting in lower pressure

Leading edge

Trailing edge

Fibre-glass skin

Movement of wing

Airflow is slower under the wing, resulting in higher pressure

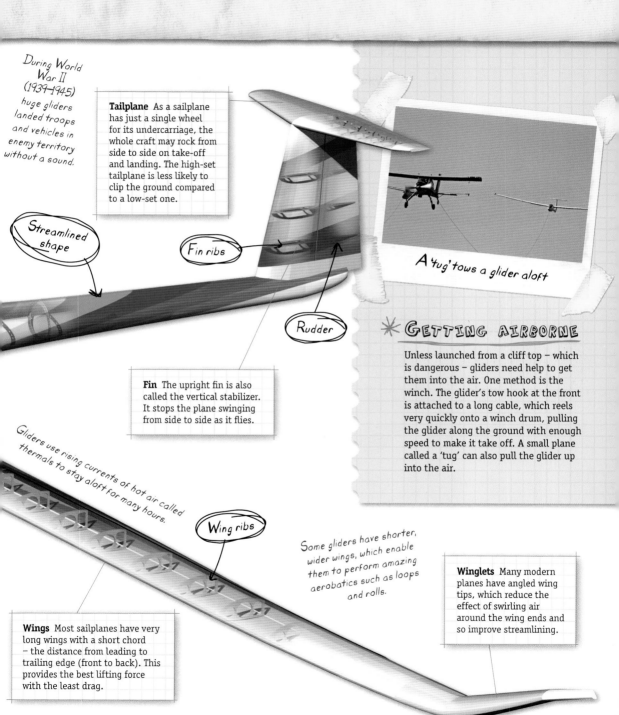

During World War II (1939–1945) huge gliders landed troops and vehicles in enemy territory without a sound.

Tailplane As a sailplane has just a single wheel for its undercarriage, the whole craft may rock from side to side on take-off and landing. The high-set tailplane is less likely to clip the ground compared to a low-set one.

Streamlined shape

Fin ribs

Rudder

A 'tug' tows a glider aloft

Fin The upright fin is also called the vertical stabilizer. It stops the plane swinging from side to side as it flies.

✳ GETTING AIRBORNE

Unless launched from a cliff top – which is dangerous – gliders need help to get them into the air. One method is the winch. The glider's tow hook at the front is attached to a long cable, which reels very quickly onto a winch drum, pulling the glider along the ground with enough speed to make it take off. A small plane called a 'tug' can also pull the glider up into the air.

Gliders use rising currents of hot air called thermals to stay aloft for many hours.

Wing ribs

Some gliders have shorter, wider wings, which enable them to perform amazing aerobatics such as loops and rolls.

Winglets Many modern planes have angled wing tips, which reduce the effect of swirling air around the wing ends and so improve streamlining.

Wings Most sailplanes have very long wings with a short chord – the distance from leading to trailing edge (front to back). This provides the best lifting force with the least drag.

WRIGHT FLYER

The time: 10:35 am, Thursday 17 December 1903. The place: A windy beach near Kitty Hawk, North Carolina, USA. The event: The first-ever flight in a controlled, powered aircraft, the *Flyer*, built by brothers Wilbur and Orville Wright. Watched by just a handful of helpers, it lasted 12 seconds – but it would change the world.

Eureka!

The Wright brothers spent many hours watching how birds twist their wings for flight control. This gave them the wing-warping idea to control the *Flyer*.

Whatever next?

After Orville's first flight, the *Flyer* made three more trips that day, with the brothers taking turns to fly. Wilbur's last flight was the longest – 260 metres in 59 seconds.

Muslin covering

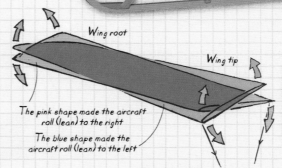

The Flyer covered 37 m on its first trip – half the length of an Airbus A380 jumbo jet.

Elevator lever
The pilot's left hand worked a lever to tilt the two front elevators and control the *Flyer*'s height.

Canard layout
Flyer had elevators at the front, which is known as a canard design.

Elevators

Hip cradle

✳ How did WING WARPING work?

Flyer's bendy wings could be twisted, or warped, along their length. This gave the wing on one side more lifting force than the other, so raising it higher as the other wing dipped. It made the plane lean or roll to the side. Modern planes have flap-like ailerons at the rear outer edges of their wings for the same purpose (see page 294).

Wing root

Wing tip

The pink shape made the aircraft roll (lean) to the right

The blue shape made the aircraft roll (lean) to the left

Wires pulled the wing to twist its shape

Skids The base of the main airframe worked like skis, or skids, to slide along the sand on landing.

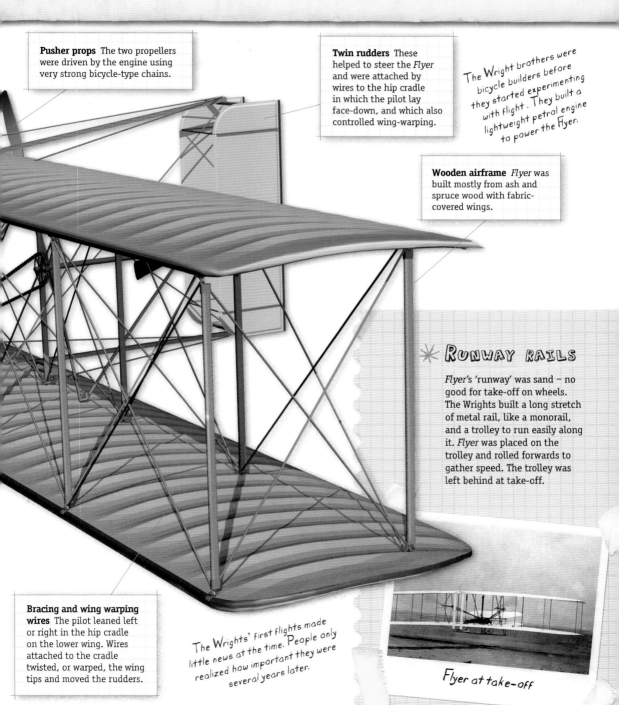

Pusher props The two propellers were driven by the engine using very strong bicycle-type chains.

Twin rudders These helped to steer the *Flyer* and were attached by wires to the hip cradle in which the pilot lay face-down, and which also controlled wing-warping.

The Wright brothers were bicycle builders before they started experimenting with flight. They built a lightweight petrol engine to power the Flyer.

Wooden airframe *Flyer* was built mostly from ash and spruce wood with fabric-covered wings.

✳ RUNWAY RAILS

Flyer's 'runway' was sand – no good for take-off on wheels. The Wrights built a long stretch of metal rail, like a monorail, and a trolley to run easily along it. *Flyer* was placed on the trolley and rolled forwards to gather speed. The trolley was left behind at take-off.

Bracing and wing warping wires The pilot leaned left or right in the hip cradle on the lower wing. Wires attached to the cradle twisted, or warped, the wing tips and moved the rudders.

The Wrights' first flights made little news at the time. People only realized how important they were several years later.

Flyer at take-off

CESSNA 172 SKYHAWK

Light aircraft are like flying versions of family cars. The most common kinds have four seats and a single car-type engine that spins a propeller. These planes cannot fly very fast or do amazing stunts. However they are strong, reliable, easy to fly and simple to service. They are also light – about half the weight of a family car.

Eureka!

The first Cessna 172s were built over 50 years ago, in 1955. From the start, the makers believed they had a world-beating design – and they were right.

Whatever next?

A future version of the Cessna 172 will be powered by a turbo diesel engine, similar to the engines in some fast cars.

Engine The plane is powered mainly by Lycoming or Continental engines with four or six cylinders. The engine works in the same way as a car engine. Fuel and air burn inside the cylinders and push the pistons along. However the cylinders are not in a line as in a car. They lie flat, with one half facing one side and the other half facing the other side. This is called a horizontally opposed layout.

Control stick This is linked to the ailerons and elevators by long metal cables. Push it forwards and the plane dives, pull it back and the plane climbs.

Spinner

Yaw
controlled by rudder

Roll
controlled by
ailerons

Rudder

Pitch
controlled by
elevators

Ailerons

Elevator

Rudder pedals Pushing the left pedal causes the rudder at the rear to swing to the left, making the plane steer to the left.

How do CONTROL SURFACES work?

Control surfaces are moveable parts on the wings and tail. As a control surface moves, air rushing past pushes against it and moves that part of the plane. This changes the plane's pitch (up and down), yaw (left or right) and roll (lean to the side).

More Cessna 172s have been built than any other aircraft – over 43,000.

More people have learned to fly in the Cessna 172 than in any other plane.

Rudder This control surface is worked by the pilot's pedals and makes the plane steer left or right. It is hinged onto the upright 'tail', which is known as the fin, and helps the plane to fly straight.

Tail plane

Elevators These control surfaces are hinged onto the tailplane, the small wing at the rear. They are moved by long cables attached to the control stick. They both move up or down together.

The name 'Skyhawk' was first used for the Cessna 172 in 1961.

Elevator cables

Rudder cables

✳ How do TAIL-LESS aircraft fly?

Delta-wing or flying-wing planes have no tailplane at the rear for the elevators. Instead, each main wing has a combined elevator-aileron control surface, the elevon.

Elevon

Control cable pulleys

The 172's normal cruising speed is 220 km/h, but versions with a souped-up engine can reach a speed of almost 250 km/h.

Ailerons These control surfaces are at the end of each wing, on the rear or trailing edge. They are worked by cables from the control stick. When the aileron on one side tilts up, the other tilts down.

Wheel fairing

F-117 Nighthawk fighter, a delta-wing aircraft

SOPWITH CAMEL

One of the best fighter planes of World War I (1914–1918), the Camel was speedy and agile in the air. As they twisted and turned in deadly aerial battles called 'dogfights', Camels from the air forces of Britain and its allies (friendly countries) shot down almost 1300 enemy planes – more than any other allied aircraft.

Twin machine guns The pilot aimed the Vickers machine guns accurately by looking along their barrels and pointing the plane straight at the target.

Biplane design A biplane has two sets of main wings one above the other. This gives lots of lifting force for a fairly small wingspan (tip-to-tip length).

Struts and braces Wooden pole-like struts held apart the two sets of wings. Taut bracing wires made the whole structure very strong yet lightweight.

Rotary engine The cylinders were arranged like the spokes of a wheel, as in a radial engine (see page 298). They moved around the central shaft rather than staying still.

Cockpit

Engine cowl

How do PROPELLERS work?

A propeller works partly by pushing air backwards, like a spinning electric fan with flat angled blades. Propeller blades are not flat. They have an aerofoil shape (see the blue, yellow and green cutaway areas) more curved on the front surface than the rear, like an aircraft wing. This produces lower air pressure in front of the blade than behind. So the blade 'sucks' itself forwards as well as pushing air backwards.

Hub or boss

Steep or coarse pitch

The angle or pitch of the blade is greatest near the hub, where the blade moves slower through the air

The blade tip moves much faster through the air, so a shallower angle works best

Shallow or fine pitch

The engine, fuel, machine guns and pilot were close together at the front. This made the Camel tricky to learn to fly but a supreme dogfighter for a fighter 'ace'.

Fabric-covered spoked wheels

Eureka!

To prevent their own bullets shooting off their propellers, early fighting planes had metal wedge shapes called deflectors fixed to the backs of the propeller blades. The bullets bounced off these at an angle rather than smashing into the wooden blade.

Whatever next?

The 2F.1 version of the Camel could take off from boats, and carried out the first ever ship-launched air raids in 1918.

The Camel took its name from the hump-like cover over the machine guns.

Fin and tailplane The fixed surfaces of these parts had bracing wires to keep them rigid and in position.

Rudder

Roundel This was the symbol of Britain's Royal Flying Corps, which became the Royal Air Force in 1918. It identified the plane so allies would not attack it.

Squadron markings

F2227

A Camel was tested as a mid-air launched fighter by attaching it under a huge airship and simply dropping it.

Wooden airframe

Nearly 5500 Camels were built, among the most of any World War I plane.

✳ Don't shoot the PROP!

Very early war planes had a hand-held gun, then a hand-operated gun on a metal arm with a swivel joint, aimed by the pilot or gunner. Sometimes in the heat of combat these flyers shot off their own propellers by mistake! The Camel had a synchronization mechanism where the spinning propeller shaft had a bulge or cam that pushed a rod each time it turned. The rod pressed against the trigger and prevented the machine gun firing for a split second each time a blade was in the way.

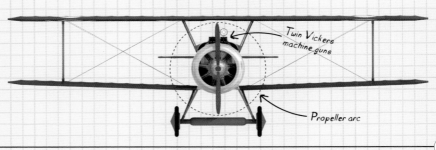

Twin Vickers machine guns

Propeller arc

RYAN NYP SPIRIT OF ST LOUIS

Right now, many people are flying across the Atlantic Ocean and some are very bored. In 1927, Charles Lindbergh had no time for boredom in *Spirit of St Louis*. He was completing the first non-stop solo flight over the Atlantic. The next day, he was a superstar.

Whatever next?

The first non-stop round-the-world flight was in December 1986 by Bert Rutan and Jeanna Yeager. Their craft *Voyager* was specially built for the trip. They took just over nine days – more than six times longer than Lindbergh – and covered about 42,400 kilometres.

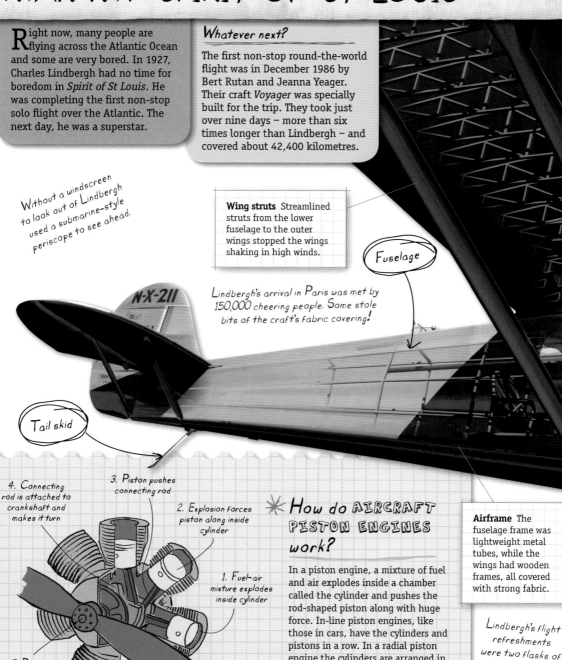

Without a windscreen to look out of, Lindbergh used a submarine-style periscope to see ahead.

Wing struts Streamlined struts from the lower fuselage to the outer wings stopped the wings shaking in high winds.

Fuselage

N·X·211

Lindbergh's arrival in Paris was met by 150,000 cheering people. Some stole bits of the craft's fabric covering!

Tail skid

4. Connecting rod is attached to crankshaft and makes it turn

3. Piston pushes connecting rod

2. Explosion forces piston along inside cylinder

1. Fuel-air mixture explodes inside cylinder

5. Propeller is mounted on crankshaft

Piston

✳ How do AIRCRAFT PISTON ENGINES work?

In a piston engine, a mixture of fuel and air explodes inside a chamber called the cylinder and pushes the rod-shaped piston along with huge force. In-line piston engines, like those in cars, have the cylinders and pistons in a row. In a radial piston engine the cylinders are arranged in a circle like the spokes of a wheel.

Airframe The fuselage frame was lightweight metal tubes, while the wings had wooden frames, all covered with strong fabric.

Lindbergh's flight refreshments were two flasks of water and four ham sandwiches.

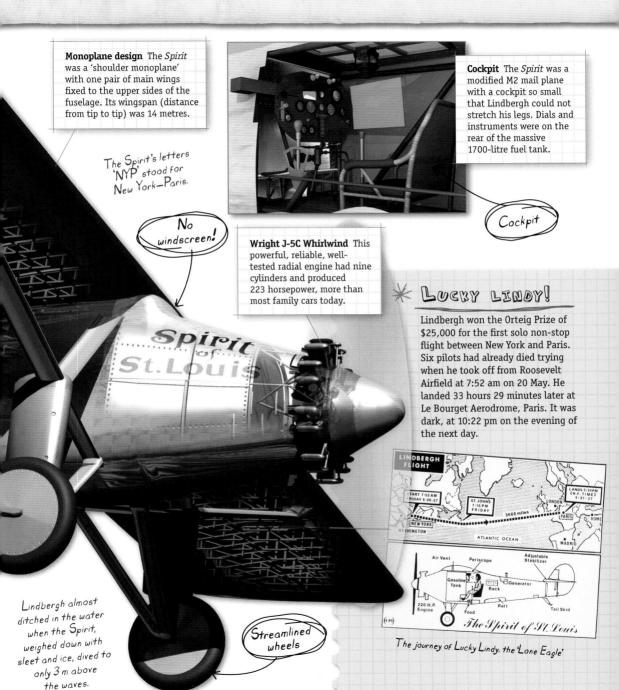

Monoplane design The *Spirit* was a 'shoulder monoplane' with one pair of main wings fixed to the upper sides of the fuselage. Its wingspan (distance from tip to tip) was 14 metres.

Cockpit The *Spirit* was a modified M2 mail plane with a cockpit so small that Lindbergh could not stretch his legs. Dials and instruments were on the rear of the massive 1700-litre fuel tank.

The *Spirit's* letters 'NYP' stood for New York–Paris.

No windscreen!

Cockpit

Wright J-5C Whirlwind This powerful, reliable, well-tested radial engine had nine cylinders and produced 223 horsepower, more than most family cars today.

Spirit of St. Louis

✳ LUCKY LINDY!

Lindbergh won the Orteig Prize of $25,000 for the first solo non-stop flight between New York and Paris. Six pilots had already died trying when he took off from Roosevelt Airfield at 7:52 am on 20 May. He landed 33 hours 29 minutes later at Le Bourget Aerodrome, Paris. It was dark, at 10:22 pm on the evening of the next day.

LINDBERGH FLIGHT

START 7:52 AM FRIDAY 5-20-27

ST. JOHN'S 7:15 PM FRIDAY

LONDON

LANDS 5:24PM (N.Y. TIME) 5-21-27

NEW YORK

WASHINGTON

3600 miles

PARIS

ROME

MADRID

ATLANTIC OCEAN

Air Vent   Periscope   Adjustable Stabilizer

Gasoline Tank   Generator   Rack

220 H.P. Engine   Food   Ratt   Tail Skid

The Spirit of St. Louis

The journey of Lucky Lindy, the 'Lone Eagle'

Lindbergh almost ditched in the water when the *Spirit*, weighed down with sleet and ice, dived to only 3 m above the waves.

Streamlined wheels

SUPERMARINE SPITFIRE

One of the world's most famous aircraft, the Spitfire fighter plane first flew in 1936 and was still being produced nine years later. It played a major part during World War II (1939–1945), especially the Battle of Britain (1940), being just about the fastest and most agile war plane of the time. Spitfires stayed in service until the 1950s.

Eureka!

The fastest Spitfires were able to chase jet-powered V1 flying bombs, fly alongside them and wiggle their wing tips to flip the bombs off course.

Over 20,000 Spitfires were built — more than any similar warplane.

Engine Early Spitfires had a Rolls Royce Merlin, as used on other aircraft of the time such as the Lancaster bomber. Later Spitfires had Rolls Royce's more powerful Griffon engine.

Fuel tank

✳ How do adjustable PITCH PROPS work?

The exact size, shape and pitch (angle) of propeller blades are carefully designed to give the best forward force or thrust. However as a prop turns faster for higher-speed flight, a different pitch works better than for slow flight. The adjustable pitch prop automatically changes the pitch of its blades to give the most possible thrust at different spinning speeds.

Coarse (steep) pitch for high speed flight

Propeller blade twists along this axis (line)

Streamlined spinner

Fine (shallow) pitch for low speed flight

Armament Early Spitfires had Browning machine guns in each wing. Later ones were also fitted with the more powerful Hispano cannons.

Propeller Different versions of the Spitfire had propellers with different numbers of blades from two to six. These became larger with more powerful engines.

The fastest wartime Spitfire had a top speed of about 730 km/h. Built for spying and photographic missions, it was painted pink to help it blend in with sunrise and sunset.

Whatever next?

Around the world about 50 Spitfires are still flying today. A few have a second seat so a passenger can enjoy the ride.

Several names were considered for the Spitfire and it was almost called the Supermarine Shrew!

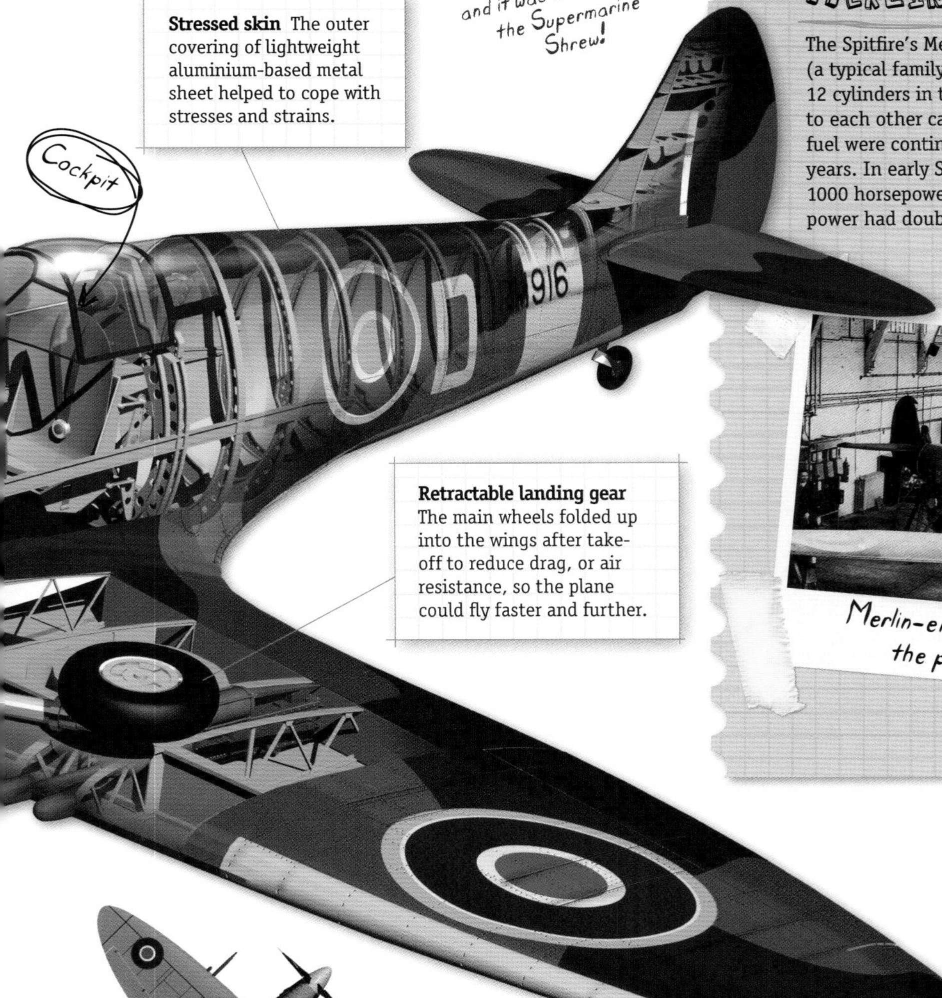

Stressed skin The outer covering of lightweight aluminium-based metal sheet helped to cope with stresses and strains.

Cockpit

✳ ROLLS ROYCE MERLIN

The Spitfire's Merlin engine was 27 litres (a typical family car is two litres). It had 12 cylinders in two rows of six at an angle to each other called a V12. Its design and fuel were continually improved over the years. In early Spitfires it produced about 1000 horsepower. Ten years later this power had doubled.

Merlin-engined Spitfires on the production line

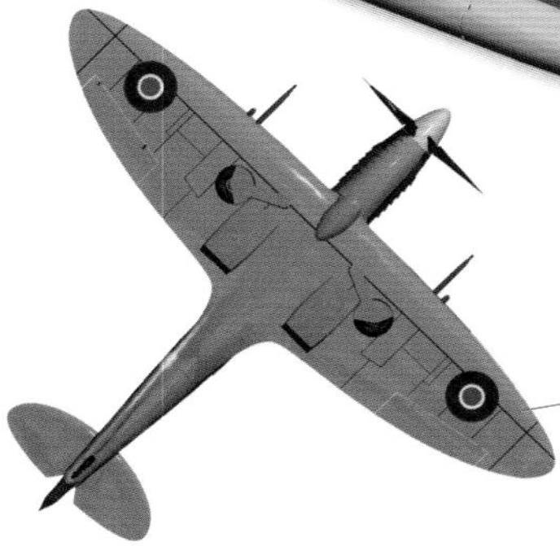

Retractable landing gear The main wheels folded up into the wings after take-off to reduce drag, or air resistance, so the plane could fly faster and further.

Curved wing tips

Wing shape The wings had a distinctive elliptical or 'oval' shape when seen from above or below (planform view).

Spitfires were famous in the Battle of Britain. However their companion fighters, Hawker Hurricanes, shot down more enemies.

SHORT SUNDERLAND S.25

Before big airports with hard runways, huge planes had trouble landing on airfields. 'Flying boat' seaplanes could use any sizeable stretch of water, such as a river, lake or sea. From World War II (1939–1945) until the 1960s, long-range Sunderlands patrolled the oceans to spot dangers such as enemy submarines, and some also carried passengers in great luxury.

Eureka!

In 1914 the world's first regular airline service began in the USA. The St Petersburg–Tampa Airboat Line used Benoist XIV flying boats. Each trip took ten minutes and carried up to three passengers.

Whatever next?

Many inventors have built flying cars that can take off from an ordinary straight road. The problem is that learning to fly takes at least 50 times longer and is more than 20 times more costly than learning to drive.

Top turret

Gun turrets The gun turrets had Browning .303 machine guns and could swivel around under electrical power to aim at the enemy.

The first Sunderland flew in 1937 and some were still in service 40 years later.

Engines The most powerful Sunderlands had four Pratt & Whitney R-1830-90B Twin Wasp engines, each with 14 cylinders.

The Sunderland's fuselage was shaped like a fast boat so it could take off and land through the waves.

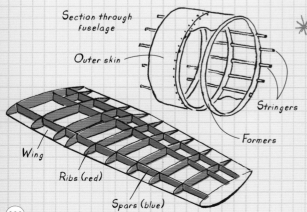

Section through fuselage

Outer skin

Stringers

Formers

Wing

Ribs (red)

Spars (blue)

✳ How does an AIRFRAME work?

The airframe is the strong 'skeleton' of an aircraft. The fuselage has hoop-shaped formers and long stringers, or longerons. The wings have curved ribs from front to back and rigid spars along their length. Both are usually covered in a thin 'skin' of the very light metal aluminium.

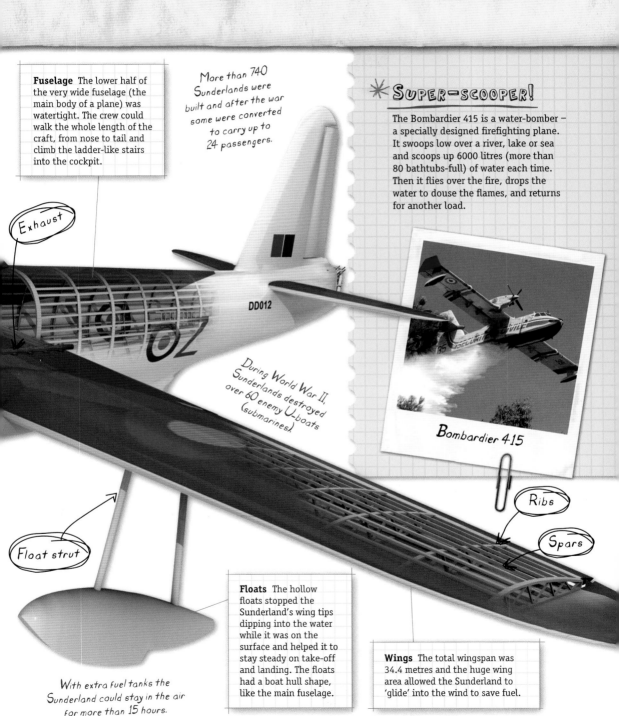

Fuselage The lower half of the very wide fuselage (the main body of a plane) was watertight. The crew could walk the whole length of the craft, from nose to tail and climb the ladder-like stairs into the cockpit.

More than 740 Sunderlands were built and after the war some were converted to carry up to 24 passengers.

Exhaust

DD012

During World War II, Sunderlands destroyed over 60 enemy U-boats (submarines).

Float strut

With extra fuel tanks the Sunderland could stay in the air for more than 15 hours.

Floats The hollow floats stopped the Sunderland's wing tips dipping into the water while it was on the surface and helped it to stay steady on take-off and landing. The floats had a boat hull shape, like the main fuselage.

*✳ SUPER-SCOOPER!

The Bombardier 415 is a water-bomber – a specially designed firefighting plane. It swoops low over a river, lake or sea and scoops up 6000 litres (more than 80 bathtubs-full) of water each time. Then it flies over the fire, drops the water to douse the flames, and returns for another load.

Bombardier 415

Ribs

Spars

Wings The total wingspan was 34.4 metres and the huge wing area allowed the Sunderland to 'glide' into the wind to save fuel.

HARRIER JUMP JET

The Harrier is the world's most successful VTOL jet aircraft. VTOL stands for Vertical Take-Off and Landing. It means the Harrier can rise straight up on take-off, hover in mid air, then come straight down to land. The first Harriers flew in the late 1960s and have been through four main versions and many small improvements. Dozens still serve in several air forces around the world.

Eureka!

One of the VTOL test craft that led to the Harrier involved two jet engines fitted into a metal frame. It hovered briefly in 1953 and was called the 'Flying Bedstead'.

Pilot Harrier pilots say that the craft flies like an ordinary plane at fast speeds, but more like a helicopter at slow speeds and when hovering or moving up and down.

Cockpit canopy

VTOL uses so much fuel that Harriers are usually STOL, Short Take-Off and Landing.

Mid-air refuelling nozzle

Nose radar This sends out powerful radio wave blips and detects their echoes bouncing off objects ahead.

* How does the HARRIER hover?

The Harrier's single Rolls Royce Pegasus jet engine sends out a continuous blast of hot gases but these do not come out of a hole at the plane's rear as usual. They rush out of four underwing nozzles, which can swivel through a right angle (90°). The nozzles point straight down for vertical flight and then slowly turn or swivel to aim straight backwards for full speed ahead.

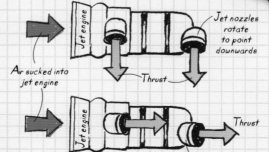

Hovering or vertical flight

Jet engine

Air sucked into jet engine

Jet nozzles rotate to point downwards

Thrust

Jet engine

Forward flight

Thrust

Jet nozzles rotate to aim backwards

Air intake Air for the jet engine is sucked in through two intakes, one on each side of the fuselage.

Whatever next?

In September 2008, Swiss aviator Yves Rossy flew across the English Channel using a back-pack powered by four jet engines. Rossy reached a speed of almost 300 kilometres per hour and completed the 34 kilometre journey in less than 10 minutes.

Harriers have starred in several big movies, including James Bond's The Living Daylights (1987) and True Lies (1994) with Arnold Schwarzenegger.

A pilot makes an emergency exit using his ejector seat

✳ FAST EXIT

Many military aircraft have ejector seats. In an emergency, the pilot pulls a lever that makes the cockpit canopy (cover) blast away and then sets off a small rocket under the seat. The rocket fires the seat with the pilot upwards to get clear of the plane – especially the tail, which comes up fast behind. The pilot can then detach from the seat and parachute down to safety.

Missile

Underwing pylon mountings

Rear-facing radar A radar dish in the tail detects planes, ships and other objects up to several hundred kilometres behind the Harrier.

Wing tip thruster

Jet thrust nozzles The blast of air from the jet engine comes out through four swivelling nozzles. There are two on either side, one in front of the other.

The Harrier can usually hover for just 90 seconds. Then its jet engine starts to overheat because it is not cooled by moving through the air.

Underwing pods Clip-on pods can carry various weapons such as rockets and missiles, or extra fuel tanks to give a greater range (distance).

LOCKHEED C-130 HERCULES

Wars don't always break out next to large airports with long, smooth runways. Transport planes such as the Hercules must be strong and tough, able to lift great loads after a short take-off from rough air strips or even from farm fields and sandy deserts. The Hercules first flew in 1954 and hundreds are still in action in more than 60 countries.

Eureka!

After landing, the Russian An-124 Condor heavy transport 'kneels' by shortening its nose wheel undercarriage. This lowers the nose to the ground, then the whole nose door swings opens for easy loading.

One Hercules was equipped with rockets slanting downwards and missile engines facing backwards so it could take off and land almost like a helicopter!

Propellers Early Hercules models had three or four blades for each propeller. The latest version, the C-130J Super Hercules, has six blades on each prop.

Flight deck The standard flight crew of five is a captain (main pilot), a co-pilot, a navigator, a flight engineer who looks after the engines and mechanical systems and a loadmaster in charge of the cargo.

More than 2200 Hercules have been made for 67 countries worldwide.

Forward-looking radar

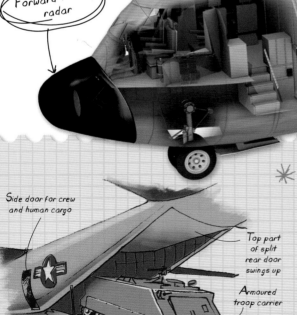

Undercarriage bay

The Hercules' many roles include mid-air refuelling tanker, flying hospital, survey plane, airborne weather station and search-and-rescue.

Side door for crew and human cargo

Top part of split rear door swings up

Armoured troop carrier

Lower rear door forms loading ramp

✳ LOADING UP

Some versions of the Hercules can carry more than 20 tonnes of cargo. Military vehicles such as jeeps and armoured cars, or more than 100 combat-ready soldiers, load themselves up the rear ramp, which lowers down to the ground. Or rollers can be fitted onto the floor to slide tray-like pallets of freight along inside the fuselage.

Whatever next?

The problem of landing a Hercules in cold, snowy places was solved by fitting it with skis in addition to the ordinary wheels.

Engines Four turboprop engines power the Hercules. These have turbine blades inside like a jet engine (see page 310) rather than pistons in cylinders.

High-set tailplane The tailplane is set high up at the end of the fuselage to allow for the loading ramp, which forms the rear, sloping part of the fuselage floor.

UF 8668

The Hercules is one of only four planes still in production more than 50 years after it was first introduced.

Cargo bay The large wings sit on top of the fuselage so that they do not obstruct the flat floor of the cargo area. This is up to 17 metres long in 'stretched' versions.

Desert colour scheme

✳ MULTI-WHEELS

The Hercules' many huge wheels with soft tyres spread its fully loaded weight of more than 70 tonnes. This means it can roll across soft ground such as a grass air strip. Hercules carry loads varying from military vehicles and weapons to emergency provisions for disaster areas.

Extra wheels spread the Hercules' weight

NORTHROP B-2 SPIRIT BOMBER

No other aircraft looks like the B-2 Spirit, a long-distance bomber and spyplane. It has no tailplane, no fin and no real fuselage either. Its flying wing shape is specially designed to be extremely difficult to detect, as it sneaks up for a surprise attack. Its first flight was in 1989 and the B-2 finally went into service with the US Air Force in 1996.

Eureka!

During World War I (1914–1918) inventors tried to make planes invisible with a covering of clear cellophane instead of cloth. However the sunlight glinted off the shiny surface.

Whatever next?

Several big aircraft makers regularly test stealth plane shapes such as the US's Boeing 'Bird of Prey', Russia's Sukhoi 'PAK-FA' and China's 'J-XX'.

Engine outlets The hot, noisy blast of gases from the four jet engines goes through ducts or openings in the wing, so it shows up less on the enemy's heat-sensing equipment.

Only 21 B-2s have been made at a cost of some $2 billion each.

A fighter plane fires decoy counter-measure flares

☀ HOT STUFF!

Heat-seeking missiles have infrared (heat) sensors that detect and lock onto a strong heat source – such as the gases blasting from an enemy jet or rocket. To counteract this an aircraft may fire decoy counter-measure flares to attract the missile away from it.

Angled wing tips

Control surfaces The B-2 has elevators and ailerons combined as elevons (see page 295). Each elevon splits into two flaps that open at the same time to work as an air brake, or deceleron.

Ultra-smooth surface The curved surfaces have no projections such as bomb pods or extra fuel tanks. This helps with streamlining and stealth.

The B-2 has a top speed of just 1000 km/h (much slower than the speed of sound). However it can fly 10,000 km without having to refuel.

Air intakes The intakes for the engines are hidden within the wing's thickness.

Cockpit

How does STEALTH work?

A stealth plane such as the B-2 is hard to find by sight, sound, infrared (heat) sensors or the radio waves of radar. The smooth curves on the top and underside and the 'double W' rear edge, break up the incoming radar signals into lots of weak beams. These reflect in many directions, rather than as a strong beam that goes back towards the radar equipment.

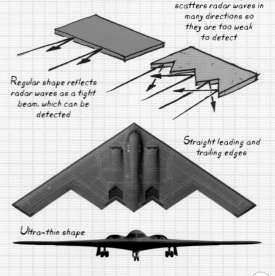

Sawtooth shape scatters radar waves in many directions so they are too weak to detect

Regular shape reflects radar waves as a tight beam, which can be detected

Straight leading and trailing edges

Ultra-thin shape

Flying wing shape With a very thin, low, wide shape and no tail or fuselage bulge, the B-2 is difficult to see from a distance. Its wings measure 52 metres across, yet its length is just 21 metres.

Leading edge radar-absorbing tape

Special paint The paint is designed to soak up or absorb the radio waves of radar, rather than bounce them back for detection. However, it is affected by too much heat or cold, so B-2s are kept in air-conditioned hangars.

With mid-air refuelling, B-2s have flown missions of up to 50 hours. Luckily for the two crew there are on-board hot meals and a flush toilet.

USAF 21001

AIRBUS A380

The world's largest passenger plane, the A380 Super Jumbo, first flew in 2005 and went into regular service in 2007. It's also known as a 'double-decker', with two passenger cabins almost the full length of its fuselage. In fact it's a triple-decker, with all the luggage on the third, lowermost deck – the cargo compartments under the passenger floor.

Eureka!

In 1940 the Boeing 307 Stratoliner was the very first airliner to have a pressurized cabin. This meant it could fly above thunderstorms without passengers suffering from lack of oxygen.

Whatever next?

Airbus plan a 'stretched' version of the A380, which will be 6.4 metres longer, with room for 150 more passengers.

Passenger cabin
There's room for 555 people in the usual three classes of seats, or 853 if they all travel in economy class seats.

Flight deck The seats, controls and instruments for the two pilots are similar to other Airbus planes such as the A340 and A320. This allows pilots to swap aircraft more easily.

At take-off a fully loaded A380 weighs 560 tonnes and needs a runway almost 3 km long.

Wheel fairing

☀ FLY-BY-WIRE

In some planes the pilot's control column ('joystick'), rudder pedals, wheel brake lever and other controls are connected by long metal cables to the parts they move, such as the elevators, ailerons and rudder. In a fly-by-wire aircraft, the pilot's controls send signals along electrical wires into a computer. This then sends out signals to electric motors and hydraulic pumps, which work the moving parts. The computer helps by alerting the pilots to problems.

The A380's fly-by-wire flight deck has eight screen displays

When the Boeing 747 first flew in 1969 it became known as the Jumbo Jet. The A380 is even bigger, so it's nicknamed the Super Jumbo.

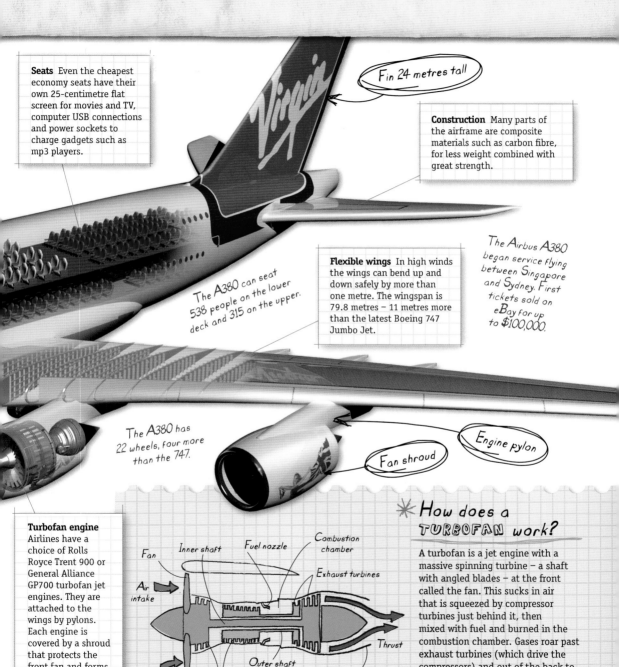

Seats Even the cheapest economy seats have their own 25-centimetre flat screen for movies and TV, computer USB connections and power sockets to charge gadgets such as mp3 players.

Fin 24 metres tall

Construction Many parts of the airframe are composite materials such as carbon fibre, for less weight combined with great strength.

The A380 can seat 538 people on the lower deck and 315 on the upper.

Flexible wings In high winds the wings can bend up and down safely by more than one metre. The wingspan is 79.8 metres – 11 metres more than the latest Boeing 747 Jumbo Jet.

The Airbus A380 began service flying between Singapore and Sydney. First tickets sold on eBay for up to $100,000.

The A380 has 22 wheels, four more than the 747.

Engine pylon

Fan shroud

Turbofan engine Airlines have a choice of Rolls Royce Trent 900 or General Alliance GP700 turbofan jet engines. They are attached to the wings by pylons. Each engine is covered by a shroud that protects the front fan and forms the outer casing.

Fan

Inner shaft

Fuel nozzle

Combustion chamber

Exhaust turbines

Air intake

Thrust

Outer shaft

Exhaust nozzle

Fan shroud

Compressor turbines

✳ How does a TURBOFAN work?

A turbofan is a jet engine with a massive spinning turbine – a shaft with angled blades – at the front called the fan. This sucks in air that is squeezed by compressor turbines just behind it, then mixed with fuel and burned in the combustion chamber. Gases roar past exhaust turbines (which drive the compressors) and out of the back to push the engine forwards. The huge front fan also works like a propeller for added thrust.

F-35B LIGHTNING

One of the world's most advanced aircraft, the F-35 Lightning fighter-bomber first roared into the skies in 2006. The F-35B is a special STOVL version – Short Take-Off and Vertical Landing. Using the lift fan just behind the pilot, it needs only a very short runway to become airborne, and it is able to land straight down.

Eureka!

The idea of a lift fan for vertical take-off and landing was first tried in the 1920s with propeller planes. However the piston engines of the time could not produce enough power to drive both the propellers and the fan.

Whatever next?

The F-35 Lightning shares 'stealth' features with the F-22 Raptor and even newer, secret 'X-planes' still at the design stage.

Rudder

Twin fins Like many modern combat aircraft, the Lightning has two fins, each with a rudder. This gives better control, especially at low speeds when taking off and landing on an aircraft carrier.

All-moving tailplane The whole tailplane (small wing at the back) tilts to work as an elevator for super-quick climbs, dives and manoeuvres.

Wheel

✳ How does a LIFT FAN work?

The F-35B's lift fan looks like a big cooling fan with blades set at an angle. It is driven by a spinning shaft from the main engine. Air is sucked in from above and forced out at high speed below to push the plane upwards. The clutch connects it to the engine for use then disconnects it for normal flight.

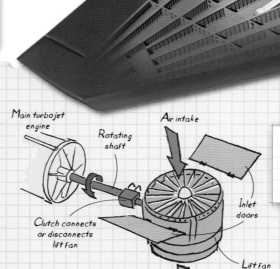

Main turbojet engine

Air intake

Rotating shaft

Clutch connects or disconnects lift fan

Inlet doors

Lift fan

Air outlet produces thrust

Turbojet The single jet engine is either a Pratt & Whitney F135 or General Electric-Rolls Royce F136.

The F-35B (the version with the lift fan) first flew in June 2008, 18 months after the F35.

Sensors Small sensors with cameras, lasers and heat detectors are scattered all over the F-35B. They pick up any objects moving nearby, from friendly planes to enemy missiles.

The name 'Lightning' has been used for previous war planes including the prop Lockheed P-38 Lightning of World War II and the English Electric Lightning jet of the 1960s.

✳ How does a TURBOJET work?

A turbojet is similar to a turbofan (see page 311). Air is sucked in at the front, gets squeezed or compressed, burns with fuel and roars out the back to produce thrust. Turbojets lack a big fan at the front, so they can go much faster than turbofans. However, they are noisier and consume more fuel.

Afterburner burns leftover fuel vapour in exhaust

Exhaust nozzle

Exhaust turbines

Central shaft

Fuel injectors

Compressor turbines

Roll nozzle

Other names considered for the Lightning were Kestrel, Phoenix and Black Mamba.

Ejector seat

Combustion chamber

Air intake

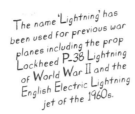
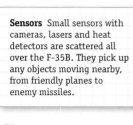

Cockpit The pilot has a 50 x 20 centimetre display, bigger than many flat-screen TVs. Some of the controls work simply by speaking through the headset microphone into the plane's computer.

Lift fan The fan is just behind the cockpit. The air inlet doors above it and the outlet doors below it all open just before use. After use, these doors close for fast forward flight.

Forward-facing radar The radar is so powerful that it must never be switched to full power on the ground. Anyone in front of it would be cooked as if in a microwave oven!

Probe

BOEING CH-47 CHINOOK

The Chinook heavy-lift helicopter is used by air forces and civilians in more than 20 countries worldwide. A helicopter's spinning rotor blades are shaped like long, thin plane wings. They provide lift in the same way as they spin around. This is why helicopters are called rotary-wing aircraft.

Eureka!

In 1939, Russian aircraft pioneer Igor Sikorsky came up with the basic helicopter design still used today. He also designed successful flying boats.

If one engine fails the Chinook can still fly with the other one driving both rotors.

Rotor The rotor's three fibre-glass blades make a circle 18.3 metres across and spin almost four times each second. Their aerofoil shape produces lift as they turn and their chop-chop-chop sound is why helicopters are called 'choppers'.

Front rotor head The front rotor spins one way, which makes the helicopter body spin the other way. The rear rotor spins in the opposite direction, and the two cancel each other out. This means there is no need for a small upright rotor as on other helicopters.

Apart from military missions, Chinooks carry people and supplies in disaster areas and are also used for logging, firefighting, and surveys.

The rotor in an autogyro relies on passing air for lift

Nose gun

Flight deck The Chinook usually has a crew of three. The chief pilot sits in the left seat, with the co-pilot in the right. The flight engineer is in the compartment behind them.

Machine gun hatch

✳ What is an AUTOGYRO?

Like a helicopter, an autogyro has a rotor, but this is not engine-powered – only the propeller is. As the propeller pushes the autogyro forwards, passing air makes the rotor whirl around for lift.

Whatever next?

The Solotrek strap-on personal helicopter has two rotors in ring-shaped casings above the pilot's head, fixed onto a chair-like frame. But it's not available in a store near you just yet!

The Chinook is named after winds in northwest North America. They are warm, dry and gusting, and blow downwards like the craft's rotor blast.

Engines There are two Lycoming turboshaft engines, one on each side of the tail fin base. They have turbines, like jet engines. They turn an axle-like shaft rather than use their hot gas blast for thrust.

Gearbox The gearing system changes the very fast revolutions of the engine to the much slower, more powerful turning force for the rotors.

Cabin Almost 26 metres long, the straight-through open cabin can take more than 50 fully equipped troops, several vehicles or 12 tonnes of cargo. Top speed is more than 300 km/h.

629089

Rear loading ramp

UNITED STATES ARMY

Missile pod

✳ How does the ROTOR HEAD work?

Connecting rods link the turning rotor blades and their ring-shaped upper swashplate to the non-turning lower plate below. As the pilot's controls lift, lower or tilt the whole swashplate, the blades also tilt, altering their amounts of lift. This makes the helicopter rise, descend, hover and go in any direction.

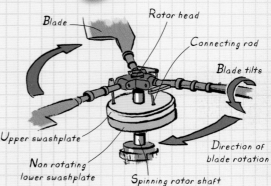

Blade

Rotor head

Connecting rod

Blade tilts

Upper swashplate

Non rotating lower swashplate

Spinning rotor shaft

Direction of blade rotation

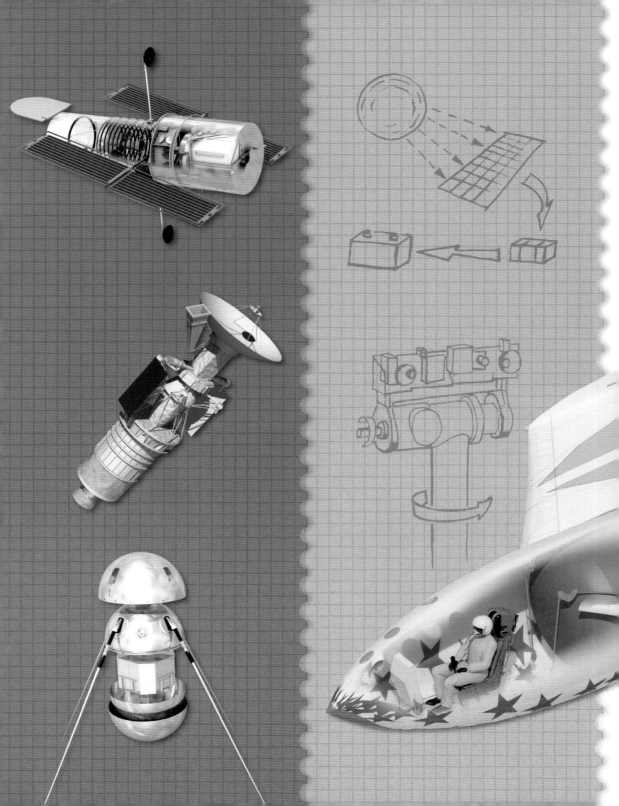

SPACE
EXPLORATION

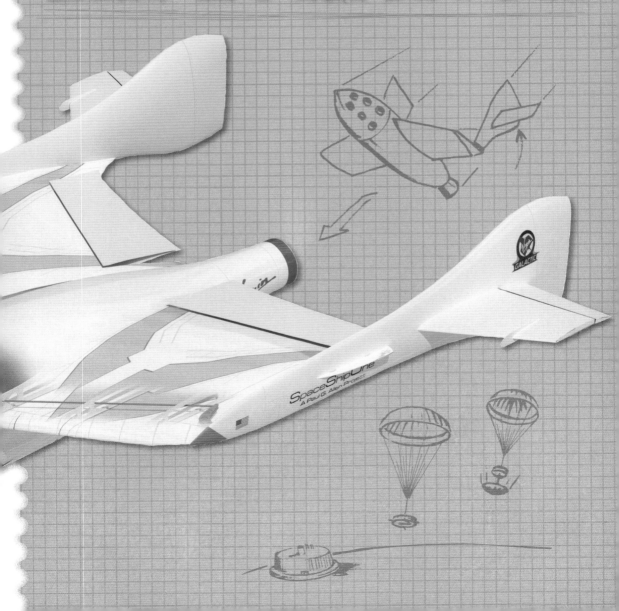

INTRODUCTION

Long ago there were no street lamps, electric lights or even candles, just glowing wood fires. Ancient humans had time to look up at the Moon, planets, stars and other twinkling specks in the night sky. Legends grew about gods and spirits in a mysterious dark world far above. From 1610, the telescope made these tiny specks bigger. Astronomers realized that they were faraway worlds moving through a vast, empty area called 'space'.

In 1635, Claude Melan drew the first detailed telescopic map of the Moon.

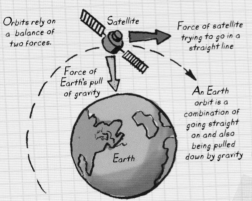

Orbits rely on a balance of two forces.

Satellite

Force of satellite trying to go in a straight line

Force of Earth's pull of gravity

An Earth orbit is a combination of going straight on and also being pulled down by gravity

Earth

INTO ORBIT

In the early 1900s, Russian schoolteacher Konstantin Tsiolkovsky suggested how a machine called a rocket could escape Earth's pull of gravity and go into orbit – an 'endless fall' round and round our planet. In the 1920s, American engineer Robert Goddard made a practical start with the first controllable rockets. World War II (1939–1945) saw the first big long-distance rocket, the V-2. Designed as a weapon of destruction, it was the first man-made object to reach space (a height above 100 kilometres).

SPACE RACE

The 1950s 'Cold War' was a trial of strength between the two world superpowers, the USA and USSR. In this 'Space Race' the USSR scored three great firsts – an orbiting satellite, an orbiting human and an orbiting space station. The USA followed a longer-term goal and developed the most powerful rocket ever, Saturn V. It sent the first humans to another world, when Apollo 11 landed on the Moon in 1969.

Saturn V rockets took eight Apollo spacecraft to the Moon between 1968 and 1972, with six landings.

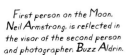

First person on the Moon, Neil Armstrong, is reflected in the visor of the second person and photographer, Buzz Aldrin.

SATURN LANDING

In 2004, seven years after launch, the Cassini-Huygens probe reached Saturn. The Huygens lander detached from the Cassini orbiter and parachuted down to Saturn's giant moon Titan – an automatic process that went without a hitch.

Huygen's descent onto Titan

Heat shield prevented burn-up on entry into Titan's atmosphere

Large parachute and then a smaller one slowed Huygen's decent

Huygens lands on Titan

The International Space Station is a temporary workplace for dozens of scientists – and a hotel for the occasional space tourist.

SPACE GETS BUSY

Today, trips to the International Space Station (ISS) grab the headlines. However space probes travel much further. They visit all the planets going around our Sun, many of their moons and smaller objects such as asteroids and comets. Their findings help us to understand how and when the Universe began. Much nearer and more practical for our daily lives are hundreds of satellites orbiting Earth. They provide television links, telephone calls and computer communications, help us to forecast the weather, monitor global warming and carry out spying missions.

Space is not as empty as it was 50 years ago. What will the next 50 years bring?

V-2 ROCKET

The V-2 missile was the first big long-distance rocket. Its earliest flight was in 1942 in the middle of World War II (1939–1945). After the war the V-2 was the first rocket to reach space, but it never went into orbit around the Earth. Almost all space rockets that followed the V-2 were based on its design.

Eureka!

The first rockets used gunpowder as fuel. Called 'fire arrows', they were invented in China around AD 1050. The first rocket with liquid fuel was launched by Robert Goddard in 1926. It reached a height of just 12 metres!

Whatever next?

The USA plans a 'Star Wars' network of satellites in space to detect enemy missiles so counter-attack missiles can be fired at them.

Warhead The nose cone was filled with three-quarters of a tonne of the explosive Amatol, based on TNT (trinitrotoluene).

Nose cone

Fuel tank

Oxidizer tank

Pump for fuel and oxidizer

Igniter sets fire to fuel

Combustion chamber where fuel burns

Nozzle

In 1951 a V-2 blasted to a record height of 213 km. That's well into space, which officially starts at 100 km.

Controls Early V-2s steered themselves on a preset course. Later versions were controlled by radio signals from the ground.

✳ How do ROCKET ENGINES work?

Burning gases provide thrust

Rockets use the basic scientific law of action-reaction. As burning gases from the rocket engine blast out backwards, they push the rocket forwards. Burning needs oxygen, but space has no air and therefore no oxygen. Rockets take liquid oxygen or an oxygen-rich chemical called an oxidizer.

Just after launch the V-2 used 'gas rudders' just below the nozzle for steering. By the time the V-2 was going fast enough, the air vanes on the fins also began to work as rudders.

Fuel tank The upper tank contained nearly 4 tonnes of a mixture of liquids. Three-quarters was ethanol, a type of alcohol that burns well but at extremely high temperatures. The rest was water, to make the burning temperature slightly lower.

The V-2's rocket engine only ran for about 65 seconds but this was enough to reach a height of 80 km. It fell back to Earth and exploded up to 300 km away from the launch site.

A V-2 rocket being prepared for launch

✳ Launching the V-2

The V-2 blasted off from a special steel launch pad shaped like a low table. This and all the other equipment required were carried by about 30 trucks to the launch site, usually hidden among trees in a forest. The V-2 itself had a special truck and trailer almost 15 metres long, weighing 11 tonnes. The launch crew took 90 minutes to set up the platform, prepare the V-2 and its fuel and guidance systems and then arm (switch on) the explosive warhead.

Streamlined body

Fuel pumps

Combustion chamber The fuel sprayed into this chamber through more than 1200 tiny nozzles, where it burnt using the oxygen.

Air vane

Nozzle

Liquid oxygen tank
The lower tank carried almost 5 tonnes of oxygen. This was so cold and under such immense pressure that it was squeezed into a liquid rather than being a gas.

Fuel for fuel pump

Fin

During World War II more than 3000 V-2s were launched at enemies.

SPUTNIK 1

On 4 October 1957 the world was stunned by amazing news – the first satellite in space. Sputnik 1 was launched by an R-7 Semyorka rocket into orbit around the Earth. It was the first of many Sputniks to test new machines and technologies in space. It lasted three months, then burned up as it fell back to Earth.

Eureka!

An orbiting comsat (communications satellite) receives and sends out radio signals as if it was on an incredibly tall mast. The first person to have the idea for comsats was science fiction writer Arthur C Clarke (1917–2008) way back in 1945.

Sputnik 1 sent out radio signals for 22 days before its batteries died. However it continued for a total of 1440 orbits and a total journey of 60 million km.

O-ring A ring-shaped joint between the inner casing halves sealed the satellite to keep in its contents of pure nitrogen gas.

Inner casing

Power supply
The three small but heavy batteries weighed as much as a small adult person. Two were for the radio transmitter and one was for the fan to control the temperature inside.

✳ How do ORBITS work?

An orbit is the curved path of an object, such as a satellite, around a planet, moon or star. It is a balance between moving forwards and falling downwards. In space, an object tends to go straight on unless a force affects it. Earth's gravity causes a force – a pull that makes the object curve around, as if falling. However the Earth's surface also curves around below the object. If the object's speed and height are exactly right, it keeps 'falling' but never reaches the ground.

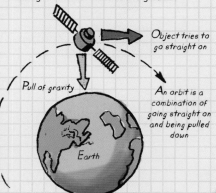

Object tries to go straight on

Pull of gravity

An orbit is a combination of going straight on and being pulled down

Earth

Ventilation fan

One month after Sputnik 1 was launched, Sputnik 2 carried the first space passenger – Laika the dog.

Whatever next?

There are more than 600 working satellites in space, hundreds more 'dead' ones and thousands of old bits of rockets, space stations and other space junk. Each new satellite is given an orbit to help it avoid all of these existing objects.

Sputnik 1 was launched by the USSR, which is now Russia and nearby nations. Their big space rival the USA was very surprised and some Americans thought the news was a trick!

Outer casing The two halves of the ball-shaped casing were made of an alloy (metal mixture) of aluminium, magnesium and titanium fixed together with 36 bolts.

Sputnik 1 started the Space Age by showing that machines, and maybe even people, could go into orbit and survive.

Antennae The four antennae, or aerials, which sent out the radio signals were made of thin 'whips' more than 2 metres long.

Sputnik 1's single transmitter weighed 3.7 kilograms. It sent out two sets of radio signal beeps, low and high, each 0.3 seconds long.

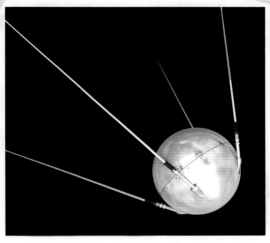

Sputnik 1 weighed 84 kg and was 58 cm across — about the size of a big beachball.

Inner casing

Heat resistant outer casing

✳ What is ESCAPE VELOCITY?

If you could launch a spacecraft into the air, Earth's pull of gravity would soon bring it back down. The harder you launch it, the higher it goes but it would never reach very far. A rocket is the only engine powerful enough to give a spacecraft enough movement energy to break free of Earth's gravity and get into space. At Earth's surface this means a speed of 11 kilometres per second, which is known as the escape velocity.

The R-7 rocket blasts off with Sputnik 1 in its nose cone

EXPLORER 1

After the shock of seeing its rival the USSR launch Sputnik 1 (see page 288), the USA increased its efforts to send its first satellite into space. Four months later on 31 January 1958, Explorer 1 blasted off from Cape Canaveral, inside the nose of a Juno I rocket. During its 111-day mission, Explorer 1 made several exciting discoveries about conditions in space.

Eureka!

Explorer 1 found a doughnut-shaped region of tiny particles trapped around Earth by the planet's natural magnetic field. The region was named the Van Allen Belt after James Van Allen, one of the Explorer mission leaders.

Whatever next?

The Explorer series of satellites carried on until 1981 when Explorer 59 studied how sunlight and polluting gases form smog.

Explorer 1's orbit was elliptical, or oval, in shape, 2550 km above Earth at its farthest but only 360 km at its nearest.

✳ How do MULTI-STAGE ROCKETS work?

A multi-stage rocket, or launch vehicle, is several rockets on top of one another. The first stage is biggest and most powerful because it has the greatest weight to lift. Also, it sets off from the ground where Earth's gravity is strongest. After it uses up its fuel it falls away, or separates. The whole launch vehicle is now lighter and higher, so gravity is weaker. This means the second stage can be smaller, and so on.

Second stage: This needs less power and fuel to keep going

Separation

First stage: This uses its fuel and then falls away, otherwise it would be 'dead weight'

Fuel tank

Oxidizer tank

Rocket engine

Cosmic ray detector
A tube-shaped detector measured the strength of cosmic rays. These are like radio waves but each one is much shorter in length.

High-power transmitter
The two transmitters sent information from the onboard sensors and detectors down to Earth as radio signals.

Temperature sensors
There were five temperature sensors – one in the nose, one in the main body and three on the outside.

Metal casing

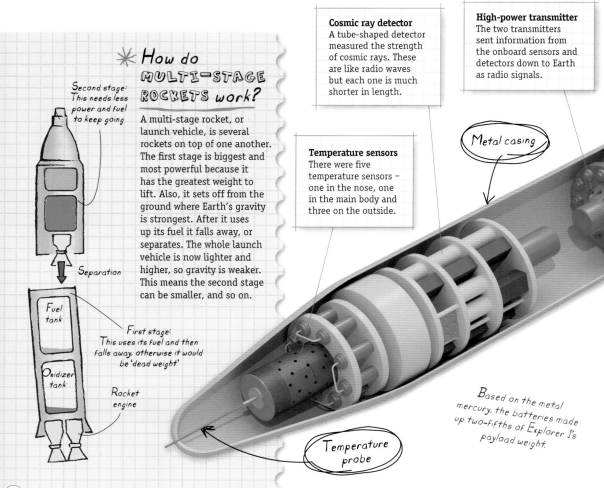

Based on the metal mercury, the batteries made up two-fifths of Explorer 1's payload weight.

Temperature probe

Antennae Four short whip-like antennae (aerials) on the outside, plus two straight antennae built into the satellite casing, sent out radio signals.

Explorer 1 was 15 cm wide and at 14 kg, it was only one-sixth of the weight of Sputnik 1.

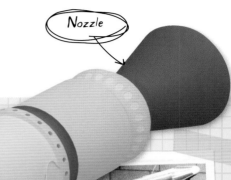

Nozzle

Fibre-glass ring

At 203 cm long, Explorer 1 was not much taller than an adult

Explorer 1 was the first satellite to use newly invented transistors, which helped to control the satellite's electronics, and also made it much lighter than using older devices called valves.

To the surprise of mission experts, when Explorer 1 got into orbit it changed the direction in which it spun – 12 times each second. No one knew why.

✷ TRACKING STATIONS

As rockets, satellites, probes and other craft travel through space they send back to Earth all kinds of information about where they are and what they have found. The information is sent in the form of radio signals. Huge dishes on Earth detect the weak signals and swivel to point at, or track, the spacecraft as they move across the sky. As the Earth spins around once every 24 hours, different tracking stations take turns around the world.

Parkes Observatory tracking station, Australia

VOSTOK 1

The first person in space was Yuri Gagarin, a Russian pilot-turned-astronaut, on the mission known as Vostok 1. On 12 April 1961 he made one orbit of Earth in his Vostok 3KA spacecraft. The trip lasted just one hour 48 minutes. It made Gagarin a hero and started the era of human space travel.

Eureka!

As far back as 1903, Russian scientist Konstantin Tsiolkovskii wrote about using rockets to reach space and that one day people might travel there. Others at the time thought he was mad!

Hatch The door into the craft was sealed after the astronaut went in. It was released after re-entry to allow Gagarin to bail out with his parachute.

The Vostok team's radio call sign for Gagarin's craft was 'Swallow', and for Yuri himself 'Cedar'.

Descent module Only the ball-shaped part of the craft containing the astronaut came back to Earth.

Visor The Visor (Vzor) was like a window-mounted periscope (angled telescope). It helped to position the craft in the correct position and angle for re-entry.

✳ How does RE-ENTRY work?

One of the riskiest parts of a return mission is re-entry, when the craft comes back from empty space down into Earth's atmosphere – the layer of air around the planet. At a speed of 10 kilometres each second, rubbing, or friction, with the thickening air rapidly makes the craft glow red-hot. The key is to enter at the right angle. Otherwise the craft skips off the atmosphere like a stone bouncing off a pond's surface, or plunges too steeply to a fiery end.

Overshoot zone

Re-entry corridor

Undershoot zone

Entry too steep, craft overheats into a fireball

Entry too shallow, craft bounces off atmosphere into deep space

Ejector seat Explosives blew Gagarin and his seat out of the craft, ready to open his parachute.

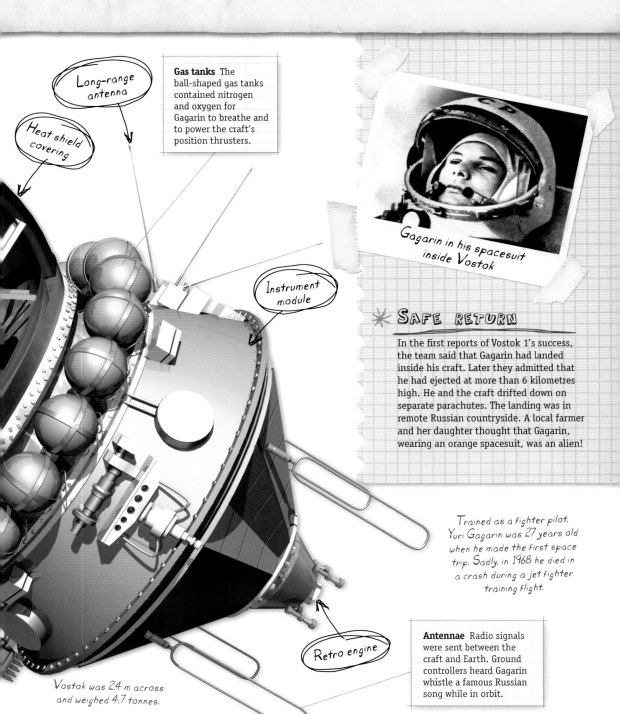

Long-range antenna

Heat shield covering

Gas tanks The ball-shaped gas tanks contained nitrogen and oxygen for Gagarin to breathe and to power the craft's position thrusters.

Gagarin in his spacesuit inside Vostok

Instrument module

✳ SAFE RETURN

In the first reports of Vostok 1's success, the team said that Gagarin had landed inside his craft. Later they admitted that he had ejected at more than 6 kilometres high. He and the craft drifted down on separate parachutes. The landing was in remote Russian countryside. A local farmer and her daughter thought that Gagarin, wearing an orange spacesuit, was an alien!

Trained as a fighter pilot, Yuri Gagarin was 27 years old when he made the first space trip. Sadly, in 1968 he died in a crash during a jet fighter training flight.

Retro engine

Antennae Radio signals were sent between the craft and Earth. Ground controllers heard Gagarin whistle a famous Russian song while in orbit.

Vostok was 2.4 m across and weighed 4.7 tonnes.

SATURN V

The biggest and most powerful rocket to take craft into space was the USA's Saturn V. It launched Apollo astronauts on their journeys to the Moon. From the first Apollo test flight in November 1969 to the last lift-off in May 1973, all 13 Saturn V flights have been successful. Most famous was the launch on 16 July 1969, which carried the first men to land on the Moon, Neil Armstrong and Buzz Aldrin, with their co-astronaut Michael Collins.

Eureka!

Apollo 13 was unlucky – an explosion damaged the oxygen supply. The crew had the idea to use the Lunar Module as a 'space lifeboat' until they went back to the Command Module for re-entry.

Whatever next?

Will people ever go back to the Moon? The USA plans to send astronauts there again between 2015 and 2020.

Russia's Energia rocket was slightly more powerful than Saturn V. However it only had two test launches and never went into full operation.

Second stage The S-II stage two had five J-2 rocket engines. It was 25 metres tall, and like the first stage, it was 10 metres wide.

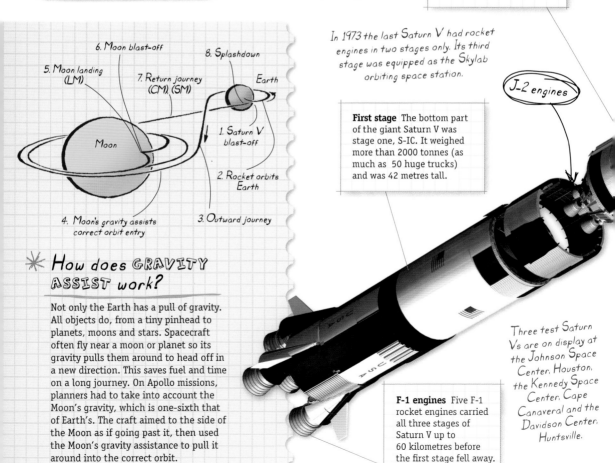

In 1973 the last Saturn V had rocket engines in two stages only. Its third stage was equipped as the Skylab orbiting space station.

First stage The bottom part of the giant Saturn V was stage one, S-IC. It weighed more than 2000 tonnes (as much as 50 huge trucks) and was 42 metres tall.

J-2 engines

Diagram labels:
- 6. Moon blast-off
- 5. Moon landing (LM)
- 8. Splashdown
- 7. Return journey (CM) (SM)
- Earth
- Moon
- 1. Saturn V blast-off
- 2. Rocket orbits Earth
- 4. Moon's gravity assists correct orbit entry
- 3. Outward journey

✳ How does GRAVITY ASSIST work?

Not only the Earth has a pull of gravity. All objects do, from a tiny pinhead to planets, moons and stars. Spacecraft often fly near a moon or planet so its gravity pulls them around to head off in a new direction. This saves fuel and time on a long journey. On Apollo missions, planners had to take into account the Moon's gravity, which is one-sixth that of Earth's. The craft aimed to the side of the Moon as if going past it, then used the Moon's gravity assistance to pull it around into the correct orbit.

Three test Saturn Vs are on display at the Johnson Space Center, Houston, the Kennedy Space Center, Cape Canaveral and the Davidson Center, Huntsville.

F-1 engines Five F-1 rocket engines carried all three stages of Saturn V up to 60 kilometres before the first stage fell away.

Lunar Module (LM) Two astronauts transferred to the LM to land on the Moon's surface. It was their base for a few days and left its lower part behind as it blasted back up to the CM.

Service Module (SM) The SM contained water, air and other life support materials, batteries, radio and scientific equipment and a small rocket. It remained joined to the CM until just before re-entry to the Earth.

Launch escape tower

Third stage Known as the S-IVB, the third stage was 17.8 metres high and 6.6 metres wide. It had one J-2 engine (like those in the second stage).

Command Module (CM) There were three astronauts on each Apollo mission. Two landed on the Moon while the other orbited the Moon in the CM. All three came back to Earth in the CM.

At 110.6 m high, Saturn V was just half a metre shorter than St Paul's Cathedral in London.

J-2 engine

✳ SPLASHDOWN!

The USA's space rival the USSR returned their craft by parachute onto land. The USA's craft parachuted into the ocean. US mission controllers tracked the Apollo Command Module back down by radio, then jet fighters followed it. After splashdown, helicopters dropped divers into the ocean who fixed a flotation device, like a big rubber ring, so the Command Module would not sink.

Saturn V launch At blast-off Saturn V weighed more than 3000 tonnes – over seven times heavier than a fully loaded jumbo jet.

The Apollo Command Module after splashdown

PIONEER 11

Space probes are craft without crew, remote-controlled by radio signals from Earth. The twin probes Pioneer 10 and 11 were launched in 1972 and 1973 on vast journeys to fly past the outer planets millions of kilometres from Earth. They took pictures on the way and are still out there, heading away from Earth at incredible speeds into the unknown depths of space.

Eureka!

After Pioneer 11's launch, mission controllers realized that they could use Jupiter's gravity to alter its course so that it would reach Saturn before two other probes, Voyagers 1 and 2.

Pioneer 11 flew within 34,000 km of Jupiter and 21,000 km of Saturn.

In Pioneer 11's amazing pictures of Saturn's rings, the rings appeared dark. Yet when seen from Earth they are bright.

Asteroid – Meteoroid detector senor

Antenna dish This bowl-shaped antenna was 2.74 metres across and pointed at Earth to send and receive radio signals.

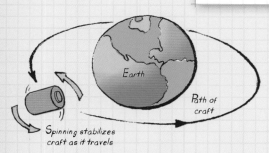

Earth

Path of craft

Spinning stabilizes craft as it travels

✳ How does SPIN-STABILIZING work?

On its journey through space a craft might be hit by tiny particles called micrometeorites and start to wobble. This is why many satellites and probes are made to spin as they travel, known as spin-stabilizing. It causes them to fly straighter by the gyroscope effect (see page 310). Spinning also spreads out the heat of the Sun's rays, otherwise the side of the craft facing the Sun would become too hot (known as the 'barbeque effect'). Pioneer 11 spun around about once every 12 seconds but kept its dish pointing back to the Earth.

Separation ring

Spin thrusters Three pairs of small rocket thrusters controlled Pioneer's spinning motion and speed by puffing out jets of gas.

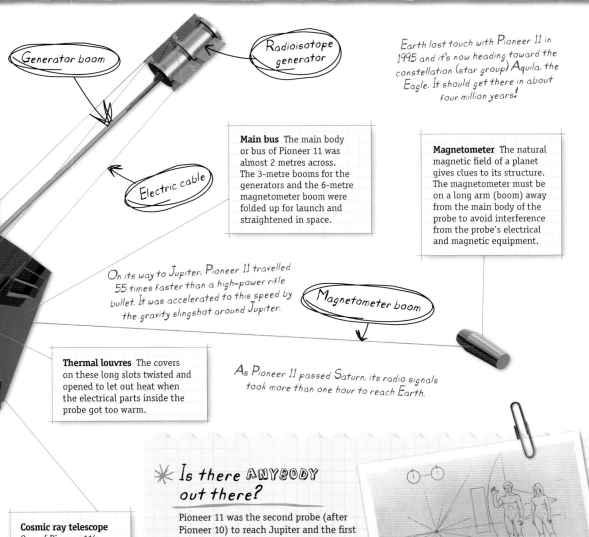

Generator boom

Radioisotope generator

Earth lost touch with Pioneer 11 in 1995 and it's now heading toward the constellation (star group) Aquila, the Eagle. It should get there in about four million years!

Electric cable

Main bus The main body or bus of Pioneer 11 was almost 2 metres across. The 3-metre booms for the generators and the 6-metre magnetometer boom were folded up for launch and straightened in space.

Magnetometer The natural magnetic field of a planet gives clues to its structure. The magnetometer must be on a long arm (boom) away from the main body of the probe to avoid interference from the probe's electrical and magnetic equipment.

On its way to Jupiter, Pioneer 11 travelled 55 times faster than a high-power rifle bullet. It was accelerated to this speed by the gravity slingshot around Jupiter.

Magnetometer boom

Thermal louvres The covers on these long slots twisted and opened to let out heat when the electrical parts inside the probe got too warm.

As Pioneer 11 passed Saturn, its radio signals took more than one hour to reach Earth.

✳ Is there ANYBODY out there?

Pioneer 11 was the second probe (after Pioneer 10) to reach Jupiter and the first to reach Saturn. Both Pioneers carry a plaque about 23 centimetres wide. This shows pictures of a man and woman, also the Solar System – our Sun and its planets – along the bottom and a chart of where the Earth is among the distant stars. In space the Pioneers will keep going for an immense time unless they hit a moon, a planet or an asteroid. Or maybe they will be found by aliens who perhaps can read the plaque and come to visit us!

Cosmic ray telescope One of Pioneer 11's many instruments, the cosmic ray telescope looked at powerful cosmic rays travelling across the Universe.

Pioneer's plaque

VOYAGER 2

In 1977, Voyagers 1 and 2 blasted off on vast journeys across the Solar System. Voyager 1 flew close to Jupiter and Saturn. Meanwhile Voyager 2 travelled more slowly to these planets, then headed onwards to become the first probe to visit Uranus and Neptune.

Eureka!

Mission controllers forgot to switch on Voyager 2's main radio equipment because they were distracted by a problem with Voyager 1. Luckily there was a back-up radio.

Whatever next?

The only probe that is planned to visit worlds beyond the outermost planet Neptune is New Horizons. It was launched in 2006 and should reach the 'dwarf planet' Pluto and its moon Charon in 2015.

Cameras Voyager 2 had two light-detecting cameras similar to those used by television crews. One took wide-view pictures and the other took narrow close-ups.

Main bus The bus or body of the probe was 1.8 metres across and 45 centimetres deep. It contained the main electronic equipment.

Cosmic ray detector

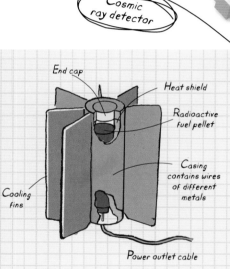

End cap

Heat shield

Radioactive fuel pellet

Casing contains wires of different metals

Cooling fins

Power outlet cable

✳ How do RADIOISOTOPE GENERATORS work?

In the depths of the Solar System, the Sun's light rays are too weak to power solar panels for electricity, and on a long trip lasting years, ordinary batteries would run out. So deep-space probes have radioisotope generators. These contain a pellet (lump) of plutonium fuel that is radioactive – it sends out energy in the form of particles and rays, including infrared (heat) rays. The heat warms wires of different metals, which are joined together to form a device called a thermocouple. This turns heat energy into electrical energy and has no moving parts so it lasts for years.

Main antenna The 3.7-metre dish received remote control commands from Earth and sent back pictures and other information as radio signals.

Voyager 2 flew within 81,000 km of Uranus and found ten unknown moons around the planet.

Voyager 2 is the only craft to visit Neptune. This planet will be far away from the probe New Horizons when when it crosses its orbit.

VOYAGER

JUPITER
SATURN
URANUS

Voyager 2's mission map

✳ GRAND TOUR

Voyager 2 is often called the 'best value' probe as it visited so many planets and moons and made important discoveries for a reasonable cost – about $500 million. Its 'Grand Tour' of outer planets was possible only because they were lined up in suitable positions, which happens once every 176 years. Voyager 2 made its closest approach to Jupiter in July 1979 and Saturn in August 1981. It used Saturn's gravity to 'slingshot' to Uranus in January 1986 and Neptune in August 1989. Both Voyager probes carried a gold-plated copper record (like an old vinyl record) with Earth pictures and sounds such as birds, whales, wind, thunder and people speaking.

Magnetometer boom This grid-like sensor detected magnetic fields of the various planets and moons that the probe passed, and the background magnetism of the Sun.

Scientists think that Voyager 2 will keep sending out radio signals until at least 2025, when it will be almost 50 years old.

Radioisotope generators

Voyager 2's twin, Voyager 1, is the most distant Earth-made object in space. It's travelling so fast that it will not be overtaken by any craft planned for the future.

Long antennae Two 10-metre whip-like aerials formed a V shape called the 'rabbit ears'. They listened for radio waves and other types of waves from deep space that give scientists clues to the origin of the Universe. The Voyagers' data is still being studied today.

SPACE SHUTTLE

Recycling is good for us and our planet – and most parts of the USA's space shuttles are recyclable. A space shuttle set-up consists of the white orbiter or 'spaceplane', two tall rocket boosters and a giant fuel tank. The first shuttle blasted off in 1981 and the last launch is expected soon after 2010, making a total of about 140 trips.

Eureka!

The shuttle's boosters produce more than two-thirds of lift-off thrust. To stop them hitting the orbiter as they separate or fall away, 16 very small rockets fire to push them clear.

Flight deck Like a big aircraft, the orbiter has two seats up front for the mission commander and the pilot.

Cargo bay This large area for satellites, space telescopes and other payloads is 18 metres long and 5 metres wide – big enough to pack in a dozen family cars.

Almost the whole orbiter re-entry is controlled by computer, except for lowering the landing wheels.

Cargo door

Orbiter

✳ How do BOOSTERS work?

Boosters are additional rockets that give extra thrust for lift-off and other activities. The shuttle has two SRBs (Solid Rocket Boosters). When their fuel is used up, exploding bolts let them detach at a height of 45 kilometres. The empty casings parachute back down for re-use. At the mission's end the orbiter re-enters without engine power and swoops down to land on a runway like a huge glider.

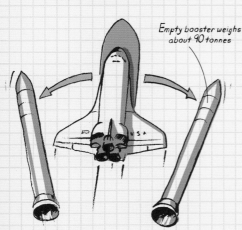

Empty booster weighs about 90 tonnes

Hubble telescope carried in cargo bay

Main engines The orbiter has three RS-24 main engines. They can swivel slightly to direct their thrust and steer the craft.

On the launch pad the whole space shuttle set-up is 56 m tall and weighs an incredible 2000 tonnes.

SRBs separate two minutes after launch

Whatever next?

After the space shuttles retire, the USA plans a two-stage rocket called Ares I. It will take a crew capsule, Orion, into space by 2015.

The six orbiters are Enterprise (used for test landings), Discovery, Atlantis, Endeavour, Challenger (destroyed after lift-off in 1986) and Columbia (destroyed during re-entry in 2003).

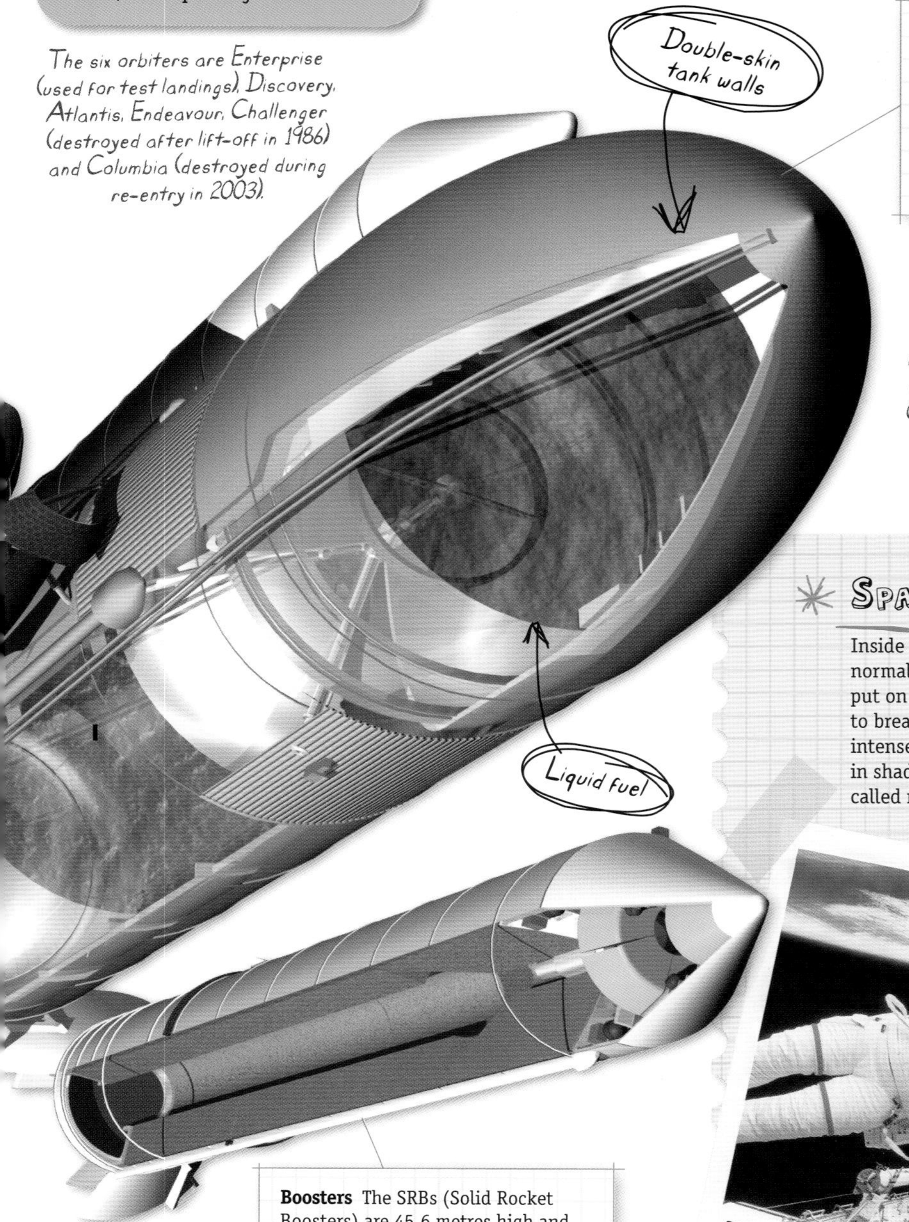

Double-skin tank walls

Fuel tank The fuel tank is 46.9 metres tall and 8.4 metres wide. It supplies fuel to the three main orbiter engines. At take-off it weighs 755 tonnes and detaches from the orbiter after nine minutes.

Shuttles usually launch and land at Kennedy Space Center, Florida. In bad weather the orbiter can land at Edwards Air Force Base, California. It flies 'piggy-back' on a Boeing 747 jumbo jet for the 3500 km journey back to Florida.

Liquid fuel

✳ SPACE walking

Inside the orbiter, the crew wear normal clothes. To go outside they put on spacesuits. These contain air to breathe and protect them from intense glare in the Sun, freezing cold in shadow, and tiny bits of space dust called micrometeorites.

Boosters The SRBs (Solid Rocket Boosters) are 45.6 metres high and weigh almost 590 tonnes. They detach from the orbiter after two minutes.

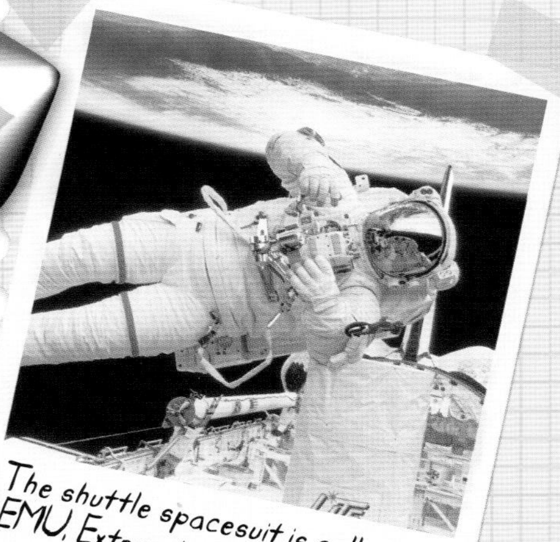

The shuttle spacesuit is called the EMU, Extravehicular Mobility Unit

MAGELLAN

In May 1989 the Magellan space probe blasted away from the space shuttle Atlantis, orbiting Earth on a 15-month journey. Its target was the planet next closest to the Sun from Earth – mysterious, cloud-shrouded Venus. In October 1994, after its hugely successful mission, controllers on Earth sent radio signals to Magellan instructing it to self destruct. It plunged down into Venus' thick poison clouds and burned away.

Eureka!

The first space probe sent to Venus was the USSR's Venera 1 in 1961 but it lost radio contact with Earth. Th ult. Finally, in 1962 Mariner 2 was the first probe to visit another planet when it flew within 35,000 kilometres of Venus.

Whatever next?

The Venus Express probe reached Venus in 2006 (see page 310). A probe called VISE may carry the first lander to Venus, probably some time after 2015.

Once in Venus' orbit, with its rocket gone, Magellan was 4.6 m long.

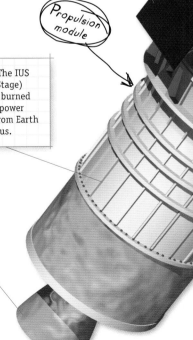

Solar panels Two solar panels folded out after launch to provide enough electricity to power Magellan for five years.

Propulsion module

Rocket engine The IUS (Inertial Upper Stage) solid fuel rocket burned several times to power Magellan away from Earth and towards Venus.

Retrorocket As Magellan neared Venus, its IUS rocket became a retrorocket. It slowed down the probe so that the planet's gravity could capture it into the correct orbit.

The Magellan probe was named after explorer Ferdinand Magellan. He led the first round-the-world sailing voyage more than 500 years earlier (although he died on the way).

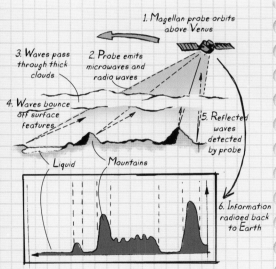

1. Magellan probe orbits above Venus
2. Probe emits microwaves and radio waves
3. Waves pass through thick clouds
4. Waves bounce off surface features
5. Reflected waves detected by probe
6. Information radioed back to Earth

Liquid   Mountains

7. Information used to make images showing surface height and nature of hard rock, loose dust or liquid

✳ How does RADAR work?

Shout at a distant wall and sound waves bounce off it and return as an echo. The time this takes shows the wall's distance. Radar is the same but with radio waves, microwaves or similar waves. Magellan sent out millions of microwave pulses and its antennae detected the reflections. The sooner these came back, the nearer the reflecting surface. The way the pulses changed as they reflected showed the nature of the surface.

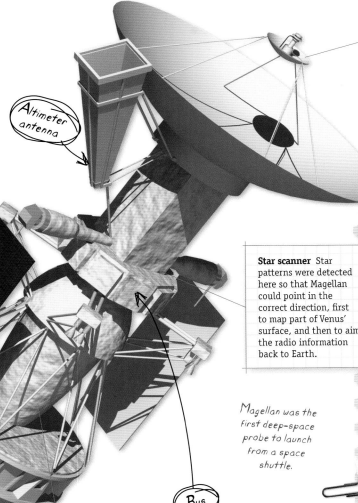

Low-gain antenna This small dish helped the main antenna to send and receive radio signals, including those for radar mapping.

High-gain antenna The main 3.7-metre antenna (aerial) dish sent out microwaves for radar mapping and communicated by radio with Earth.

Altimeter antenna

Star scanner Star patterns were detected here so that Magellan could point in the correct direction, first to map part of Venus' surface, and then to aim the radio information back to Earth.

Magellan was the first deep-space probe to launch from a space shuttle.

Bus

Thermal blanket Most of Magellan's delicate electronic equipment was wrapped in a shiny covering. This reflected the Sun's heat and other rays, which are much stronger around Venus than on Earth.

Magellan was built from the spares and leftover parts of several other probes including the Voyagers and Galileo.

✳ RADAR VISION

Seen from Earth, Venus is covered by thick clouds. Magellan's radar signals passed through these clouds to reveal the hidden landscape below. The probe's inital orbit was lop-sided, ranging from over 8500 kilometres away from Venus to less than 300 kilometres. As it swooped low each time it made a narrow radar picture of a surface strip up to 28 kilometres wide and 70,000 kilometres long, from a different angle on each orbit.

Thousands of Magellan's radar images were used to make this picture of Venus

HUBBLE SPACE TELESCOPE

In 1990 space shuttle Discovery took a massive payload into space – the HST, Hubble Space Telescope. The HST is still there today although only a few parts continue to work. Why take a bus-sized, 11-tonne telescope into an orbit 580 kilometres high? On Earth, even on a cloudless night, telescopes have to look through the blurry atmosphere. In space it's always dark and crystal clear.

Eureka!

HST is named after US astronomer Edwin Hubble (1889–1953). He made the great discovery that the Universe is expanding as stars and galaxies fly away from each other an incredible speeds.

The central tube-shaped part of the HST is 13.2 m long and 4.2 m wide.

Secondary mirror
The smaller mirror is 30 centimetres across and weighs 12 kilograms.

People were planning space telescopes as early as the 1940s, but the HST was the first to be made.

Door

Solar panels About 8 metres long, these turn sunlight into electricity to power all of the HST's equipment. They also charge batteries for the 36 minutes of each 97-minute orbit when the HST is in shadow, on the far side of the Earth from the Sun.

✳ How does the HST work?

The HST's optical (light-detecting) telescope is called a Cassegrain reflector. Light comes in through the open end door and bounces or reflects off the huge primary mirror, which curves inwards like a bowl. The light rays shine onto the secondary mirror, which curves outwards like a dome. It reflects them through a hole or aperture in the middle of the primary mirror, onto the scientific sensors and other instruments.

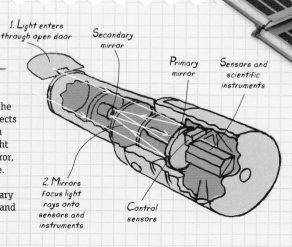

1. Light enters through open door

Secondary mirror

Primary mirror

Sensors and scientific instruments

2. Mirrors focus light rays onto sensors and instruments

Control sensors

Whatever next?

Taking over from 'Hubble' should be 'Webb', the James Webb Space Telescope. Due for launch after 2012, it's main mirror will be about 6.5 metres across!

Antenna

The HST has helped scientists to solve some of astronomy's big puzzles, such as how stars are born. However its other findings mean there are new mysteries about the size and shape of the Universe.

The Hubble sees galaxies far away across the Universe

Primary mirror The main mirror that collects starlight is 2.4 metres across and weighs 830 kilograms. It took three years to cast, shape and polish.

Reflective casing

☀ SHORT-SIGHTED TELESCOPE

Soon after launch, mission experts realized that the HST's view was slightly fuzzy – because its main mirror was not exactly the correct shape. In 1993 a space shuttle mission took astronauts and equipment to fix the problem. More shuttle missions in 1997, 1999 and 2002 serviced the equipment and made further improvements. Then from 2004, parts began to fail. The HST is slowly 'dying'.

Sun sensor

The HST zooms through space at almost 8 km every second.

Rear shroud

Scientific instruments Several sets of scientific equipment analyze the incredibly weak light and other waves coming in from deep space.

CASSINI-HUYGENS

Saturn is our Solar System's second-biggest planet, sixth farthest from the Sun and famous for its glittering rings. In July 2004, two-part Cassini-Huygens was the fourth Earth craft to visit the planet. As the orbiter Cassini circled Saturn, the lander Huygens detached and touched down on Saturn's huge moon, Titan.

Eureka!

Saturn's beautiful rings were first glimpsed by the great scientist Galileo Galilei in 1610 with his newly built telescope. He saw them only as vague bulges on either side of the planet and called them 'Saturn's ears'.

Whatever next?

In 2011 the US plans to send a probe called Juno to Saturn's neighbour, Jupiter – which is also the biggest planet. It should arrive about five years after launch.

Depending on the orbits of Earth and Saturn, radio signals can take more than 80 minutes to travel between us and Cassini.

Cameras Cassini carries about 12 cameras and other scientific instruments. Some see visible light (like our eyes), others detect infrared (heat) and ultra-violet waves.

CASSINI

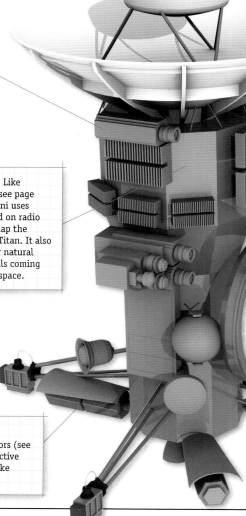

Parachute slowed decent

Heat shield prevented burn-up on entry, then detached

Large parachute and then smaller one slowed descent

Huygens lands on Titan

Radar bay Like Magellan (see page 302), Cassini uses radar based on radio waves to map the surface of Titan. It also 'listens' for natural radio signals coming from deep space.

✳ How do PROBES land?

On 25 December 2004, Huygens left Cassini and began its 21-day drift to huge Titan, which is half as big again as our own Moon. Unlike most other moons, Titan has an atmosphere of gases. During the descent through its atmosphere, Huygens was protected by a 2.7-metre heat shield or 'decelerator'. It was also slowed down by parachutes, first by a large one 8.3 metres across, then by a smaller 3-metre parachute. After two and a half hours, Huygens finally landed with a bump – still well and working.

Power supply Three radioisotope generators (see page 298) use radioactive plutonium fuel to make Cassini's electricity.

✳ ON ANOTHER WORLD

Huygens' six sets of instruments gathered pictures and information for two and a half hours as the lander fell towards Titan, then for more than an hour on the surface. Cameras took more than 750 pictures and sensors detected the atmosphere's gases and winds. Most of the information was sent by radio to the Cassini probe orbiting above, which relayed it to Earth. Some of Huygens' faint signals were received direct by huge radio telescopes on Earth.

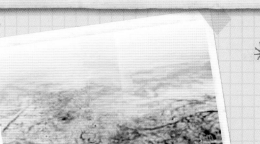

Four-metre main antenna

One of the hundreds of pictures Huygens took of Titan

Magnetometer Mounted on an 11-metre boom, the magnetometer measures Saturn's natural magnetism and how it affects the planet's rings.

On the way to Saturn, Cassini-Huygens made use of four gravity assists – one from Earth, two from Venus and one from Jupiter.

Huygens electronics Most of Huygens' equipment was dormant or 'asleep' on the six-and-a-half year trip to Saturn. It was 'woken' every six months by mission controllers for a quick check-up.

HUYGENS: EXPLODED VIEW

The orbiter is named in honour of Italian-French astronomer-scientist Giovanni Domenico Cassini (1625–1712). He discovered four of Saturn's moons and a gap between the rings, now named the Cassini Division.

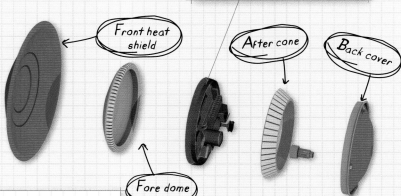

Front heat shield

After cone

Back cover

Fore dome

Huygens lander Disc-shaped Huygens, just 1.3 metres across but weighing 318 kilograms, was bolted to Cassini's side.

The lander is named after Dutch astronomer and all-round scientist Christiaan Huygens (1629–1695), who identified Saturn's rings and discovered the first of its moons.

SPIRIT AND OPPORTUNITY

More than half of all space missions to Mars have failed. Great successes were the USA's Mars Exploration Rovers, MERs. In June and July 2003 two rockets launched the twin rovers, which are remote-controlled robot vehicles. They landed on Mars three weeks apart in the following January. They have been trundling around since, taking pictures and gathering information.

Eureka!

Mars has more spacecraft on its surface than any other planet, (apart from Earth) among them are:
- Mars 2 and 3 (1971)
- Vikings 1 and 2 (1976)
- Mars Pathfinder and its Sojourner rover (1997)
- Spirit and Opportunity
- Perhaps Beagle 2
- Phoenix (2008, opposite)

Whatever next?

Russia and China plan a mission called Phobos-Grunt to visit Mars' tiny moon Phobos and bring back samples of its rocks.

Navcam On the rover's mast are several cameras including two navcams to see rocks, boulders and hollows.

☀ How do PANCAMS work?

Twin panoramic cameras (mounted above the Navcam) on the rover's mast swivel and tilt to see a panoramic or all-around view. They detect shapes and colours in great detail. The two cameras look from slightly different angles, known as stereoscopic vision. From their two views the rover's computer can judge the distance of objects – just like our own eyes and brain.

Solar panels These produce electricity for up to four hours each Martian day (which is 37 minutes longer than an Earth day).

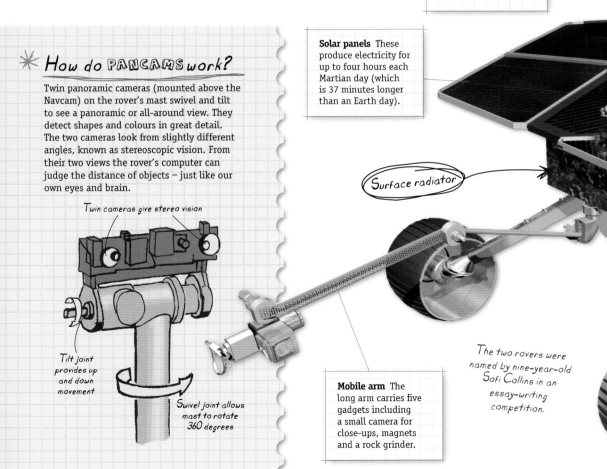

Surface radiator

Twin cameras give stereo vision

Tilt joint provides up and down movement

Swivel joint allows mast to rotate 360 degrees

Mobile arm The long arm carries five gadgets including a small camera for close-ups, magnets and a rock grinder.

The two rovers were named by nine-year-old Sofi Collins in an essay-writing competition.

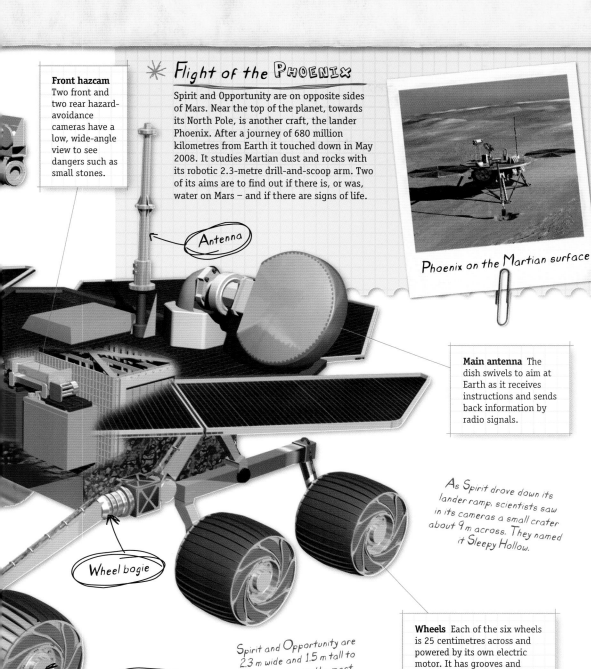

Front hazcam
Two front and
two rear hazard-
avoidance
cameras have a
low, wide-angle
view to see
dangers such as
small stones.

✳ Flight of the PHOENIX

Spirit and Opportunity are on opposite sides
of Mars. Near the top of the planet, towards
its North Pole, is another craft, the lander
Phoenix. After a journey of 680 million
kilometres from Earth it touched down in May
2008. It studies Martian dust and rocks with
its robotic 2.3-metre drill-and-scoop arm. Two
of its aims are to find out if there is, or was,
water on Mars – and if there are signs of life.

Antenna

Phoenix on the Martian surface

Main antenna The
dish swivels to aim at
Earth as it receives
instructions and sends
back information by
radio signals.

As Spirit drove down its
lander ramp, scientists saw
in its cameras a small crater
about 9 m across. They named
it Sleepy Hollow.

Wheel bogie

Wheel motor

Spirit and Opportunity are
2.3 m wide and 1.5 m tall to
the cameras on the mast.
They weigh 180 kg.

Wheels Each of the six wheels
is 25 centimetres across and
powered by its own electric
motor. It has grooves and
cleats (ridges) to grip slippery
rocks or soft dust.

VENUS EXPRESS

Each spacecraft has a limited 'launch window' or time to blast off. This depends on many things such as if the weather is suitable for the rocket to leave, to whether the target planet or moon is in the best position from Earth. Venus Express almost missed this window. It left Earth in November 2005, nearly too late. However it still managed to get into Venus' orbit in May 2006.

Eureka!

Venus Express has found out more about its planet's amazing 'greenhouse effect' due to all the carbon dioxide in its atmosphere (CO_2 is the main global warming gas here on Earth).

Whatever next?

Japan plans a mission called Planet-C to Venus in the next few years. It will study the lightning storms and volcanoes there.

Venus is by far the hottest planet in the Solar System. A warm day in midsummer can be 480°C!

Gold coat Much of the probe is covered by a 23-layered sheet called MLI (Multi-Layer Insulation) to keep out the Sun's intense heat.

Venus Express was developed from the Mars Express mission and uses many similar parts. It also has spare bits from the Rosetta probe, launched to study the comet Churyumov-Gerasimenko.

Solar panels Venus is much closer to the Sun than the Earth is. The solar panels were carefully designed to cope with double the light energy, since Earth-type panels would overheat in the Sun's fearsome glare.

Satellite spins as it travels in orbit

Gyroscope always remains upright in spinning satellite

☀ How can GYROSCOPES help with control?

A moving object tends to keep going unless a force acts to slow it down or change its direction. A gyroscope is a heavy, very fast-spinning wheel or ball with great movement energy, so it resists being tilted or changing position. Inside a satellite, an electrical gyro whizzes around for years, staying in the same position even as the satellite around it spins or changes direction. Measuring the angle between the gyro and the satellite shows which way the satellite is pointing.

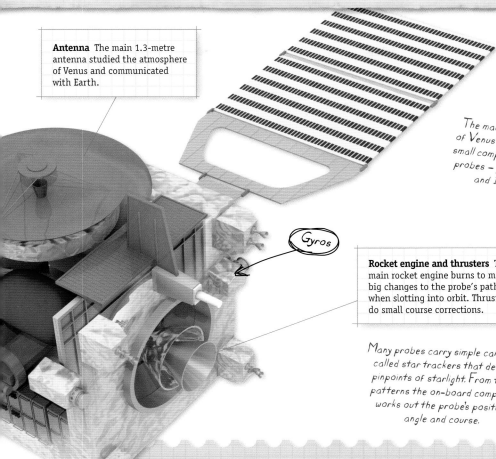

Antenna The main 1.3-metre antenna studied the atmosphere of Venus and communicated with Earth.

The main body, or bus, of Venus Express is very small compared to similar probes – just 1.8 m long and 1.4 m high.

Gyros

Rocket engine and thrusters The main rocket engine burns to make big changes to the probe's path, as when slotting into orbit. Thrusters do small course corrections.

Many probes carry simple cameras called star trackers that detect pinpoints of starlight. From their patterns the on-board computer works out the probe's position, angle and course.

Positioning thrusters

✳ Lost in SPACE

In 1966 the USSR's Venera 3 was the first spacecraft to land on another planet – Venus. However all contact was lost, perhaps because it crash-landed or the planet's thick gases may have crushed it into a crumpled ball. In 2003 all contact was lost with Beagle 2 as it left its orbiter craft Mars Express for a landing on the surface. The fate of Beagle 2 is still a mystery. One day humans may arrive and find its smashed remains.

Beagle 2 as it should have landed

SPACESHIPONE

The X-Prizes are awards for great leaps forward in science and technology. In 1996 the Ansari X-Prize was offered for a craft able to carry three people into space twice in two weeks. However it had to be a private craft, built by a team of individuals or a company, not by a government or whole country. In 2004 SpaceShipOne, developed by Scaled Composites of California, USA, won the prize. Their reward – a cool $10 million.

Eureka!

Pegasus was the first private (non-government) rocket, a solid-fuel rocket booster built by Orbital Sciences. In 1990 the first of its 40-plus launches took up two satellites. Unlike SpaceShipOne it never carried people.

Whatever next?

SpaceShipOne was a forerunner of the much bigger SpaceShipTwo, the first 'spaceliner'. It is planned to carry passengers regularly on space trips and will be operated by Virgin Galactic.

SpaceShipOne retired soon after its spaceflights and is on display at the Smithsonian Institution's National Air and Space Museum in Washington DC, USA.

Pilot On its three space trips, SpaceShipOne carried just one person, the pilot, who didn't need to wear a spacesuit. The craft had enough room and power for three people.

Oxidizer tank

Porthole windows

Controls The pilot's controls were very similar to a small aircraft, with a control column or 'joystick' and two rudder pedals.

✳ How does FEATHERING work?

SpaceShipOne had a new way of slowing down and remaining steady during re-entry. The outer parts of its wings swung up, or 'feathered', so that the craft could come down at a steep angle with its heat-resistant underside facing the correct way. This also stopped SpaceShipOne from tilting or spinning. The wings swung back again for the final glide down and landing.

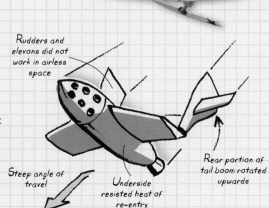

Rudders and elevons did not work in airless space

Steep angle of travel

Underside resisted heat of re-entry

Rear portion of tail boom rotated upwards

After gliding tests, the first powered trip of SpaceShipOne was 17 December 2003. This was exactly 100 years after the Wright brothers' first aircraft flight.

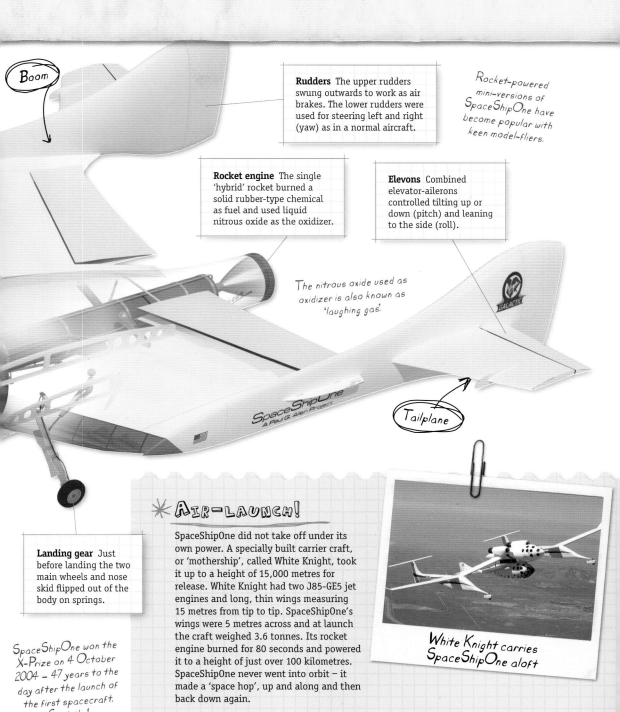

Boom

Rudders The upper rudders swung outwards to work as air brakes. The lower rudders were used for steering left and right (yaw) as in a normal aircraft.

Rocket-powered mini-versions of SpaceShipOne have become popular with keen model-fliers.

Rocket engine The single 'hybrid' rocket burned a solid rubber-type chemical as fuel and used liquid nitrous oxide as the oxidizer.

Elevons Combined elevator-ailerons controlled tilting up or down (pitch) and leaning to the side (roll).

The nitrous oxide used as oxidizer is also known as 'laughing gas'.

Tailplane

Landing gear Just before landing the two main wheels and nose skid flipped out of the body on springs.

SpaceShipOne won the X-Prize on 4 October 2004 – 47 years to the day after the launch of the first spacecraft, Sputnik 1.

✷ AIR-LAUNCH!

SpaceShipOne did not take off under its own power. A specially built carrier craft, or 'mothership', called White Knight, took it up to a height of 15,000 metres for release. White Knight had two J85-GE5 jet engines and long, thin wings measuring 15 metres from tip to tip. SpaceShipOne's wings were 5 metres across and at launch the craft weighed 3.6 tonnes. Its rocket engine burned for 80 seconds and powered it to a height of just over 100 kilometres. SpaceShipOne never went into orbit – it made a 'space hop', up and along and then back down again.

White Knight carries SpaceShipOne aloft

INTERNATIONAL SPACE STATION

The first space stations in orbit around Earth where people could stay for days or weeks, were the USSR's Salyut series from 1971 and the USA's Skylab in 1973. Much bigger was Russia's Mir, which lasted from 1986 until it burned up (without crew) on re-entry in 2001. The only current space base is the International Space Station, ISS. Building began in 1998 and will finish around 2010.

Eureka!

The ISS began as an idea to combine three separate planned space bases – USA's Freedom, Russia's Mir-2 and the European Space Agency's Columbus.

Whatever next?

The ISS is planned to stay in service until at least 2016. Next could be a Moon base, possibly finished around 2025.

The ISS travels at 27,700 km/h and completes almost 16 orbits every 24 hours.

✳ How do SOLAR PANELS work?

A solar panel, or array, has thousands of button-sized PV (photovoltaic) cells. Each takes in the energy of sunlight and changes it into electricity. The electric current is fed through a control unit to batteries. These charge up during half of each orbit when the ISS is on the sunny side of Earth, for use during the other half.

Airlock

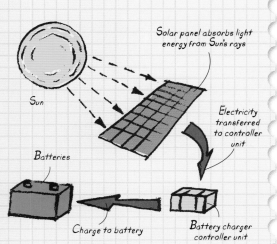

Solar panel absorbs light energy from Sun's rays

Sun

Electricity transferred to controller unit

Batteries

Charge to battery

Battery charger controller unit

Soyuz There is always at least one Russian Soyuz spacecraft docked at the ISS as a 'lifeboat' in case of an emergency, such as crew illness. Soyuz takes almost two days to launch and chase after and link onto the station, but it can be back down on Earth in less than four hours.

The ISS has an elliptical (oval) orbit at a height of between 275 and 425 km. It can be seen from Earth with the unaided eye, if you know where to look!

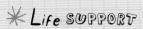 Life SUPPORT

Canadarm2 This remote-control arm, nearly 18 metres long, runs on rails along the main truss. It moves equipment and even space-walking astronauts.

All the basics of life must be taken up to the ISS by spacecraft such as the USA's space shuttles, Russia's Soyuz (with crew) and Progress (without crew), and Europe's Jules Verne (another 'robot' craft without crew). Supplies include water, food and even air to breathe. However there is plenty of recycling. Filters clean the air and an Elektron machine makes fresh oxygen from water. In fact all the water from the shower, sink, astronaut's breathed-out air and even their urine is re-used – after cleaning, of course.

A state-of-the-art toilet on board the ISS

Solar panels Also called photovoltaic arrays, the solar panels swivel as the ISS orbits so they point at the Sun. Each panel is about 34 metres long.

Main truss The truss is the 'backbone' of the ISS to which all the other modules and parts are fixed. It is made up of about 12 sections called segments with code names such as S1 and P6.

P1 truss segment

Space shuttle Visiting spacecraft join the ISS at docking ports. The connection is airtight so that the crew can enter the ISS through an airlock.

The ISS sinks downwards about 2000 m each month. It has to be pushed back up again using small booster rockets on its visiting spacecraft.

349

INDEX AND GLOSSARY

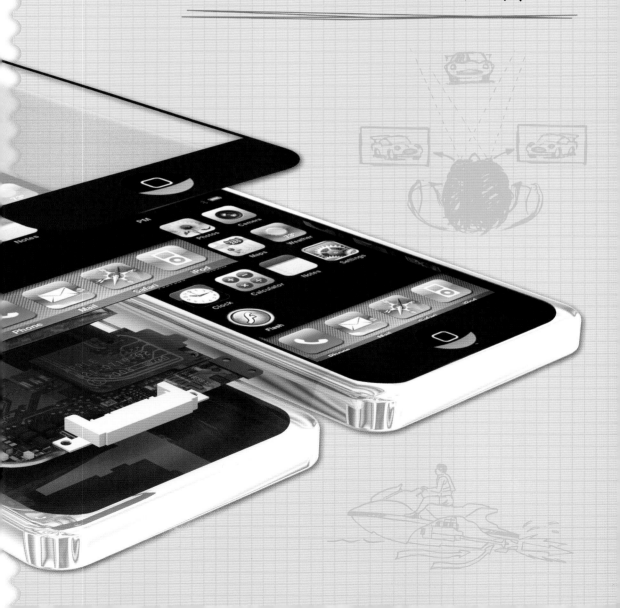

GLOSSARY

Aerofoil

The cross-section shape of most aircraft wings, being more curved or humped on the upper surface than the lower surface, which provides a strong lifting force. Also the cross-section shape for various water vessel parts such as the propellers (water screws) and the foils of hydrofoils.

Aileron

The control surface of an aircraft, usually on the trailing (rear) edge of the wing, that makes it lean left or right (roll or bank).

Airframe

The strong inner framework or 'skeleton' of an aircraft.

Alloy

A combination of metals, or metals and other substances, for special purposes such as great strength, extreme lightness, resistance to high temperatures, or all of these.

Analogue

Signals that carry information or data by varying in strength or size, such as by the varying strength (voltage) of an electric current.

Anode

The positive (+) electrical contact that is part of an electrical pathway or circuit.

Antenna

Part of a communications system that sends out and/or receives radio signals, microwaves or similar waves and rays. Most antennae, also called aerials, are either long and thin like wires, bar-shaped, or dish-shaped like a bowl.

Articulated

In vehicles, having a joint or bendy part rather than being rigid all the way along.

Atmosphere

The layer of gases – air – around a very large space object such as planet Earth.

Atoms

The smallest pieces or particles of a material or substance, each made of a central nucleus with electrons going around it.

Azimuth

To do with movements and angles in the horizontal plane, that is, left and right, level with the water's surface. On a ship, an azimuth thruster can swivel to point in various directions horizontally, but it cannot tilt vertically to point up or down.

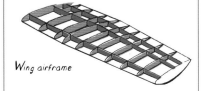

Wing airframe

Ballast

A heavy substance, such as water, concrete or metal, added to a craft or vehicle to make it more stable and to stop it toppling over, for example, in high winds or when turning at speed. Many boats and ships have ballast tanks low in the hull that can be flooded with water if the vessel is not fully loaded. This allows them to float at the correct level and remain steady while moving and turning.

Articulated steering

Barrel

The long, tube-shaped main part of a gun or similar weapon, in front of the breech and ending at the muzzle.

Battens

Long, thin strips of wood, plastic or similar that help to hold out a flexible surface, such as a hang-glider wing or yacht sail.

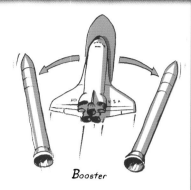

Booster

Bearing

A part designed for efficient movement to reduce friction and wear, for example, between a spinning axle and its frame.

Biofuels

Energy-rich substances (fuels) that are made from recently living things, such as wood, the gases from decaying or rotting plant and animal matter, plant oils and animal droppings.

Biomass

Living or recently living matter from plants and animals that can be made into biofuel (see above).

Biplane

An aircraft with two sets of main wings, usually one above the other.

Blade

One of the long, slim parts of a propeller (airscrew), helicopter rotor or turbine.

Blu-ray

A type of optical (light-based) disc, similar to a DVD, which uses blue laser light. This has shorter waves compared to the usual red DVD laser and so it can read smaller pits on the disc. This enables a Blu-ray disc to hold more information than a standard DVD – up to 50 GB (gigabytes).

Bluetooth

A wireless system for using radio waves to communicate and send information over relatively short distances, usually tens of metres.

Boom

A long, slim, arm-like part, sometimes called a jib, of a crane or similar machine that can usually move up and down, from side to side and perhaps in and out. In watercraft it is the pole or spar along the base, or foot, of a sail. It prevents the bottom area of the sail from flapping out of control.

Booster

An added-on rocket that gives extra thrust, for example, when blasting off from a planet's surface, or when leaving an orbital path to travel into deep space.

Bow

In watercraft, the forward-facing part of the hull.

Bracing wires

Thin metal wires or cables that are stretched tightly between various parts of an aircraft, especially the wings, to hold them steady.

Breech

The rear part of a gun or similar weapon, at the opposite end to the muzzle, where the bullets or similar ammunition are loaded.

Bridge

In watercraft, the control room of a large boat or ship, housing the wheel (steering wheel), engine throttles, instrument displays and other important equipment.

Bulkhead

An upright wall or partition across the width of a structure, such as across the hull of a ship or the fuselage of an aircraft.

Bullet

Usually a short, rod-shaped, solid metal or plastic object with a pointed front end, fired out of a gun or similar weapon.

Bullet

Bus

The main body or central part of a craft such as a space probe or satellite, to which the other parts and modules are attached.

Calibre

In weapons, the inside width of a tube such as a gun barrel.

Canard design

An aircraft layout with the small wings or tailplane in front of the large main wings rather than behind them.

Cartridge

A package loaded into a gun consisting of the bullet or shell, along with its casing, the main explosive and the primer.

Cathode

The negative (−) electrical contact that is part of an electrical pathway or circuit.

CCD

Charge-coupled device, a microchip that turns patterns of light rays into patterns of electronic signals.

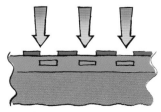

CCD chip

CD laser beam

CD

Compact disc, a plastic-based disc usually 12 centimetres across, with a very thin metal layer. This layer stores information or data in the form of microscopic pits, which are detected or 'read' by a laser beam. Most CDs have a memory capacity of 650–750 MB (megabytes).

Chassis

The main structural framework or 'skeleton' of a car, that gives it strength, and to which other parts are fixed, like the engine and seats.

Chord

On an aircraft, the measurement from the front or leading edge of the wing to its rear or trailing edge.

Cleat

A device or structure for attaching lines or ropes, which may be shaped like a cylinder, a 'T', a 'V' or a similar design.

Cockpit

The control compartment of an aircraft where the pilot sits. On larger aircraft with two or more flying crew it is sometimes called the flight deck or control cabin.

Cocoon

A long bag, similar to a sleeping bag, for the pilot of a hang-glider or similar craft.

Cofferdam

An empty space between two bulkheads, for ballast or for safety, for example, to stop leakage of dangerous substances into the rest of the vessel.

Cogs

The name for the teeth of a gear wheel, or for whole gearwheels (which are sometimes called cogwheels).

Combustion chamber

A chamber where fuel burns (combusts) to produce roaring, high-pressure hot gases, as in a rocket engine.

Con-rod

Connecting rod, an engine part that links the piston to the main crankshaft.

Constant-velocity

(CV) joint, a mechanical joint or linkage that carries a turning action from one part to the other at the same regular (or constant) speed (velocity).

Crank

A bent part of a spinning shaft or axle, or an arm-like part sticking out from it, like the crank of a bicycle with the pedal fitted to it.

Crankcase

The main body of a petrol or diesel engine, below the pistons and cylinders, containing the crankshaft and con-rods.

Crankshaft

The main turning shaft in an engine, which is made to rotate by the up-and-down movements of the pistons.

Cylinder

In an engine or mechanical part, the chamber inside which a well-fitting piston moves.

Damper

A part that reduces or dampens movements, such as jolts or to-and-fro vibrations. On vehicle suspensions it is sometimes called the shock absorber.

Disc brake

Derailleur

The gear-change mechanism on many bicycles that moves the chain sideways so it goes from one sprocket to another. It also takes up slack along the length of the chain to keep it taut when it moves between different-sized sprockets.

Diesel engine

An internal combustion engine (one that burns or combusts fuel inside a chamber, the cylinder) that uses diesel fuel, and causes this to explode by pressure alone rather than by a spark plug.

Differential

A part that makes road wheels turn at different speeds as a vehicle goes round a bend. The wheel on the outside of the curve must spin slightly faster because it has farther to go than the inner wheel and would otherwise judder or skid.

Digital

Carrying information or data in the form of coded on-off signals, usually millions every second.

Disc brake

A braking system where two stationary pads or pistons press onto either side of a rotating flat disc attached to the wheel, to slow it down.

Dope

In electronics, to add tiny amounts of a substance, the dopant, to large quantities of another one, to alter the way electricity flows.

Drag

The force or resistance of air pushing against something moving through it.

Drive shaft

A spinning shaft from an engine or motor that drives or powers another part, such as the propeller of a water vessel, the caterpillar tracks of a bulldozer or the wheels of a car.

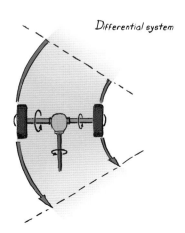

Differential system

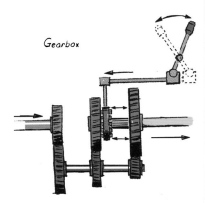

Gearbox

DVD

Digital versatile disc (sometimes digital 'video' disc), a plastic-based disc usually 12 centimetres across, with a very thin metal layer. This stores information or data in the form of microscopic pits, which are detected or 'read' by a laser beam. Most DVDs have a memory capacity of 4.7 GB or 4700 MB. Double-sided dual-layer versions can hold more than 17 GB.

Electrode

An electrical contact, or part of an electrical pathway or circuit, that is either positive (+), the anode, or negative (−), the cathode.

Electrolysis

To split apart or break up particles of a substance, usually a fluid (liquid or gas), by passing an electric current through it.

Electron

Tiny particles inside atoms with a negative electrical charge or force, which move around the central area (nucleus) of the atom. Lots of electrons moving along between atoms make an electric current.

Elevator

The control surface of an aircraft, usually on the tailplane (small rear wing) that makes it tilt up or down (pitch).

Elevon

The control surface of a tail-less or 'flying wing' aircraft or spacecraft, which is a combined elevator and aileron.

Envelope

In ballooning, the main casing of the balloon that contains the hot air or lighter-than-air gas.

Escape velocity

The minimum speed or velocity needed to leave the pull of gravity of an object and escape into space.

Geothermal energy

Fin

The upright part at the rear of most aircraft, also known as the vertical stabilizer and often called the tail.

Fossil fuels

Fuels that were formed over a very long time, usually millions of years, from once-living things that were trapped in rocks and changed by fossilization. The main fossil fuels are coal, oil (petroleum) and gas (natural gas).

Frequency

How often something happens over a certain unit of time, usually one second. For example, low-frequency sound waves vibrate about 50–100 times each second.

Friction

When two objects rub or scrape together, causing wear and losing movement energy by turning it into sound, heat and other forms.

Fuel

A substance with lots of energy in the form of its matter or substance, as chemical energy. We usually release this energy for use by burning. In some cases fuels are used in other ways – in a fuel cell, hydrogen fuel is converted into electricity.

Fuselage

The main body or central part of an aircraft, usually long and tube-shaped.

Gears

Toothed wheels or sprockets that fit or mesh together so that one turns the other. If they are connected by a chain or belt with holes where the teeth fit, they are generally called sprockets. Gears are used to change turning speed and force, for example, between an engine and the road wheels of a car, or to change the direction of rotation.

Generator

A device or machine that changes kinetic or mechanical energy – the energy of movement – into electricity.

Geo-

To do with rocks and the Earth. For example, geothermal energy is the heat (thermal) energy from rocks that are found deep below the surface of the Earth.

Giga-

One thousand million, as in 1 GB (gigabyte), which is 1,000,000,000 bytes of information or data. For a typical MP3 digital music player, 1 GB provides about 16 hours of sound.

Gyroscope stability

Gores

Curved strips that make up the envelope (main part) of a balloon.

GPS

Global Positioning System, a network of more than 20 satellites in space going around the Earth. They send out radio signals about their position and the time, allowing people to find their location using GPS receivers or 'satnavs'.

Gravity

The natural pulling force or attraction that all objects have, no matter what their size. Bigger or more massive objects have more gravity than smaller ones.

Gyroscope

A device that maintains its position and resists being moved or tilted because of its movement energy. It can be used to measure speed and direction of movement. It usually consists of a very fast-spinning ball or wheel in a frame.

HD

High definition, in television screen technology, is where the tiny coloured spots or pixels are considerably smaller and closer together than on a normal screen, to provide much more fine detail.

Heat shield

A special part of a spacecraft made to absorb and resist the heat of entry or re-entry as the craft comes from space into an atmosphere.

Hold

In larger ships and boats, the place where cargo, freight and stores are kept.

Hub

The central part (boss) of a propeller, wheel or similar spinning object, where it turns on its shaft or axle.

Hull

The main body or central part of a water vessel, and also of some land vehicles such as tanks.

Hybrid vehicle

A vehicle, such as a car, with more than one method of moving or propulsion, such as a petrol engine and an electric motor.

Hydraulic

Machinery that works by using high-pressure liquid such as oil or water.

Hydro-

To do with water. For example, hydroelectricity is generated from the energy of moving water.

Hydrofoil

A watercraft that uses wing-like foils to create a lifting force as they move forwards, and so make the hull rise, either partly or completely above the surface.

Impeller

A spinning part similar to a fan or turbine, with angled blades, which forces a gas or liquid into an area at high pressure.

Incinerate

To burn something thoroughly, usually at very high temperature, so that almost nothing is left except ashes.

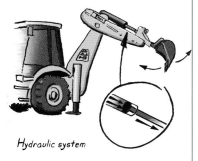

Hydraulic system

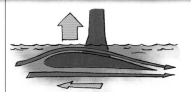

Hydrofoil

Infra-red

A form of energy, as rays or waves, which is similar to light but with longer waves that have a warming or heating effect.

Insulate

To prevent something, usually electricity or heat, moving or to greatly slow its movement. Electrical insulators such as plastic and glass stop electricity flowing, and thermal insulators such as fibre-glass and foamed plastic slow the passage of heat.

Jib

A smallish, usually triangular sail in front of the mainsail(s), towards the front of the vessel. This is also the term used for the working arm of a crane.

Keel

A large flap or flange sticking down below the centre of the hull, with its flat surfaces facing to each side. Keels are used mainly in sailing vessels to give greater control and stability. The term is also used for the central part of a vessel's structure, like its 'backbone' running from front to rear.

Kilo-

One thousand, as in 1 KB (kilobyte), which is 1000 bytes of information or data. For a typical MP3 digital music player, 1 KB is about one-sixteenth of one second of sound.

Laser

A special high-energy form of light that is only one pure colour. All of its waves are exactly the same length, and they are parallel to each other rather than spreading out as in normal light.

Launch vehicle

The part of a space mission that launches the payload and other parts, lifting them up into space – usually called the 'rocket'.

Launch window

The limited time when a space mission can take off, or be launched. Before and after this time period the mission will no longer be possible, for example, because its target planet is too far away.

LCD

Liquid crystal display, a technology for showing images on a screen using semi-liquid crystals that 'twist' or polarize light rays. For example, mobile telephone screens use LCD.

Lens

A shaped piece of clear glass, plastic or a similar transparent substance that bends or refracts light rays. It changes their direction so that they either come together (converge) or spread apart or diverge.

Luff

To raise up and lower down in a vertical direction, as with the boom or jib of a crane.

Lunar

Anything that relates to a moon, usually the Moon (Earth's moon).

Magnetometer

A scientific instrument that detects magnetic forces, such as the natural magnetic fields of planets.

Mast

On a watercraft, this is the upright or almost upright pole or spar that holds up and supports various items such as sails, flags and radar and radio equipment.

Mega-

One million, as in 1 MB (megabyte), which is 1,000,000 bytes of information or data. For a typical MP3 digital music player, 1 MB provides about one minute of sound.

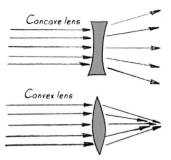

Concave lens

Convex lens

Microchip

A small sliver or 'chip' of a substance, usually silicon or germanium. It has many microscopic electronic components and devices, such as resistors and transistors, built into it.

Mine

An explosive device that can be used on land and in water. In water, it's a floating weapon that explodes when it touches or comes near to another object. Land mines are buried in the ground and explode upon victim contact.

Module

A main part or section of a spacecraft, for example, containing all the radio equipment, or the batteries, or housing scientific instruments such as telescopes.

Monoplane

An aircraft with one main pair of wings, rather than two (biplane), three (triplane) or more.

Moon

A space object that orbits a planet, like Titan orbiting Saturn. 'The' Moon (with a capital M) travels around the Earth.

Motor

A machine that converts electricity into mechanical power to drive another device.

Multi-stage rocket

A rocket or launch vehicle with several sections that fire or burn one after the other, falling away when their fuel is used up.

Muzzle

The open end of a gun or similar weapon, where the bullet or other ammunition comes out.

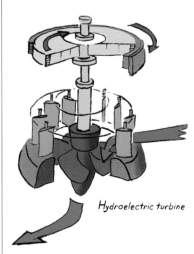

Hydroelectric turbine

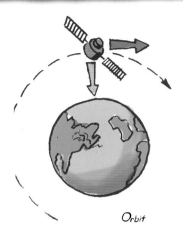

Orbit

Nozzle
A cone- or trumpet-shaped device from which fast-moving liquid or gas comes out, such as in a jet ski, rocket engine or gas burner.

Nucleus
The central part of an atom, which is made up of minute particles called protons and neutrons, and around which even smaller particles called electrons move.

Optical
Working with light rays, instead of other waves or rays (such as radio waves, microwaves or infra-red 'heat' rays).

Optical telescope
A telescope that works using light rays, instead of other waves or rays (such as radio waves).

Orbit
A curved path around a larger object, such as a spacecraft going around Earth, or the Earth orbiting the Sun. Orbits can be circular, elliptical ('oval'), teardrop-like and other shapes.

Payload
The load or cargo part of a space mission, such as a satellite or space probe, as opposed to the launch vehicle or rocket that takes it up into space.

Petrol engine
An internal combustion engine (one that burns or combusts fuel inside a chamber, the cylinder) that uses petrol fuel and causes this to explode using a spark plug.

Photovoltaic
(PV) cell, a small electronic device that changes the energy of light into electrical energy.

Piston
A wide, rod-shaped part, similar in shape to a food or drinks can, that moves along or up and down inside a close-fitting chamber, the cylinder.

Pitch prop

Pitch
When an aircraft points up or down, to climb or descend. Also the angle of a propeller blade compared to the propeller's direction of movement.

Pixels
Picture elements, the tiny spots or areas of different colours and brightness that together make up a bigger picture or image.

Planet
A very large space object that orbits or travels around a star, like the eight planets, including the Earth, that orbit the Sun.

Planing (hydroplaning)
In watercraft, a way of moving by skimming over the water's surface with almost no part in the water, rather than by pushing through it.

Plasma
A substance that is similar to a gas, but where its tiniest particles (atoms) become extremely hot and have an electric charge and lots of energy.

Pneumatic
Machinery that is operated by high-pressure gas such as air or oxygen.

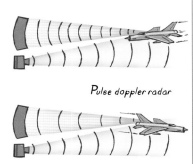

Pulse doppler radar

Power

In everyday life 'power' often means electricity, as in a power station, which generates electric current. 'Power' is also sometimes used with a similar meaning to force or pressure. As an official scientific term 'power' is the rate of changing or transmitting energy, or the rate that objects are moved or work is done, in units of time. It is measured in watts or horsepower.

Primer

A small amount of explosive that is set off or ignited by a spark, or by being hit, which then makes the main explosive blow up and fire the bullet or shell.

Probe

A craft without crew that is remote-controlled from Earth, which usually undertakes a long-distance deep-space mission.

Propeller

A spinning device with angled blades, like a rotating fan, which turns to draw in fluid such as water or air at the front, and thrust it powerfully backwards. Also called a water-screw in water vessels or an airscrew in aircraft.

Pusher prop

A propeller or airscrew at the rear of an engine that pushes air backwards, rather than one at the front that pulls its way through the air.

Rack

In gear systems, such as in cars and similar vehicles, this is a long strip with teeth or cogs, as used in rack-and-pinion steering.

Radar

A system that sends out radio waves that reflect off objects such as aircraft or ships, and detects echoes to find out their position.

Radiator

In cars and similar vehicles, a part designed to lose heat, for example, from an engine. It has a large surface area, usually made up of lots of fins or vanes. Hot water from the engine circulates through it, to become cooler before flowing back to the engine.

Radio

A system by which signals and messages are sent by invisible waves of combined electricity and magnetism, where each wave is quite long, from a few millimetres to many kilometres. (Light waves are similar but much shorter.)

Radio telescope

A telescope that works using radio waves, microwaves or similar waves, instead of the light rays detected by an optical telescope.

Radio waves

Invisible waves of combined electricity and magnetism where each wave is quite long, from a few millimetres to many kilometres. (Light waves are similar but much shorter in length.)

Radioactive

Giving off or emitting certain kinds of rays and/or particles known as radiation, which can cause harm to people and other living things.

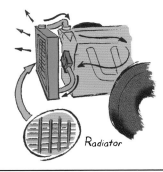

Radiator

Radioisotope
generator

Radioisotope generator

A device that turns the radioactive energy (rays) given off by certain substances into electricity.

Re-entry

When a spacecraft comes back into the layer of gases (atmosphere) around a planet or moon.

Retractable

When something folds away or retracts into a compartment, as with aircraft wheels, to leave a smooth surface.

Retrorocket

A rocket engine that fires to slow down a spacecraft, for example, as it enters orbit or touches down on a planet or moon.

Return mission

A space trip where the craft comes back to its starting place, usually Earth, rather than travelling away into deep space.

Rib

The short, curved parts inside a wing, from the front or leading edge to the rear or trailing edge.

Rigging

Lines (as the ropes are called on ships), masts, sails and other equipment that make a sailing ship travel along under wind power.

Rocket

A type of engine or motor that burns fuel using oxygen or an oxygen-rich chemical (oxidizer). It produces a blast of hot gases that provide a force called thrust.

Roll

When an aircraft leans or banks to one side.

Rover

In space, a wheeled vehicle that can travel around and explore a planet or moon, such as the lunar rovers used by astronauts on the Moon, or the remote-controlled Spirit rover on Mars.

Rudder

The control surface of an aircraft or watercraft, usually on the upright fin or 'tail' of an aircraft or below the rear hull of a boat, that makes it steer left or right (yaw).

Satellite

Any object that goes around or orbits another. For example, the Moon is a natural satellite of the Earth. The term is used especially for artificial or man-made orbiting objects, particularly those going around the Earth.

Satnav

Satellite navigation, finding your way and location using radio signals from the GPS (Global Positioning System) satellites in space.

Shell

A bullet-like object fired out of a gun or similar, which usually contains explosives that blow up when they hit the target.

Shroud

A collar- or tube-like structure around a spinning impeller (propeller-like fan), which restricts and controls the direction and force of the fluid passing through it.

Satellite navigation
system

Thruster

Silencer box
Part of an exhaust system that makes the noise of the exploding gases from the engine quieter, also called a muffler.

Slicks
Tyres that have little or no pattern of grooves, or tread, usually used on dry road surfaces.

Solar
To do with the Sun.

Solar panel
A device that turns sunlight directly into electricity, as used on many satellites and near-space probes, using lots of PV (photovoltaic) cells. It is a large flat device and is sometimes called a solar array.

Space station
A base in space, usually orbiting a planet, where people can live and work for weeks, months or even years.

Spar
The long, rigid, beam-like part inside a wing, from root to tip, that gives it strength.

Spinner
The cone-shaped covering over a propeller's central part, the hub (boss), to protect it and improve streamlining.

Sprocket
A wheel with teeth around the edge, often called a gear wheel. Unlike gears, sprockets do not fit together or mesh directly, but have a chain or belt or similar object between them.

Star
A huge space object that gives out heat and light. The nearest star to the Earth is the Sun.

Stealth technology
The design of an aircraft, ship or similar object so it is difficult to detect by sight, sound, heat sensors or radar equipment.

Stern
In watercraft, the rear or blunt end of the hull, or main body.

STOL
Short Take-Off and Landing, when an aircraft can take off and land within a very small distance.

Suspension
Parts that allow the road wheels of a vehicle to move up and down separately from the driver and passengers, to smooth out bumps and dips in the road. Also any similar system that gives a softer, more comfortable ride.

Tailplane
The two small rear wings on most aircraft and some helicopters, also known as the horizontal stabilizers. They carry the elevators and are usually next to the fin or 'tail'.

Telescopic
When one part or section of a structure slides inside another, as in a telescope, an extending ladder or certain kinds of cranes.

Thermal
To do with heat energy and temperature.

Suspension strut

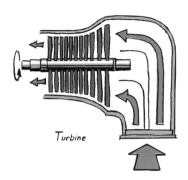

Turbine

Throttle

A control that allows more fuel and air into an engine for greater speed, sometimes called an accelerator.

Thrust

The force that pushes an object forwards, such as the propellers or jet engines of an aircraft or the rocket blast that moves a spacecraft.

Thrust bearing

A bearing for a shaft or axle that is designed to cope with other forces as well as the usual spinning movement of the shaft or axle.

Thruster

A small propeller, nozzle or jet-like part that produces a pushing force, usually to make small adjustments to the position or direction of travel of a craft or vehicle.

Torpedo

A self-powered exploding weapon launched at the water's surface or below, usually to hit a watercraft such as a ship, boat or submarine.

Tracking station

A place with a large radio receiver, such as a dish, which detects radio waves or similar signals from a spacecraft and follows or tracks its course.

Tractor unit

In an articulated truck, the part with the engine or cab that does the pulling, also called the prime mover.

Transmission

The parts that transmit the turning force from the engine (crankshaft) to the wheel axles, including the gears, gearbox and propeller shaft.

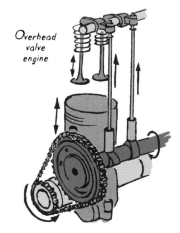

Overhead valve engine

Transom

The flat rear panel across some watercraft, which is usually almost vertical and faces backwards.

Traverse

When a gun or similar weapon aims by moving from side to side (horizontally) rather than up and down (vertically).

Turbine

A set of angled fan-like blades on a spinning shaft, used in many areas of mechanics and engineering, from pumps to jet engines and the turbogenerators in electricity-generating power stations.

Turbo

An engine, pump, generator or similar device that works using a turbine.

Turbofan

A jet engine with fan-like turbine blades inside and one very large turbine or 'fan' at the front that works partly as a propeller.

Turbojet

A jet engine with fan-like turbine blades inside, which produces a powerful blast of gases from the rear end.

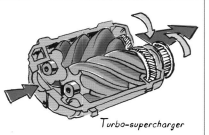
Turbo-supercharger

Turboprop

A jet engine with fan-like turbine blades inside, which turns a propeller for thrust rather than using its jet blast of gases.

Turboshaft

A jet engine with fan-like turbine blades inside, which spins a shaft for power rather than using its jet blast of gases.

Undercarriage

An aircraft's landing wheels, skids, floats or similar devices that support it on the ground.

Valve

A part that controls the flow or passage of a substance, like a water tap or the movement of fuel and air mixture into an engine.

VTOL

Vertical Take-Off and Landing, an aircraft that can lift off and touch down by moving vertically, straight up and down.

Winch

A winding mechanism that turns or reels in a rope or cable, slowly but with great force.

Winglet

A small angled-up or 'bent' part at the tip of an aircraft's wing.

Wingspan

In aviation, the distance of an aircraft's main wings from one tip to the other.

Wireless

When electronic devices can communicate or transfer information without wires, usually by waves such as radio, microwaves or infra-red rays.

Yaw

When an aircraft steers or turns to the left or right, or when a machine swivels around on an upright shaft, as in a wind turbine.

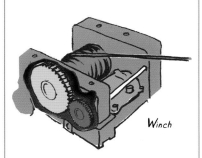
Winch

INDEX

INDEX

INDEX

INDEX

INDEX

INDEX

INDEX

INDEX

Z

ACKNOWLEDGEMENTS

All panel artworks by Rocket Design

The publishers would like to thank the following sources for the use of their photographs:

Alamy: 14 sciencephotos; 57 DBURKE; 69 Motoring Picture Library; 80(t) Interfoto; 81(c) David Wall; 87 Tom Wood; 88 Justin Kase z07z; 92 David Gowans; 136 Mint Photography; 140 Ruby; 149(c) Purestock; 172 Peter Jordan; 175 vario images GmbH & Co.KG; 201 Jim Parkin; 204 Jim West; 235 John Novis; 244 greenwales; 308 Emil Pozar III

Aviation Images: 310 M Wagner

Corbis: 12(t/r) Carl & Ann Purcell; 13(r) Fred Prouser/ Reuters; 20 TScI/NASA/Roger Ressmeyer; 22 Reuters; 28 Ed Kashi; 38 Roger Ressmeyer; 47(b) Clifford White; 51 Mike King; 61 Diego Azubella/epa; 63 Chris Williams/ Icon/SMI; 65 Transtock; 66 Walter G. Arce/ASP Inc.Icon SMI; 75 Thinkstock; 76 George Hall; 81(b/r) Yoav Levy/ MedNet; 82 Rick Wilking/Reuters; 85 Narendra Shrestha/ epa; 95 Paul A. Souders; 104 Jim Sugar; 114(t) Hulton-Deutsch Collection; 119 Walter G Arce; 122 Bettmann; 135 Hulton-Deutsch Collection; 144 Bettmann; 148(t) Bettmann; 148(b) Corbis; 156 Jeon Heon-Kyun/ epa; 165 Shawn Thew/epa; 168 Pawel Supernak/epa; 182(t) Bettmann, (c) Patrick Pleul/dpa; 236 Joseph Sohm/Visions of America; 238 Harald A. Jahn; 246 Kim Kulish; 260 Andy Newman/epa; 262 Atlantide Phototravel; 271 Paul A. Souders; 273 Lester Lefkowitz; 295 Aero Graphics, Inc.; 299 Bettmann; 301 Hulton-Deutsch Collection; 303 Antonio Cotrim/epa; 307 Handout/ Reuters; 321 Bettman; 325 Roger Ressmeyer

Dreamstime.com: 13 Fotosav; 185 Vladikpod; 187 Orientaly; 193 Orangeline; 203 Amaranta; 224 Ichip

Fotolia: 12(c) Avava; 13(t) Henrik Andersen; 31 Monkey Business; 33 Peter Baxter; 41 Andy Dean; 55 Sculpies; 110 Gorran Haven; 194 Paul Fearn; 196 Jose Gil; 223 Lottchen; 250(b) Alexander Rochau; 251(b) Snowshill; 253 Forgiss; 255 linous; 277 Aaron Kohr; 287 Charles Shapiro; 291 Igor Zhorov

Getty Images: 70 Tim Graham; 73 James Balog; 91 John Li/Stringer; 97 Shaun Curry/Stringer; 114(b) AFP, (c) Curventa; 121 Mike Hewitt/Staff; 126 David Taylor/ Staff; 143 Time & Life Pictures; 155, 160, 162 Time & Life Pictures; 177 Getty Images; 206, 208 AFP; 229 Boris Horvat; 231 Harald Sund; 314 Johnny Green

iStockphoto.com: 199 Joe Gough; 289 Dennis Van Duren

Photolibrary.com: 151 Larry McManus; 166 Philip Wallick; 183(c); 178 US.Navy; 189 Glow Images; 196 Con Tanasiuk; 211 Bernd Laute; 217(c) Manfred Bail; 251(c) Bernard van Dierendonck

Rex Features: 26 James King-Holmes; 34 Action Press; 36 ©.W.Disney/Everett; 43 David Hay Jones; 47(c) The Travel Library; 49; 53 KPA/Zama; 59 Motor Audi Car; 80(b) Sipa Press; 99 MH/Keystone USA; 100 Sipa Press; 103 Phil Yeomans; 106 Kenneth Ferguson; 109 Nils Jorgensen; 115(b) VIZO; 117 Mission; 128 Gavin Hellier/ Robert Harding; 130 Kevin Holt/Daily Mail; 133 Newspix; 149(c); 153; 159 Greg Mathieson; 190 Nicholas Bailey; 212 Paul Grover; 221 Sipa Press; 240 Jon Santa Cruz; 257 Neale Haynes; 259 Stuart Clarke; 265 Sipa Press; 267; 275 Sipa Press; 281 ©.W. Disney/Everett; 284 Jonathan Hordle; 285 Hugh W. Cowin; 293 C.WisHisSoc/Everett; 305; 327; Everett Collection; 337 Denis Cameron; 345 Sipa Press; 347 Scaled Composites

Science Photo Library: 17 Chris Martin-Bahr; 46(t) LIBRARY OF CONGRESS; 138 NASA; 183(r) Ria Novosti; 227 US Department of Energy; 243 Andrew Lambert Photography; 278 Alexis Rosenfeld; 318; 323 Ria Novosti; 333 NASA; 341 European Space Agency; 349 NASA

Topfoto.co.uk: 125 Topham Picturepoint

All other photographs are from Miles Kelly Archives and NASA

Every effort has been made to acknowledge the source and copyright holder of each picture. Miles Kelly Publishing apologizes for any unintentional errors or omissions.